BAR MITZVAH

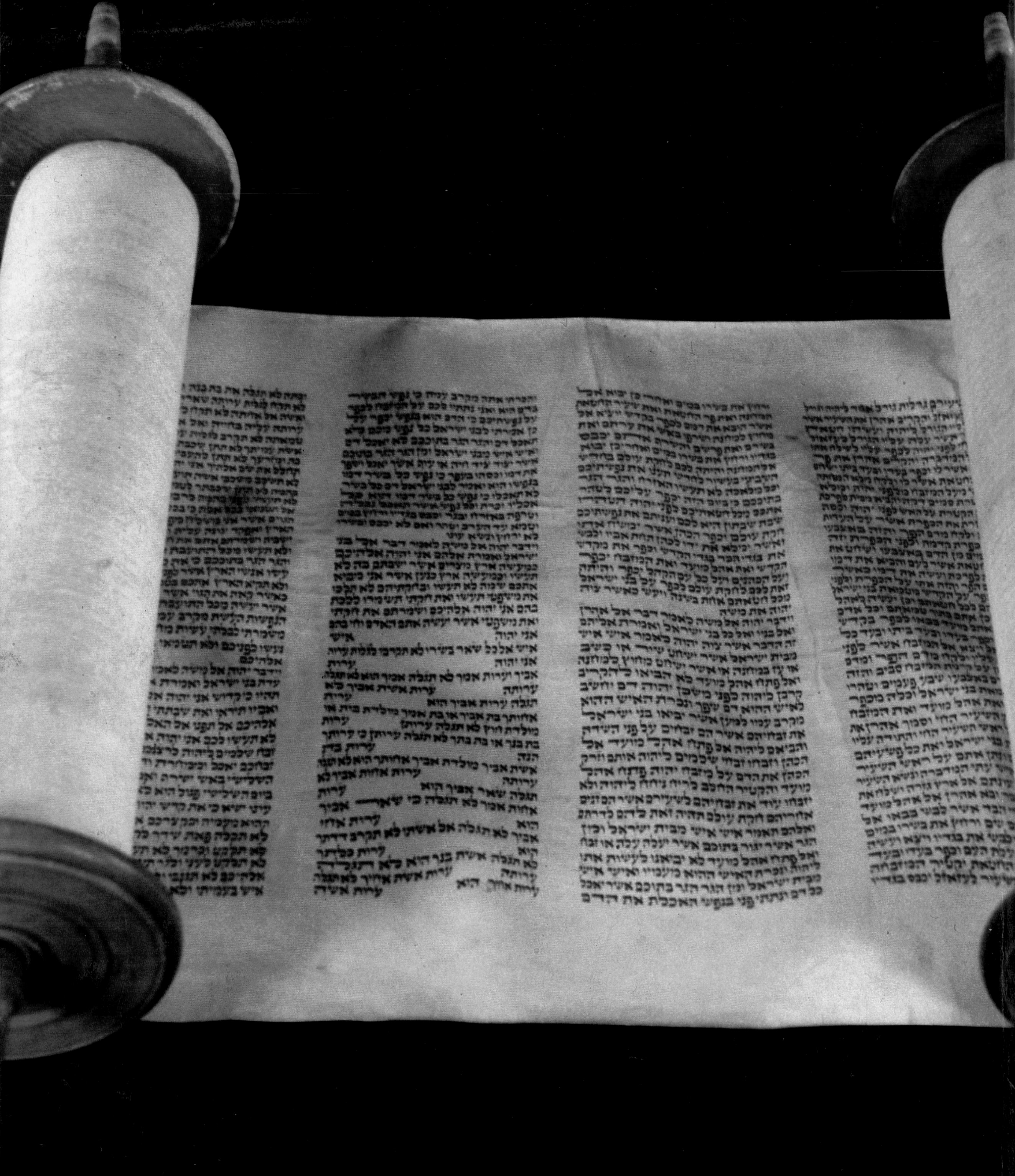

BAR MITZVAH

BY SARAH SILBERSTEIN SWARTZ
WITH AN INTRODUCTION BY PAUL COWAN

DOUBLEDAY & COMPANY, INC.
GARDEN CITY, NEW YORK
1985

The author would like to acknowledge the following people
for their contributions to this book:

Toni Olshen for her creative research and comments;
Stuart Schoenfeld for his guidance and consultations;
Patrick Crean for his editorial support and encouragement;
Elaine Newton for her helpful suggestions;
Jessica O'Brien for her patience and expertise with the typewriter.

Designed by David Wyman
Edited by Patrick Crean
Production by Paula Chabanais Productions
Text Consultation by Stuart Schoenfeld
Text Research by Toni Olshen
Picture Research by Katherine Bourbeau
Typesetting by Trigraph Inc
Cover and title page photographs by Jim Allen
Cover model: Jeremy Fine
Prayer shawl courtesy of Negev Bookstore, Toronto
Cover and title page Torah courtesy of
First Narayever Congregation, Toronto

Printed in Italy

Library of Congress Cataloging in Publication Data

Bar Mitzvah.
Summary: Excerpts from memoirs, biographies, novels,
short stories, religious, ethical, and psychological
literature, and visual art provide the bar mitzvah boy
with examples from his Jewish heritage.
1. Bar mitzvah—Addresses, essays, lectures.
[1. Bar mitzvah] I. Swartz, Sarah Silberstein, 1947-
BM707.B36 1985   296.4'424   85-4412
ISBN 0-385-19826-4

Produced by Somerville House Books Ltd.
24 Dinnick Crescent, Toronto, Ontario, Canada M4N 1L5

First Edition

Somerville House Books would like to thank Adrian Zackheim
for his editorial sense, support, and enthusiasm,
and D.C. for his cultural and historical contribution.

TABLE OF CONTENTS

INTRODUCTION

Dear Bar Mitzvah Boy,

In this book you will read many moving accounts of bar mitzvahs in Europe, in Israel, and among people who were part of another generation of American Jews. Some of these writings contain appealing memories. They are part of the past that created us.

This day—your bar mitzvah day—is occurring in an America our ancestors could never have imagined. Unlike some of the people who have contributed to this book, we are free in this land to do whatever we wish, to create ourselves in whatever image appeals to us. We can enter the school we choose; live in the most attractive place we see; marry whomever we want; pursue the profession that interests us most. And we can choose how Jewish we want to be. For that matter, we can choose whether we want to identify as Jews at all.

Like many of you, I have benefitted immensely from this freedom—and paid a price, too. I grew up right after the Holocaust, in a family which believed that, as Jews, our debt to the six million dead demanded that we fight for justice wherever we could. But my family also believed that the observant Judaism our ancestors practised—including the mitzvot that are described so lovingly in this book—was archaic and a little embarrassing. They were so removed from the tradition that it never occurred to them that I would have a bar mitzvah—which is why I feel some envy for you today.

As a result of this upbringing, I felt pride and ethical responsibility because I was a Jew. But I also felt a bewildering distance from Judaism. In those days, my parents had an apartment on Fifth Avenue in New York. As a 10- or 11-year-old boy, growing up before Israel's independence was celebrated, I'd gaze out the window at the St. Patrick's Day parade or Columbus Day parade, and wonder where my parade was. I felt different from other Americans—even from my closest gentile friends—but disconnected from my own past. Growing up in a large, noisy, loving family, I felt like an orphan in history.

That feeling burned inside me like an ember. In high school and college I had an unabating curiosity to learn whatever I could about Jews and Judaism. I read novels and history books; I tried to understand my religion; I dropped out of college for a year and lived in Israel. But I was reluctant to put what I learned into practice. I couldn't see any reason to restrict my diet, in accordance with kosher laws. It seemed strange to refrain from working on the Sabbath; boring to go to synagogue. Besides, I was worried that my non-religious friends would think I was

peculiar. I was worried that Jews who knew more than I did would laugh at my ignorance.

In those days, Judaism represented a suit of clothes that didn't fit. I wanted to roam America as I pleased, free from the demands of any religion or community. I loved my independence.

But when I was married and had children, a curious new feeling swept over me—one I couldn't have imagined when I was a teenager. I began to experience the independence I'd always treasured, as loneliness: sometimes I felt as I had when I was a boy, gazing out at the St. Patrick's Day parade. My wife—a social worker and photographer—and I—a reporter—both had work we enjoyed. We had many close friends. My daughter and son had playmates they loved. But it still seemed as if our family was an island. As a journalist, I had seen how warm ceremonies and stable communities gave texture and meaning to the lives of many of the people I wrote about. I yearned to weave those qualities into my own life: to possess what I had tried to escape just a few years earlier. Soon, the Jewish life I had been reading about since I was a boy seemed to offer a whisper of a promise. It offered the amber glow of peace.

I began to experience that promise more than a decade ago, with the Sabbath. In those years—as in these—many people my age were getting divorced. My children were five and three when they noticed what was happening to many of their friends' parents. They worried that their parents would get divorced, too. As a matter of fact, my wife and I had—and have—a happy marriage, but there are no words that can guarantee stability to an anxious child. So we began to light Friday night candles as a way of showing our love for each other and for our kids. It was an anchor in our week—a ritual that embodied light and warmth and joy. At first, though, it was difficult for me to put a yarmulke on my head and utter the barely familiar blessings. That act had little to do with my self-image. But soon those Friday nights became the part of the week that I anticipated most eagerly.

After a few years, the full Shabbat—from sundown Friday to sundown Saturday—came to represent a sacred space in a very worldly week. It allowed me to be part of the friendly community in my synagogue. It encouraged me to study the Torah—to see new depths in my ancient religion. It was a time when I could relax with my family, when I could read whatever I pleased. The people at the newspaper where I worked didn't care if I observed Shabbat as long as I did my job well the rest of the week. In fact, some of them seemed to envy me. I felt contentment when

Shabbat began, a sense of personal renewal when it was over.

I began to discover that Judaism can be a source of comfort and celebration—that it provided more means for enjoying and consoling myself than the Humphrey Bogart-like reporter's life I'd been living ever could. When my parents died, I found that observing the week-long mourning period—the *shivva* period—surrounded by loving friends, who took care of me and my family, helped ease my grief. When my children reached 13, I was thrilled to participate in their bat and bar mitzvahs: those events helped me express my love for them. Besides, every year it has seemed more satisfying to have exuberant holidays like Purim, introspective ones like Yom Kippur, and communal ones like Passover, as part of my life. Their very different rituals help me feel a wide range of emotions. They put me in touch with new aspects of my community—and of myself.

These traditions and holidays, I realized, would never have existed if all Jews had been like my younger self—full of Jewish feelings, but reluctant to express them in action. In other words, the laws I'd once seen as old-fashioned—the dietary laws, the practice of putting on tefillin that is described in these pages—had served to keep the religion I loved alive. These inexplicable, lovely observances were the cornerstone of the miracle that has allowed a small, embattled, hardy, exuberant group of people to endure for 4,000 years.

Without Jewish law there wouldn't be Jews. Without Jews who prospered in North America, Europe, and Israel, those who were oppressed in Ethiopia, Iran and the Soviet Union would have been abandoned. As my parents taught me when I was a boy, Jewish history and the Jewish people had claims on me as a human being. But I felt those claims more deeply—and was able to respond to them more fully—through the observances that seemed off-limits when I lived in my parents' house, and which began to give me such pleasure when I lived in my own. For example, when I wound the thongs of my tefillin around my arm in the morning, I felt securely wedded to a people that had existed since the Exodus. When I went to synagogue and heard the Torah read each Shabbat, I realized that Jews in the United States and France, Canada and Argentina, Israel and even the Soviet Union were listening to the very same words—and that they would welcome me as a brother if I visited their cities.

These mitzvot made me feel like part of a community that stretched back in time to Abraham and wove through most of the countries of my contemporary world. When I began to heed them, I had to face a question that had been brewing in my mind for most of my life—a question that became particularly acute when the prospect of observing religious laws seemed confining, not nourishing. Should I continue to explore Judaism, the living link with my ancestors, with the six million, with my people all over the globe? Or should I resist it, and be a conscious participant in the obliteration of 4000 years of history? Put that way, of course, it wasn't really a question. It was a summons to a way of life. The challenge was to respond to it fully without relinquishing the American freedom I had come to love. That challenge was a blessing bestowed on me by my country and my religion. It was a chance to be part of a generation of Jewish pioneers who could explore and develop our faith and enrich our community here in the land of our birth.

Some of you who are reading this book might feel the emotions I am describing right now. Others might, like me, feel them in 10 or 20 years. Some may never feel them at all.

Some of you will see this book as the perfect symbol of the rite of passage you have just experienced. Others may regard it as just one small drop in the ocean of presents you received after you read your Torah portion and your haftorah. But I urge you to treasure it, and to fill in the pages about yourself, your family, and your community as soon as you can. For in time, your bar mitzvah and this book will represent the precious legacy you want for yourself—and, one day, for your children.

Mazel Tov,

Paul Cowan,
New York.

vii

In memory of my father, Menachem Silberstein,
who taught me how to be a Jew,
just by being himself.

PART ONE
THE JEWISH INDIVIDUAL

''Today I am a man of duty.''

All Beginnings Are Hard

All beginnings are hard.

I can remember hearing my mother murmur those words while I lay in bed with a fever. "Children are often sick, darling. That's the way it is with children. All beginnings are hard. You'll be all right soon."

I remember bursting into tears one evening because a passage of Bible commentary had proved too difficult for me to understand. I was about nine years old at the time. "You want to understand everything immediately?" my father said. "Just like that? You only began to study this commentary last week. All beginnings are hard. You have to work at the job of studying. Go over it again and again."

The man who later guided me in my studies would welcome me warmly into his apartment and, when we sat at his desk, say to me in his gentle voice, "Be patient, David. The midrash says, 'All beginnings are hard.' You cannot swallow all the world at one time."

I say to myself today when I stand before a new class at the beginning of a school year or am about to start a new book or research paper: All beginnings are hard. Teaching the way I do is particularly hard, for I touch the raw nerves of faith, the beginnings of things. Often students are shaken. I say to them what was said to me: "Be patient. You are learning a new way of understanding the Bible. All beginnings are hard." And sometimes I add what I have learned on my own: "Especially a beginning that you make by yourself. That's the hardest beginning of all."

Chaim Potok, from *In the Beginning*.

(Above) A Russian immigrant boy from Kiev celebrates his first Hanukah in America.

(Preceding page) A young man, wearing tallit and tefillin, reads his prayer book in a kibbutz synagogue.

Bar Mitzvah marks an important beginning in your life. It is your initiation into Jewish adulthood and into the Jewish community. On becoming thirteen years of age, you are recognized as a "man of duty" or more literally a "son of the commandments." According to Jewish tradition, gone are the carefree days of childhood, when you could do as you pleased without considering the consequences, when your physical and spiritual welfare was provided for by your parents. Now, you are responsible for yourself.

Whether you have a customary Bar Mitzvah ceremony, an alternative Bar Mitzvah, or no recognizable Bar Mitzvah ceremony at all, at age thirteen you are seen as an adult in the eyes of Jewish law. And as a Jewish adult, you are the recipient of responsibilities and privileges, both religious and personal. Certain religious rituals are symbols of your new adult responsibilities. You are counted as a member of the *minyan*, the necessary quorum for prayer. You are eligible for an *aliyah*, the privilege of being called to read from the Torah during synagogue services. And, traditionally, you are obligated to wear a *tallit*, the prayer shawl, and to don *tefillin*, phylacteries, for morning prayers. You are also obligated to observe fast days such as Yom Kippur and your oath is legally binding.

Whether you accept traditional Jewish practices or whether you find your own ways of experiencing your Jewishness, you are on the threshold of becoming a Jewish "man of duty" for your entire life–a person with certain responsibilities and moral obligations to yourself, your family, your community, as well as to the rest of the world. You are not only responsible for your own conduct, but you must also act with respect for yourself and others. Filling this role doesn't happen all at once. Intellectual and spiritual maturity is a long involved process which takes time and experience. Bar Mitzvah is merely the symbolic beginning of this evolution.

Ancient rabbinical sources stated that it was at age thirteen that a male began to acquire the faculty for sound reasoning and good judgment, as well as the ability to control his desires. It was at this age, according to a Midrash, a commentary on the Bible, that Abraham rejected the idols of his father. It was also at age thirteen that Jacob and Esau went their separate ways–Jacob to study Torah, Esau to worship idols. Current psychologists agree that at puberty young people begin not only to understand themselves better, but also to understand what is expected of them by society.

Many ancient civilizations celebrated the passage from childhood to adulthood at puberty. These initiation rites, which welcomed the younger generation into the adult community, were a means of perpetuating that society. Becoming a man meant becoming a citizen of the community with the responsibility of affirming and preserving it. Initiation required a certain amount of preparation, and the ceremony usually reflected what had already been learned and absorbed in childhood. Often, the rites were a test of physical endurance, and the young man's ability to persevere through the ordeal confirmed him as a full-fledged member of the community.

The Bar Mitzvah ceremony probably originated as a type of initiation rite. In typical Jewish fashion, however, the emphasis is on the spiritual and intellectual, rather than on the physical. Bar Mitzvah is an educational experience for which the young man has been preparing himself arduously for months–if not for years. Historically, the cultural, intellectual, and emotional preparation for Bar Mitzvah began long before age thirteen. A boy was first taught the Hebrew alphabet at age three, studied the Bible at age five, and learned rabbinical commentaries at age ten. He was taken to the synagogue on a regular basis by age four, and, from then on, was formally educated in Jewish culture and values. All of this culminated in the Bar Mitzvah ceremony. The Bar Mitzvah was in a sense the young man's ordeal by intellect, after which he was accepted as a full-fledged member of the Jewish community.

"Mitzvah" literally means commandment or law. There are

many "mitzvot" of conduct and observance within the Jewish tradition. "Bar" means son in the Aramaic language, but in context it means "responsible for." At age thirteen, you are traditionally responsible for the commandments of God. You are part of the 4,000-year continuum of Jewish heritage and its framework of values, and it is your privilege to live a Jewish way of life.

The Beginning and Ending of Childhood

Circumcision, ordained in Torah, and Bar Mitzvah, established by custom, have become inviolate for most Jews. Actually, there is a relationship between them, intuitively recognized by Jews. Any child of a Jewish mother is automatically a Jew. Circumcision formally seals him in this status. As it occurs, the father assumes his responsibility to bring him into the covenant. Bar Mitzvah, equally automatically, concludes the first stage of the child's life. As it is observed in celebration, the father proclaims that he is now relieved of the responsibility for the religious conduct of his son. The young Jew now has to stand on his own feet. Circumcision and Bar Mitzvah are the two pillars of the structure that bridges the years of childhood.

Leo Trepp

A birth blessing, handwritten by a Galician Jew in 1902 for his brother-in-law's son, born in New York City.

The following Jewish folktale tells the story of an extraordinary Bar Mitzvah boy named Joseph and his initiation into manhood. On the day of his Bar Mitzvah, he has a dream which leads him on an adventure during which he must demonstrate a multitude of adult virtues: courage, belief, perseverance and intellect. Joseph is a typical Jewish hero, a hero of the intellect.

A Dream of Promise

Time was, our people, the people of the Book, the Hebrew people, were close to God and had faith to dream.

In those days, there grew up among them a boy, a poor boy, an orphan boy. His name was Joseph.

Joseph lived on the edge of a remote, windswept little hamlet overlooking the endless, empty steppes; by the shadow of a burnt-out, hollow sycamore that serviced as lookout against the enemy and gallows for the wicked; in the cellar of a tumbledown poorhouse, at the bottom of a potter's field.

Early each morning, dressed in his threadbare black caftan, black pantaloons, hose and half-boots, and black high-crowned velvet hat, Joseph left his cellar for the House of Study.

There, among the shelves stuffed with books from floor to ceiling, he studied, from dawn to dusk and dusk to dawn, sometimes in the company of his fellow-scholars but, at other times, when the hour was too early or too late, alone. He rested only long enough to take his turn warming himself at the bench behind the stove. He stopped only when called upon to perform the duties that earned his keep—caring for the books and scrolls, waiting on the worshippers at the ritual baths, running through the village to rap his little hammer at the windows of the faithful to summon them for midnight prayer.

Then, at last, in that early morning hour when spirits, demons, and imps are said to lurk about in the air, just before the crowing of the cock, Joseph returned to the depths of his cellar.

Slight and slender was the boy Joseph, like the scroll that is carried through the House of Study on the sabbath and festivals, pale as the scroll's parchment of white calf leather, mysteriously silent as its china-ink letters and words that he searched and studied every day.

But, from under Joseph's crown of copper curls, there flowed an open radiant face, with eyes of amber that threw out sparks, and, when he read, or recited psalms or sang lamentations, his voice was that of a lion.

In his thirteenth year, Joseph came of age and was confirmed in the faith.

In the House of Study on that festive day, as the worshippers told out their prayers, they swayed back and forth in ecstasy, they clapped their hands and stamped their feet, they shouted out in exultation. Joseph danced, his every step a mystery powerful as the eternal motion of the spheres in the heavens.

As the celebrations reached into the night, Joseph fell asleep on the bench behind the stove. In the atmosphere of wonder and miracles that suffused the House of Study, enveloped in the drowsy scent of burning wax and blessed spices, he had a dream.

In his dream, an angel appeared. The angel bade him leave at once for the capital city of the land; there, he was to seek out the king and ask him for a treasure—the treasure that is the inheritance of the dreamer, the dreamer of faith.

In the morning, Joseph told the strange dream to his fellow scholars, but they only laughed.

"A dream is all very fine and pretty. And it costs nothing, to be sure. But of what use is it?" they mocked. "You can eat it,

The angel appears in Joseph's dream in this drawing by Ruben Zellermayer.

perhaps?'' snorted one. "It will clothe you, maybe?'' snickered another. "It's a roof over your head, possibly?'' simpered a third.

Time passed, and the strange dream came to Joseph a second time. Again, his fellow scholars only sniffed and sneered at him.

"May your vain dreams be scattered in the wind!'' scolded the rabbi of the House of Study. "Go, work. Better yet, study. Best of all, pray.''

But when, after some time, the dream came to Joseph a third time, he made immediate preparations to obey the call.

"So be it!'' he cried. "I will follow the dream. For faith is clearer than sight. And trust is surer than understanding.''

And with a staff in his hand, and all his belongings in a bundle on his back, Joseph set out by foot for the capital city.

The journey was long and the way beset with hardships and perils.

Most of the time he travelled. But now and again, to earn his keep for the way, he stopped off to work—as a porter in the bazaar, a boiler of pitch, a chicken plucker.

After a season, Joseph at last reached the capital city.

On the eve of the day set for audience with the king, he set out for the royal palace. All night long he waited in the shadow of its walls, and early next morning, he entered its court to join a seething, humming crowd that swirled and streamed its endless way toward the king's chamber.

At sunset, as the guards prepared to close the doors, the crowds erupted and boiled over like a volcano. In their frenzy, they broke rank, pushing and pressing, so that Joseph was again and again lifted off his feet and propelled pell-mell toward the king's throne.

In a moment, he found himself swept into the royal presence; suddenly he was face to face with the king.

Watery, red-rimmed eyes peered out at Joseph from behind a milky-white shag that framed a face withered and hollow like an ancient goat's.

"Speak!" the king bleated. "Speak! Speak!"

"If it please you, Sire," Joseph fell to his knees at the king's feet, "I had a dream, a dream of promise. An angel bade me journey to the capital city and hasten before you to ask for a treasure—the treasure that is the inheritance of the dreamer, the dreamer of faith."

And Joseph fell forward on his face.

Waves of stillness rippled out over the king's chambers; a hush settled on the crowd.

The king's scribe now ceased his scratching on the parchment, and wiped his quill on a shirtsleeve. The king's counsellor shrugged uncomprehendingly. Doffing his cocked hat, he mopped his brow with it and fanned himself. The king fixed Joseph with his rheumy eyes. Now and then, as if on the point of speaking, his gums moved like a goat chewing the cud.

"Are you then a sorcerer, boy, that you listen to voices and follow visions?" he gasped at last.

"Or a benighted fool, to wear out your boots to humor a dream?" the counsellor prodded Joseph's prostrate form with the toe of his slipper.

"Or a lunatic in a cloud cuckooland?" guffawed the scribe. "Why, if *I* had believed what a dream once showed *me*.... Treasure, treasure, treasure! Under the cellar stove of a tumble-down poor-house at the bottom of a potter's field—of *all* places, now, I *ask* you! By the shadow of a burnt-out hollow sycamore—well, mightn't *that* be just anywhere from here to the back of beyond? On the edge of a lonely little hamlet overlooking the endless, empty steppes—why, I could *still* be scratching around for pie in the sky, this very *day!*"

And the guards seized Joseph and threw him out of the king's chambers.

And so, with a staff in his hand and all his belongings in a bundle on his back, Joseph departed the capital city and set out for home once more.

The journey was long and the way beset with hardships and perils.

Most of the time he travelled. But now and again, to earn his keep for the way, he stopped off to work—as a water-carrier, a peddler of herring, a chimney sweep's help.

After a season, Joseph at last reached his hamlet again.

He went straight down into the depths of his cellar and dug under the old stove.

There, he found the treasure.

With the treasure, Joseph built a House of Study, with room to lodge the poor, the orphaned, and the aged. He became rabbi of the House and, in time, his teaching drew followers from across the land. Whenever he welcomed a new disciple, he told his story, saying:

"Search for your dream, take it to your heart, make it your own by faith. This dream is your priceless treasure.

"The treasure must be found, but no one can find it for you, you must find it for yourself.

"Your treasure is to be found neither in books, nor from hearsay, nor even by travel to the very ends of the earth; for it is in no other person, place, or thing: your treasure is in yourself."

Meguido Zola.

"At age thirteen one becomes subject to the commandments."

Talmud *Avot 5 : 21.*

"What does it mean to be thirteen? The night before my son became a bar mitzvah, I decided that I would say good night and 'tuck him in,' something that I had not done for years. I went to his room and found that he had already fallen asleep with his light on. As I tiptoed in to turn off the light, I saw that under one arm he clutched his old teddy bear, and in the other he held a copy of Playboy magazine. That's what it means to be thirteen."

Sharon Strassfeld and Kathy Green, *The Jewish Family Book*.

RELIGIOUS JEWISH IDENTITY

"These are the things whose fruits a person eats in this world while the capital remains for him in the world to come: honoring one's parents, the practice of loving-kindness, hospitality to strangers, and making peace between a person and his neighbor. And the study of Torah surpasses them all."

Babylonian *Talmud*, tractate *Kiddushin*.

The experience of Bar Mitzvah often raises the issue of Jewish identity. This, coupled with your increasing self-examination and expanding intellect, has probably brought you to the question: "What does it mean to be a Jew?"

From a religious viewpoint, Jews are the descendants of Abraham who have a special covenant with God, which involves a strong belief in God and an eternal commitment to carrying out God's commandments. The Jewish conception of God is of a moral diety who demands ethical conduct and justice for all people. Acting in accordance with biblical and rabbinical law, as stated in the Torah and the *Talmud*, is a Jew's central obligation.

TORAH

Religious Jews rely on the Torah to guide them in their conduct. The following is an explanation by a rabbinical authority of the significance of Torah to Orthodox Jewry.

The Living Torah

Torah is the embodiment of the Jewish faith. It contains the terms of his Covenant with God. It is what makes a Jew a Jew.... If it possesses any enduring value and truth, the Torah must be seen as a record not of man's spiritual genius, but of God's will communicated to mortal and finite man. No interpretation of Judaism is Jewishly valid if it does not posit God as the *source* of Torah.

What is Torah? Technically it refers to the Five Books of Moses. This is the Written Torah (*Torah SheBiktav*). The scroll upon which it is written and which is kept in the Holy Ark of the synagogue is called a scroll of the Torah (*Sefer Torah*). In a sense, this is the constitution of the Jewish people. But this constitution was promulgated not by men, but revealed by God. By Torah is also meant the Oral Torah (*Torah She-B'al Peh*) "which Moses received at Sinai, and transmitted to Joshua, and Joshua to the Elders, and the Elders to the Prophets, and the Prophets to the Men of the Great Assembly..." (Ethics of the Fathers 1:1).

The Oral Torah included the finer points of the commandments, the details of the general principles contained in the Scriptures and the ways by which the commandments were to be applied. For example, the Torah forbids "work" on the Sabbath. What constitutes "work"? How shall "work" be defined for purposes of the Sabbath? Except for several references to such

"Judaism is one religion based entirely on learning. Its very essence is the Torah, a scroll, a book." Isaac Bashevis Singer.

tasks as gathering wood, kindling fire, cooking and baking, the Written Torah does not say. The Oral Torah does.

The Written Torah commands that animals needed for food be killed "as I have commanded thee." How shall this slaughtering take place? What regulations govern such slaughtering? The Written Torah does not say. The Oral Torah does.

The Written Torah commands us to "bind them as a sign upon your hands and as frontlets between your eyes." This reference to *tefillin* leaves us in the dark as to how they were to be made up, what they were to consist of, how they were to be donned. The Written Torah does not say. The Oral Torah does.

The Written Torah prescribes capital punishment for various crimes. What legal rules and procedures had to be followed before such a verdict could be handed down? What were the limitations? The Written Torah does not say. The Oral Torah does.

Ultimately, this Oral Torah was reduced to writing. During the second century C.E., it was incorporated into the Mishna, which in turn became the cornerstone for the Gemara which consists of the monumental records and minutes of the case discussions and legal debates conducted by the Sages. Mishna and Gemara together make up the Talmud.

The Torah, whether Written or Oral, is the teaching that directs man how to live. Although it speaks primarily to Israel (Jewry), it also has directives for all men. It is concerned with every aspect of human life. Ritual laws, generally thought of as "religious observances," are only part of the total complex of commandments. The commandments of the Torah, its statutes and regulations, cover the entire range of human and social behavior. It asserts its jurisdiction in areas of behavior which in other religions are generally thought of as belonging to the ethical or moral domains or to the jurisdiction of secular civil and criminal codes of law. Even its non-legal and non-statutory sections stress spiritual truths and convey insight into the still finer extra-legal ethical and moral norms of behavior.

The rest of the books of the Hebrew Bible, written over a period of many centuries, consists of the Prophets (*Neviim*) and the Sacred Writings (*Ketuvim*). These books convey the teachings of the Prophets in the context of Israel's history over a period of about seven hundred years. They tell of the Prophets' visions of God and of their ongoing struggles to promote greater allegiance among the people to the teachings of the Torah; of their struggles against the many false prophets and priests who so often misled the people and turned them away from God and the Torah. Among these books is the inspirational Psalms that reflects man's deepest religious sentiments.

The Torah, with the Neviim and the Ketuvim are together referred to as *Ta Nakh*. (This is what non-Jews call the "Old Testament" but which to the Jew has always been the *only* Testament.) In the broadest sense, however, the study of Torah refers not only to the Scriptures and the Oral Torah, but also to the entire body of rabbinic legislation and interpretation based upon the Torah that developed over the centuries. For the Torah was always a living law, constantly applied by a living people to real conditions that were often changing. Though these are obviously the result of human efforts, they are an integral part of the entire body of religious jurisprudence to which the Torah itself grants authoritative status: "And you shall observe and do according to all that they shall teach you. According to the law which they shall teach you and according to the judgment which they shall tell you, you shall do" (Deut. 17:10-11).

Rabbi Hayim Halevy Donin.

The following parable carries a message about the importance of preserving the Torah and its place in the continuity of Jewish culture.

The Guarantors

It is told, in one of the ancient books, of the time when God was ready to give the Torah to the children of Israel.

As Israel stood ready to receive this precious gift, the Holy One, Blessed be He, said: "I will give you My Torah. But first you must bring Me good guarantors, that I may know you will guard it well."

And the children of Israel said: "Let our fathers be our guarantors: Abraham, Isaac, and Jacob."

And God said: "Your fathers are not acceptable to Me. Abraham is unacceptable, Isaac is unacceptable, and Jacob is unacceptable. But offer Me good guarantors, and I shall yet give the Torah to you."

Then the children of Israel said: "Master of the Universe, we offer you our prophets as guarantors."

And God replied: "The prophets are unacceptable to Me. Bring Me good guarantors that I may give the Torah to you."

And then the children of Israel said: "Let our children and our children's children be our guarantors."

And the Holy One, Blessed be He, said: "Your children and your children's children are good guarantors. For their sake will I give the Torah to you."

Adapted from the *Aggadah* by Azriel Eisenberg.

(Above) Tallit being woven on looms.   (Preceding pages) Torah covers from the Portuguese synagogue in Amsterdam. The synagogue was protected from the Nazis by being declared a national monument.

TEFILLIN AND TALLIT

Hear, O Israel, the Lord our God, the Lord is One.

And thou shalt love the Lord thy God with all thy heart, and with all thy soul, and with all thy might. And these words, which I command thee this day, shall be upon thy heart; and thou shalt teach them diligently unto thy children, and shalt talk of them when thou sittest in thy house, and when thou walkest by the way, and when thou liest down, and when thou risest up. And thou shalt bind them for a sign upon thy hand, and they shall be frontlets between thine eyes. And thou shalt write them upon the door-posts of thy house, and upon thy gates.

Deuteronomy 6:4-9.

And the Lord spoke unto Moses, saying: "Speak unto the children of Israel, and bid them that they make them throughout their generations fringes in the corners of their garments, and that they put with the fringe of each corner a thread of blue. And it shall be unto you for a fringe, that ye may look upon it, and remember all the commandments of the Lord, and do them; and that ye go not about after your own heart and your own eyes, after which ye use to go astray; that ye may remember and do all My commandments, and be holy unto your God. I am the Lord

your God, who brought you out of the land of Egypt, to be your God: I am the Lord your God."

Numbers 15:37-41.

These passages from Deuteronomy and Numbers in the Torah, with their commandments to love and honor God, are the basis of two important personal observances followed by traditional Jewry: the binding of the tefillin and the wearing of the tallit. Every day at the morning prayer service, except for the sabbath and festivals, the tefillin are bound on the arm and then on the head, while appropriate blessings and prayers are recited. Every day of the year (never in the evenings, except on Yom Kippur), the tallit, with its blue or black stripes and its tassels, is worn to services. Applied to the body, these two rituals are personal expressions of one's own relationship with God, symbolic reminders of one's religious convictions in everyday life.

The Hebrew word *tefillah* comes from a root meaning prayer or self-examination. Tefillin are cubes which contain passages from the Torah, handwritten on parchment by a scribe. They are attached to the head, the root of intellect, and the arm, the instrument of action, with leather straps.

Tefillin is the religious symbol most closely identified with becoming Bar Mitzvah. Since a boy under thirteen years of age is not allowed to put on tefillin, it is the most visible religious ritual that sets the men apart from the boys. However, it is customary for a twelve-year-old to begin putting on the tefillin one to three months prior to the Bar Mitzvah and not to wait until the actual birthdate.

Instructions for Putting on Tefillin

• One should stand while putting on or taking off tefillin.

• While putting on the tefillin, one should not engage in conversation or allow one's attention to be diverted. One neither answers "Amen" nor responds to the Kaddish nor joins in Kedushah. If one is in the midst of putting on one's tefillin and hears either Kaddish or Kedushah being recited, one should merely stop to listen without joining in the responses.

• Take out the hand tefillin (*shel yad*) from the bag, unwind the leather straps (*retzuot*), and remove the ornamental case.

• Place the hand tefillin on the left arm. A left-handed person puts tefillin on his right arm.

• The hand tefillin is set on the biceps of the arm in such a way that the broad side of the lip or edge is set toward the top of the arm and not the bottom.

• Before tightening the strap around the biceps, check to make sure that the knot is adjacent to the box and has not slid away.

• Recite the following blessing:

> *Barukh atah Adonai eloheinu melekh ha olam, asher kidshanu b'mitzvotav, v'tzivanu l'hani ah tefillin.*
>
> *Blessed be Thou, Lord our God, King of the universe, who sanctified us with His commandments, and commanded us to put on tefillin.*

• Tighten the strap and wind it seven times around the forearm below the elbow with a counter-clockwise motion. (This accords with Ashkenazic practice. In the Hassidic-Sephardic tradition, the knot on the hand tefillin faces away from the person, so that the strap must be wound around the arm with an outward clockwise motion.) Make sure that the black side of the leather strap is on the outside. Then wrap the remaining length of strap around the palm of the hand.

• Take out the head tefillin from the bag. Unwind the straps, remove the ornamental case, and place the tefillin upon the head.

• Tefillin must come in direct contact with the body—on the head as well as on the arm—without any intervening materials.

• Before adjusting the tefillin on the head, recite the following blessing and declaration:

> *Barukh atah Adonai eloheinu melekh ha olam, asher kidshanu b'mitzvotav, v'tzivanu al mitzvat tefillin.*
> *Barukh shem kvod malkhuto l'olam va ed.*
>
> *Blessed art Thou, Lord our God, King of the universe, who has sanctified us with His commandments, and commanded us concerning the mitzvah of tefillin.*
> *Blessed is the name of His Glorious Majesty forever and ever.*

• Adjust the tefillin to rest comfortably and correctly on the head as illustrated. The head tefillin should be placed above the forehead in such a way that it lies above the hairline and is centered between the eyes. The knot on the headstrap should be centered behind the head at the base of the skull. The straps are brought forward and allowed to hang loosely in front of the chest.

• Unwrap the strap from around the middle of the palm and wind it three times around the middle finger: once around the middle part of the finger and twice around the lower part

closest to the knuckle. The remainder of the strap is then carried around the ring finger and rewound around the palm. While doing this, or immediately thereafter, say the following:

> *I will betroth you to me forever; I will betroth you to me in righteousness and justice, in kindness and mercy; I will betroth you to me in faithfulness and you shall know the Lord (Hosea 2:21-22).*

When removing the tefillin, reverse the procedure:

• Unwind the strap around the fingers, rewinding it about the palm.

• Remove the head tefillin and wrap it up neatly.

• Unwind the strap around the palm and the forearm and slip off the hand tefillin. Wrap it up neatly.

It is customary to kiss the tefillin when taking them out of their bag or before putting them back in.

Rabbi Hayim Halevy Donin.

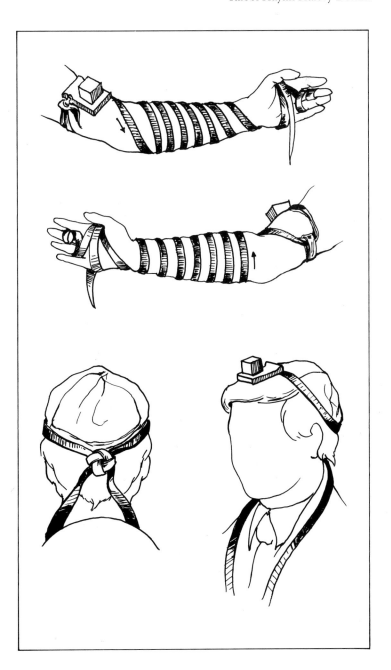

"When a man puts on the phylactery of the hand, he should stretch out his left arm as though to draw to him the Community of Israel and to embrace her with the right arm."

Canticles, Song of Songs, Leviticus, 55a.

Gift

I will make him a little red sack
    For treasure untold,
With a velvet front and a satin back,
    And braided with gold,
    His *Tefilin* to hold.

I will stitch it with letters of flame,
    With square characters:
His name, and his father's name;
    And beneath it some terse
    Scriptural verse.

Yes, singing the sweet liturgy,
    He'll snare its gold cord,
Remembering me, even me,
    In the breath of his word,
    In the sight of the Lord.

Abraham M. Klein.

(Above) A tallit bag from North Africa, with cut-out silver ornament on blue velvet. Circa 1715.

(Opposite page) Checking correctness of tefillin.

The tallit is a four-cornered garment with fringes attached to each corner. It is the fringes on the corners, the *tzitzit*, that provide the prayer shawl with its religious significance. They are a reminder of God's commandments according to the biblical passage in Numbers: "Make...fringes on the corners of their garments...and remember all the commandments of the Lord...." Although four-cornered robes were common in ancient times, changing styles would have rendered this important commandment obsolete. Therefore, a specially made four-cornered prayer shawl was devised to accommodate the fringes.

The shorter fringes, often found on the sides of tallit, are not tzitzit, but only ornaments without significance. The actual tzitzit are tied to the tallit in a very specific way. There is much mysticism, as well as symbolic meaning, attached to the procedure. For example, the 39 windings that go into the making of each of the four fringes equals the numerical value of the Hebrew words for "The Lord is One."

Instructions for Putting on a Tallit

- Spread open the tallit and hold it in both hands while standing. Recite the following blessing:

    Barukh atah Adonai eloheinu melekh ha olam, asher kidshanu b'mitzvotav, v'tzivanu l'hitatef b'tzitzit.

    Blessed be Thou, Lord our God, King of the universe, who sanctified us with His commandments, and commanded us to wrap ourselves in the tzitzit.

- Throw the tallit over your shoulders in much the same way as you would a cape.

- Before adjusting the tallit so that it rests comfortably on the shoulders, it is customary momentarily to wrap the tallit around one's head immediately following the above blessing.

The tallit is always put on before the tefillin in accordance with the principle of always ascending in holiness. First we *cover* ourselves with a tallit, and then move to *bind* ourselves with the symbols of holiness. The tallit is given priority also because of the general rule: That which is observed more often precedes that which is observed less often. In this case, a tallit is worn all seven days of the week, while tefillin are worn only on weekdays. At the end of the service, the procedure is reversed. The tefillin are removed first, and the tallit is taken off last. The rule to remember is first on, last off!

Rabbi Hayim Halevy Donin.

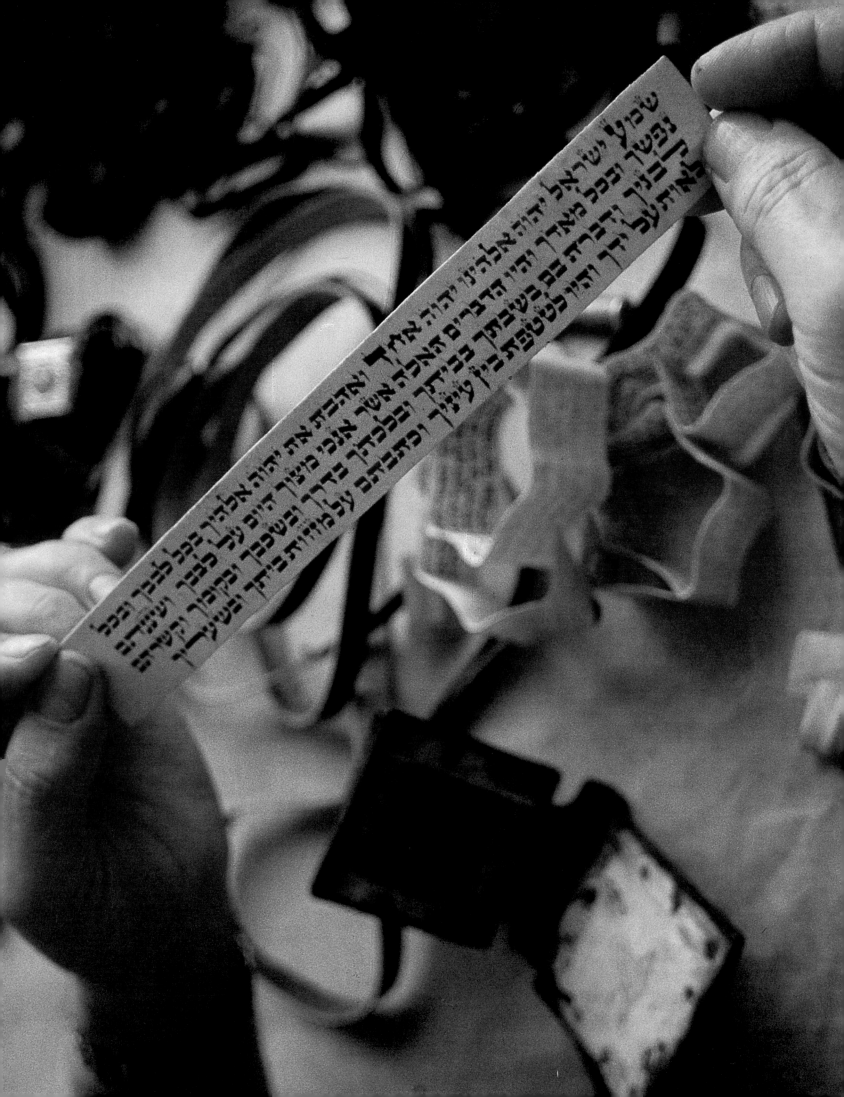

PERSONAL JEWISH IDENTITY

"In life, you discover that people are called three names: One is the name the person is called by his father and mother; one is the name people call him, and one is the name he acquires for himself. The best one is the one he acquires for himself."

Tanchuma, Vayakhel, 1.

There are many ways, other than by observing religious ritual, of identifying oneself as a Jew. One can identify oneself with Jewish history, Jewish nationhood or Jewish culture. Or one can take on certain identity traits that are based on Jewish values.

The term "identity" refers to a psychological awareness of oneself as an individual, and of one's uniqueness among other people. It was in fact first used as a psychoanalytic concept by Sigmund Freud, with reference to his own Jewish identity. A non-practising Jew, Freud stated that his interest in Judaism stemmed from a common identity and a readiness to stand up to a common enemy.

My language is German. My culture, my attainments are German. I considered myself German intellectually, until I noticed the growth of anti-Semitic prejudice in Germany and German Austria. Since that time, I consider myself no longer a German. I prefer to call myself a Jew.

* * *

No reader of [the Hebrew version of] this book [*Totem and Taboo*] will find it easy to put himself in the emotional position of an author who is ignorant of the language of holy writ, who is completely estranged from the religion of his fathers–as well as from every other religion–and who cannot take a share in nationalist ideals, but who has yet never repudiated his people, who feels that he is in his essential nature a Jew and who has no desire to alter that nature. If the question were put to him: 'Since you have abandoned all these common characteristics of your countrymen, what is there left to you that is Jewish?' he would reply: 'A great deal, and probably its very essence.' He could not now express that essence clearly in words; but some day, no doubt, it will become accessible to the scientific mind.

Sigmund Freud.

Another great thinker of the same era, Albert Einstein, was much less hesitant and more jubilant about his Jewish identification.

The pursuit of knowledge for its own sake, an almost fanatical love of justice, and the desire for personal independence–these are the features of Jewish tradition which make me thank my stars that I belong to it.

* * *

The essence of the Jewish concept of life seems to me to be the affirmation of life for all creatures. For the life of the individual has meaning only in the service of enhancing and ennobling the life of every living thing. Life is holy; i.e. it is the highest worth on which all other values depend. The sanctification of the life which transcends the individual brings with it reverence for the spiritual, a peculiarly characteristic trait of Jewish tradition.

There remains, however, something more in the Jewish tradition, so gloriously revealed in certain of the psalms; namely, a kind of drunken joy and surprise at the beauty and incomprehensible sublimity of this world, of which man can attain but a faint intimation. It is the feeling from which genuine research draws its intellectual strength, but which also seems to manifest itself in the song of birds. This appears to me to be the loftiest content of the God-idea.

Albert Einstein.

Other Jews, both infamous and ordinary, have expressed their Jewish identity in different ways. Here are some examples.

Why I Am a Jew

I am a Jew because born of Israel and having lost it, I felt it revive me more alive than I am myself.

I am a Jew because born of Israel, and having found it again, I would have it live after me even more alive than it is within me.

I am a Jew because the faith of Israel demands no abdication of my mind.

I am a Jew because the faith of Israel asks every possible sacrifice of my soul.

I am a Jew because in every age when the cry of despair is heard the Jew hopes.

I am a Jew because in all places where there are tears and suffering the Jew weeps.

I am a Jew because the message of Israel is the most ancient and the most modern.

I am a Jew because Israel's promise is a universal promise.

I am a Jew because for Israel the world is not finished; men will complete it.

I am a Jew because for Israel man is not yet created: men are creating him.

Edmond Fleg.

Judaism–a Nation or a Religion?

Are the Jews a nation or a religion? The Jews are, and always have been, both. This is unique in today's world, but in the ancient world, of which the Jews are the one surviving intact culture, it was common for a nation to have a religion that was unique to it. To this day, the Jews remain a nation defined by its religion: even secular Jews recognize that one cannot be a Christian or Muslim Jew, that by becoming a member of the Christian or Muslim *religion*, one is no longer a member of the Jewish *nation*. Similarly, all Jews recognize that a member of any nation can become a member of the Jewish nation only by converting to the Jewish religion. On the other hand, a completely irreligious Jew is as much a Jew as the most religious one, because Jews are also a nation. Thus, an American Jew is a member of two nations, the American and the Jewish–though his only country or state is the United States. Attempts by Jews or non-Jews to tear the national or religious limb from Judaism have resulted in the assimilation or destruction of Jews.

Dennis Prager and Joseph Telushkin.

JEWISH VALUES AND OTHER CHARACTERISTICS

"At one time in Lithuania–perhaps not so much today– Torah was held in higher esteem than money. A boor, no matter how rich, was nothing more than a boor. Never would he be voluntarily accorded a place of honor or listened to open-mouthed. Oh, no! To be worthy of that, one had to be learned, good, pious, and come of a good family. Prestige depended not on the moneybags but upon the mind and the heart."

Mendele Mokher Sforim.

FAITH

Certain ethics are central to Judaism. Though most have a religious base, they are often deeply ingrained, even in those who do not practise traditional Judaism. Faith is one of these important Jewish values. The following story tells of a Bar Mitzvah boy's strong faith.

The Law

On and off, that whole summer, I wondered what my uncle Willi was going to do about his son. The boy, Danny, was going to be thirteen on the twelfth of July, and as early as February, I remembered, Willi was talking about having his Bar Mitzvah at their Temple in Queens; the whole works–a service in the morning and a party for the family and their friends in the afternoon at their home.

"Nothing ostentatious, you understand," he told me. "Drinks and hors d'oeuvres. You know: franks, little pigs in a blanket, or lox on pieces of toast."

I said that I thought that the party was a nice idea but, though it was really none of my business, maybe that was enough.

"I mean why the whole service? You don't want to make him go through all of that speechmaking."

"Ah, but he insists," said Willi.

"Does he?"

"So help me. He says he wouldn't think of having one without the other, and his doctor says it's all right. The doctor says if he really wants to speak, then by all means. Treat him normal."

"What doctor?"

"Rhinehart. Didn't I tell you? Rhinehart's been treating him since the Fall."

"Who's Rhinehart?"

"I thought you knew. Didn't Helene tell you? Speech therapy. One of the big speech men in New York. He's connected with the Medical Center. Just since September, and he's done wonders."

"I didn't know. I'm glad to hear it."

"When will it be?"

"The weekend after the Fourth. That Saturday, in the morning. The Fourth is on a Monday. That Saturday, the ninth," he said.

"Sure."

"Ten o'clock in the morning. Don't you forget now. Mark it down," he said.

I never thought he'd go through with it. For as long as I could remember, his son had a terrible stammer. Just to say "hello" was an effort. He had a habit of closing his eyes as though he'd been told to visualize the word beforehand. It was agonizing to watch: the shut eyes, the deep breath, the pulse beating in his neck, the chin jerking spasmodically, and the spit gathering in the corners of his mouth.

"H-h-h-hello, Joe," he'd greet me. "How-how-how are ya?"

Relaxed, silent, he seemed another kid, somehow altogether different-looking, resembling his mother, with a placid oval face, and large dark eyes, beautiful eyes, with long curly lashes, and delicate hands with bitten nails that were always in his mouth. To avoid speaking as much as possible, he had developed the facility of listening attentively, fixing those eyes on you, with a faint smile on his lips, nodding or shaking his head as the occasion demanded, so that he gave the impression of following whatever you said with a kind of ravenous intensity that made you self-conscious of being able to speak normally yourself. An intelligent defense. That he was really brilliant, there wasn't any doubt.

"An 'A' average in school," Willi told me, throwing his arm about the boy's shoulders. "He loves history," he added, as a kind of concession to me. A pause, as though I was supposed to test the boy's knowledge. Helene, his mother, glanced at me with alarm. I remained silent, smiling with a nod, and it seemed to me that the boy himself gave me a look of gratitude that went unnoticed by his father. At the time, I was teaching American history to the tenth grade in a private school on the Upper East Side. It was easy to imagine Danny's suffering in class, called upon by his teacher to recite, straining to express himself, while the other kids laughed behind their hands, or mimicked him, spraying the air with spit.

Anyhow, that was in February, as I've said. Came the summer and I didn't see much of them at first. I spent most of my time in the Forty-second Street Library doing research for my Ph.D. thesis on the Alien and Sedition Act. A couple of times in May Willi called me on the phone to invite me out to dinner, but I was too busy. He was really the only family I had left, but with one thing and another, we were never really close. My mother's younger brother, a man in his middle forties, short and powerfully built, running now to fat, with red cheeks and a fringe of dark hair about the crown of his head that resembled a monk's tonsure, he always reminded me of the picture of the jolly monk on the labels of imported German beer. He had been born in Germany, as a matter of fact. My mother had written and tried to persuade him to leave the country in 1935, but he intended to study law at Heidelberg, so the Nazis caught him and deported him to Bergen Belsen where he managed to survive the war, coming to this country in 1947, just before my mother's death. He had written a book about his experiences–*Mein Erlebnis*– that was never actually published, but everyone who knew him felt they had read it anyhow, from the way he constantly spoke of what had happened to him. When he spoke about the concentration camps, he sounded as if he was quoting by heart from a manuscript. He generally loved to talk, and if it was a blow to his pride that his son had so much trouble in getting a word out straight, he never let on, as far as I could see.

"Stammering? What's a stammer?" I once heard him tell the boy. "It's a sign of greatness....Yes, I mean it. Demosthenes stammered, and Moses. *Moshe Ribenue*. Mose our Teacher himself."

"M-M-Moses?"

"The luckiest thing that ever happened, believe you me."

"H-h-how l-lucky?"

"How many Commandments are there?"

His son held up his ten fingers.

"Ten! There you are!" said his father. "Believe me, if he didn't have a stammer he would have given us a hundred.... Luck, eh? Luck or not?"

The boy laughed. His father had a way with words, there was no doubt of it, making a good living as a paper-box salesman for a company at New Hyde Park on the Island. I imagine he cleared over twenty thousand a year. He lived nicely enough, in one of those red-brick, two storey, semi-detached houses on Eighty-first Avenue in Queens, with a little rose garden in the back and a pine-paneled bar and rumpus room in the cellar where he intended to have the party after the Bar Mitzvah. I finally went out for dinner the second week in May. We had a drink downstairs.

"You can't help it," he said. "I figure about thirty, thirty-five people. What can I do? Helene's family, friends from the office, the kid's friends from school, the rabbi and his wife. Thirty-five, maybe more....Helene says with that many we'll have to serve lunch. I thought maybe a cold buffet. We'll eat down here. I'm having it air-conditioned."

"It's a nice idea."

"It'll be a nice party, you wait and see. How about another Scotch?"

"Just a drop."

"Chivas Regal. Twenty years old. Like velvet water."

"Just a splash of water," I told him. "Where's Danny?"

"What's the time?"

"Just six."

"Be home any minute. He's at Hebrew school."

"How's he doing?"

"Wonderful. That rabbi does wonders. The boy can already read. Of course, it's all modern. To help him he has a recording of the Haftorah he has to say, put out by some company in New Jersey."

"Sounds like a wonderful idea."

"He's reciting from Numbers."

"I don't know too much about it."

"It's some of the Laws, and how they should organize themselves in the march though the desert."

"And Danny likes it?" I asked.

"You should hear him. The rabbi, the doctor, Rhinehart—I told you: everybody helps. Ask him yourself."

He came home about six-thirty, with his notebook under his arm. He had grown a little since I saw him last, become a little leaner, with bigger hands and feet, bony wrists. There was a slight down on his cheeks and upper lip, but so far as I could tell his speech was about the same. He went through the convulsions just to say hello—the suspended breath and shut eyes, the blue veins swelling on the sides of his neck. When we sat down at the dinner table, he remained standing by his place, with a loaf of bread covered by a linen napkin set before him, and a black silk skull-cap on the back of his head.

"*B-b-b-b-aruch atah a-adonoi*," he mumbled—the Hebrew blessing of the bread—and when he finished, he looked pale and wiped the spit from his lips with the back of his hand.

"How was that?" Willi asked me.

"Nice."

"Practice. Practice makes perfect."

His son lowered his quivering eyelids. Helene served the roast chicken and wild rice, with little brown potatoes.

"You never learned the language?" Willi spoke to me again.

"I was never Bar Mitzvahed; no."

"Neither was I."

"Really?"

"In Germany, when I was growing up, it was—unfashionable to be given a Jewish education." He tore at a chicken wing with his teeth. "Once in a while in the camp I would run into somebody who could speak Hebrew. It's really an ugly language. It's just that...I don't know. It was nice to hear it spoken. It was *verboten*, of course, but still...how can I explain? It was something out of our past, the really distant past. It somehow seemed to me to be the only part of our consciousness that was left—uncontaminated. Not like Yiddish....I always hated Yiddish. I used to pride myself on my command of German, the way I wrote particularly, a really educated style, but I learned to hate it. Sometimes for weeks I couldn't bring myself to say a word. The language of the S.S....."

"T-t-t-tell about H-H-Heinz," interrupted his son.

"Eat your chicken," his mother said. The tone of her voice made me look at her with surprise: black hair with a faint reddish tinge, and long curling eyelashes that shadowed her prominent cheekbones. Lucky enough to have been spared the later horrors, she too was a refuge, coming from Germany in 1936. I suddenly sensed that she disapproved and was even a little frightened of Willi's imposition of the whole thing on the boy's consciousness. In front of me, though, "eat your chicken" was all that she said. We finished the rest of the meal in silence—lemon meringue pie and coffee—and Willi, the boy, and myself went into the living room and sat down on the sofa.

"Cigar?" Willi asked .

"No thanks."

He belched and lit up, and began to pick his front teeth with the folded cellophane. "How about a little brandy?"

"That'd be nice."

"Napoleon: the best," he said, pouring some into two snifters that the boy had brought in from the kitchen. "Wonderful....Too good. I'm getting too fat, I know. Soft," he said, patting his paunch. "The doctor tells me I ought to lose at least twenty pounds. An irony, eh? Did you know that when I got out of Belsen I weighed ninety pounds? Ninety, mind you, and now, like all other Americans, I'm to die of overweight."

His eyes gleamed as though he derived some sort of satisfaction out of the thought.

"A living skeleton," he went on. "You must have seen photos after the liberation of a place like that. I don't have to tell you...."

But he did, as I knew he would; he went on and on, while his son listened, his legs tucked under him, biting on one fingernail after the other.

"You can't know—thank God—not you, or Danny here, or Helene....No one who was not there can even guess what it was like to be so hungry, to be literally starving to death on two slices of bread a day, and a pint of watery soup with a snip of turnip in it, if you're lucky. Twice a week a spoonful of rancid butter, and an ounce of sausage or cheese....And the worst of it knowing that it's endless, knowing that no matter how hungry you are today there's absolutely no possibility of getting anything more to eat tomorrow but that the anguish will simply grow and grow and grow....Words...."He shrugged. "You aren't really listening and I can't blame you. What good are words to describe such things?"

He sucked on his cigar and screwed up his eyes to watch the

smoke, as thick and white as milk, gather in the cone of light above the lamp on the coffee table. "There were two obsessions that everyone had. Ask anyone who was in such a place. Have you ever read any books about them?...Food first: dreaming about food, sitting down to a meal like we just had, and eating till you burst, and second: just staying alive so that you would be able to describe what was happening to you. Everyone wanted to write a book. Seriously. Just to tell the world, as though to convince ourselves as well that such things were really happening, that we were actually living through them. I wrote *Mein Erlebnis* in six weeks...."

He waved the smoke away, and again his narrowed eyes had that peculiar gleam. The boy sat perfectly motionless, with his lips slightly parted in expectation of his father to continue, and for the first time I began to understand the nature of Willi's compulsion to talk so much about what he had endured. Triumph. There was a flash of triumph in his eyes as he regarded his son. It was as if I were listening to a mountain climber—what's his name, the one who climbed Everest—or the first man who will land on the moon and live to tell about it. He talked and talked, partly, I am sure, because it was essentially a personal victory that he was describing—and gloating over, in spite of himself. It was a display of prowess before his son; the supreme success, perhaps even the high point of his life, that he among all those millions managed to live through it all.

From the kitchen came the swish of water and the hum of the automatic dishwasher. Helene came into the living room with a bowl of fruit.

"An apple, Joe?"

"No thanks."

Willi peeled a banana, and to be polite perhaps, or maybe because of his wife's feelings about talking as he did in front of the boy, he began to ask me about my work.

"The Alien and Sedition Act, eh?" he said. "Yes....Yes, interesting and significant....When was it again?"

"S-s-seventeen n-ninety-eight," said Danny.

Willi questioned me with a raised eyebrow. "That's right," I told him.

He grinned. "I told you he loves his history."

"He's right a hundred per cent."

"Who was it?" Willi went on. "President Adams, wasn't it? Against the Bill of Rights—the first suspension of habeas corpus."

"And M-M-Marshall," began the boy.

His father laughed with his mouth full of banana. "You can see for yourself he knows much more about it than me." The boy smiled, flushed to his temples with pride. "Still, I remember: No freedom of speech, hundreds of editors thrown into jail for criticizing the government, the prisons packed with dissenters." From his voice, he sounded as though he momentarily somehow enjoyed it.

"About twenty-five, all told," I said.

"You don't say. Just twenty-five?"

"That's it."

He grinned again. "How about that! America, you see?" he said to his wife. "Imagine. A whole stink over that."

"There was more to it than that," I told him.

"Of course, but still—a crisis! Genuine indignation over the fate of just twenty-five men...."

"Yes, partly," I told him, suddenly weary, bleary-eyed from the dinner and the drinks.

"And the Jews?" he asked me.

"I don't understand."

"There was no particular repression of the Jews, as such?"

"I never thought about it, to tell you the truth."

He laughed. "Seriously," I went on. "The law was directed against foreigners, mostly—the British and the French. French spies, for example. There was a lot of spying going on, and the law forced a lot of foreigners to leave the country."

"But nothing was specifically directed against the Jews."

"No. Why should there have been?"

Another laugh. "What's so funny?" I asked him.

"Don't you know the joke?"

"Which one?"

"You must have heard it....The S.S.man in Berlin who grabs a Jew by the collar and kicks him in the shins. 'Tell me, Jew, who's responsible for all of Germany's troubles?' The Jew trembles. His teeth absolutely chatter; his knees knock together. 'The Jews, of course,' he answers. 'Good,' says the S.S.man. 'The Jews and the bareback riders in the circus,' the little Jew goes on. 'Why the bareback riders in the circus?' the S.S.man asks. 'Aha,' comes the answer. 'Exactly! So *nu*? Why the Jews?'"

The boy laughed, slapping his thigh, guffawing until the tears came into his eyes, as if he were delighted to find a release in a sound that he could express without impediment.

"Yes, yes," Willi continued, taking a last bite of the banana and throwing the peel into an ashtray. "He laughs, and it's true, the absurdity, and yet there's something more. There's a reason....Why the Jews? There's the psychology of a Heinz to contend with, and not an isolated pathological case either, but common. More common than you'd care to know."

The boy shifted his position, leaning toward his father with one hand on the arm of the sofa, and both feet on the floor.

"Have a piece of fruit," Helene told me.

"No thanks. Who's Heinz?" I asked.

"*Herr Hauptsturmfuehrer Berger,*" said Willi. "You know the type. Tall and blond, beautiful, really, the very image of manly perfection that you can see for yourself, today, just by going to the movies....A movie star, so help me; six foot two at least, with straight blond hair, white flashing teeth, a positively captivating smile—dimples at the corners of his mouth—beautiful blue eyes....The uniform? Perfection. Designed for him; tailor-made for that slim, hard body, broad shoulders...." He spread his stubby hands in the air, reminding me more than ever of that monk making an invocation. "Black, all black and belted with what do you call them? Riding pants. Jodhpurs, and gleaming black boots...."

"But I still don't understand," I said. "Who is he?"

"Was," corrected Willi. "He was a guard in the camp. After the war the British caught him and he was tried and hanged.... Was....Unfortunate. I mean it, too. Seriously. No one had the good sense to study him instead: how he used to stand, for example—very significant—with the thumb of one hand, his left hand, I remember, stuck in his belt, and the other grasping a braided riding whip that he would tap against those boots. The boots, the belt, the buckle, the buttons, all flashing in the sun— enough to blind you, believe me. White teeth, that dimpled smile....He was convicted of murder. One day he killed a child, a little girl of seven....In the camp, some of the barracks had three tiers of wooden beds along the wall, bare planks to sleep on, *boxen* in the jargon. We slept together packed like sardines. Often someone would die in the night, but it was impossible to move. We would sleep with the dead, but no matter....Where was I?"

"The child," I said.

"Ah, yes. One of the *boxen* in the women's barracks was coming apart; one leg was coming off. Three tiers, mind you; hundreds of pounds of timber....For some reason the child was on the floor, directly beneath it, on her hands and knees. Perhaps he–Heinz–had ordered it so. I don't know. I don't think so. She must just have been looking for something. A crust of bread, a crumb, perhaps, and in walks the *Hauptsturmfuehrer* smiling all the while as though to charm the ladies, immediately sizing up the situation; perfect. The child beneath the rickety bed, the girl's mother, Frau Schwarz, in one corner, binding up her swollen legs with a few rags.

"'*Gnädige Frau*...' he greets her–the mother, who stands up nervously twisting a rag about her wrist.

"Hilda!" she screams....Not even a Jewish name, mind you; a good German name....'Hilda!' The child begins to rise, but it's too late. With a flick of his boot, a movement of that polished toe, our Heinz has already acted, kicking out the loose timber, bringing down the whole thing on the child's back....A broken back.

"'Mama!' she cries. 'I can't move! My legs!' For a day and a half like that until she goes into convulsions and dies in her mother's arms. The woman comes to me and reproaches herself because she hasn't got the courage to commit suicide.

"'After all,' she says, 'I have the means....' She's referring to the rags that she has woven into a noose. 'Just the courage is lacking. Mr. Levy, what's the matter with me?' She goes mad, and before she dies she wanders about the camp asking everyone to strangle her....She even comes to Heinz. It was just outside the latrines. I witnessed this myself. Apparently he doesn't even remember who she is. He shoos her away, those beautiful blue eyes clouded for just an instant in complete bewilderment.

"'*Verrüct*,' he tells me. 'Insane.' With a shrug. I'm busy on my hands and knees scrubbing the concrete floor with a brush and a pail lye and water, not daring to look up, blinded by those boots.

"'Here, here, Levy. No; to the left. Put some elbow grease into it.'

"A fanatic for order and cleanliness, you understand. He used to speak with me a great deal. I couldn't imagine why. Perhaps because we were both about the same age. He would constantly ask me questions about the Jews–technical questions, so to speak, about our beliefs, about the Torah, for example, all the Laws. He seemed sincerely interested and as far as I could tell, he was genuinely disappointed when he realized that I knew next to nothing and had been educated like himself as a good, middle-class German–*Gymnasium*, and two semesters at Heidelberg. One day he was absolutely flabbergasted to find out that for the life of me I couldn't even recite the Ten Commandments. I couldn't get more than five, and not in order, either. 'Tsk! Tsk! Levy.' He shook that beautiful head and began reciting them all.

"'I am the Lord thy God who brought thee forth out of the land of Egypt, out of the house of bondage....Thou shalt have no other gods before me.' Etc., etc. All of them, the whole business....Imagine the scene. It was a Sunday, I remember, rest day, the one day off from man-killing labor the whole week. I had gone outside the barracks to get a little sun. Imagine it, I tell you. A vast desert, our own Sinai surrounding us, rolling sand dunes, green wooden shacks set in rows. In the distance, the silver birch trees of the women's camp like a mirage. The wire mesh gate of the main entrance to my right that always reminded me of the entrance to a zoo. Here and there, scattered on the ground, all heaped together, the mounds of bodies, the living dead and the dead–stiff, open eyes, gaping mouths, all heaped together, indistinguishable. It was early Spring, and warm, with a weak sun, gray clouds, cumuli, with a flat base and rounded outlines, piled up like mountains in the western sky. I remember that distinctly–cumuli....It was a matter of life and death,

An eerie roll-call of ragged inmate shirts bears witness to the Holocaust in this concentration camp memorial at Maidanek.

learning to tell one type of cloud from another—the promise of a little rain. There was never enough water. Just two concrete basins to supply the entire camp. We were slowly dying of thirst in addition to everything else. I remember thinking that if the rain does come I shall try and remain outside the barracks as long as I can after roll call, with my mouth open. Crazy thoughts. What was it? Chickens, young *Truthahnen*—turkeys drown that way in the rain, too stupid to close their mouths....Insane, disconnected thoughts while, according to regulation, I stood rigidly at attention, with my chin in, and chest out, my thumbs along the crease in my striped prison pants, as Heinz drones on and on.

"'Honor thy father and thy mother....Thou shalt not murder....' On and on to the end, and then, with what I can only describe as a shy expression on his face, the explanation:

"'We live in Saxony,' he tells me. 'Absolutely charming, Levy. Do you know East Prussia? Ah, the orchard and the flower beds—roses, red and white roses, growing in front of the church. My father's church. A pastor, Levy, and his father before him and before that. Three generations of pastors. When I was young, I thought I would go into the Church myself. I have the religious temperament.'

"'Yes, sir, *Jawohl, Herr Hauptsturmfuehrer*.'

"'Does that astonish you?'

"'Not at all, *Mein Herr*.'

"'It does, of course....Sundays....Ah, a day like today. The church bells echoing in the valley and the peasants in their black suits and creaking shoes shuffling between those rose beds to listen to Papa thunder at them from the pulpit, slamming down his fist. "Love, my friends! It is written that we are to love our neighbors as ourselves." The fist again. "Love!" he shouts, and I would begin to tremble, literally begin to shake....Why, Levy? I often asked myself. You ought to know. Jews are great psychologists. Freud....'

"'I don't know, *Herr Hauptsturmfuehrer*.'

"'A pity....He would preach love and all I could see from that front pew was that great fist—the blond hair on the backs of the fingers, the knuckles clenched, white....That huge fist protruding from the black cuff like the hand of God from a thunder cloud....' That was his image, I swear it. So help me, a literary mind. '*Die grosse Faust ist aus der schwarzen Manschette heraus gestreckt wie Gottes-hand aus einer Sturmwolke*. Yet to be honest,' Heinz went on, 'he never struck me. Not once in my whole life, and I was never what you could call a good child, Levy. Secret vices, a rebellious spirit that had to be broken....And obedience was doubly difficult for the likes of me, but, as I've said, whenever I misbehaved, he never once laid a hand on me....Love.... He spoke about love and was silent. Talk about psychology! That silence for days on end; all he had to do was say nothing and I would lie in my bed at night, trembling. Can you explain that, Levy? I would lie awake praying that he would beat me instead, smash me with that fist, flay my back with his belt rather than that love, that silent displeasure. He had thin, pale lips, with a network of wrinkles at the corner of his mouth....No dimples. I get my dimples from my mother....To please him, I would learn whole passages of the Bible by heart; your Bible, Levy.'

"He tapped his whip against the top of his boots.

"'Tell me, Levy....'

"'Yes, sir?'

"'I know the Jews; a gentle people. Tell me honestly. Did your father ever beat you?'

"'No, sir.'

"'Not once?'

"'Never, sir.'

"'A gentle people, as I've said, but lax in your education, wouldn't you say?'

"'Yes, sir.'

"'Well, then we must remedy that....'"

For the first time, the flow of words faltered. Willi paused to relight his cigar, and then, as though it had left a bad taste in his mouth, snubbed it out in the ashtray and picked a fleck of tobacco from the tip of his tongue. "Like some dog," he finally went on. "As if he were training some animal....That whip across the back, the bridge of the nose, the eyes....All afternoon I stood at attention while those clouds gathered and it began to rain, until I could repeat it all word for word. 'I am the Lord thy God who brought thee forth out of the land of Egypt.' He hit me in the adam's apple. I could hardly speak. The rain came down my face...."

Another silence. The automatic dishwasher had long since stopped. Helene bit into an apple and looked at her watch. Before she had a chance to speak, the boy shook his head.

"Never mind," she told him. "It's late. Past ten. Time for bed."

"Ten?" I repeated, standing up. "I've got to go myself."

"Say good night to Joe," said Helene to her son.

"You w-w-w-wanna hear my r-r-record?" He asked me. "It'll only t-t-take a minute."

"O.K.; for a minute."

His room was at the head of the stairs. I followed him up and he shut the door.

"Y-you never heard about H-H-Heinz before?"

"Never."

"I have; o-often. It used to give me b-bad dreams."

On top of his desk was a phonograph record. He put it on the portable phonograph that stood in one corner of the room. For a time, sitting on the bed while the boy put on his pajamas, I listened to the deep voice chanting in the unintelligible tongue.

"D-don't you understand?"

"Not much," I said.

"How—how come you were never B-B-Bar Mitzvahed?"

"I wasn't as lucky as you. My father was dead, and, my mother didn't care one way or the other."

"M-Mama doesn't care either," he said, tying his bathrobe around his waist. He rejected the record and stood by the window that faced the rose garden, biting his thumbnail.

"D-d-do you believe in G-G-God?"

"I don't know."

"I do—do."

"You're lucky there too."

"D-don't you ever pray?"

"No."

"I d-d-do; often."

I imagined that, rather like his laughter, that too must have been a wonderful relief; praying in silence, grateful and convinced that he was able to communicate something without a stammer.

"D-d-do you know what I p-pray for?" he asked me.

"What?"

"A-actually it's a s-s-secret."

"You can tell me if you like."

"S-sometimes, y-you know, when I think of all th-those people at the Temple—at the B-B-Bar Mitzvah, I mean—I get into a sweat."

"It'll be all right."

"There'll be h-hundreds of people there, M-Mama's whole family, G-G-Goldman's parents, and all his family, and all their friends."

"Who's Goldman?"

"He's a f-f-fink. Sammy Goldman. We're being B-B-Bar Mitzvahed together. He's rich. His father owns a chain of delicatessens. He's t-told everybody about me. He didn't want to g-go with me. He has p-pimples from p-p-p-playing with himself."

"It's late," I told him. "I really ought to go."

"It's another m-m-month or so. More. Time enough. Anything can h-h-happen in time, don't you think?"

"It depends."

"If you b-b-believe enough?"

"Maybe so."

"The st-st-stammer, you know, is all psychological. Dr. Rhinehart says so. It c-came all of a sudden. W-when I started school."

"I didn't know."

"Oh yes. And if it c-c-came that way, it can g-g-go too; suddenly, I mean. That's l-l-logical, don't you think?"

"Anything is possible," I told him.

He smiled abruptly, and opened his mouth again, giving me the impression that he wanted to say something more. But for some reason, maybe because he was tired, he got stuck; his chin jerked spasmodically as he tried to force the word from his mouth, and then he shrugged and gave up, holding out a moist palm to say good night and good-by.

"Good luck," I told him.

About a week later his father gave me a ring. He had a customer in the garment district, on Seventh Avenue and Thirty-seventh Street, and he thought that if as usual I was working at the Forty-second Street Library, we could meet for a bite of lunch. I said fine. It was a hot day. His cheeks were purplish from the heat and he breathed heavily. We had a sandwich and a soda at Schrafft's and then he walked me back to the library where we sat for a while on the granite steps under the trees around the flagpole at the north entrance on the avenue. The place was jammed with shopgirls and clerks taking in a few minutes of the sun before they had to go back to work. We sat and watched the flow of crowds going into the stores; the cars and the buses and the cabs, the cop at the intersection, wearing dark glasses and a short-sleeved summer uniform, waving traffic on.

"How's the work?" Willi asked me.

"Coming along. How's the family?"

"Fine. They send their best."

"Send my love."

"I will." He smoked a cigar and coughed. The air was thick with fumes. "You know, Danny doesn't say much, but he can't fool me."

"About what?"

"He's worried about the Bar Mitzvah. Speaking in front of all those people. I told him to take it slow and everything would be all right. What do you think?"

"You know best."

"Helene thinks I'm doing the wrong thing."

"It's hard for me to say."

"You heard me that night....Sometimes I go on and on. She says I shouldn't fill his head with that sort of thing, but I say that he has a right to know."

"You may be right."

"He doesn't understand everything, of course....That story about Heinz, for example....But he will in time....It was a revelation to me. You know, sometimes, in the camp, before I met Heinz, I used to wonder why it was all happening. Why the Jews, I mean....

"Oh, there are other factors, of course....But don't you

see? The Commandments. All the Laws...." He flicked away his cigar ash. "The Law, more than anything....He taught me that, that day in the rain. They were murdering, humiliating us because whether it was true or not we had come to—how shall I say it?—embody, I suppose...In some strange way, we had come to embody that very Law that bound them too—through Christianity, I mean—and in destroying us...Heinz, for example, hating his father, the pastor, who preached love—love thy neighbor, from Leviticus, you know....Of course, there's the fist: love and hate all mixed together. I really don't understand that part myself, but I do know that what all of them hated, somehow was the yoke that we had given them so long ago. The Law that makes all the difference, that makes a man different from a beast, the civilized..." He coughed. "Can't you see what I mean?"

"I'm not sure. I think so."

"It's hard for me to keep it all straight myself....I just feel that the least we can do is pass it on, the way we always have, from father to son. The Bar Mitzvah....Of course, now with Danny, he doesn't really complain, but he suffers, I know. I'm not sure just what to do."

"What can I tell you?"

"Nothing, I know. I just wanted you to understand....You know the irony is that he hates me."

"Don't be absurd."

"It's true—at least partly. Oh, he loves me too, but Rhinehart says that stammering is very often—it's very complicated—a kind of expression of hostility, resentment, to those whom you're supposed to love....It all started you know when he began school. He was very bright. I've always demanded too damn much of him."

"It'll be O.K."

"Oh, I know it, eventually. It's only that in the meantime... I told him yesterday that if he wanted to call the whole service off, I'd be glad to do it in a minute."

"What'd he say?"

"Nothing doing. What he's been saying all along. Definitely not....As a matter of fact, he smiled."

"Did he?" I said. "What are you going to do?"

"Go ahead, I guess. But I made it as clear as I could that at any time he wants to drop the speech and just have the party at home, it was more than O.K. by me."

"Well," I told him, "I've got to get back to the books."

"I know. I didn't mean to keep you."

"Thanks for lunch."

"My pleasure....Joe, you're the only blood relative I've got left. People talk. I just wanted you to understand."

I nodded, and left him standing there, smoking and coughing, in the dazzling pattern of light and shadow cast by the sunlight streaming through the dusty leaves of the trees.

The weeks went by. Once or twice he called again to have me out to dinner, and I asked him whether or not the service was still on. "Sure," he'd answer. "He's studying away." I was too busy getting my notes into shape to go out and see them. My work was going fairly well. I decided to attack the whole problem from the point of view of Chief Justice Marshall—the origin of judicial review—but with all of it, I got a good chunk of the reading done by the beginning of July, so that over the Fourth I was able to get away and spend the weekend visiting a classmate of mine at Columbia and his wife who had taken a cottage for the summer at Cape Cod. I got back Tuesday night. The service was scheduled for the following Saturday, so I called Willi to make absolutely sure once and for all that Danny was going to speak in the Temple.

"You bet," he told me. "You know, I think I've got a

budding rabbi on my hands."

"How do you mean?"

"Religious? My God, you ought to see him. He gets up at six in the morning to pray."

The service was to be held at Temple Shalom on Seventy-eighth Avenue. I hadn't bought a present yet and I was stumped. For the life of me I couldn't think of anything original. In the end, I went to the bank and bought him a series-E savings bond for $25.00. Somehow it didn't seem enough, so in addition I bought him fourteen silver dollars—one extra for good luck—and had them packed in a velvet box with a clasp. I thought the kid might get a kick out of it.

Saturday at last: hot and muggy, a promise of rain, with a peculiar diffused light shining from behind the low gray clouds. It was too hot to sleep much the night before. I was up at six-thirty and out of the house by a quarter to eight. At first I thought that maybe I'd go out to the house and we'd all go to the Temple together. I don't know why; I decided against it. I loafed around instead, wasting time, and by the time I took the subway and arrived at Queens it was a quarter to ten. The crowds were already arriving at the Temple, Goldman's relatives, most of them people I didn't know, all dressed up in dark summer suits and light dresses, flowered prints and silks. It was so muggy that the powder flaked on the women's cheeks. I finally recognized Helene's brother and sister-in-law in the crush—a chiropodist who lived in Brooklyn. We chatted for a minute before they went inside.

"Willi here?" I asked.

"Not yet. I didn't see any of them," he said. "Maybe we ought to call up and find out of they're really coming. Between you and me, I never thought the kid would go through with it."

I waited alone just outside the big oaken doors. The air was stifling, and the sun had shifted and faded from behind the clouds darkening the streets. It began to rain. I went into the vestibule, and about three minutes of ten the family arrived.

"A rabbi, I told you," said Willi, folding his dripping umbrella. "He didn't want to take a cab on *Shabbos*. We had to walk here in the rain."

Helene took off her wilted straw hat. "Ruined," she said. The boy said nothing. With a white-silk prayer shawl over his arm, he was dressed in a dark-blue suit that emphasized the pallor of his face. All the color had gone from his cheeks; his lips were drawn and white.

"Congratulations," I told him.

He nodded. "We're late," said his father. "We ought to get seated." He took his wife by the elbow and they went inside. The boy hung back and pulled at my sleeve.

"D-d-d-do you think they'll laugh?" he asked.

"Of course not."

He shook his head and shrugged.

"I p-p-p-prayed and p-p-prayed."

We all sat in the front pew, to the left of the Ark. There were baskets of red roses set on the marble steps. The bronze doors of the Ark were open and the rabbi, young and prematurely gray at the temples, conducted the morning service. He was sweating and, while the cantor sang, he surreptitiously plucked a handker-chief from the sleeve of his robe and dabbed at his upper lip. The service went on, mostly in Hebrew, chanting and responsive reading, the drone of voices and the tinkle of silver bells as Willi and Mr. Goldman were called upon to elevate the Torah over the heads of the congregation and lay it open on the mahogany podium set on the edge of the steps. The rain beat against the stained glass windows. Danny sat to my right, picking at the cuticle of his thumb. When it came time for the recitation of the

Haftorah, the Goldman kid went first. He would do well and he knew it—chanting the Hebrew in a high sing-song voice that was just beginning to crack; rather good-looking, and tall for his age, with reddish blond hair, full lips, and pimpled cheeks. His father, seated on the stage to the rabbi's left and next to Willi, beamed at the audience. Then it was Danny's turn. The crowd shifted perceptively in their seats, and as he stood up two women in the row behind us nervously began to fan themselves with their prayer books. Evidently he was right: the Goldman boy had told everyone about his stammer. You could sense it. You could hear everyone in the place take a deep breath as he mounted the three steps with the fringed end of his shawl dragging along the floor. He stood behind the opened Torah, and with a bitten forefinger found his place. The rustle of silks; the audience had shifted again, with a faint murmur. The wooden pews creaked and the noise must have startled him, because he suddenly glanced up. For a moment he was up to his old tricks, trying to stare them down, but it was no use. No one said anything. All at once he was just listening to the sound of their labored breathing. They pitied him and he knew it, and they hated him, in spite of themselves, for the embarrassment that he was causing them, and he was aware of that too. The rabbi wiped the sweat from his upper lip. With his left hand rubbing the side of his nose, Willi sat looking at his feet. Then, for a moment more, wide-eyed, and with trembling lips he continued to stare down at the crowd until he caught my eye. He blinked and shrugged his shoulders again, and hunched forward, as though before he began to stammer the blessing he had made up his mind to assume the burden of what the reiteration of the Law of his Fathers had demanded from the first.

Hugh Nissenson.

The Essence of Judaism

Rabbi Simlai taught: Moses gave 613 commandments to the Israelites. Then David came and reduced them to eleven as it is written (Psalm 15): "Lord, who shall dwell in Your tabernacle? Who shall abide on Your holy mountain? He who walks uprightly, works righteousness, and speaks the truth which is in his heart. He carries no slander upon his tongue nor does he do harm to anyone. He makes no false charges against his neighbor. He has contempt for evil men but he honors those who revere the Lord. He keeps his promise at all costs. He does not loan his money for excessive interest, nor does he take a bribe to injure the innocent. He who lives like this shall never be shaken."

Then came Isaiah and reduced the commands to six, as it is written (Isaiah 33:15-16): "He who walks in righteousness and speaks truthfully; who despises profit through oppression and keeps his hands free from bribes; who refuses to hear of shedding blood or to witness evil. He shall dwell on high; his defence shall be the fortress of rocks. His bread shall be given him, his waters shall be assured."

Then Micah came and further reduced the commands to three (Micah 6:8): "It has been told to you, O man, what is good and what the Lord requires of you—only to act justly, to love mercy and to walk humbly with your God."

At last came the prophet Habakkuk who summed them all up in one word (Habakkuk 2:4): "The righteous man shall live by his faith."

The *Talmud*.

(Right) "Allegoria" by Ben Shahn (1898-1969).

Ben Shahn

TZEDAKAH

"He who gives charity secretly is greater than Moses."

The *Talmud*.

In Judaism, actions are even more important than faith. Most Jewish laws from the Torah are guidelines for human interactions. "Mitzvah," the word for commandments, is also the word for good deeds. Thus doing good deeds is a religious duty.

Perhaps the most important concept in Judaism dealing with human interactions is "tzedakah." Tzedakah means to be charitable, just and ethical. It is one's obligation rather than one's choice to help others. The great Jewish philosopher of the twelfth century, Moses Maimonides, divides the givers of tzedakah according to rising degrees of merit.

Eight Levels of Tzedakah

1. Those who bestow tzedakah but complainingly.
2. Those who do so cheerfully but give less than they should.
3. Those who contribute only when they are asked and the sum they are asked.
4. Those who give before they are requested to.
5. Those who give tzedakah but do not know who benefits by it, although the recipient is aware from whom he has received it.
6. Those who give tzedakah and do not disclose their names to those who have received it.
7. Those who do not know to whom their contribution will be given, while the recipients do not know from whom they have received it.
8. Those who extend a loan or bestow a gift upon the needy, or who take a poor man into partnership, or help him to establish himself in business, so that he should not be compelled to apply for charity. Such people practice the highest degree of tzedakah.

Moses Maimonides.

Giving anonymously sits high in the Jewish hierarchy of tzedakah. Here is an account of traditional tzedakah as practised in the shtetl of nineteenth-century Eastern Europe—and in the suburbs of twentieth-century Brooklyn.

Tzedakah in Brooklyn

For almost a year after I met him, Rabbi Singer wanted to be written about pseudonymously. He wasn't publicity-shy. He believed that truly holy people refrained from taking credit for their own mitzvahs. But the better I came to know him, the more important it seemed to use his name. In the past, I'd written many articles filled with pseudonymous characters, and readers assumed I was creating composites. Now, I wanted them to see that the man I admired so much was a real, breathing person. Misha Avramoff and Rabbi Singer's son, David, agreed with me, and urged him to let his name be used. Despite his reservations, he said he would, largely to please us.

But he wanted me to understand why even the most charitable people could hurt others if they flaunted their good deeds. As he told me about his grandfather, Gershon Singer, the rabbi of Pilzno, who exemplified the qualities Rabbi Singer wanted to bring to the Lower East Side, I came to the rueful, haunting realization that those of us who had been in the Peace Corps and the civil-rights movement might have done our work better if we'd had some of his training in the social value of humility.

Every Thursday night, the rabbi of Pilzno would walk by all the Jewish houses in town, accompanied by his shamess. Their mission? To inspect the chimneys of the congregants. They looked for houses where there wasn't any smoke. Those families couldn't afford enough kindling to heat the Shabbos meal. So Gershon Singer would fetch a charcoal and a chicken for Shabbos.

But the mitzvah must never be discovered. The rabbi must remain anonymous. The people who received the food must never be embarrassed by the knowledge that he was aware of their poverty.

So, between 1 and 5 A.M., when all the Jews of Pilzno were asleep, the rabbi and the shamess would pile the chicken and the charcoal into a wheelbarrow and place them in front of the house. Then they would hurry away, before their goodness could be detected.

One Thursday night between Passover and Shavuot, Rabbi Singer asked me to accompany him to Brooklyn so that I could see a modern-day version of his grandfather's attitudes toward charity. First, we stopped for dinner at his apartment. After we washed our hands and said the *motzi* (the traditional blessing over the bread), we began to eat the lavish meal of chicken liver, matzo-ball soup, roast beef, kidney beans, and potato pancakes his wife had prepared. As we ate, he elaborated his grandfather's feelings—and, I realized, his own. "He didn't want to be a show-off. Of course, sometimes it is all right to be a show-off because if you give to others, they give too. But the highest point of charity should be anonymity. The taker shouldn't know who gave the gift and the giver shouldn't know who took it."

After dinner, he took me to a tree-lined residential street. Inside a large garage about fifty hasidic men were filling grocery boxes with chicken, fish, wine, bread, and vegetables, and loading them into cars on the street outside. Soon they would distribute the cartons to needy Jews. They would drive away before the recipients could see them.

In one corner of the garage a stocky young diamond cutter had replaced his black suit with a blood-flecked butcher's apron and was cutting up carp. Three more Hasidim, still dressed in gabardine, wrapped fish in plastic bags and placed the bags in boxes. Then a young man whose father had died three weeks earlier came in. They'd been waiting for him before they davened maariv (the evening service); they would provide a minyan for him to recite the mourner's Kaddish.

All work stopped. Everyone picked up his *siddur* (prayer book), and, facing the eastern wall of the garage—symbolically facing Jerusalem—rocked back and forth in prayer. Then, in a few minutes, work resumed.

The organizer, middle-aged, European born, a civil servant, stood by shelves full of packages. Writing in Yiddish, he inscribed each box with the address of the people who would receive it. But not with the names. To spare the recipients any embarrassment, even the drivers who delivered the food would remain ignorant of their identities. My presence plainly made the organizer uncomfortable. Some of the younger people argued that publicity might help with fund raising, but he made me promise not to mention the organization's name—or even the area it worked in—because the anonymity meant more to him than the prospect of contributions.

Paul Cowan.

KNOWLEDGE

"If you have acquired knowledge, what do you lack? If you lack knowledge, what have you acquired?"

The *Midrash*.

The importance to Judaism of learning and study has already been mentioned. In an earlier age, a boy devoted himself entirely to sacred study, because in many cases secular education was closed to him. Today, there is more often a greater emphasis on general academic learning. The following legend is a fanciful explanation of this timeless Jewish love and respect for learning.

The Legend of the Honey

There once lived a man named Simon ben Yehuda. If one were to look at Simon, and then look at his neighbors, one would say: here is one like all the others, and the others are like him. For Simon seemed to be an ordinary, industrious man who led a simple life.

But, as it is said, you cannot know a man unless you look into his heart. And it was only the angels in heaven who knew the pureness and greatness of Simon's heart. For Simon gave to the poor without hope of reward from God or his fellow man. He forgave his enemies and bore no hatred. He was modest and carried his goodness deep within himself.

One day, high in heaven, a group of angels met and decided that Simon's goodness should be rewarded. For seven days and seven nights they talked. What could they do for Simon? He had a wife whom he loved dearly, and a son precious beyond measure to both of them. Simon was happy. But at last an idea came to the angels. What better reward for Simon than to have a son who would be a seer and sage among his people? Then the angels sent messengers across the wide world to gather together the purest honey from the best bees, bees who had fed on none but the loveliest flowers in the world's gardens.

When Simon's son reached the proper age, his father brought him to school for the first time. As the boy sat in front of his books, a strange sweet smell came to him. He touched a book, and put his finger to his mouth, and then he tasted the most wonderful sweetness he had ever known. For the messenger of the angels had covered the pages with the rare honey they had gathered.

So Simon's son learned to love the book that was set before him. And as the angels knew, from this love there grew a love for learning, and a great hunger to know all that was known by man. So began his days of study, days that led to honor and fame as a seer and sage among his people.

This is the story that is told, and this is why the custom arose of dabbing honey on the pages of a child's first book.

Jacob Benlazar.

Dabbing honey on a child's first book was a custom practised by traditional Jews in Eastern Europe. Here is an account of a young boy's first day of Jewish studies and the rituals involved in this important event.

First Day at Cheder

That I might not look upon anything unclean on the way, my father wrapped me up in a *talith* and carried me in his arms to the cheder, which was about a mile distant from my home. I was received by the teacher, who held out to me the Hebrew alphabet on a large chart. Before starting in with the lesson I was given a taste of honey and was asked whether it was sweet, which of course I answered in the affirmative. I was then informed that I was about to enter upon the study of the Law, and that it was sweeter than honey. After that I was shown the first letter, *alef*, and was told to mark it well on my mind. I was doing that with the greatest seriousness, when suddenly a coin fell upon the alphabet. The teacher informed me that an angel had dropped it from heaven and through the ceiling, because I was a good little boy and wanted to learn.

David Blaustein.

(Right) Portrait of a rabbi and his students by Alfred Eisenstaedt.

HUMOR

"Humor is the truth in an intoxicated condition."

G. J. Nathan, *The Theatre*.

An exceptional sense of humor has always stood out as a strong Jewish characteristic. It is said that true Jewish humor mirrors the history of the Jewish people–their joys and tragedies, their aspirations and discouragements, their values. To be able to laugh at one's own miseries, to see the ridiculousness in one's own behavior, and to avoid pompousness by pointing out others' and one's own pretensions are some basic traits of Jewish humor.

Making the fools the real heroes of life is a typical Jewish approach. Perhaps the most famous example of this are the stories which come down to us from Eastern European tradition about the "wise" people from the town of Helm.

The Wise Men of Helm

Deep in the forests of Poland, quite hidden from all the world, lay the little town of Helm. The people who lived there were Jews, and like all other Jews, they had long beards and curly side-locks around their ears. They wore long, shiny, black coats that reached to their ankles and striped prayer-shawls with thick fringes. Just like Jews all over the world at that time. Yet, frankly, there was something peculiar about the Helmites, something odd about the way they did things. Truth to tell, they weren't really quite like other people.

There was that winter, for instance, a cold, bitter winter, when the Helmites had no fire-wood to warm their homes. They suffered much through the long months, and, determined that such a thing should never again happen in Helm, the very next year they built a high brick wall all around the town to keep out the cold.

Then there's that other story about how they decided to invite the most famous organist of the great city of Warsaw to play for them. They hadn't ever heard an organ before, so they awaited him with eager anticipation, never realizing that there wasn't a single organ in all of Helm.

It was after this that people began to wonder about the Helmites. They said they were just fools. Then they asked one another how so many fools came to collect in one place, and therein too lies a tale:

Once upon a time an angel, carrying a sackful of foolish souls back to heaven for repair, lost his way in a storm and flew over Helm. The town, as you know, lies in a valley, completely surrounded by high mountains. On the top-most peak of the highest mountain stood a tall, pointed tree. Suddenly, as the angel struggled through the storm, the bottom of the sack caught and tore on the tree-top, and alas, all the poor, damaged souls spilled out of the ripped sack, rolled down the mountain side into Helm and there they stayed from that day on.

But the foolishness of Helm was so fabulous that it couldn't be explained away by just one tale, so here's another: Once a great wind blew over the town, a wild, swirling wind, sweeping with it a stream of air from the strange isle of Abdera. Now it is well-known among certain scientists who spend most of their lives bothering with these things that the air of Abdera has a very unusual quality. One whiff of it makes a man a simpleton for life. And no sooner did the Helmites begin to breathe this air than they and their children and their children's children all became fools.

Naturally, the wise men of Helm never dreamed that the world looked upon them as fools until one day Berel the Beadle left the town to journey to Shedlitz. There, for the first time, a Helmite learned what the world thought of Helm. Hardly able to believe his ears, Berel hurried home in alarm to report to Mottel the Mayor.

Frantically, Mottel called a Town Meeting, and for seven days and seven nights, the leading citizens of Helm thought and thought and thought. On the seventh night of the seventh day, when their brows were as wrinkled as prunes, Mottel suddenly shot up from his seat, exclaiming, "Why didn't I think of it before! It's simple. We Helmites aren't fools. It's just that foolish things are always happening to us." Thereupon a sigh of relief arose from the assembly and all the brows became smooth again. Delighted with this wise explanation, the Helmites immediately decided to send forth a messenger to proclaim it to the world.

But for this important mission, no ordinary Helmite would do–only the cleverest youth in town. Meetings were held to make the selection, discussions took place and finally a contest was announced with Mottel the Mayor as judge. Day in and day out, the young men of Helm appeared before Mottel who found them all so filled with true Helmite wisdom that he was sorely tried to choose from amongst them. However, when Gimpel the son of Mendel appeared before him, he knew that here at last stood the true representative of Helm.

For was it not about Gimpel that this story was told? Once while eating a slice of white bread thickly spread with gleaming yellow butter, it slipped from his hands and fell to the floor. Now, it's pretty well known that when a slice of bread falls, it always lands on the buttered side. But Gimpel's didn't, and when he was asked why, he brightly replied, "It's obvious–the butter was spread on the wrong side."

Now give heed to the extraordinary way in which Gimpel the son of Mendel answered the Mayor's questions:

"Why is the sea salty?" asked Mottel.

Without a moment's hesitation came Gimpel's reply, "Naturally, because of the herring. The herring is salted–and that makes the water salty, too."

Pleased, the Mayor pricked up his ears and put the second question, "If the distance from Helm to Shedlitz is four miles, what is the distance from Shedlitz back to Helm?"

"Eight miles," came Gimpel's prompt reply.

"And can you tell us why?" asked Mottel the Mayor, smiling eagerly.

"Certainly," Gimpel answered. "It's simple. There are four months from Chanukah to Passover and eight months from Passover back again to Chanukah."

Now the Mayor grinned with pleasure and flung the final question. "Why are summer days long and winter days short?"

In a flash, Gimpel answered, "That's easy, in the summer, the days expand because of the heat, and in the winter, they contract because of the cold."

The Mayor nearly jumped out of his skin with delight–even for Helmites, this was truly a great mind.

Soon, attired in the best the town had to offer, Gimpel was sent forth into the world to proclaim the message of Helm. Years passed and when he finally returned and recounted the amazing way he had been received by the peoples of all the strange lands through which he had journeyed, the Helmites then and there decided that the world was unquestionably inhabited by a pack of fools. All except Helm, of course.

Adapted by Solomon Simon.

Old world characters by Tully Filmus (1908-   )

THE PERSONAL MEANING IN BAR MITZVAH

Bar Mitzvah at the Western Wall in Jerusalem.

There are many ways of experiencing Bar Mitzvah. Having a traditional Bar Mitzvah in your community synagogue is one way. Making your own traditions, based on the values, attitudes and lifestyles of you and your family, is another. Many families have chosen alternative forms to celebrate Bar Mitzvah. Some families travel to Israel and celebrate their Bar Mitzvah at the Western Wall, or at a synagogue in Jerusalem. Others prefer inviting friends and family to a resort or country retreat to observe the Bar Mitzvah in a rustic, intimate setting. Yet others choose the familiarity of their home and backyard.

Stephen Bernstein, son of Rabbi Philip Bernstein, prominent rabbi and former advisor on Jewish Affairs to the American military, chose to celebrate his Bar Mitzvah amid the ruins of Frankfurt, Germany, in 1947. At this event, Rabbi Bernstein addressed his son and the small Bar Mitzvah congregation with the following speech.

An Extraordinary Bar Mitzvah

Stephen chose it so. He had been trained for his confirmation in Rochester during the month of November, but when he learned that my responsibilities would keep me here longer he decided to postpone the event, to learn a new portion and to have the service far from his own friends and our families in the normal, peaceful environment of our own community, so as to share it with me and with you. You will forgive me, therefore, a pardonable sense of gratification and pride on this blessed occasion.

This must be also a very extraordinary and heart stirring event for many of the Jews who are here this morning. The very fact that no Bar Mitzvah has been held in Frankfurt since 1940, the very fact that since liberation there was not a single Jewish boy in this once-great city of Frankfurt who reached the age of thirteen, tells more forcefully than I could dare put into words what happened to the Jewish children. This very building in which we gather was once a Jewish school, alive with the voices and activities of Jewish boys and girls. Stephen, then, becomes the symbol of the childhood that was and is no more.

This must be a poignant occasion, also, for the surviving members of the Jewish community of Frankfurt. This was one of the great Jewish communities of the world. The Judaism of Frankfurt, which combined the noblest of our tradition with modern enlightenment, was renowned throughout the world. The very fact that we could find no adequate standing synagogue in which to conduct this ceremony reveals the fate of Judaism here. Frankfurt was the home of great Jewish families who combined material success and patriotism with devotion to their faith.

It is of special significance that this hall in which we meet was the last institution used by the Jewish community for religious services from 1942 until liberation by the American Army. On November 10, 1938, the synagogues of Frankfurt were desecrated, burned, destroyed. The Jewish community then conducted its services in this hall of this school. Here, in these bitter years between 1938 and 1942, with ominous, black clouds gathering overhead and irresistibly pressing down upon them, the remaining members of this community assembled to worship God according to the traditions of their fathers, and to seek strength to withstand their oppressors, and to find solace for their losses.

Synagogue destroyed by fire.

But, in the fall of 1942, the end came. Then began the deportations to Litzmannstadt, Lodz, where they were imprisoned in the ghetto and, ultimately, exterminated. At this point, services were discontinued in the Philantropin Building. There was a brief period of a few weeks when they were conducted in a private home. Then the Gestapo ordered them to cease entirely. For three years there were no Jewish religious exercises in Frankfurt, save for the anguished prayers that must have welled up from the heart of the miserable, terror-stricken people.

Even the very physical circumstances under which we meet today are extraordinary. This is now a hospital for German war-wounded. Some of the very men who participated in these dreadful things are now round-about. There is a window in which the *Magen David*, the Star of David, has been defaced by some Nazi hand.

Yes, we are surrounded by memories today, by tragic memories of a greatness that was and is no more, and of a people who are no longer among the living.

But, that is of the past. The very fact that we are gathered here to worship this morning is a source of hope for the future. On every side you see the wages of the terrible sin which was here committed by the mighty and the wicked. Our eyes confirm the rightness of the prophetic words which Stephen just read to us:

> For the sword hath devoured round about thee
> Why is the strong one overthrown?
> He stood not because the Lord did thrust him down.

The oppressor may triumph for a moment. He may enjoy for a short time the rewards of his gangsterism, but his house is built on sand. It cannot withstand the irresistible moral laws of history. But Israel survives. This very Bar Mitzvah in these very extraordinary circumstances demonstrates the indestructibility of our people and our faith. *"Am Yisrael Chai."*

In the prophetic portion that was just read, the Lord says, "Fear not, for I am with thee." That is a magnificent promise and an imperishable source of hope. It is also justification for pride. It makes me proud I am a Jew. Despite the misfortunes of my people, I would not exchange that heritage for anything in the world.

It is this heritage which we formally transmit to you today, Stephen. When I place my hands upon your head in benediction, I will be the humble instrument through which will flow the stream of history and memories of the great and the good in Israel, the ideals and the aspirations of our people, the strength and the lift of our faith. It is something which places upon you a solemn responsibility to be worthy of its precepts, to be loyal to its ideals, and to express them in a life of service.

"So be the Lord with you as I will let you go."

Philip S. Bernstein.

The following article describes a modern bar mitzvah held amongst the ruins of a lost Jewish community on a small Caribbean island.

A Bar Mitzvah in St. Eustatius

Standing on an improvised *bima* in the ruins of what had been a beautiful synagogue on the tiny Caribbean island of St. Eustatius, Larry Pine knew he would always remember his bar mitzvah.

He looked out at the "congregation"–40 relatives and friends who had flown down from New Jersey, a delegation from the Jewish communities of the nearby islands of St. Thomas, St. Maarten and Curaçao, dignitaries from the Dutch Government in the Lesser Antilles, and the solemn-faced residents of "Statia"–as the island is known locally–their black heads covered with the white *kippot* Larry's mother had brought. The overflow crowd lined the crumbling brick walls, and the children sat on the stairs leading to what had once been the women's gallery.

Behind Larry was an Ark containing two Torahs. They had been flown in on one of the small jets that form the island's only link to the outside world. A portable Ark, made of two sections, had come from St. Maarten. When word had spread throughout Antilles Jewry about the boy from Maplewood, New Jersey, who wanted to enter manhood in the ruins of the centuries-old Honen Dalim Synagogue, Rabbi Aaron L. Peller, of Curaçao's Congregation Mikve Israel-Emanuel, readily agreed to officiate. And David de Robles of St. Maarten, a descendant of the last rabbi to conduct services at Honen Dalim volunteered to bring the portable Ark and a Torah by plane. Because that particular Saturday morning's service required two Torahs, Rabbi Peller also brought one from Curaçao.

After reading from the Torah, Larry spoke about his Haftora portion from *Ezekiel*, the prophet of the return to Zion from the Babylonian Exile. "It was particularly fitting," he said, "because we find ourselves in a place that offered comfort to Jews fleeing from an unfriendly country. They didn't come in great numbers to this part of the New World, but one or two at a time, during the seventeenth and eighteenth centuries.

"Although the Jewish population of Statia numbered about 225 at the most, the Dutch Government gave them permission in 1737 to build a synagogue. I hope that, by being here today, we bring a spirit of renewal to this temple and give thought to those who looked for safety here..."

Larry's parents, Rhoda and Murray Pine, remembered the Jews who once worshipped in this synagogue. The doctor and his wife, looking for a quiet Caribbean island on which to vacation, had first come to Statia, a tiny speck on the map, five years before. Year after year they had returned to the lush, tropical island, drawn by a sense of history as pervasive as the scent of jasmine and bougainvillaea, and by the link they felt with the Jews who had lived there so long ago.

"Today," thought Rhoda on the day of the bar mitzvah, "we are contributing to that history. We're the first new congregants of Honen Dalim in nearly two hundred years."

St. Eustatius, discovered by Columbus on his second trip to the New World, was settled by the Dutch in 1635. By the 1770's, the "Golden Rock," as it came to be known, was the richest free port in the Americas, the mecca for honest traders and privateers. Since it belonged to a neutral nation, all European countries dropped their cargo or their loot at Statia. Along a two-mile stretch of its shore, as many as 60 ships a day unloaded a steady stream of cargo into small boats heading for the overflowing warehouses that lined the shore.

Many of the merchants, warehouse owners and auctioneers on the island were Jews who had settled there in small numbers as far back as 1660. Their ancestors had fled to Amsterdam to escape the Spanish Inquisition and had come to Statia by way of Curaçao. By 1737, the Jews of Statia had their own cemetery and had built a synagogue with help received from Curaçao and Amsterdam. When the synagogue was destroyed by a hurricane in 1772, it was quickly rebuilt, with help from Amsterdam, Curaçao and the members of Congregation Shearith Israel in New York City, with whom the Jews of Statia now had business and family ties. (John Loeb Jr., the New York investment banker, is a descendant of Samson Mears, once the treasurer of Honen Dalim.)

During the American War of Independence, a good part of the weapons, ammunitions and supplies needed by the Americans was transshipped via Statia, and a great deal of it was supplied by Jewish merchants, who paid the severest penalties for dealing with the Americans.

When England declared war on Holland in December 1780, British Admiral George Rodney was ordered to attack Statia–a move which coincided with his own wishes to "clean out that nest of vipers from the face of the earth." Not only did he seek vengeance on Statia for supporting the American colonists–especially the Jews, with their excellent connections in the Carribean and North America as well as Europe–but he also couldn't forgive the Dutch Government for firing an 11-gun salute to the American brigantine, Andrew Doria, on November 16, 1776, thereby giving recognition to the rebels' new flag.

Rodney seized the island on February 3, 1781, in a surprise attack with a huge fleet of ships. The Dutch, English and French merchants were deported to their homelands and allowed to take their families and household possessions with them. For the Jews, however, Rodney had special treatment. He ordered 101 merchants, without their wives and children, to appear at the weighhouse for deportation to an undisclosed destination. They were stripped of all their money, even the linings of their clothing being ripped out in a search for hidden coins, yielding Rodney's men a total of 8,000 pounds sterling. Thirty of the Jews were deported immediately to St. Kitts and Antigua; 71 were locked up for three days, then sent home to witness the sale of their confiscated possessions. The women, children, and remaining men were left in abject misery, reduced to pauperage.

After Rodney's devastation of Statia Lower Town, the island declined as a transshipment center. Most of the Jewish population left for St. Thomas. Congregation Honen Dalim's last service was held in 1792. Since then, no more than two or three Jews at a time have lived on Statia. The population today–about 1,500–is mostly descendants of slaves.

One of the Jews living in Statia during the Pine family's winter holidays in the past five years was Marty Scofield. He and his friend, John May, own and manage two inns at Gallows Bay–the Mooshay Bay Public House and the Old Gin House. "The idea for holding Larry's bar mitzvah at Honen Dalim started as an off-the-wall idea at first, but 15 minutes into the conversation with Marty we knew it could be done," recalls Rhoda Pine.

While the Pines went home and made arrangements ("getting a block of 40 plane seats for our relatives and friends was the hardest part," said Rhoda), Marty got busy at his end. After obtaining permission from the Dutch Governor of the island to use the old synagogue, he enlisted the enthusiastic cooperation of Ismael Berkel, president of the St. Eustatius Historical Foundation, to spruce up the place with potted plants and folding chairs.

A young boy reads Kaddish in a surviving synagogue in Cuba, another Caribbean Jewish community in peril.

The Pines wanted an invitation extended to all the Statians who wished to attend. For this chore, Marty Scofield turned to Vivian Graham, his former colleague at the J. Walter Thompson Agency, now spending her retirement with her husband on the island.

"Since we have no newspaper or radio station on Statia, we used a truck with a loudspeaker to get any important information out," says Graham. "We had a man go up and down the island announcing the invitation and letting the people know that this was a solemn occasion and they were to dress and act the way they did in church."

At last the great day arrived, and Graham, talking into her tape recorder, repeated the remarks of Rabbi Peller, the young spiritual leader of the Curaçao synagogue: "I feel a great sense of historical continuity for the Jews who once flourished here. . . . Once again, the Jews of Statia have gone to Curaçao for help. We responded, and all of us here have shown the world that the Jewish people, even where a synagogue is in ruins, can hold a living event in the interest of a young man. . . . The people of Statia came to join us because they care about keeping tradition, about preserving religion. . . . This is an historic day for the congregation, for the island and for the life of this young man."

After the ceremony, the guests stepped through the paneless windows into the courtyard beyond. There a *kiddush* table was set. At first, the Statians hung back shyly. Then, at the family's coaxing, they tasted the *gefilte fish*, drank the sweet wine and ate their fill of the *challeh* and honey cake. And when it was over, they thanked their hosts warmly.

"It made me proud to be here," said one of the Statian women. "I felt good about that young boy coming to our island for so serious a thing."

"I used to worry over the way people would misuse this site," said Monte Euson, the island's historian and chief librarian. "They'd come up here and take bricks away from the walls when they needed them. But I don't think they will after today. It has given us a high respect for our synagogue, now that we know what really took place here so long ago."

Larry felt he was being given the star treatment when, after the ceremony, many of the local children came up with the xeroxed *siddurs* used during the services and asked for his autograph.

For Rhoda Pine, Larry's mother, the most touching moment was provided by her sister-in-law, who is not observant and rarely goes to temple.

"It made me feel religious again," she told Rhoda. "We really *are* part of something very special."

Bernice Scharlach.

Considering your own personal feelings about being Bar Mitzvah, and choosing the way you would like to express them, is ultimately what makes your Bar Mitzvah celebration a success. The following story, told by David Cohen, a contemporary Israeli writer, shows the beauty in even the most unconventional Bar Mitzvah. The story is told through the vehicle of the Baal Shem Tov, the legendary founder of Hasidism.

Bar Mitzvah Joy

It was the custom of the Baal Shem Tov to journey by wagon to remote settlements, and bring the hearts of the simple folk of Israel closer to God. One time he came upon a distant settlement cut off from any city or town. The people of the place were very simple Jews, villagers, workers of the fields and the forest. They toiled very hard, and had time only for a snatched prayer at *Shacharit*, *Mincha* and *Maarev*. And even then they did not know the meaning of the words. They would bemoan their loneliness, and saw themselves as outcasts, abandoned by the rest of Israel.

Among the people of the settlement there was one, a tax-collector, rich and respected, who was recognized as their leader and head. This tax-collector had an only son, who did not go about with the rest of the Jewish boys, for they knew no Torah, and besides, they were laborers, just like their fathers. And when this boy became thirteen years old, his father, the tax-collector, called a big feast, and invited all the Jews of the village. They dressed themselves in their Sabbath best, and came to the Bar Mitzvah celebration.

At that time the Baal Shem Tov was traveling in the neighborhood. The tax-collector came before him, and begged him to honor the occasion with his presence. The Baal Shem Tov accepted. He came and sat at the head of the table, and studied the weather-beaten faces of the villagers, their black, gnarled hands. They sat at the table, covered with all good things, like apprehensive children, afraid of their elders. The heart of the Baal Shem Tov went out in pity to these simple folk. He began to delight them with beautiful *Nigunim*, the melodies of shepherds in the Carpathian hills, and with pleasing tales. The villagers drank in every note of the *Nigun*, and every word of the story. Their happy faces shone, and they fingered their grizzled beards. Tears of joy sparkled in their eyes.

The tax-collector saw all this, and was filled with anger and amazement at the Baal Shem Tov for not talking to him or to his son, who after all had the true spirit of the Torah. Instead, he paid attention only to the coarse villagers, who were not even fit to be called human beings. The tax-collector, anxious to rebuke the Baal Shem Tov, stood up and announced: "All that we have eaten and drunk up until now is only a beginning, merely the introduction. The real feast will begin upon the arrival of the Rabbi, and the honored guests from the distant town. Only before them will the Bar Mitzvah deliver his *droshe*, the interpretation of the Torah. Only they are fit to hear the words of the Torah."

The Baal Shem Tov pretended not to hear. He turned to the Bar Mitzvah boy, and regaled him with Torah and ethics. He awakened in the boy's heart a love for the Creator. While his words were sinking into the boy's thoughts, the Baal Shem Tov glued his eyes on the open window, towards the broad stretches of field and forest. He concentrated on a far, faraway point. The villagers watched the face of the Baal Shem Tov change. Slowly his face changed color, and, then, suddenly, he burst into a hearty laugh. He laughed once, twice, and the laugh sounded like an outburst from the innermost depths. His face laughed, his eyes laughed, his beard laughed. The simple village folk, drawn in by this laughter, began too to laugh. And it seemed as if everything was laughing: the fields, the forest, the lake, even the heavens above, and the burning sun—all the world joined in a hearty ringing laugh. And the Baal Shem Tov was making all sorts of strange movements and grimaces. He neighed like a horse, and mooed like a cow, crowed like a rooster and bleated like a sheep. And all, all were convulsed in laughter.

At that moment a carriage drew near, and in it was the Rabbi of the town, together with his retinue. When they entered the house, they heard the laughter, and the sounds of the beasts of house and field. They were frightened and inquired: "What is the meaning of all this?" Then the Baal Shem Tov told them what he had seen.

"In a distant village, lying at the foot of the Carpathian Mountains, there dwells a widow with an only son, and today is the day of his Bar Mitzvah. The boy never studied Torah, for the village is very far from any settlement. But he donned the *Tefillin*, the phylacteries which his father left him as an inheritance. He wound them around his arm, and placed them on his forehead, just as his father had taught him to do. His mother had told him that it was a custom among Jews for the Bar Mitzvah boy to be called up before the congregation to read from the Torah, and that a *Minyan*, a quorum of Jews, must listen to the Blessings, and answer: Amen. The boy listened to his mother's words carefully. He went into the barn, and gathered all the barnyard animals and fowl. With his great love he brought them all together, and they constituted his *Minyan*. He smoothed the horse's mane, stroked the back of the cow, patted the goat and the dog. The boy stood in their midst, and the animals, the congregation, heard from his own lips the good news that today he was being received into the Law. The animals answered Amen, each in their own way, with a neighing, a bleating, a braying and a barking. The angels heard this, and they too joined in with their Amen. The joy and laughter rolled from heaven to heaven, and ascended to the Holy Seat itself."

The Baal Shem Tov concluded. He turned to the Rabbi, to all those present, and to the Bar Mitzvah boy, and said: "Because of the orphan boy from the Carpathian Mountains, the very gates of Heaven are open. Come, now let us hear the Bar Mitzvah's *droshe*!"

David Cohen.

"Hasidic Dance" by Arthur Szyk, painted in 1936 in Lodz, Poland.

(Right) "I and the Village" by Marc Chagall (1887-1985).

Another Bar Mitzvah innovation, which is becoming more prominent, is the celebration of belated Bar Mitzvahs for those adults who have not gone through the Bar Mitzvah ceremony at age thirteen. This is an account of a truly unique adult Bar Mitzvah, that of "Bill," a 66-year-old man, who had been institutionalized as mentally retarded for 44 years.

Coming of Age at 66–A Most Unforgettable Bar Mitzvah

Bill's story is tied up with the larger immigrant experience. Bill was the child of Russian-Jewish parents who emigrated to Minneapolis at the turn of the century. Bill was born in 1913; his mother was widowed six years later. Social agencies diagnosed the child as "subnormal" and "feebleminded" in the language of the day, and the desperately impoverished mother was persuaded to commit her son to the Faribault State School for the Feebleminded and Epileptic. It is now agreed that Bill may have been less severely retarded than he now seems to be, but the prejudices and assumptions of the time, along with the language difficulties, made it easy to label him. Institutionalized and treated since childhood as seriously retarded, he failed to develop normally.

During the 44 years that Bill was in institutions, his religious background was obscured. He went to Jewish and Christian services indiscriminately, responding to the music and the ritual, as he still does. In 1964, when work-release programs were opening locked doors of institutions, Bill was placed in a boarding home in Minneapolis. He was working as a handyman in a country club when Bev and Barry Morrow met him. It was the Morrows who managed to have the old records scrutinized. They confirmed Bill's Jewish identity.

Bev and Barry Morrow arranged for Bill to come to Iowa City when they moved here several years ago. He boards with a kind woman, Mae Driscoll, who helps him keep his things in order and prepares his lunch. Bill keeps his pet bird Chubby in his room, feeding and caring for it. "I found a good home," says Bill, "and I've been home ever since."

Every morning Bill boards the city bus and heads for his job. The University of Iowa School of Social Work may be the only school in the country with a mentally handicapped staff member. Bill's title is formidable: Special Developmental Disabilities Consultant. He putters around the lounge, making fresh coffee, sanding furniture, straightening up, chatting with children who wander up from the Early Childhood Development Center, ready to pass the time of day with anyone who happens by. "Shabbat Shalom," he says cheerfully to everyone, any day of the week. Someone has put up a sign: "Wild Bill's Bar and Grill."

"It started as a generous gesture on our part," observes Barry Morrow. "But Bill is a major educational resource. He offers friendship, warmth and music. On a lazy afternoon, Bill is as good a person to spend time with as anyone I know. Over a cup of coffee, he teaches social work students the very essence of their profession."

*   *   *

As befits a member of a distinguished faculty, Bill can list honors and awards on his vita. He has a bronze plaque naming him "Handicapped Iowan of the Year—1976" that was presented to him by the Governor at a formal banquet. He has an award from the American Academy for Cerebral Palsy and Developmental Medicine. But perhaps his greatest achievement is that he holds no bitterness. He remembers being badly treated at Fairbault, but of those days he will say only, "That was bad."

"He's not trapped by his past," observes Jim Cosper, who loves to spend time with Bill. "What some would take as a sign of retardation, I think may be a sign of advancement."

*   *   *

Bill's bar mitzvah has come to be a mythological event for the synagogue of Agudas Achim. "Let us tell you about Bill's bar mitzvah," we tell anyone who will listen. It taught us that the form of all ceremonies need not be precisely the same, that the rules can be broken yet the essentials kept.

It is important to say bluntly that Bill's was not a second-class ceremony, a pathetic gesture for a retarded patient. Though Bill could not understand the words, he understood the essentials. He understands that he has a lot of friends who had gathered to welcome him. He is proud of his bar mitzvah certificate, which hangs framed on his wall. He is proud of his tallis, which he wears as often as he can. He feels a legitimate part of the community; "I had a bar mitzvah," he tells visitors cheerfully.

Every Friday night and Saturday morning, Rabbi Portman or another friend stops by to bring Bill to services. He loves the music and ritual: it is very important to him to have a friend keep him on the correct page.

"He is the most consistent shul-goer in the community," observes Debbie Cosper. "If I don't go, Bill will worry that I'm sick, and I worry that no one will help Bill find his place. So I go, and then Jim goes, and that makes three."

Bill watches Rabbi Portman count the adults, and he is as pleased to be needed for the minyan as we are to have him there. He has a good ear, and his approximation of the aliyah has come a lot closer over the years. Nearly every Saturday Bill carries the Torah. And after services Bill's harmonica is a joyous celebration of the Sabbath.

*   *   *

Iowa City is a university town, and ours is a homogenous community. Most of us are middle-aged, in our thirties and forties. We tend to be highly educated; many of us teach at the University. We are doctors, lawyers, writers. We are vulnerable to the sin of pride in our intellectual accomplishments; "What do you *do?*" we demand of the stranger at the Oneg.

But we cannot demand of Bill, "What do you do?" We have to find something else to say. He has a wonderful ability to disarm the pompous. "I think he's the easiest person to talk to because he accepts you right away," says Debbie Cosper. "He doesn't care what your status is. Getting to know him means getting to know a *person*, rather than a doctor, a lawyer...." She pauses, gropes for the right phrase. "I watch new people who haven't met him before. The encounter is a test of whether you are a *mensch*."

Our encounter with Bill has been profound. We have not been used to thinking of mentally handicapped people as assertive or aggressive, but we have learned from Bill that they can be. No one pushes Bill around; he goes where he chooses.

Bill gives our congregation depth of age. He gives us our minyan. He gives us music. He has instructed us in encountering another human being directly, without the trappings of status or ascribed roles. And he teaches us philosophy.

"The Lord," says Bill, "helps those who *can't* help themselves."

*   *   *

At age 66, Bill Sackter celebrates his bar mitzvah with friends.

It was Saturday afternoon, and the sun was setting. At the Hillel sanctuary the folding doors were opened, the chairs moved out of the way, an improvised Bimah set up in the center of the floor.

"We wanted something informal," Rabbi Jeffrey Portman observed later, "and Havdalah seemed just right. We also wanted to arrange it in the round, to increase access to the Torah, since that is the part of the service Bill likes best."

The familiar words of the Mincha/Ma'ariv service began, and we shuffled, awkwardly into a vague circle. Gathered were well over a hundred people, children and adults, Jewish and non-Jewish. Familiar faces from the congregation, from the faculty, staff and students of the School of Social Work. Our ceremony would be a formal welcome into the Jewish community of a man who had been institutionalized as feebleminded sixty years before.

The Torah service began. Rabbi Portman handed the Torah to Bill, who wrapped his arms around it. The usual verses were too complex a musical line, but Bill knows and loves Hine-ma-tov, so we sang that, over and over again as Bill carried the Torah slowly around our circle, making sure that everyone, including children, got to touch it. "Hine-ma-tov, Hine-ma-tov," hummed Bill. "Behold it is good."

"Y'a'mod Simcha Ben Abraham, ha bar mitzvah." Jonathan Goldstein, the professor of ancient history who regularly reads our Torah, called Bill by the Hebrew name that Rabbi Portman had devised for him: Simcha for happiness. They said the words of the aliyah together: Rabbi Portman loud and clear; Bill echoing along in his own Hebrew.

The president of the synagogue made the same speech he makes to every bar and bat mitzvah, presenting a certificate testifying to the successful completion of Hebrew preparation. Martha Lubaroff, the president of the Sisterhood, presented a tallis. Bill's parents are long since dead, but his court-appointed conservator, Barry Morrow, was there.

"There have been many occasions like this when I've stood beside you, Bill, but somehow tonight seems like the most important. I know you missed many things when you were growing up—your bar mitzvah was one. Tonight you have been reunited with your religious heritage and the faith of your parents."

It was time for the bar mitzvah to make a speech. Bill moved to the Bimah. "Thanks to all my friends for coming. God bless you. Thank you very much." Pausing a moment, he reached for his harmonica, and, facing the Torah, for all the world like the Fool in the Isaac Bashevis Singer story, Bill Sackter played his harmonica before the Lord.

Linda Kerber.

39

"In Judaism faith is the capacity of the soul to perceive the abiding." Leo Baeck.

While according to Jewish tradition one becomes an adult the day of one's thirteenth birthday (or more precisely on the first day of one's fourteenth year), often one's personal experience of becoming an adult may occur at some time before or thereafter. Experiencing emotional crises often brings on responsibility and maturity more quickly. Sam Levinson, comedian and writer, describes his personal crisis and coming of age.

The Day I Became a Man

It was shortly after my Bar Mitzvah. Papa and I were alone in the house the day Mama died. It was Friday morning, always a stressful time for a Jewish woman, who had to purify her home for the arrival of the Sabbath, which they called "the Bride." Death knew where to find Mama any Friday morning–on her knees washing the floor. And that was where she died. Following ancient orthodox ritual, a group of elderly women were called in to wash Mama's body and put her to rest on the floor, some candles near her head.

After the family was called together (brother Joe, the doctor, signed her death certificate), she was placed in a hearse, which carried her to the steps of Papa's synagogue, from which the rabbi wailed some verses beseeching God's mercy. The hearse then proceeded down the block. No one told us to, but we did what we had seen done before. Tradition. We lined up behind the hearse in a funeral cortege, Papa and I first, behind us the family.

It was summer. The sun was shining. I could not understand how the sun could shine in such darkness. Birds sang gayly from the telephone wires. I hated the sunshine and I hated the birds. The sidewalks were lined with neighbors, mostly women in their stained aprons also caught in the middle of preparing for the Sabbath, knowing they had been spared for now, sobbing and pointing at me: "Left over, a child, a child, a child." As I walked behind the slowly moving black wagon, my head bowed down, I saw fragments of my childhood coming toward me from between the wheels, chalk drawings of hearts, baseball bases, boxes for hopscotch, crisscrosses of ticktacktoe, parts of tops and checkers. Out of nowhere, or perhaps from somewhere where the sun had some reason to shine and birds to sing, a rubber ball came bouncing between the wheels. It hit the inside of one wheel and was sent spinning against the opposite wheel, back and forth, picking up momentum with each bump, seeming to be not only unaware of danger but leaping back again and again for more, taunting the wheels. Then at the height of its joyousness a soft pop, a squish, and it lay there baby pink on the inside, gashed on the outside. Its last breath rose gently to my nostrils. It was the smell of death. I knew that the time had come for me to put away the things of my childhood. That day I became a man.

Sam Levenson.

"If there is any miracle in the world, any mystery, it is individuality."   Leo Baeck.

Each in His Own Way

Every person born into this world represents something new, something that never existed before, something original and unique. "It is the duty of every person in Israel to know and consider that he is unique in the world in his particular character and that there has never been anyone like him in the world, for if there had been someone like him, there would have been no need for him to be in the world. . . ."

The wise Rabbi Bunam once said in old age, when he had already grown blind: "I should not like to change places with our father Abraham! What good would it do God if Abraham became like blind Bunam, and blind Bunam became like Abraham? Rather than have this happen, I think I shall try to become a little more myself."

The same idea was expressed with even greater pungency by Rabbi Zusya when he said, a short while before his death: "In the world to come I shall not be asked, 'Why were you not Moses?' I shall be asked, 'Why were you not Zusya?'"

Martin Buber.

A spirit of individual choice and a strong belief in oneself have always been stressed in Jewish tradition. Ultimately, your Bar Mitzvah and your Jewish identity depend on *you* and what *you* want them to be. The following pages will give you an opportunity to think about the aspects of yourself and your Bar Mitzvah that make you truly individual and unique. Fill in the pages, including copies of any readings, blessings, and prayers which were a part of your ceremony. These pages are a memento of a very important time in your life.

FACTS ABOUT YOU

Name: _____   Hebrew Name: _____

Date of Birth: _____   Place of Birth: _____

Address: _____

Height: _____   Weight: _____

Date of Bar Mitzvah Ceremony: _____   Hebrew Date: _____

Portion of Torah read: _____

Portion of Haftorah read: _____

_____

Some Favorite Things:

_____

Some Favorite Activities:

PERSONAL THOUGHTS AND SPECIAL MOMENTS

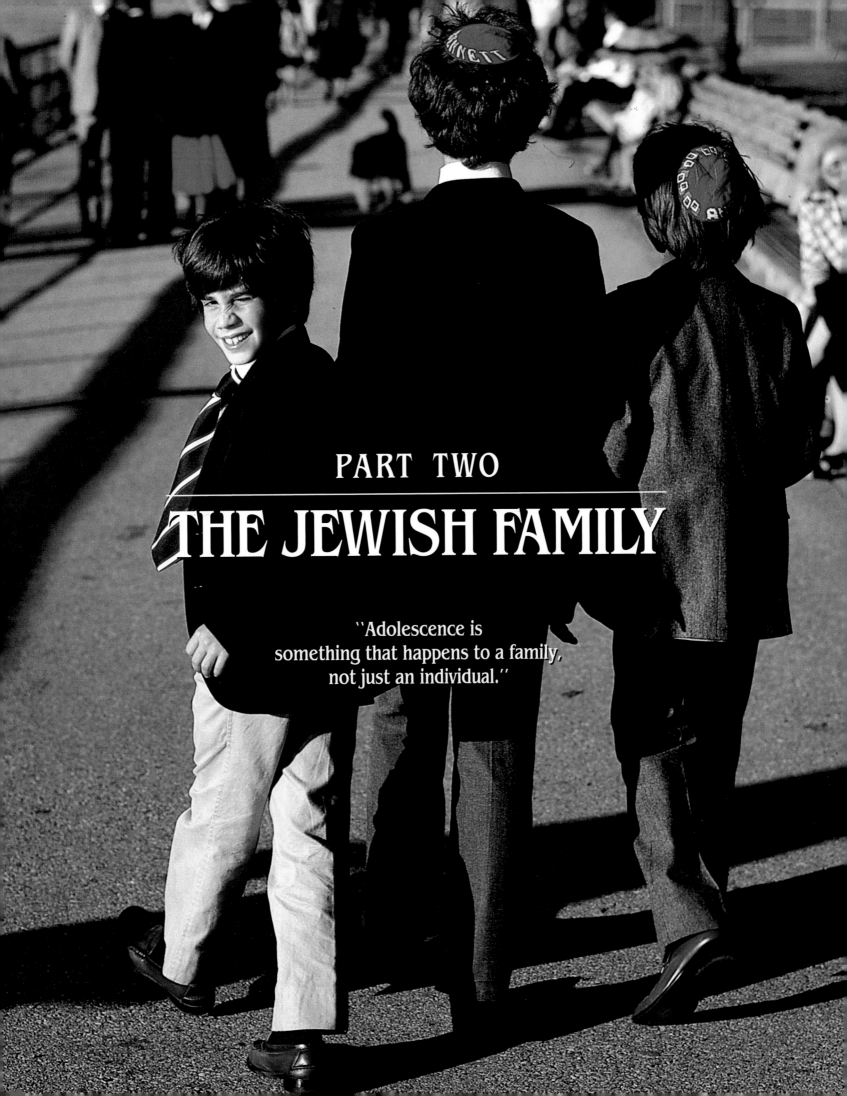

PART TWO
THE JEWISH FAMILY

"Adolescence is
something that happens to a family,
not just an individual."

Once in a Year

Once in a year this comes to pass:
My father is a king in a black skull cap,
My mother is a queen in a brown perruque,
A princess my sister, a lovely lass,
My brother a prince, and I a duke.

Silver and plate, and fine cut-glass
Brought from the cupboards that hid them till now
Banquet King David's true lineage here.
Once in a year this comes to pass,
Once in a long unroyal year.

Abraham M. Klein.
From a longer poem, Hagaddah.

Psalm XXXVI: a Psalm Touching Genealogy

Not sole was I born, but entire genesis:
For to the fathers that begat me, this
Body is residence. Corpuscular,
They dwell in my veins, they eavesdrop at my ear,
They circle, as with Torahs, round my skull,
In exit and in entrance all day pull
The latches of my heart, descend, and rise–
And there look generations through my eyes.

Abraham M. Klein.

In many ways, Bar Mitzvah is a family affair. The choices of how you decide to experience your Bar Mitzvah–which Jewish traditions you wish to practise, which rituals you will change, what form your celebration will take–have probably been the topics of family discussion for a long time. But even more important, you are the person you are today because of your family.

Your parents have taught you, either directly or through their actions, what they feel is important in life. They have given you practical, moral and emotional guidance, as well as physical care, since you were born. They have guided your education, and have probably introduced you to the Jewish customs or observances which you practise. Your siblings have influenced your life as well; and your extended family–if you are fortunate to have grandmothers, grandfathers, aunts and uncles–have probably also made an impact on your life.

There has always been a great emphasis on the importance of the family in Jewish tradition. In the shtetls of Eastern Europe, where life outside the Jewish ghettos was hostile, the Jewish home provided a refuge from hate and persecution. The traditions within the home were perhaps more important in preserving the Jewish way of life than the school or the synagogue. When the family celebrated Jewish holidays, Jewish values were passed from one generation to the next. The close bonds between family members gave each person, adult and child alike, the strength to deal with the intimidating outside world.

The following story, by Samuel Joseph Agnon, highly respected Hebrew writer, conveys this special Jewish sense of family. The story is from the point of view of a man who reminisces about his parents and his boyhood in a Galician shtetl in Eastern Europe. His tale climaxes on the day of his Bar Mitzvah when he faces a moral dilemma and makes a very adult decision.

from The Kerchief

Whenever father returned from the fair he brought us many gifts. He was very clever, was father, knowing what each of us would want most and bringing it to us. Or maybe the Master of Dreams used to tell father what he showed us in dream, and he would bring it for us.

There were not many gifts that survived long. As is the way of the valuables of this world, they were not lasting. Yesterday we were playing with them, and today they were already thrown away. Even my fine prayer-book was torn, for whatever I might have had to do, I used to open it and ask its counsel; and finally nothing was left of it but a few dog-eared printed scraps.

But one present which father brought mother remained whole for many years. And even after it was lost it did not vanish from my heart, and I still think of it as though it were yet there.

*   *   *

That day, when father returned from the fair, it was Friday after the noon hour, when the children are freed from school. Those Friday afternoon hours are the best time of the week, because all the week round a child is bent over his book and his eyes and heart are not his own; as soon as he raises his head he is beaten. On Friday afternoon he is freed from study, and even if he does whatever he wants to, nobody objects. Were it not for the noon meal the world would be like Paradise. But mother had already summoned me to eat and I had no heart to refuse.

Almost before we had begun eating my little sister put her right hand to her ear and set her ear to the table. "What are you doing?" mother asked her. "I'm trying to listen," she answered. Mother asked, "Daughter, what are you trying to listen to?" Then she began clapping her hands with joy and crying, "Father's coming, father's coming." And in a little while we heard the wheels of a wagon. Very faint at first, then louder and louder. At once we threw our spoons down while they were still half full, left our plates on the table and ran out to meet father coming back from the fair. Mother, may she rest in peace, also let her apron fall and stood erect, her arms folded on her bosom, until father entered the house.

How big father was then! I knew my father was bigger than all the other fathers. All the same I used to think there must be someone taller than he–but now even the chandelier hanging from the ceiling in our house seemed to be lower.

Suddenly father bent down, caught me to him, kissed me and asked me what I had learnt. Is it likely that father did not know which portion of the week was being read? But he only asked to try me out. Before I could answer he had caught my brother and sister, raised them on high and kissed them.

*   *   *

The wagoner entered bringing two trunks, one large and the other neither large nor small but medium; and that second trunk seemed to have eyes and smile with them.

Father took his bunch of keys from his pocket and said, "We'll open the trunk and take out my tallith and tefillin." Father was just speaking for fun, since who needs tefillin on Friday afternoon, and even if you think of the tallith, my father had a special tallith for Sabbath, but he only said it in order that we should not be too expectant and not be too anxious for presents.

But we went and undid the straps of the trunk and watched his every movement while he took one of the keys and examined it, smiling affectionately. The key also smiled at us; that is, gleams of light sparkled on the key and it seemed to be smiling. Finally

Market day in Hrubieszow, Poland, 1925.

he pressed the key into the lock, opened the trunk, put his hand inside and felt among his possessions. Suddenly he looked at us and became silent. Had father forgotten to place the presents there? Or had he been lodging at an inn where the inn people rose and took out the presents? As happened with the sage by whose hands they sent a gift to Caesar, a chest full of jewels and pearls, and when he lodged one night at the inn, the inn folk opened the chest and took out everything that was in it and filled it with dust. Then I prayed that just as a miracle was done to that sage so that that dust should be the dust of Abraham our father, which turned into swords when it was thrown into the air, so should the Holy and Blest One perform a miracle with us in order that the things with which the innkeepers had filled father's trunk should be better than all presents. Before my prayer was at an end father brought out all kinds of fine things. There was not a single one among his gifts which we had not longed for all the year round. And that is why I said that the Master of Dreams must have revealed to father what he had shown us in dream.

The gifts of my father deserve to be praised at length, but who is going to praise things that have vanished and are lost? All the same, one fine gift which my father brought my mother on the day that he returned from the fair, deserves to be mentioned in particular.

*   *   *

It was a silk brocaded kerchief adorned with flowers and blossoms. On the one side it was brown and they were white, while on the other they were brown and it was white. That was the gift which father of blessed memory brought to mother, may she rest in peace.

Mother opened up the kerchief, stroked it with her fingers and peeped at father; he peeped back at her and both of them remained silent. Finally she folded it again, rose, put it in the cupboard and said to father, "Wash your hands and eat." As soon as father sat down to his meal I went out to my friends in the street and showed them the presents I had received, and was busy outside with them until the Sabbath began and I went to pray with father.

How pleasant that Sabbath was when we returned from the synagogue! The skies were full of stars, the houses full of lamps and candles, people were wearing their Sabbath clothes and walking quietly beside father in order not to disturb the Sabbath angels who accompany one home from the synagogue on Sabbath Eves: candles were alight in the house and the table prepared and the fine smell of white bread, and a white table-cloth spread and two Sabbath loaves on it, covered by a small napkin out of respect; so they should not feel ashamed when the blessing is said first over the wine.

Father bowed and entered and said, "A peaceful and blessed Sabbath, and mother answered, "Peaceful and blessed." Father looked at the table and began singing, "Peace be unto you, angels of peace," while mother sat at the table, her prayer-book in hand, and the big chandelier with the ten candles one for each of the Ten Commandments, hanging from the ceiling, gave light. They were answered back by the rest of the candles, one for father, one for mother, one for each of the little ones; and although we were smaller than father and mother, all the same our candles were as big as theirs. Then I looked at mother and saw that her face had changed and her forehead had grown smaller because of the kerchief wound round her head and covering her hair, while her eyes seemed much larger and were shining towards father who went on singing, "A woman of valor who shall find?"; and the ends of her kerchief which hung down below her chin were quivering very gently, because the Sabbath angels were moving their wings and making a wind. It must have been so, for the windows were closed and where could the wind have come from if not from the wings of the angels? As it says in the Psalms, "He maketh his messengers the winds." I held back my breath in order not to confuse the angels and looked at my mother, may she rest in peace, and wondered at the Sabbath Day, which is given us for an honor and a glory. Suddenly I felt how my cheeks were being patted. I do not know whether the wings of the angels or the corners of the kerchief were caressing me. Happy is he who merits to have good angels hovering over his head, and happy is he whose mother has stroked his head on the Sabbath Eve.

* * *

When I awakened from sleep it was already day. The whole world was full of the Sabbath morning. Father and mother were about to go out, he to his little synagogue, and she to the House of Study of my grandfather, may he rest in peace. Father was wearing a black satin robe and a round shtreimel of sable on his head, and mother wore a black dress and a hat with feathers. In the House of Study of my grandfather, where mother used to pray, they did not spend too much time singing, and so she could return early. When I came back with father from the small synagogue she was already seated at the table wearing her kerchief, and the table was prepared with wine and brandy and cakes, large and small, round and doubled over. Father entered, said, "A Sabbath of peace and blessing," put his tallith on the bed, sat down at the head of the table, said, "The Lord is my shepherd, I shall not want," blessed the wine, tasted the cake and began, "A Psalm of David; The earth is the Lord's and the fulness thereof." When the Ark is opened on the New Year's Eve and this Psalm is said there is a great stirring among the congregation. There was a similar stirring in my heart then. Had my mother not taught me that you do not stand on chairs and do not clamber on to the table and do not shout, I would have climbed onto the table and shouted out, "The earth is the Lord's and the fulness thereof," like that child in the Gemara (Talmud) who used to be seated in the middle of a gold table which was a load for sixteen men, with sixteen silver chains attached, and dishes and glasses and bowls and platters fitted, and with all kinds of food and sweet-meats and spices of all that was created in the Six Days of Creation; and he used to proclaim, "The earth is the Lord's and the fulness thereof."

Mother cut the cake giving each his or her portion; and the ends of her kerchief accompanied her hands. While doing so a cherry fell out of the cake and stained her apron; but it did not touch her kerchief, which remained as clean as it had been when father took it out of his trunk.

* * *

A woman does not put on a silken kerchief every day or every Sabbath. When a woman stands at the oven what room is there for ornament? Every day is not Sabbath, but on the other hand there are Festivals. The Holy and Blest One took pity on His creatures and gave them times of gladness, holidays and appointed seasons. On festivals mother used to put on a feather

hat and go to the synagogue, and at home she would don her kerchief. But on the New Year and the Day of Atonement she kept the kerchief on all day long; similarly on the morning of Hoshana Rabba, the seventh day of Tabernacles. I used to look at mother on the Day of Atonement, when she wore her kerchief and her eyes were bright with prayer and fasting. She seemed to me like a presented prayer-book bound in silk.

The rest of the time the kerchief lay folded in the cupboard, and on Sabbaths and festivals mother would take it out. I never saw her washing it, although she was very particular about cleanliness. When Sabbaths and festivals are properly kept the Sabbath and festival clothes are preserved. But for me she would have kept the kerchief all her life long.

What happened was as follows. On the day I became thirteen years old and a member of the congregation, my mother, may she rest in peace, bound her kerchief round my neck. Blessed be He who is everywhere, who has given His word to guardians. There was not a spot of dirt to be found on the kerchief. But sentence had been passed already on the kerchief, that it was to be lost through me. This kerchief, which I had observed so much and so long, would vanish because of me.

* * *

Now I shall pass from one theme to another until I return to my original theme. At that time there came a beggar to our town who was sick with running sores; his hands were swollen, his clothes were rent and tattered, his shoes were cracked, and when he showed himself in the street the children threw earth and stones at him. And not only the children but even the grownups and householders turned angry faces on him. Once when he went to the market to buy bread or onions the stall-women drove him away. Not that the stall-women in our town were cruel; indeed, they were tender-hearted. Some would give the food from their mouths to orphans, others went to the forest, gathered twigs, made charcoal of them and shared them free among the beggars and poor folk. But every beggar has his own luck. When he fled from them and entered the House of Study, the beadle shouted at him and pushed him out. And when on the Sabbath Eve he crept into the House of Study, nobody invited him to come home with them and share the Sabbath meal. God forbid that the sons of our father Abraham do not perform works of charity; but the ministers of Satan used to accompany that beggar and pull a veil over Jewish eyes so that they should not perceive his dire needs. As to where he heard the blessing over wine, and where he ate his three Sabbath meals—if he was not sustained by humankind he must have been sustained by the Grace of God.

Hospitality is a great thing, since buildings are erected and wardens appointed for the sake of it and to support the poor. But I say it in praise of our townsfolk, that although they did not establish any poorhouse or elect any wardens, every man who could do so used to find a place for a poor man in his own house, thus seeing the troubles of his brother and aiding him and supporting him at the hour of his need; and his sons and daughters who saw this would learn from his deeds. When trouble would befall a man he would groan; the walls of his house would groan with him because of the mighty groaning of the poor; and he would know that there are blows even greater than that which had befallen him. And as he comforted the poor, so would the Holy and Blest One in the future comfort him.

* * *

Now I leave the beggar and shall tell only of my mother's kerchief, which she tied round my neck when I grew old enough to perform all the commandments and be counted a member of the congregation. On that day, when I returned from the House of Study to eat the midday meal, I was dressed like a bridegroom and was very happy and pleased with myself because I was now donning tefillin. On the way I found that beggar sitting on a heap of stones, changing the bandages of his sores, his clothes rent and tattered, nothing but a bundle of rags which did not even hide his sores. He looked at me as well. The sores on his face seemed like eyes of fire. My heart stopped, my knees began shaking, my eyes grew dim and everything seemed to be in a whirl. But I took my heart in my hand, nodded to the beggar, wished him peace, and he wished me peace back.

Suddenly my heart began thumping, my ears grew hot and a sweetness such as I had never experienced in all my days took possession of all my limbs; my lips and my tongue were sweet with it, my mouth fell agape, my two eyes were opened and I stared before me as a man who sees in waking what has been shown him in dream. And so I stood staring in front of me. The sun stopped still in the sky, not a creature was to be seen in the street; but the merciful sun looked down upon the earth and its light shone bright on the sores of the beggar. I began loosening my kerchief to breathe more freely, for tears stood in my throat. Before I could loosen it, my heart began racing with wonder, and the sweetness, which I had already felt, doubled and redoubled. I took off the kerchief and gave it to the beggar. He took it and wound it round his sores. The sun came and stroked my neck.

I looked around. There was not a creature in the market, but a pile of stones lay there and reflected the sun's light. For a little while I stood there without thinking. Then I moved my feet and returned home.

*   *   *

When I reached the house I walked round it on all four sides. Suddenly I stopped at mother's window, the one from which she used to look out. The place was strange; the sun's light upon it did not dazzle but warmed, and there was perfect rest there. Two or three people passing slowed their paces and lowered their voices; one of them wiped his brow and sighed deeply. It seems to me that that sigh must still be hanging there, until the end of all generations.

I stood there awhile, a minute or two minutes or more. Finally I moved from thence and entered the house. When I entered I found mother sitting in the window as was her way. I greeted her and she returned my greeting. Suddenly I felt that I had not treated her properly; she had had a fine kerchief which she used to bind round her head on Sabbaths and festivals, and I had taken it and given it to a beggar to bind up his feet with. Ere I had ended begging her to forgive me she was gazing at me with love and affection. I gazed back at her, and my heart was filled with the same gladness as I had felt on that Sabbath when my mother had set the kerchief about her head for the first time.

The end of the story of the kerchief of my mother, may she rest in peace.

Samuel Joseph Agnon.

(Right) "Baber's Family Celebrating the Sabbath in Edmonton" by William Kurelek (1927–1977). Collection: The Ontario Heritage Foundation. Courtesy of the Isaacs Gallery, Toronto.

FAMILY BONDS

In America, Jewish immigrants depended on family bonds and Jewish traditions to survive the poverty and loneliness which they experienced in their new environment. Charles Angoff, American writer and son of Jewish immigrants, conveys the comfort and strength provided by family and Jewish home traditions when he describes his own Bar Mitzvah.

Memoirs of Boston

I was Bar Mitzva on Thursday. My father woke me up at 6:30 in the morning and took me to *shul*. There were about thirty people at the service. I was called to the Torah for the first time–and that was *Bar Mitzva*. Some of the other congregants came over to me and wished me *mazel tov*. My father bashfully put his arm around me and also congratulated me. Then he and I walked a bit and he went off to work. I turned toward home feeling terribly lonely. I had become a full, mature Jew–and most of Boston was asleep, and didn't care. The few people who passed me on the street didn't care either. When I reached our house, as soon as I put my hand on the doorknob my mother opened the door and threw her arms around me and kissed me and hugged me and kissed me again. Her arm around me, she took me to the kitchen, and there on the table was the *Shabbes* tablecloth. To my mother it was *yom tov*. She had the usual *boolkes* on a platter, but there was also a platter of the kind of cinnamon cakes I liked, and a smaller platter of ginger jam, another favorite of mine. Also a cup of cocoa. "Eat, Shayel, eat," said my mother. I suggested she have some cocoa too. "No, I'm not hungry." I ate. I was conscious that she was looking at me with great appreciation of what had happened to me. Her oldest son was now a full man in Israel. I was embarrassed, but I was also delighted. I finished my cocoa, and mother said, "Have another cup." The last time she had suggested I have another cup of cocoa was when I was convalescing from a cold that had almost turned into pneumonia. I had another cup. When I was finished with my special breakfast, mother said, "Father had to go to work. He had to. You understand."

"Sure," I said.

"But we'll have a small reception on Saturday night, after *mincha*. We've invited the relatives and some friends. So we'll have a little reception."

"Oh," I said, too moved to say anything else.

She got up, came to me, patted my head and then kissed me slowly. "Maybe you're a little sleepy, Shayel. Maybe you want to sleep a little more. I'll wake you up in time for your school."

"Yes, I think I'll have a little more sleep," I said.

I didn't want any more sleep. I lay down on the bed. I was profoundly happy. Everything was good. Everything was very good.

Charles Angoff.

In spite of the strong support from family, sometimes the occasion of your Bar Mitzvah can be quite challenging, or even overwhelming. Bar Mitzvah can be experienced as a command performance for the family, and they can also be your harshest critics. Rabbi Gunther Plaut, author and Reform rabbi, humorously recalls the trauma of his Bar Mitzvah.

Bar Mitzvah Ordeal

I was Bar Mitzvah like everyone else and prepared myself by paying an occasional visit to the rabbi of the upstairs synagogue. . . .

The Bar Mitzvah ceremony itself–a traumatic rite for any youngster–left me only two memories: one, naturally, of the many books I received; the other of my reading the Haftarah. I had complained to Father–not too seriously, of course, but complained nonetheless–that my portion (the beginning of First Kings) was unduly long. Why was I born to be punished in such a fashion? He shrugged his shoulders in his usual fashion and said, "I have it from high authority that the Heavenly Court will consider your complaint at its next session."

When the ordeal was finally over I went to sit with my father.

"You know, it wasn't really as long as all that," I ventured, whereupon he, placing his glasses on the top of his head–an inevitable sign that something of great importance was about to come–replied, "Of course it didn't appear long, because you left half of it out."

I'm not sure that I did, but I must have skipped something; at any rate, I did not pass with flying colours. I often told the story to an aspiring youngster coming to me prior to his Bar Mitzvah, trembling from head to toe wishing the trial were already ended. I told him that he should not worry about making mistakes; that the only punishment that could possibly be meted out was that he be condemned to become a rabbi.

Rabbi W. Gunther Plaut.

The Boston Jewish quarter at the turn of the century.

FAMILY TRANSITIONS

Traditionally, the father of the Bar Mitzvah recites a blessing during the ceremony in which he gives up his responsibility for his son's actions: "Blessed be He who has relieved me of the responsibility for this boy." Today, though this prayer may still be recited, the real emphasis is on *you* and your growing independence. As you mature, both you and your family must adjust to the changes in your relationships. You will always be your parents' child, but you are becoming your own independent person too. The transition, from being dependent on your parents to setting out on your own, is sometimes very painful—maybe even more so for your parents.

Jewish parents are known for their concern and high expectations for their children. They care deeply about what will happen to their children and the values they will live by. This is a mixed blessing. The large percentage of Jewish doctors, lawyers, scientists, university professors, etc. is perhaps a tribute to this point. On the other hand, self-assertion and the ability to make one's own choices in life are an important part of growing up. After all, it was only after Abraham asserted himself by smashing his father's idols (at the age of thirteen) that he became the first Jew. Isaac Babel's story "Awakening," written at the turn of the century about life in Odessa, Russia, shows that some things never change. Parents may have their expectations, but young people must come to their own conclusions and live with the consequences—whether it is 4,000 years ago, 100 years ago, or today.

Awakening

All the folk in our circle—brokers, shopkeepers, clerks in banks and steamship offices—used to have their children taught music. Our fathers, seeing no other escape from their lot, had thought up a lottery, building it on the bones of little children. Odessa more than other towns was seized by the craze. And in fact, in the course of ten years or so our town supplied the concert platforms of the world with infant prodigies. From Odessa came Mischa Elman, Zimbalist, Gabrilowitsch. Odessa witnessed the first steps of Jascha Heifetz.

When a lad was four or five, his mother took the puny creature to Zagursky's. Mr. Zagursky ran a factory of infant prodigies, a factory of Jewish dwarfs in lace collars and patent-leather pumps. He hunted them out in the slums of the Moldavanka, in the evil-smelling courtyards of the Old Market. Mr. Zagursky charted the first course, then the children were shipped off to Professor Auer in St. Petersburg. A wonderful harmony dwelt in the souls of those wizened creatures with their swollen blue hands. They became famous virtuosi. My father decided that I should emulate them. Though I had, as a matter of fact, passed the age limit set for infant prodigies, being now in my fourteenth year, my shortness and lack of strength made it possible to pass me off as an eight-year-old. Herein lay father's hope.

I was taken to Zagursky's. Out of respect for my grandfather, Mr. Zagursky agreed to take me on at the cut rate of a rouble a lesson. My grandfather Leivi-Itzkhok was the laughing-stock of the town, and its chief adornment. He used to walk about the streets in a top hat and old boots, dissipating doubt in the darkest of cases. He would be asked what a Gobelin was, why the Jacobins betrayed Robespierre, how you made artificial silk, what a Caesarean section was. And my grandfather could answer these questions. Out of respect for his learning and craziness, Mr. Zagursky only charged us a rouble a lesson. And he had the devil of a time with me, fearing my grandfather, for with me there was nothing to be done. The sounds dripped from my fiddle like iron filings, causing even me excruciating agony, but father wouldn't give in. At home there was no talk save of Mischa Elman, exempted by the Tsar himself from military service. Zimbalist, father would have us know, had been presented to the King of England and had played at Buckingham Palace. The parents of Gabrilowitsch had bought two houses in St. Petersburg. Infant prodigies brought wealth to their parents, but though my father could have reconciled himself to poverty, fame he must have.

"It's not possible," people feeding at his expense would insinuate, "it's just not possible that the grandson of such a grandfather..."

But what went on in my head was quite different. Scraping my way through the violin exercises, I would have books by Turgenev or Dumas on my music stand. Page after page I devoured as I deedled away. In the daytime I would relate impossible happenings to the kids next door; at night I would commit them to paper. In our family, composition was a hereditary occupation. Grandfather Leivi-Itzkhok, who went cracked as he grew old, spent his whole life writing a tale entitled "The Headless Man." I took after him.

Three times a week, laden with violin case and music, I made my reluctant way to Zagursky's place on Witte (formerly Dvoryanskaya) Street. There Jewish girls aflame with hysteria sat along the wall awaiting their turn, pressing to their feeble knees violins exceeding in dimensions the exalted persons they were to play to at Buckingham Palace.

The door to the sanctum would open, and from Mr. Zagursky's study there would stagger big-headed, freckled children with necks as thin as flower stalks and an epileptic flush on their cheeks. The door would bang to, swallowing up the next dwarf. Behind the wall, straining his throat, the teacher sang and waved his baton. He had ginger curls and frail legs, and sported a big bow tie. Manager of a monstrous lottery, he populated the Moldavanka and the dark culs-de-sac of the Old Market with the ghosts of pizzicato and cantilena. Afterward old Professor Auer lent these strains a diabolical brilliance.

In this crew I was quite out of place. Though like them in my dwarfishness, in the voice of my forebears I perceived inspiration of another sort.

The first step was difficult. One day I left home laden like a beast of burden with violin case, violin, music, and twelve roubles in cash—payment for a month's tuition. I was going along Nezhin Street; to get to Zagursky's I should have turned into Dvoryanskaya, but instead of that I went up Tiraspolskaya and found myself at the harbor. The alloted time flew past in the part of the port where ships went after quarantine. So began my liberation. Zagursky's saw me no more: affairs of greater moment occupied my thoughts. My pal Nemanov and I got into the habit of slipping aboard the S.S. *Kensington* to see an old salt named Trottyburn. Nemanov was a year younger than I. From the age of eight onward he had been doing the most ingenious business deals you can imagine. He had a wonderful head for that kind of thing, and later on amply fulfilled his youthful

"Jewish Home Life in Montreal" *by William Kurelek (1927-1977). Collection: The Ontario Heritage Foundation. Courtesy of the Isaacs Gallery, Toronto.*

At the birth of a baby, children chant the "Shema Israel" prayer.

promise. Now he is a New York millionaire, director of General Motors, a company no less powerful than Ford. Nemanov took me along with him because I silently obeyed all his orders. He used to buy pipes smuggled in by Mr. Trottyburn. They were made in Lincoln by the old sailor's brother.

"Gen'lemen," Mr. Trottyburn would say to us, "take my word, the pets must be made with your own hands. Smoking a factory-made pipe–might as well shove an enema in your mouth. D'you know who Benvenuto Cellini was? He was a grand lad. My brother in Lincoln could tell you about him. Live and let live is my brother's motto. He's got it into his head that you just has to make the pets with your own hands, and not with no one else's. And who are we to say him no, gen'lemen?"

Nemanov used to sell Trottyburn's pipes to bank-managers, foreign consuls, well-to-do Greeks. He made a hundred percent on them.

The pipes of the Lincolnshire master breathed poetry. In each one of them thought was invested, a drop of eternity. A little yellow eye gleamed in their mouthpieces, and their cases were lined with satin. I tried to picture the life in Old England of Matthew Trottyburn, the last master-pipemaker, who refused to swim with the tide.

"We can't but agree, gen'lemen, that the pets has to be made with your own hands."

The heavy waves by the sea wall swept me further and further away from our house, impregnated with the smell of leeks and Jewish destiny. From the harbor I migrated to the other side of the breakwater. There on a scrap of sandspit dwelt the boys from Primorskaya Street. Trouserless from morn till eve, they dived under wherries, sneaked coconuts for dinner, and awaited the time when boats would arrive from Kherson and Kamenka laden with watermelons, which melons it would be possible to break open against moorings.

To learn to swim was my dream. I was ashamed to confess to those bronzed lads that, born in Odessa, I had not seen the sea till I was ten, and at fourteen didn't know how to swim.

How slow was my acquisition of things one needs to know! In my childhood, chained to the Gemara, I had led the life of a sage. When I grew up I started climbing trees.

But swimming proved beyond me. The hydrophobia of my ancestors–Spanish rabbis and Frankfurt money-changers–dragged me to the bottom. The waves refused to support me. I

would struggle to the shore pumped full of salt water and feeling as though I had been flayed, and return to where my fiddle and music lay. I was fettered to the instruments of my torture, and dragged them about with me. The struggle of rabbis versus Neptune continued till such time as the local water-god took pity on me. This was Yefim Nikitich Smolich, proofreader of the *Odessa News*. In his athletic breast there dwelt compassion for Jewish children, and he was the god of a rabble of rickety starvelings. He used to collect them from the bug-infested joints on the Moldavanka, take them down to the sea, bury them in the sand, do gym with them, dive with them, teach them songs. Roasting in the perpendicular sunrays, he would tell them tales about fishermen and wild beasts. To grownups Nikitich would explain that he was a natural philosopher. The Jewish kids used to roar with laughter at his tales, squealing and snuggling up to him like so many puppies. The sun would sprinkle them with creeping freckles, freckles of the same color as lizards.

Silently, out of the corner of his eye, the old man had been watching my duel with the waves. Seeing that the thing was hopeless, that I should simply never learn to swim, he included me among the permanent occupants of his heart. That cheerful heart of his was with us there all the time; it never went careering off anywhere else, never knew covetousness and never grew disturbed. With his sunburned shoulders, his superannuated gladiator's head, his bronzed and slightly bandy legs, he would lie among us on the other side of the mole, lord and master of those melon-sprinkled, paraflin-stained waters. I came to love that man, with the love that only a lad suffering from hysteria and headaches can feel for a real man. I was always at his side, always trying to be of service to him.

He said to me:

"Don't you get all worked up. You just strengthen your nerves. The swimming will come of itself. How d'you mean, the water won't hold you? Why shouldn't it hold you?

Seeing how drawn I was to him, Nikitich made an exception of me alone of all his disciples. He invited me to visit the clean and spacious attic where he lived in an ambience of straw mats, showed me his dogs, his hedgehog, his tortoise, and his pigeons. In return for this wealth I showed him a tragedy I had written the day before.

"I was sure you did a bit of scribbling," said Nikitich. "You've the look. You're looking in *that* direction all the time; no eyes for anywhere else."

He read my writings, shrugged a shoulder, passed a hand through his stiff gray curls, paced up and down the attic.

"One must suppose," he said slowly, pausing after each word, "one must suppose that there's a spark of the divine fire in you."

We went out into the street. The old man halted, struck the pavement with his stick, and fastened his gaze upon me.

"Now what is it you lack? Youth's no matter–it'll pass with the years. What you lack is a feeling for nature."

He pointed with his stick at a tree with a reddish trunk and a low crown.

"What's that tree?"

I didn't know.

"What's growing on that bush?"

I didn't know this either. We walked together across the little square on the Alexandrovsky Prospect. The old man kept poking his stick at trees; he would seize me by the shoulder when a bird flew past, and he made me listen to the various kinds of singing.

"What bird is that singing?"

I knew none of the answers. The names of trees and birds,

their division into species, where birds fly away to, on which side the sun rises, when the dew falls thickest—all these things were unknown to me.

"And you dare to write! A man who doesn't live in nature, as a stone does or an animal, will never in all his life write two worthwhile lines. Your landscapes are like descriptions of stage props. In heaven's name, what have your parents been thinking of for fourteen years?"

What *had* they been thinking of? Of protested bills of exchange, of Mischa Elman's mansions. I didn't say anything to Nikitich about that, but just kept mum.

At home, over dinner, I couldn't touch my food. It just wouldn't go down.

"A feeling for nature," I thought to myself. "Goodness, why did that never enter my head? Where am I to find someone who will tell me about the way birds sing and what trees are called? What do I know about such things? I might perhaps recognize lilac, at any rate when it's in bloom. Lilac and acacia—there are acacias along De Ribas and Greek Streets."

At dinner father told a new story about Jascha Heifetz. Just before he got to Robinat's he had met Mendelssohn, Jascha's uncle. It appeared that the lad was getting eight hundred roubles a performance. Just work out how much that comes to at fifteen concerts a month!

I did, and the answer was twelve thousand a month. Multiplying and carrying four in my head, I glanced out of the window. Across the cement courtyard, his cloak swaying in the breeze, his ginger curls poking out from under his soft hat, leaning on his cane, Mr. Zagursky, my music teacher, was advancing. It must be admitted he had taken his time in spotting my truancy. More than three months had elapsed since the day when my violin had grounded on the sand by the breakwater.

Mr. Zagursky was approaching the main entrance. I dashed to the back door, but the day before it had been nailed up for fear of burglars. Then I locked myself in the privy. In half an hour the whole family had assembled outside the door. The women were weeping. Aunt Bobka, exploding with sobs, was rubbing her fat shoulder against the door. Father was silent. Finally he started speaking, quietly and distinctly as he had never before spoken in his life.

"I am an officer," said my father. "I own real estate. I go hunting. Peasants pay me rent. I have entered my son in the Cadet Corps. I have no need to worry about my son."

He was silent again. The women were sniffling. Then a terrible blow descended on the privy door. My father was hurling his whole body against it, stepping back and then throwing himself forward.

"I am an officer," he kept wailing. "I go hunting. I'll kill him. This is the end."

The hook sprang from the door, but there was still a bolt hanging onto a single nail. The women were rolling about on the floor, grasping father by the legs. Crazy, he was trying to break loose. Father's mother came over, alerted by the hubbub.

"My child," she said to him in Hebrew, "our grief is great. It has no bounds. Only blood was lacking in our house. I do not wish to see blood in our house."

Father gave a groan. I heard his footsteps retreating. The bolt still hung by its last nail.

I sat it out in my fortress till nightfall. When all had gone to bed, Aunt Bobka took me to grandmother's. We had a long way to go. The moonlight congealed on bushes unknown to me, on trees that had no name. Some anonymous bird emitted a whistle and was extinguished, perhaps by sleep. What bird was it? What was it called? Does dew fall in the evening? Where is the constellation of the Great Bear? On what side does the sun rise?

We were going along Post Office Street. Aunt Bobka held me firmly by the hand so that I shouldn't run away. She was right to. I was thinking of running away.

Isaac Babel.

The Most Rebellious Jewish Child

Ever since Joseph and his brothers, and probably earlier, Jewish children have tended to rebel against their parents and their faith. Although common to most youth, this rebelliousness is especially problematic for the Jews, who are not yet as numerous as the stars in heaven and the sand on the beaches, according to demographers.

Marty (after his great-grandfather, Mordecai) Bennett (away from his grandfather Benetinsky) ran off soon after his Bar Mitzvah to become a Zen Buddhist. After a number of years, he became a Sufi Muslim and joined an *ashram*. Just a few months later, he was attracted to Jews for Jesus, and then moved on to become a follower of Reverend Sun Moon. Losing interest, he fell in love with a Hare Krishna woman, and joined that group; but when he discovered that sex was frowned upon, he went to Israel, which moved his long-suffering parents to ecstasy. However, he joined Bahá'i, whose world headquarters is in Haifa. Shortly thereafter he befriended some Hassidim, and began to study at a *Yeshiva* in Jerusalem. At this point, his parents had him kidnapped and de-programmed back in the States. Said Mrs. Bennett: "I didn't raise *my* son to be a rabbi."

Allan Gould and Danny Siegel.

"Do not limit your children to your own learning, for they were born in another time."

The *Talmud*.

The following letter, written in 1938 by a struggling Jewish immigrant to North America, whose children have already grown up, describes the confusion which many parents experience when their children *do* live up to their parents' expectations. The letter was written to the "Bintel Brief" advice column of the Yiddish newspaper *The Jewish Daily Forwards*. Note the editor's response.

Bintel Brief

Dear Editor,

I come to you with my family problem because I think you are the only one who can give me practical advice. I am a man in my fifties, and I came to America when I was very young. I don't have to tell you how hard life was for a "greenhorn" in those times. I suffered plenty. But that didn't keep me from falling in love with a girl from my home town and marrying her.

I harnessed myself to the wagon of family life and pulled with all my strength. My wife was faithful and she gave me a hand in pulling the wagon. The years flew fast and before we looked around we were parents of four children who brightened and sweetened our lives.

The children were dear and smart and we gave them an education that was more than we could afford. They went to college, became professionals, and are well established.

Suddenly I feel as if the floor has collapsed under my feet. I don't know how to express it, but the fact that my children are well educated and have outgrown me makes me feel bad. I can't talk to them about my problems and they can't talk to me about theirs. It's as if there were a deep abyss that divides us.

People envy me my good, fine, educated children but (I am ashamed to admit it) I often think it might be better for me if they were not so well educated, but ordinary workingmen, like me. Then we would have more in common. I have no education, because my parents were poor, and in the old country they couldn't give me the opportunities that I could give my children. Here, in America, I didn't have time and my mind wasn't on learning in the early years when I had to work hard.

That is my problem. I want to hear your opinion about it. I enclose my full name and address, but please do not print it. I will sign as,

Disappointed.

Answer:

It is truly a pleasure to have such children, and the father can really be envied. But he must not feel he has nothing in common with them any longer, because they have more education than he. There should be no chasm between father and children, and if there is, perhaps he himself created it.

In thousands of Jewish immigrant homes such educated children have grown up, and many of them remain close to their parents. Also there is no reason why the writer of this letter shouldn't be able to talk to his fine, good children about various problems, even though they are professionals and have outdistanced him in their education.

Hasidim, young and old, listen to a rabbi's speech.

FATHERS AND SONS

The Zhitomer rabbi was once walking along with his son when they saw a drunken man and his drunken son both stumbling into the gutter.

"I envy that father," said the rabbi to his son. "He has accomplished his goal of having a son like himself. I don't know yet whether you will be like me. I can only hope that the drunkard is not more successful in training his son than I am with you."

Adapted by Francine Klagsbrum.

The relationship between fathers and sons, separated by different generations and different lifestyles, is often volatile but moving. Here is an eloquent statement, made by Leonard Kriegel, writer and himself a father, about his relationship with his father.

Fathers and Sons

The sons of immigrant fathers usually chose American models of manhood. I loved no one as I loved my father. He was—and I write this without sentimentality—a good and simple man, imbued with a sense of decency and a working-class Jew's need for dignity. And yet, I was also ashamed of my father, as, I suspect, a good many sons of immigrant fathers were ashamed. My father was many things, but every breath he took reminded me that he was not an American. He spoke with an Eastern European accent, was ignorant of American ways, cared nothing for the things that meant so much to me—baseball, football, movies, the rich life of the streets. For him, this America was both blessed in its abundance and cursed in its lack of memory. It was a country in which he worked "like a horse" in one small appetizing store after another, for one immigrant boss (more successful than he!) after another, serving one Yiddish-speaking neighborhood clientele after another. Had he been more successful, had he even managed in time to own his own small appetizing store, I might have come to terms with my father's American strivings. But he was not successful, not, certainly, as this America understood the word. From the time I was five, both of us recognized that I could never choose to be the Jewish son to him that he had been to the father he had left in Ottynier.

Where I failed my father was the mirror image of where I thought he failed me. If he was not American enough, I was too American. If he loved to listen to the chazan on Yom Kippur and Rosh Hashanah (even in his religion, America betrayed him—for he worked on Shabbos, worked or starved, because Jewish housewives in America shopped and smoked on Saturdays, too), I loved to listen to Benny Goodman and Artie Shaw. If his love of Yiddishkeit seemed to me mere superstition, my skill in baseball and my toughness as a fighter simply puzzled him; such talents were worthless in his eyes. When he would discover that I had "cut" Saturday services at the Mosholu Jewish Center in order to play football, his despair would permeate even the beatings he gave me (these were the only times my father ever laid a hand on me). America was a series of confusions for him, particularly in what it had made of his sons.

His dream was that we would become educated men. I suppose it was a dream realized, for both of his sons were to become college professors, "men of learning," as he loved to phrase it. And yet, even our learning was secular, far more in tune with the demands of this America than my father could

possibly conceive. My brother read history and I read Hemingway and Faulkner and Farrell—and my father dreamed of Pesach in the old country, of his own father's seders.

My father died four months after his eldest grandson's, my son's, bar mitzvah. At his funeral I delivered a brief eulogy, aware that I was speaking to my sons, far more American than their grandfather could conceive, more relaxed with this country than their father could understand. They had been to this America born and they had nothing to prove to it. Their grandfather's accent was not for them a secret source of shame, merely a curious remnant of a life they loved to hear about but recognized as more distant from their own lives than what they witnessed on the nightly re-runs of *Star Trek*, which I watched with them....

All my life, I had chosen to be American....I defined manhood in terms opposite to those my father understood. For I was trying to get beyond him, to claim an existence that he viewed as more than a man needed and less than a Jew deserved. And now I wonder whether, caught by their own emerging manhood, my sons will endow me with the qualities of an alien culture against which they must struggle to create a presence as men. I wonder and I wait. I think about my father, their grandfather, that good and simple man. And if my fate as a man seems finally to approach his, then I can, at least, console myself by asking, what better fate can an American son desire than to become, finally, a Jewish father?

Leonard Kriegel.

Sometimes, sons rebel against their parents' idea of Jewish identity. In other situations, sons challenge what they feel is their parents' lack of Jewish identity.

In 1917, at the age of 36, Franz Kafka, Czech-born German-Jewish novelist, wrote the following letter to his father. Estranged from what he felt was the bourgeois Judaism of his father, Kafka himself identified strongly with secular Jewish culture and Zionism.

My Father's Bourgeois Judaism

I found little means of escape from you in Judaism. Here some escape would, in principle, have been thinkable, but more than that, it would have been thinkable that we might both have found each other in Judaism or even that we might have begun from there in harmony. But what sort of Judaism was it I got from you? In the course of the years I have taken roughly three different attitudes to it.

As a child I reproached myself, in accord with you, for not going to the synagogue enough, for not fasting, and so on. I thought that in this way I was doing a wrong not to myself but to you, and I was penetrated by a sense of guilt, which was, of course, always ready to hand.

A family portrait in Prague, at the turn of the century.

Later, as a young man, I could not understand how, with the insignificant scrap of Judaism you yourself possessed, you could reproach me for not (if for no more than the sake of piety, as you put it) making an effort to cling to a similar insignificant scrap. It was indeed really, so far as I could see, a mere scrap, a joke, not even a joke. On four days in the year you went to the synagogue, where you were, to say the least, closer to the indifferent than to those who took it seriously, [you] patiently went through the prayers by way of formality, [you] sometimes amazed me by being able to show me in the prayer book the passage that was being said at the moment, and for the rest, so long as I was in the synagogue (and this was the main thing) I was allowed to hang about wherever I liked.

And so I yawned and dozed through the many hours (I don't think I was ever again so bored, except later at dancing lessons) and did my best to enjoy the few little bits of variety there were, as, for instance, when the Ark of the Covenant was opened, which always reminded me of the shooting galleries where a cupboard door would open in the same way whenever one got a bull's eye, only with the difference that there something interest-

ing always came out and here it was always just the same old dolls with no heads.

Incidentally, it was also very frightening for me there, not only, as goes without saying, because of all the people one came into close contact with, but also because you once mentioned, by the way, that I too might be called up to read the Torah. That was something I went in dread of for years. But otherwise I was not fundamentally disturbed in my state of boredom, unless it was by the *bar mitzvah*, but that meant no more than some ridiculous learning by heart, in other words, led to nothing but something like the ridiculous passing of an examination, and then, as far as you were concerned, by little, not very significant incidents, as when you were called up to read the Torah and came well out of the affair, which to my way of feeling was purely social, or when you stayed on in the synagogue for the prayers for the dead, and I was sent away, which for a long time, obviously because of being sent away and lacking, as I did, any deeper interest, aroused in me the more or less unconscious feeling that what was about to take place was something indecent.–That was how it was in the synagogue, and at home it was, if possible even more poverty-stricken, being confined to the first evening of Passover which more and more developed into a farce, with fits of hysterical laughter, admittedly under the influence of the growing children. (Why did you have to give way to that influence? Because you brought it about in the first place. And so there was the religious material that was handed on to me, to which may be added at most the outstretched hand pointing to "the sons of the millionaire Fuchs," who were in the synagogue with their father at high holidays. How one could do anything better with this material than get rid of it as fast as possible was something I could not understand; precisely getting rid of it seemed to me the most effective act of "piety" one could perform.

Franz Kafka.

Bar Mitzvah

My father comes to see me on Friday night.
He scrubs my ears,
brushes my smelly suit,
and drops two vitamins down my mouth.
On Saturday he shows up with sleepless eyes,
makes breakfast
and polishes my shoes.
He takes my best shirt out of the closet
and gently dresses me like a divorced mother.
He takes my hand,
and we quickly pass by a church door.
Hunched over, almost touching the ground, we walk back and
        forth down endless streets,
chasing off flies as they land on our faces.
Three old men, a tray of sardines and tomatoes, wine,
a loaf of white bread wait for us at the Brena Synagogue.
The rabbi makes me climb up to the *bimah*
the old men smile at me,
praying through their beards.
The rabbi nods for me to start the prayers,
instead I kneel down,
ashamed, my father blushes,
an old man points to a few words in the Bible,
I begin to stammer,
I look at my father out of the corners of my eyes,
my old, gray father celebrating this rite curled up like a fetus.

Isaac Goldemberg.

Lies My Father Told Me

On Sundays, when it didn't rain, Grandpa, Ferdeleh and myself would go riding through the back lanes of Montreal. The lanes then were not paved as they are now, and after a rainy Saturday, the mud would be inches deep and the wagon heaved and shook like a barge in a stormy sea. Ferdeleh's pace remained, as always, the same. He liked the mud. It was easy on his feet.

When the sun shone through my windows on Sunday morning I would jump out of bed, wash, dress, run into the kitchen where Grandpa and I said our morning prayers, and then we'd both go to harness and feed Ferdeleh. On Sundays Ferdeleh would whinny like a happy child. He knew it was an extra special day for all of us. By the time he had finished his oats and hay Grandpa and I would be finished with our breakfast which Grandma and Mother had prepared for us....

Then began the most wonderful of days as we drove through the dirt lanes of Montreal, skirting the garbage cans, jolting and bouncing through the mud and dust, calling every cat by name and every cat meowing its hello, and Grandpa and I holding our hands to our ears and shouting at the top of our lungs, "Regs, cloze, botels! Regs, cloze, botels!"...

On week-days, Grandpa and I rose early, a little after daybreak, and said our morning prayers. I would mimic his sing-song lamentations, sounding as if my heart were breaking and wondering why we both had to sound so sad. I must have put everything I had into it because Grandpa assured me that one day I would become a great cantor and a leader of the Hebrews. "You will sing so that the ocean will open up a path before you and you will lead our people to a new paradise."

I was six then and he was the only man I ever understood even when I didn't understand his words. I learned a lot from him. If he didn't learn a lot from me, he made me feel he did.

I remember once saying, "You know, sometimes I think I'm the son of God. Is it possible?"

"It is possible," he answered, "but don't rely on it. Many of us are sons of God. The important thing is not to rely too much upon it. The harder we work, the harder we study, the more we accomplish, the surer we are that we are sons of God."

At the synagogue on Saturday his old, white-bearded friends would surround me and ask me questions. Grandpa would stand by and burst with pride. I strutted like a peacock.

"Who is David?" the old men would ask me.

"He's the man with the beard, the man with the bearded words." And they laughed.

"And who is God?" they would ask me.

"King and Creator of the Universe, the All-Powerful One, the Almighty One, more powerful even than Grandpa." They laughed again and I thought I was pretty smart. So did Grandpa. So did my grandmother and my mother.

So did everyone, except my father. I didn't like my father. He said things to me like, "For God's sake, you're smart, but not as smart as you think. Nobody is that smart." He was jealous of me and he told me lies. He told me lies about Ferdeleh.

"Ferdeleh is one part horse, one part camel, and one part chicken," he told me. Grandpa told me that was a lie, Ferdeleh was all horse. "If he is part anything, he is part human," said Grandpa. I agreed with him. Ferdeleh understood everything we said to him. No matter what part of the city he was in, he could find his way home, even in the dark.

"Ferdeleh is going to collapse one day in one heap," my father said. "Ferdeleh is carrying twins." "Ferdeleh is going to keel over one day and die." "He should be shot now or he'll collapse under you one of these days," my father would say.

Neither I nor Grandpa had much use for the opinions of my father.

On top of everything, my father had no beard, didn't pray, didn't go to the synagogue on the Sabbath, read English books and never read the prayer-books, played piano on the Sabbath and sometimes would draw my mother into his villainies by making her sing while he played. On the Sabbath this was an abomination to both Grandpa and me.

One day I told my father, "Papa, you have forsaken your fore-fathers." He burst out laughing and kissed me and then my mother kissed me, which infuriated me all the more.

I could forgive my father these indignities, his not treating me as an equal, but I couldn't forgive his telling lies about Ferdeleh. Once he said that Ferdeleh "smelled up" the whole house, and demanded that Grandpa move the stable. It was true that the kitchen, being next to the stable, which was in the back shed, did sometimes smell of hay and manure but, as Grandpa said, "What is wrong with such a smell? It is a good healthy smell."

It was a house divided, with my grandmother, mother and father on one side, and Grandpa, Ferdeleh and me on the other. One day a man came to the house and said he was from the Board of Health and that the neighbours had complained about the stable. Grandpa and I knew we were beaten then. You could get around the Board of Health, Grandpa informed me, if you could grease the palms of the officials. I suggested the obvious but Grandpa explained that this type of "grease" was made of gold. The stable would have to be moved. But where?

As it turned out, Grandpa didn't have to worry about it. The whole matter was taken out of his hands a few weeks later.

Next Sunday the sun shone brightly and I ran to the kitchen to say my prayers with Grandpa. But Grandpa wasn't there. I found my grandmother there instead–weeping. Grandpa was in his room ill. He had a sickness they called diabetes and at that time the only thing you could do about diabetes was weep. I fed Ferdeleh and soothed him because I knew how disappointed he was.

That week I was taken to an aunt of mine. There was no explanation given. My parents thought I was too young to need any explanations. On Saturday next I was brought home, too late to see Grandpa that evening, but I felt good knowing that I would spend the next day with him and Ferdeleh again.

When I came to the kitchen Sunday morning Grandma was not there. Ferdeleh was not in the stable. I thought they were playing a joke on me so I rushed to the front of the house expecting to see Grandpa sitting atop the wagon waiting for me.

But there wasn't any wagon. My father came up behind me and put his hand on my head. I looked up questioningly and he said, "Grandpa and Ferdeleh have gone to heaven...."

When he told me they were *never* coming back, I moved away from him and went to my room. I lay down on my bed and cried, not for Grandpa and Ferdeleh, because I knew they would never do such a thing to me, but about my father, because he had told me such a horrible lie.

Ted Allan.

(Page 61) "Portrait of Esther Andrews Dreyfous and Daughter Hannah". Anonymous American, 1828.

MOTHERS AND CHILDREN

"God could not be everywhere, so he created mothers."

Folksaying.

Though Jewish mothers have been maligned at times as being overbearing, they have in fact been the strength and backbone of the Jewish family. The traditional Jewish mother has been an important facilitator for both her children and her husband. In Eastern Europe, it was the mother who managed the household, raised the children in a Jewish way, and often ran the family business as well, while the man of the house studied Torah and Talmud all day according to Jewish custom. Later, amidst the poverty of immigrant America, it was again the mother who assumed responsibility for providing as decent a life for her children as she could, sometimes under adverse conditions. She learned to be resourceful and diplomatic, but firm.

Mother Fights the Landlord

My mother fought the landlord again that winter. The rent was due, and by a coincidence my brother, my sister, my mother and I all needed shoes. We had worn the old ones until they were in shreds. It was impossible to patch them any longer. My mother decided to pawn the family's diamond ring–the one my father had bought in a prosperous period.

I went with my mother to Mr. Zunzer's pawnshop. In summer it had swinging wicker doors like a saloon. Now we entered through heavy curtained doors that shut out the daylight.

It was a grim, crowded little store smelling of camphor. There were some gloomy East Side people standing around. The walls were covered with strange objects: guitars, shovels, blankets, clocks; with lace curtains, underwear and crutches; all these miserable trophies of the defeat of the poor.

Everything worth more than a quarter was taken in pawn by Mr. Zunzer, [our landlord] from an old man's false teeth to a baby's diapers. People were sure to redeem these little necessities.

If he made ten cents on a transaction he was satisfied, for there were hundreds of them. At the end of a week there was a big total.

It was said in the neighborhood he also bought stolen things from the young thieves and pickpockets.

We waited for our turn. An old Irish worker in overalls, with merry blue eyes and a rosy face, was trying to pawn some tools. He was drunk, and pleaded that he be given a dollar. Mr. Zunzer gave him only half a dollar, and said, "Get the hell out." The white-haired man jigged and sang as he left for the saloon.

A dingy little woman pawned a baby carriage. An old Jewish graybeard pawned his prayer book and praying shawl. A fat Polish woman with a blowsy, weepy face pawned an accordion. A young girl pawned some quilts; then our turn came.

The landlord wore a black alpaca coat in the pawnshop, and a skull cap. He crouched on a stool behind the counter. One saw only his scaly yellow face and bulging eyes; he was like an anxious spider. He picked up the ring my mother presented him, screwed a jeweler's glass into his eye, and studied it in the gaslight.

"Ten dollars," he said abruptly.

"I must have fifteen," said my mother.

"Ten dollars," said the landlord.

"No, fifteen," said my mother.

He looked up irritably and stared at her with his near-sighted eyes. He recognized her in the pawnshop gloom.

"You're my tenant, aren't you?" he asked, "the one that made all the trouble for me?"

"Yes," said my mother, "what of it?"

The landlord smiled bitterly.

"Nothing," he said, "but you are sure to come to a bad end."

"No worse end than yours," said my mother, "may the bananas grow in your throat!"

"Don't curse me in my own shop!" said the landlord. "I'll have you arrested. What do you want here?"

"I told you," said my mother, "I want fifteen dollars on this ring."

"It is worth only ten," said the landlord.

"To me you must give fifteen," said my mother boldly.

The landlord paled. He looked at my mother fearfully. She knew his secret. My mother mystified and alarmed him with her boldness. He was accustomed to people who cowered.

He wrote out a ticket for the ring, gave my mother fifteen dollars. She crowed over her victory as we walked home. Next day she bought shoes for my brother, my sister Esther, and myself. Her own shoes she forgot to buy. That's the way she generally arranged things.

Michael Gold.

Mothers

Did she overfeed? Her mind was haunted by memories of a hungry childhood. Did she fuss about health? Infant mortality had been a plague in the old country and the horror of diphtheria overwhelming in this country. Did she dominate everyone within reach? A disarranged family structure endowed her with powers she had never known before, and burdens, too; it was to be expected that she should abuse the powers and find advantage in the burdens. The weight of centuries bore down. In her bones, the Jewish mother knew that she and hers, simply by being Jewish, had always to live with a sense of precariousness. When she worried about her little boy going down to play, it was not merely the dangers of Rivington or Cherry streets [in New York] that she saw–though there *were* dangers on such streets; it was the streets of Kishinev and Bialystok and other towns [in Russia] in which the blood of Jewish children had been spilled.

Irving Howe.

Mama Was a Woman

It was years, said my big brother Harry, before I realized that mama was a woman, that she was like other women. Do you remember those corselets she used to cram herself into, with the bones, when we were going out? Daddy or I used to tighten and tie the laces for her. It's funny, it didn't strike me till not so long ago that she wore them because she wanted to look beautiful and slim, for herself, that she was a female and had a female life of her own, a female vanity. I always thought she was just a mother, all for us.

Adele Wiseman.

SIBLINGS

In spite of personal differences between family members, love within the family has always been a basic Jewish premise. The ideal of loving your friend or neighbor is in fact based on the concept of "brotherly love." You may fight with your brothers and sisters, but on a more basic level you are connected to each other in a very unique way. You are sharing a family life together which no one else has experienced or will experience. You share the same parents, the same home and usually a very similar upbringing.

The following excerpt, from the novel *Marjorie Morningstar* by Herman Wouk, gives a contemporary impression of how a sister feels at the Bar Mitzvah of her younger brother.

The Bar Mitzvah

It was strangely impressive, after all, when Seth stood before the Holy Ark draped in his new purple-and-white silk prayer shawl on Saturday morning, chanting his reading from the Book of Malachi.

The temple was full, and hushed. Perversely, perhaps with a touch of injured self-effacement, Marjorie sat far in the back. Her mother had tried to get her to sit on the front bench with the rest of the family, but Marjorie had said no, she would stay in the rear to welcome any late-coming friends or relatives.

Seth's voice rang clear and manly over the massed rows of black skull-caps and white prayer shawls, sprinkled here and there with the frilly hats and rich furs of women. It was a Conservative temple, so the men and women sat together. For years in the Bronx Marjorie had railed at the orthodox practice of separating the sexes; in the twentieth century women weren't second-class citizens, she said. This was one reason why the parents had joined a Conservative temple on moving to Manhattan. Another and more powerful reason was the desire to climb. The wealthiest Jews were Reform, but the Morgensterns were not ready for such a bold leap away from tradition, to praying with uncovered heads, smoking on the Sabbath and eating pork. The Conservative temple was a pleasant compromise with its organ music, mixed sexes, shortened prayers, long English sermons, and young rabbi in a black robe like a minister's. Mr. Morgenstern, indeed, was a little uncomfortable in the temple. Now and then he would grumble that if Abraham Lincoln could wear a beard, so could an American rabbi. When he had to recite memorial prayers for his father he always slipped into a small old orthodox synagogue on a side street, feeling perhaps that this was the only form of worship that really counted either with God or with his father's ghost. He quieted his conscience by paying the membership fee in both places.

His one reason for putting up with the temple was the hope of instilling some trace of religion in his daughter. But Marjorie had little use for any version of the faith. She regarded it as a body of superstitious foolishness perpetuated, and to some degree invented, by her mother for her harassment....

But today, despite herself, the girl found awe creeping over her as her brother's voice filled the vault of the temple, chanting words thousands of years old, in an eerie melody from a dim lost time. A cloud passed away overhead and morning sunlight came slanting through the dome windows, brilliantly lighting the huge mahogany Ark behind Seth with its arch of Hebrew words in gold over the tablets of the Law: *Know before Whom you stand*.

Marjorie had thrilled the first time her father translated the motto for her; and that thrill came back now as the letter blazed up in the sunlight. Seth sang on, husky and calm, and it occurred to Marjorie that after all there might be a powerful propriety in the old way of separating the men and the women. This religion was a masculine thing, whatever it was, and Seth was coming into his own. The very Hebrew had a rugged male sound to it, all different from the bland English comments of the rabbi; it sounded like some of the rough crashing passages in *Macbeth* which she so loved.

A celebration by the water, as this young girl on roller skates blows the Shofar.

She caught her breath as Seth stumbled over a word and stopped. The silence in the pause was heavy. He squinted at the book and a murmur began to run through the temple. Seth glanced up, smiled at the bench where his parents sat, and placidly resumed his chanting. Marjorie unclenched her fists; the people around her chuckled and nodded at each other. She heard a woman say, "He's a good boy." She could have kissed him. Her little jealous pique was lost in a rush of love for her baby brother, the prattler with blond curls and huge eyes, fading in the tones of the chant as though he were being borne away by a ship. Time had taken him away long ago, of course, but only in this moment did she quite realize that it was so, and that it was for ever.

Later, at the buffet lunch in the mobbed social hall of the temple, a knot of boys came tumbling past Marjorie through the crowd, yelling and pushing each other, clutching sandwiches and soda bottles. In the middle of them was Seth, flushed and glittering-eyed, his arms full of presents wrapped in tinsel and colored paper. She darted through the boys, threw her arms around her startled brother and kissed his cheek. "You were wonderful, Seth! Wonderful! I was so proud of you!"

Recognition and warmth dawned through the boy's glaze of triumphant excitement. "Did I do all right, Margie? Really?"

"Marvelous, I tell you, perfect."

"I love you," said Seth, in a most incongruous quiet tone, and kissed her on the mouth, leaving a taste of wine. The boys jeered at the lipstick smear on Seth and shoved and bore him away, and Marjorie stood transfixed, alone in the merry crowd, in a turmoil of surprised emotion. Seth had expressed no open affection for her since the day he had learned to talk.

Herman Wouk, from *Marjorie Morningstar*.

Though the biblical stories of Cain and Abel, Jacob and Esau, and Joseph and his brothers illustrate the real-life difficulties in sibling relationships, the relationship between Moses and his brother Aaron, as described in the Bible, offers a more loving picture. Separated for years, they greet each other warmly when they meet. Together they undertake to get the Jews out of Egypt. Biblical commentators explain that Aaron felt no jealousy on hearing that his younger brother would become leader, and Moses was delighted to learn that his elder brother would be appointed high priest. This story is a reminder of the positive side of having a sibling. The following Jewish folktale is another story of brotherly love.

Brotherly Love

Long, long ago, on the site of old Jerusalem, the holy city, there lived two brothers. They were farmers, and they tilled the land which they had inherited from their father. The older was unmarried and lived alone. The younger was married and lived with his wife and four children. The brothers loved each other dearly and did not want to divide the fields between them. Both ploughed, planted, and harvested the crop together. After they cut the wheat they shared equally in the produce of the earth.

One night during the time of the harvest, the older brother lay down to sleep. But his thoughts were troubled. "Here I am, all alone, with no wife and no children," he told himself. "I need not feed or clothe anyone. But my brother has the responsibility of a family. Is it right that we share our harvest equally? His need is greater than mine."

At midnight he arose and took a pile of sheaves from his crop, carried them to his brother's field, and left them there. Then he returned to his tent quietly and went to sleep in peace.

That same night his brother too could not sleep. He thought about his older brother. "Here I am," he said to himself. "When I grow old my children will take care of me. But what will happen to my brother in *his* old age? Who will take care of *his* needs? It isn't fair to divide the crops equally."

So he arose and took a load of sheaves and brought them to his brother's field and left them there. Then he returned home and went to sleep in peace.

When morning came both brothers were amazed to find their crops exactly as they had been the night before. They wondered greatly but did not speak to each other about this strange event.

The next night each brother repeated his action. When morning came, again they were amazed to find the same number of sheaves as they had left the night before.

But on the third night, when each brother was carrying a pile of sheaves to the other, they met at the top of the hill. Suddenly they understood. Overcome, they dropped their sheaves and embraced and cried with tears of gratitude and happiness. Then they turned to their tents.

The Lord saw this act of love between brothers and blessed the place where they met that night. And when in the course of time King Solomon built the Temple, it was erected on that very spot, from which peace and love flow to the whole world.

Adapted by Azriel Eisenberg.

"A brother helped by a brother is like a fortified city." Book of Proverbs.

ALTERNATIVE FAMILIES

Every family is unique and different. Not every family has a mother, a father, four grandparents, and siblings born to the same parents. If you were adopted, or if your parents are divorced, or if one of your parents has died, you may have more or less than two parents, depending on your own particular situation. Alternative families can be just as warm and supportive as traditional families. The success of any family depends on how much love and effort is put into it by each member.

The following story is about a young man who loses his mother before his Bar Mitzvah, and must go on, not only with his Bar Mitzvah ceremony, but with the uncertainties of a life without much parental support.

Man in Israel

The boy breathlessly opened the door and ran down the stairs. From his back pocket he pulled a wrinkled black skull-cap. Ignoring the three crystal marbles that fell out of it, he jammed it on his head. He opened the book he was carrying to the page where the paper airplane had been inserted, and walked quickly to the far end of the dusky room. He held the book out in front of him and began to read rapidly. A voice from the darkness stopped him.

"How can *you* see to read in this dim light?" The voice had a note of laughter in it.

"It's easy," the boy answered eagerly. "I know it by heart."

"Very nice. But what made you so sure I would be here?"

The boy seemed shocked. "You're always here," he answered. "You couldn't be anywhere else."

"I'm a fixture, like these curtains, eh?" A white-haired man drew back the heavy folds that covered most of the window. A rush of sunlight came into the room and shone on the panes of the bookcases that lined its walls. The man winced several times. "You know," he said as he shut the brown-edged volumes lying on his desk, "it's only when you boys come in that I realize the sun is shining outside." He slowly set his body down in the huge cane-backed chair, and took a tuning fork from a drawer. "Now a little more slowly," he said, "and we'll see how well you really know it." He struck the fork against the metal inkstand and held it to his ear.

The boy cleared his throat and began to chant in a high, clear voice. Each word was broken into many syllables, and each of these was sung at one of several different pitches. The monotonous rise and fall of his voice was accompanied by a swaying of the body and constant bending of the knee. "Bo-ru-uch a-to-oh a-do-no-oy...Blessed art thou, O Lord..." The boy droned on and on, his dark curly head rocking in the mid-afternoon light. When he had said the final "Amen" he shut the book and stared at it, waiting expectantly.

"Very good," said the old man. "Really very good. I can see you've been working hard." His wrinkled face lit up with a smile, as he brushed the cuff of his black broadcloth suit. "Well, are you very excited about becoming a man tomorrow? How does it feel to be a boy for the last day?"

"I don't know," he answered, cupping his hands. "I wasn't thinking about that. But I am excited–" He pressed his fingers so hard against the top of the desk that the blood ran out of them and they were deadly white. "I can hardly wait for tomorrow–"

His voice broke and he became silent.

The old man stretched his arms across the desk and covered the boy's hands with his own. He looked into the dark brown eyes that seemed absorbed in another world. "What is it, David?"

The boy's words came out in a breathless rush. "Rabbi, didn't I just read my part of the Torah good? I didn't even make one mistake, did you see?"

"Not even one mistake," he answered warmly.

"That's because I've been studying hard," the boy answered. "I haven't played baseball, nothing–I've been studying, and I know it perfect." He did not speak of it boastingly, but as the natural outcome of his industry. His eyes widened and he leaned forward anxiously. "Do you remember, you said if I do it perfect my mother will come to my bar-mitzvah? Will she come now?"

The rabbi nodded his head slowly. "Yes, your mother will come. She does not have far to travel. It is only a few months that she has been gone."

"Six months. It was the day after I got my new sled." He checked the memories that leaped into his mind and repeated the question, seeking some guarantee that his effort would not go unrewarded.

"Yes, David, she will be there. Everyone who loves you will come. Tomorrow in the synagogue you will see your mother."

"Can I talk to her?"

"If you want to."

David wished to be sure of everything in advance. "And I'll be able to see her," he said. "I'll be able to touch her."

"If you decide that you must," the rabbi answered. He pushed back his chair slowly and stepped to the window. "But I can't blame you for wanting her so much. Only twelve years old, and going to be confirmed."

"My friends in school keep saying that you have to be thirteen. They don't believe me."

"The custom is that if either parent is dead the boy is confirmed a year earlier. But of course the children would not know that." He put out his arm and caressed David's head. The skin around his wrist hung in loose folds, and was covered with freckles and silver hairs. David hoped it would not fall off just then.

"David," he was saying, "you're a fine boy and I'm glad to be your rabbi. Tomorrow you will sing for the congregation and I will be very proud of you. Now I am sure they must be waiting for you at home, so run along." He gently propelled the boy forward. "Remember, eight o'clock at the synagogue with your father."

"Yes sir, we'll be there early."

"Sholom–Peace be with you, David."

"Sholom." He went back up the dark stairs and into the sunlight of the warm June day. He walked home leisurely, his slight form idling up the street. From his back pocket he took a ruler, which he pressed against a tall iron fence. He increased his pace, pressing harder with the ruler, and keenly enjoying its ack-ack-ack-ack sound. Just like a machine gun, he thought, relishing the noise. Tomorrow he would be a man and this would be kid stuff, so he might as well get the most out of it.

(Right) "Bar Mitzvah" by Robert Guttman (1880-1942).

Eventually he turned the corner of his block. At the curb in front of the house was his father's car, and leaning against it was Uncle Ralph. His shirt collar was for once buttoned, and he was even wearing a tie. David suddenly remembered that today too was a special day, almost as special as tomorrow. Uncle Ralph must have been waiting a long time and Papa would be angry. He ran up to the car and tried to sound out of breath to show that he had run all the way.

Uncle Ralph didn't seem at all impatient. The thin lips curved gently upward on his pale face, and he spoke to David in his usual carefree way.

"Hi, Davy. How did the lesson go?"

"Good, Uncle Ralph. The rabbi said it was perfect." He lowered his voice and looked up at the windows of Aunt Millie's apartment to make sure no one was sitting at them. "Uncle Ralph, do you think Mama will come?"

"Yes, David, she'll be there. Nothing will stop her."

Uncle Ralph was a college graduate, so it was safe to assume that he knew what he was talking about. Between Uncle Ralph and the rabbi, David could feel sure. They were both much more learned than Papa, but he could not forget his father's derisive laughter.

David moved a little closer and spoke in a whisper. "I couldn't tell this to the rabbi, Uncle Ralph, but—you know what Papa says. He says that you're a dreamer and the rabbi's just an old man, and he just laughed about the whole thing. Do you think he's right?"

"There are lots of things my brother doesn't see, but that doesn't mean that you can't." The smile had disappeared, and had been replaced by silent furrows on his forehead. "He's waiting inside." He reached through the window of the automobile and pressed the horn lightly. "He'll be out in a minute."

"I'm afraid, Uncle Ralph. I don't want to go."

He patted the boy on the back. "There's nothing to be afraid of."

"But why do we have to do it? I don't want to see her lying in the ground."

"Listen, Davy, for hundreds of years people have been doing this. Before every wedding or confirmation, the celebrant visits the graves of his dead parents and invites them to the ceremony. It shows the dead that you're thinking of them. You want your mother to know that, don't you?"

"Yes, but—" He hesitated, unwilling to say the words. "I might start to cry like last time, even though I don't want to, and Papa would laugh."

"Then don't pay any attention to him. If you feel like crying, do it. Forget that your father and I are there. You'll be alone with your mother." He opened the door of the car. "Get in, Davy. Here comes your father."

Mr. Harris stepped briskly into the car and sat down behind the wheel. He said nothing as he started the motor and drove down the street. He chewed the wet stem of the stubby amber cigar holder and exhaled thick puffs of grey smoke. David always wondered why the smoke never stained his father's snowy white shirt collars and elegant bow ties, and the creamy yellow straw hat he put on immediately after the snow melted. David was happy that his father never looked poor, the way Uncle Ralph and Aunt Millie did, even though he owed everybody money and did things that other people didn't like. "You've got to be hardheaded, and to hell with what people think," he always said. But now he said nothing, and concentrated only on speeding through the maze of billboards and filling stations that indicated they were leaving the city behind. After many miles of greenery broken by an occasional building, they turned off the main road

and pulled up before the heavy iron gates of the cemetery.

Mr. Harris parked the car and spoke for the first time during the trip. "Don't forget your siddur," he said, as they stepped out of the automobile.

"I have it, Papa," David said, pointing to the small black prayer book under his arm.

Uncle Ralph opened the door in the gate. They went through it and walked up the gravel path.

Mr. Harris took a last long puff at his cigar and crushed it. "I hope that old rabbi has taught you to say a decent kaddish for all the money I've given him." He polished the amber stem with his large plaid handkerchief and dropped it into his vest pocket. "Your mother's grave is over there, to the right. Now I don't want you to act like a baby. Remember, you're a man." He thrust his index finger at David. "Just say it as fast as you can and we'll go right home."

"Yes, Papa." The boy stepped slowly toward the tombstone his father had indicated. He tried not to look at it, and kept his eyes on the open page of the book. He began to recite the prayer for the dead. "Yisgadal v'yisgadash shmai raboh–Magnified and sanctified be his great name–." The stark white of the stone protruded above the pages of the book. It had only recently been erected, and bore none of the traces of the elements that stained those around it. He lifted his eyes from the page and read the legend on the stone: HELEN HARRIS, Beloved Wife and Mother, Died January 27...

He remembered coming in from school that day and finding Mother in bed. A heart attack, and he had to be very quiet and couldn't go near her, even though there were so many important things to say, just as there had been every day. Papa was angry because he had to stay home with her that night. And the next day they had told him that she was dead, and nobody except himself seemed to think it was strange or untrue. The day after that they had buried her and he had tried hard not to act like a baby, but he had not been able to keep the tears back, and Papa had scolded him for not behaving like a man in front of the relatives, though everybody except Papa had been crying, too.

He looked down at the warm green grass that covered the shallow mound. He had once seen a movie in which a ghost floated out of a grave, and he wondered if this was what his mother would do tomorrow. He scanned the sod to see that there were no stones that could get in her way. Then it occurred to him that this was just like the grass in the park, and it was silly to think that Mother could be lying under it. It was funny to think even that she was dead, because though for six months everyone had seemed to think she was, he had always hoped that they would turn out to be wrong. Yet the stone with her name on it seemed to make it definite. Papa would never have spent all that money if she weren't really dead.

Uncle Ralph had said that he must invite her to the ceremony. He didn't know what to say, and he couldn't ask Uncle Ralph with Papa standing right near them. It was silly to tell her about it. She must know that he was going to be confirmed tomorrow, and that he wanted her to be. How could he possibly tell her how much he needed her?

He did not want his father to see that he was crying. He turned away and brushed his sleeve against his eyes. But his father had seen. He threw David's arm against his side.

"Don't do that! You're not a baby any more."

Uncle Ralph grabbed his brother by the shoulder and threw him back roughly. "For God's sake, stop picking on him, here of all places!"

"I'll pick on him long enough to make sure he doesn't become a misfit...an eternal student like you. My son will be a man in a world of men."

"A thief in a world of thieves, if you have your way." Ralph bent down and put his hands around David's shoulders. "If you want to cry, David, don't let anybody stop you. This is one of the few times the world will let you. There's no reason to hide your feelings now. You'll be doing that the rest of your life. Go ahead and cry."

The boy was lost between the opposing commands of the two men he most respected. He found himself unable to give full expression to his feelings or completely to suppress them, and knew at the same time that he was displeasing both men. Turning blindly from the grave, he ran down the path to the car and threw himself into a corner of the back seat. The trip home was as silent as the ride out had been.

Millie Gordon opened the living room window to its full width. "I'm afraid the synagogue will be terribly hot tomorrow. I hope they have the fans going." A small electric fan sat on the window sill and whirred busily, giving off a tiny breeze, but from the night outside came no movement at all. Millie wiped her bony hands on the brightly flowered apron that was tied about her narrow waist. "Well, I have to go back to the kitchen and finish the gefilte fish. It'll be better than the fish I made for my own son's bar-mitzvah, but you can't do too much for an orphan."

Ralph threw to the floor the newspaper he had been reading. "Must you speak that way? You say that in front of your own children, too."

She picked up the newspaper, folded it neatly, and put it on the table. "Well, isn't he an orphan? It's a pity, too. Twelve years old and without a mother." She lifted her apron and applied its hem to her eyes.

Mr. Harris took the cigar from his mouth and grinned broadly. "Not for much longer, Millie." He flicked the ash into a tray, and waited with the cigar poised in mid-air, savoring the startled expressions on the faces of his brother and sister.

Millie clapped her hands and coquettishly danced about his chair. "Tell me, come on, tell me. I'm dying to know who she is."

Mr. Harris drew a long, leisurely puff, and exhaled it even more slowly, determined to enjoy the suspense. "You wouldn't know even if I told you. Suffice it to say"—he hooked his thumb into the belt loop on his trousers—"that she is a wealthy widow."

Millie ran her fingers through her brother's thinning hair. "I'm glad to hear you've found somebody. Ordinarily, I might think that six months is too soon to remarry, but after all, David needs a home of his own, and so do you." The tone of her voice changed slightly and she patted her hair into place. "Not that I mind having him here, but with my three, and with Lou working nights, I have plenty to keep me busy."

He squeezed her hand. "I know, Millie, I know, but it won't be much longer. A month at the most."

"So soon?" she giggled. "When do I give her the stamp of approval."

"Tomorrow," he answered. "I've invited her to the bar-mitzvah."

"Wonderful," Millie chirped. "Now I must go into the kitchen and make the best fish I ever made. After all, if a wealthy lady is going to eat it—"

Mr. Harris gloated at his brother. From the look on Ralph's face, the news must have upset him a great deal. He was probably jealous. He would remain the poor, eternal student trying to hide his envy of his rich brother behind a mask of contempt. Well, he thought, let him sit on his high horse and be happy with his books, if he likes it.

From the kitchen came the sounds of Millie's knife chop-ping the fish on a wooden board. There was the sharp, tempting odor of horseradish and beets being strained together. He sat back and contentedly envisioned the delights his sister was preparing for his son's confirmation. There would be thick slabs of soft peppery fish, and fluffy yellow slices of challah bread, and pickled onions and sweet jellied consomme. He closed his eyes to get a better view.

The angry tone of Ralph's voice awakened him. He opened his eyes and saw Ralph looking down at him. A scowl had come over his usually calm face, and his skin looked almost grey. His hands hung tensely at his sides, and he was mumbling over and over, "You must be crazy. You must be crazy."

Mr. Harris drew back slightly; he did not want his brother to think that he was afraid of him. "What's the matter with you, Ralph? You look as though you need a doctor."

"To bring another woman to the synagogue tomorrow!" He spoke with loathing in his voice.

"There's nothing wrong in that," he shrugged. "Helen's been dead six months. I can't stay single forever."

"Nobody's asking you to. But tomorrow of all days!"

"And what's wrong with that? She's going to be the boy's mother eventually. She may as well start now."

Ralph's eyes swept over the carefully dressed form of his brother. "You don't deserve to be that boy's father. You don't understand him."

Mr. Harris' voice grew louder. "I don't baby him, or tell him fairy tales, if that's what you mean."

"But he's hardly had time to realize that his mother is dead. Six months are like six days to him. He expects to see her tomorrow." He laughed harshly. "And what will he see? His father with a strange woman. That will be a nice surprise for him, won't it?"

"Thanks to you," shouted Mr. Harris. "If you and that doddering old rabbi hadn't filled his head with stories, there'd be no trouble. If you had only let him face the facts like a man."

"There's time enough to face facts when he's older. Let the boy be a normal boy. Hoping to see his mother won't hurt him. If he wants her badly enough, he'll really think she's there. But if he sees you with someone else. . .the shock won't be good for him."

"It will be the best thing for him," Mr. Harris corrected. "It will put an end to his being a child about this and make him a man. It's my chance to undo the harm you two fools have done." He put on his jacket and went to the door. "Goodnight, Millie," he called. "Be there early tomorrow."

"Don't worry. I'll have him there neat as a pin," she answered from the kitchen.

"Good night, Ralph," he said bluntly, his hand on the doorknob. "I hope you'll be there on time."

"I'll be there, but please, for Davy's sake, tell her not to come!"

"See you tomorrow," he said, slamming the door behind him.

David stood before the ark, the large upright chest in which the scrolls of the law were kept. He examined the golden lions embroidered on the red velvet drapes that covered it. This was the first time he had been at the altar, and the synagogue which he had seen so many times before looked strangely different to him. People seemed to know it was a special day in his life. Yet there was no feeling of grave gaiety as there had been at the confirmations of his friends. When he had stood in the doorway watching the children enter the synagogue, he had noticed their parents shaking their heads at him and clucking their tongues. He had realized then that they were sorry for him because he was an orphan.

Sitting in the front pew were Aunt Millie, dressed up in a black hat and gloves, and her husband, Uncle Lou, looking as tired as he usually did. Between them were their three children, temporarily neat and shiny.

David looked down at his new suit and gleaming black shoes. Aunt Millie had told him that he must keep clean all day; she had checked the pockets to make sure there was nothing in them that did not belong. She had put an intricately folded white handkerchief in his lapel pocket, and warned him that he must not use it for blowing. She had straightened his tie many times, and repeatedly combed his hair. Only after the entire family had passed on his appearance was he deemed worthy of taking a place at the altar.

Papa sat next to Aunt Millie, wearing a black tie and a black felt hat, and without even the usual cigar didn't look much like himself. He was smiling, and turning around to receive the congratulations of the neighbors. Uncle Ralph smiled too, though he seemed nervous. He kept stealing little glances at his brother as though he were nervously waiting for something to happen.

David turned back to the ark. In there, he said to himself, are the scrolls of the law, and in a few minutes I will read from them, and then—then I'll see my mother. He longed to see the velvet curtains part so that the scrolls might be taken out and he could begin reading from them. But the rabbi sang on and on through the Sabbath prayers, and the congregation provided him with a wailing accompaniment.

Even the rabbi looked different today, he thought. He wasn't just the old man who sat in a dark study and read the holy books all week long. He was a majestic figure who would reveal to him the beauties of Israel. Over his shoulders was a heavily fringed woolen prayer shawl, striped with thick black bands, like the smaller one that David wore today as a symbol of his manhood. The rabbi's hair shone in the light that came streaming through the yellow windows, and instead of looking worn as he usually did, he now seemed the nearest earthly being to God. Surely, if he had promised mother would come, there was nothing to fear.

The rabbi nodded slowly at him. David suddenly became conscious of the crazy jumping in his heart. This was the signal to open the ark, and the next few minutes would be the most important ones he had ever lived. He had waited so long for this moment, and now that it had come, his hands were shaking so that he could barely hold the pulley ring tightly enough to get the curtain open. The heavy Torah was tenderly lifted and set down on the altar. The thickly beaded covering was gingerly pulled off, and the ribbon that kept it from unrolling was loosened. The rabbi seized the handles at the bottom of the two long wooden spools on which was wound a wide roll of parchment, and the congregation joined him in proclaiming its devotion to the word of God. The rabbi set the scroll down before him, and deftly maneuvered the heavy spools so that there was a wide expanse of parchment between them. This was the reading that David had so diligently studied. His skill would demonstrate to the congregation that he had earned the right to be considered a man, and would reflect on the ability of his teacher. The rabbi took a silver pointer in the shape of a hand and held it out to David.

The boy slowly advanced toward the altar. His legs didn't seem to want to take him there, and he was having a hard time forcing them. His tongue felt thick and heavy, as though he would not be able to make it say the words it had taken so much trouble to learn. He wished that the rabbi were holding out a glass of water instead of the silver pointer. He made a vigorous attempt to clear his throat, and with another step found himself before the altar. He caressed it with his hands, seeking strength in its rugged oak.

He looked into the rabbi's face for some sign of encouragement, but there was none. It was calm and almost stern, as befitted the countenance of the patriarch of the tribe. He set the cold metal rod in David's hand, and forced his fingers tight around it.

David felt a new strength come to him with the contact. It seemed as though some of the rabbi had entered his body. He drew himself up to his full height. His eyes widened and sharpened as he drank in the scene of which he was now the focal point. The gleaming brass of the candelabra, the worn dark wood of the pews, the lions and doves painted on the ceiling, and the ruby light that swung above him; the white shawls on the men, the musty smell of the hangings, and the myriad black figures that stared out of the parchment at him, united in an ecstatic pleasure that made him feel he was standing on the threshold of a great new experience.

Eagerly, he raised the pointer and held it on the scroll. In a solemn musical voice, he chanted the Scripture reading. His words were the only sound in the high room, and for that moment it seemed that the world had stopped moving and was listening to him. His song built into a crescendo which he ended with a surging "Amen." Breathlessly, he waited for the congregation's response. It came in an enthusiastic echo, and he knew that he had read perfectly, and that this very moment the promise of Uncle Ralph and the rabbi must come true.

He shut his eyes tightly, pressing hard against the handles of the scroll. Before him lay only diffused spots of light. He pressed his eyelids tighter and tighter together until the spots ran into each other and his mother's face began to fade in. Her eyes, her hair, and then her mouth became clear. He longed to reach out and touch her. He raised his arms slowly and his hands began to feel warm as they approached the radiance of her face.

Something crashed to the ground and David opened his eyes. He had knocked the silver pointer from the altar, and it had noisily fallen to the floor. Uncle Ralph was bending down to get it, and he brushed it against his lips, but he seemed to have been upset by something else. David noticed a look of shame on his face as he quickly thrust the pointer into the rabbi's outstretched hand. His eyes mirrored the anger inside of him as they drew the rabbi's attention toward the center of the synagogue.

A woman with a fluffy furpiece hanging from her arm was walking slowly down the aisle. Little drops of sunlight danced on the jewels that hung from her neck and ears. Her tall hat was covered with flowers. Papa had stepped up to meet her, and was ushering her into the front pew.

The scene became blurred, and even though David's eyes were wide open he could see nothing. A warm wetness was sliding over his cheeks, and he hoped nobody would see. He licked away the salty drops that were hanging on his lips. He tried to wink back the tears that clouded his vision like the rain did on the windshield of Papa's car. He braced himself against the altar as he began the speech that they were waiting to hear.

"Worthy parent," he said, barely able to make out his father smiling at the strange lady, "and dear friends—" He must stop crying and act like a grown-up, and then Papa would pay attention to him. "Today I am a man in Israel—"

Philip Perl.

Not all Jewish families have an entirely Jewish background. If you are the child of a mixed marriage or of a marriage in which one parent has been converted to Judaism, the question of your Jewish identity depends on you and the attitudes of your family. Though Orthodox Jewish law states that one is a Jew only if one has been born to a Jewish mother or has been converted to Judaism, the more commonly used definition is that one who regards oneself as a Jew *is* a Jew. According to the Book of Ruth, King David was a descendant of a mixed marriage between Boaz, a Jew, and Ruth, a Moabite.

Families of mixed backgrounds have coped with their cultural and religious identity in different ways. The following is a description written by a mother, a Jewish convert of Italian descent, about her son's Bar Mitzvah.

A Bar Mitzvah With Italian Flare

My family enjoyed "our" bar mitzvah, and they enjoyed their participation in it. Eight months prior to the bar mitzvah, they made their airline reservations. They were taking no chances! Once safely in Los Angeles, they pitched in, helping to cook and keep everything under control. They loved the service. Proudly, they came up to open the ark. They wept with pride as I was called to the Torah for an aliyah. They beamed as David chanted his blessings. During the service, my husband Ben and I spoke to David, reflecting not only on his beginnings but on our own as well. We, along with our families, cried and laughed and were filled to overflowing with the complex mixture of feelings that come at special times marking passages from one stage of life to another.

A bar/bat mitzvah service presents many opportunities for your family's participation, depending on the custom of your synagogue. Your family might read certain English sections of

"King David" by Marc Chagall (1887-1985).

A carved cameo brooch depicting the heroine of the biblical Book of Ruth.

the service, join in reciting the Shehecheyanu, or offer a special prayer for their grandchild. In the course of your planning the service with the rabbi, you should be sure to discuss your desire to have maximum involvement on the part of your family.

There were extra touches which enriched David's bar mitzvah immeasurably. My family is Italian. For the invitation, therefore, I found a picture of the young King David holding his harp, from an eighteenth-century Italian folk art haggadah and duly noted the provenance on the back of the invitation. We made certain, long before the party, that our band could play tarantellas and a couple of other Italian songs as well as the predominantly Jewish/Israeli music in which they specialized. When, during the party, the band struck up a tarantella, my family was surprised, then delighted. In an instant they were up and leading everyone in a dance which went on and on and on. My very Italian family was totally at home at "our" bar mitzvah. And so was I!

Lydia Kukoff.

ANCESTORS AND GENERATIONS

Why is the family so important in Jewish culture and religious life? And from where do we get our strong Jewish sense of family? These questions can perhaps be best answered by going back to the Bible and the origins of Judaism. The base for Judaism has always been the family. The history of the Jewish people began with the history of a family which grew into a tribe, and eventually developed into a nation. The family histories of Genesis have been studied by Jews for thousands of years. They have influenced the way Jews think about family life.

Family Relationships in the Bible

"I will maintain my covenant between me and you, and your offspring to come, as an everlasting covenant throughout the ages, to be God to you and to your offspring to come."

Genesis 17:7.

The Bible is a family centered book. There are pages and pages of geneologies going all the way back to Adam. The Bible assumes that the tribe, a large extended family, is the basic unit of society.

At the center of Genesis, when we learn the origins of the Jewish people, there is a detailed history of three generations–Abraham, his wife Sarah, and his sons Ishmael and Isaac; Isaac, Rebecca and their sons Jacob and Esau; Jacob, his wives Leah and Rachel, and his twelve sons. The lives of these generations, referred to traditionally as the "avot" and the "emot," the fathers and the mothers, were not easy. We see them struggle, as parents and children, with the special responsibilities of the covenant.

The Bible suggests that Abraham was not the only monotheist of his time. Melchizedek, king of Salem, is specifically mentioned (Genesis 14:18-20). Abraham is unique because he is the founder of a family that carries the monotheistic revelation across the generations and to the nations of the world. The covenant, which is symbolized by the rite of circumcision, is made not only with Abraham, but also with his descendants.

Genesis introduces Abraham as an adult. Stories about Abraham's youth are told in the Midrash. In the Midrash, Terah, Abraham's father, is a maker of clay idols. Abraham is presented as an independent thinker, a critic, a rebel against the way of life of his father. Abraham takes a hammer, smashes all the idols except the largest and places the hammer in the hand of the remaining idol. Terah angrily asks what happened. Abraham blames the largest idol and Terah replies, "What nonsense! You know idols neither speak nor move!" Abraham asks his father, "Why then do you serve them?" In Genesis, Abraham's decisive break with his father's values is pointedly made when God commands him, "Go forth from your native land and from your father's house. . . . (Genesis 12:1)

Abraham is a strong personality. He builds up a substantial household, plans and executes a daring rescue of his nephew Lot, and negotiates with kings as equals. His religious life combines strength and compassion. In a famous and remarkable passage, he bargains with God. When God reveals to Abraham his plan to destroy the wicked cities of Sodom and Gomorrah, Abraham pleads that the righteous not be swept away with the wicked. God agrees to spare the cities if fifty righteous persons are found. In a series of stages, Abraham asks God to lower the

number, eventually to ten, and God agrees. In this story, as elsewhere in Genesis, Abraham is presented as a self-assured, deeply religious person who successfully meets the trials he faces. His greatest trial comes late in life and involves his son.

Abraham and Sarah grow old without having a child. An angel delivers the message that Sarah shall have a child and that the covenant shall be passed on through his descendants. At the age of ninety, Sarah conceives and delivers Isaac.

This miraculous, joyous birth is followed some years later–according to the rabbinic commentator Ibn Ezra, when Isaac was thirteen–by the most difficult experience of Abraham's life. God, the Bible states, "put Abraham to the test." (Genesis 22:1) God says to Abraham, "Take your son, your favored one, Isaac, whom you love, and go to the land of Moriah, and offer him there as a burnt offering. . . . At the last minute, after a journey of three days, when Isaac is already bound upon the altar and Abraham has the knife in his hand, an angel of the Lord calls to Abraham, "Do not raise your hand against the boy, or do anything to him." (Genesis 22:12) Abraham sees a ram caught by its horns in a thicket and offers it as a burnt offering. The trial is over; the angel affirms to Abraham that his descendants shall be numerous and blessed.

This story of the "Akedah," the binding of Isaac, is one of the most vivid in the Bible and it is also considered one of the hardest to understand. It may be read as a dramatization of the Jewish rejection of child sacrifice, which was common among non-Jews in biblical times. It may be read as a test of Abraham's trust in God. It may be read as an inspiration for the martyrdom which later generations of Jews accepted rather than renouncing their faith.

It is also a story about a father and son. Jewish tradition portrays Abraham as a revolutionary, the founder of a new faith. Isaac, the son of Abraham's old age, does not come to God on his own, as Abraham did. God does not reveal himself to Isaac before the Akedah. Instead, Isaac's religion is taught to him by his father and mother. Until the Akedah, Isaac's relationship to God is indirect rather than direct. At the Akedah, where Isaac is first bound and then released by the command of God, God's desire that Isaac shall live and carry on what Abraham has begun is made dramatically clear.

Isaac, the favored son of his father, the only child of his mother's old age, has grown up in an emotional atmosphere. His father is a prophet who has been privileged to talk with God. Now Isaac is part of that relationship too; he has been through the Akedah.

The Bible tells us less about Isaac's relationship with his mother, but it appears to have been a close one. Isaac does not marry until after Sarah's death. Abraham arranges for Rebecca to be brought from Mesopotamia as Isaac's bride. "Isaac," we read, "brought her into the tent of his mother Sarah, and he took Rebecca as his wife. Isaac loved her, and thus found comfort after his mother's death." (Genesis 24:67)

Isaac and Rebecca have two sons, the twins Esau and Jacob. Their life-long rivalry begins with a struggle over which will be first born. Esau grows to be a cunning hunter, a man of the outdoors, the favorite of his father. Jacob grows up a quiet man, the favorite of his mother.

Isaac is not the awesome person his father Abraham was and Isaac's sons are less docile than Isaac. Esau is a wild man who

"The Sacrifice of Isaac" by Rembrandt (1606-1669).

(Overleaf) "The Benediction of Jacob" by Rembrandt.

indulges his passions and disdains the religious heritage of his family. He sells his birthright to Jacob for a meal of bread and lentils.

Jacob is a schemer. Having purchased the birthright, Jacob is encouraged by Rebecca to trick his aged and blind father into blessing Jacob as the more favored son. Esau swears revenge. Fearing his brother's anger, Jacob heeds the advice of his mother and flees to her brother Laban in Haran.

Jacob flees his family home having acquired the birthright of the first born and the blessing of his father. The son of Isaac, the grandson of Abraham, has his first encounter with God during this flight. Jacob's scheming to have priority over his brother takes on a clearly religious meaning. The God of Abraham and Isaac reveals himself to Jacob, promises to protect him and stay with him, and to continue the covenant with its blessings for all peoples through Jacob and his descendants.

In Haran, Jacob's life of struggle continues. He matches wits with his uncle Laban, for whom he works for twenty years. Jacob marries Laban's daughters Leah and Rachel, has eleven children and prospers. Laban becomes jealous and hostile. God tells Jacob to return to his native land. Jacob gathers his family and possessions, and once again flees.

As he nears the Jordan River, Jacob sends a message of reconciliation to his brother Esau, but learns from his messenger that Esau is approaching with four hundred men. Fleeing the hostility of his father-in-law, fearing the old enmity of his brother, Jacob prays to God for deliverance. Jacob sends presents to Esau and, as night falls, sends ahead his family and is left alone.

This night is a spiritual passage for Jacob. All night until daybreak, Jacob wrestles with an angel. The story is told briefly and leaves unanswered many questions about just what happened. When morning dawns, the struggle has left Jacob with a limp and a new name, Israel, for the angel has told him, "You have striven with beings divine and human and have prevailed." (Genesis 32:29)

His new name and his limp are signs that he returns to the land of his fathers a different person than the one who left. Jacob had left Canaan youthful, ambitious, trusting that his cleverness as well as God's protection would bring him triumph over his adversaries. Jacob returns as Israel, a middle-aged man with the responsibility of a large family, aware of the limits to what individual cleverness can accomplish, seeking a peaceful reconciliation and coexistence with his former rival.

Jacob, after his night of struggle, attempts no trick to deceive his brother. He goes to Esau ahead of his family and bows "low to the ground seven times" (Genesis 33:3) until he is near his brother. Whatever Esau's original intentions, he does not fulfil his youthful vow of vengeance. Instead, he runs to greet Jacob, embraces him, kisses him, and they both weep. The brothers are reconciled. Afterward they go their separate ways and see each other only once, when they bury their father Isaac.

Jacob, like his father and grandfather, has a favorite son— Joseph, the elder son of Rachel. In the last part of Genesis, the attention shifts to the story of Joseph and his brothers. Though Jacob is in the background, his presence is strongly felt. Jacob in his old age conveys strong mixed feelings of loss and faith. Long ago, his beloved mother had sent him away from home, fearing for his safety. Jacob never sees her again. His unexpectedly peaceful return to Canaan is turned to bitterness when his beloved Rachel dies in childbirth. He believes his favored son, Joseph, has been devoured by wild beasts. Despite his prosperity and his remaining large family, Jacob in his old age sits in mourning and will not be comforted. Yet God is with him. Jacob has received the covenant of Abraham and Isaac. He has had his own personal experiences of God's revelation.

Jacob has unhappy experiences as a father. While his children were young, he seems to have been a distant father, preoccupied with his struggle with Laban. Jacob treats his younger sons Joseph and Benjamin as favorites, not because of their personal qualities, but because of his love for their mother Rachel. His older sons' personalities appear to have been shaped not by the mature wisdom of Israel, but by the model of Jacob's youth: they plot, they deceive, they seek to overthrow their father's favorite.

In the story of Joseph and his brothers there is, as in previous generations, rivalry for preference. Unlike previous generations, Joseph and his brothers come to a complete reconciliation. Ishmael and Isaac become the founders of two peoples and their paths diverge. The twins Esau and Jacob reconcile their enmity as adults and separate. The sons of Jacob remain intact as one family. The brothers repent for the evil they did to Joseph and Joseph forgives them. They all grow to spiritual maturity through their relationship as brothers. The rivalries of previous generations are replaced with a strong sense of interdependence and mutual responsibility.

Joseph has been providentially sent to Egypt to save his family and many others from the years of famine. Jacob and his sons are brought by Joseph to Egypt. There, as the Passover Haggadah puts it, "They increased and multiplied and became a great nation." The household of Jacob becomes many households, the nation of the children of Israel, who continue to think of themselves as *k'lal Yisroel*, all Israel, an extended family.

Stuart Schoenfeld.

Here is a contemporary story of the covenant and the continuity of Jewish generations, set in Israel.

The Three-Fold Covenant

My neighbor is an immigrant from Germany who came to Palestine some time ago among the other refugees from race-hatred and persecution. It was just at that time that we came to live in our new flat in one of Jerusalem's modern suburbs. He lives on the lower floor, and I on the one above.

We have no personal acquaintance with each other. It has always been rather hard for me to get to know my neighbors. Several times a day I pass the door of his flat, and the name engraved in outstanding Hebrew letters on a brightly polished brass plate gleams at me from the door as though it were alive, proclaiming "Richard Oppenheimer."

Sometimes my neighbor and I meet in the hall in the mornings when I am starting out for work and he, too, is going off about his business. The moment he sees me he raises his hat in my direction and uncovers his flaming red hair, smiles at me and says:

"*Shalom. Guten Morgen.*"

And the echo of his thick, trumpeting voice fills the entire entrance hall.

"*Shalom.*" I return his greeting, raising my hat as well in politeness.

Apart from these infrequent morning meetings and our polite greetings, there is no contact between us. Were it not for the aroma of his pot-bellied cigars ascending to me every now and then through his open window I would not know that he was there at all. He is a peaceful sort with quiet ways, and his home is just as quiet. There are no noisy children; nor does as much as the hoarse voice of a phonograph or radio disturb us. If anything, it is he who must be aware of the presence of his neighbor. Not that I have either phonograph or radio or even noisy children in my flat; but I live above him and there can be no scrape of a shifted table or movement of a chair or even noisy tread in my flat which does not sound in the flat below like a clap of thunder.

Turning over the paper one morning, I noticed that as is the custom here, somebody had sent congratulations to Richard Oppenheimer through the columns of the paper on the birth of a son. Which Richard Oppenheimer could be meant? My neighbor? Yes, my neighbor and none other. The person offering congratulations was H. Levy and I knew H. Levy to be my neighbor's business partner, for on their big shop for the sale of pharmaceutical products and cosmetics in the main street the name "Oppenheimer and Levy" was written up large for all to see. I read through the congratulation once, twice, and yet a third time, and pondered upon the mysterious ways of our lives. In the very house in which I was living a woman had lain writhing in birth pangs and I had known nothing of it; a son had been born to my neighbor; and although no more than the thickness of a ceiling separated us, I had become aware of the fact only through the pages of a newspaper. Through my brain passed a sudden vision of the woman taken with the first pains, of the bewildered husband taking her to the hospital.

My thoughts went directly on to other things, I forgot my neighbor and the son that had been born to him, and began to consider my daily work.

I forgot my neighbor; but that evening I remembered him again. I had just sat down to eat supper when there was a knock at the door. I opened it and in came my neighbor, Mr. Richard Oppenheimer.

"*Shalom. Guten Abend.*"

I invited him in. He stood silent and nervous for a few moments with a narrow forehead, his bronze eyes squinted slightly, his red lips looked as though they were swollen, his body was well-set and soldierly, and the back of his neck, I noticed, was fleshy and scarred. In my Polish birthplace they used to call such a countenance an Esau face. I could see that he found it hard to express himself. So I came to his aid.

"Please sit down, Mr. Oppenheimer; can I do anything for you?"

"Thanks. Yes, yes," he stammered and this time his voice was gentle and restrained, entirely different from the voice that sometimes used to trumpet a greeting at me in the hall below. "Yes, yes; I have a request to make of you....The Circumcision will take place tomorrow—I suppose you know that my wife has had a son...."

"Yes, I heard about it, Mr. Oppenheimer. Congratulations." I shook his hand, and it immediately became easier for him to speak.

"I'll tell you quite frankly. I don't know what has to be done. I'm in a fix. I don't know how to say the blessing tomorrow at the ceremony...." His reddish face grew still more flushed and something childlike and innocent about him touched me to the heart; for nothing is so touching as a strong face suddenly softening.

I took my prayer-book from the bookcase and opened it to the Circumcision Service.

"Here you are," said I.

"Hm, hm," he cleared his throat and half-smiled in still greater confusion. "But what's to be done? I don't know how to read Hebrew...Not so much as a single letter. Maybe you'd be good enough to write down the blessing for me in Latin characters." In his nervousness he began fiddling with his fingers.

I was nonplused. There was something astonishing and even startling in this confession of helplessness on the part of a man like my neighbor. He always went about with such firmness and self-assurance. His morning greeting said: I know everything. I can achieve everything; and now this confession of helplessness, of inability to read the prayer-book. I suddenly felt sorry for him and strove to overcome my astonishment. Sitting down, I wrote out the blessing in Latin characters as he had requested, in block capitals so that he would be able to read it easily. Then I read it out to him three or four times. He in turn repeated it after me in Hebrew with a weird German accent....When he began to grow a little familiar with the blessing I rose, thinking it was finished. I offered him my hand but he did not take it.

"I have yet another request of you; pardon me, for giving you so much trouble," he stammered in a gentle voice. "Another slight request. The name, sir. We find it hard to choose a name for him. You know that my name's Richard. But for our son we want a nice Hebrew name, something out of the Bible...Please, do you think you could find us a nice name from the Bible?"

I took the Bible off my table and opened it at random to Numbers. The first words my eyes struck were "Elizur, son of Shedeur."

"Elizur," I read from the book.

"Elizur, Elizur." My neighbor was as happy as though he had found a valuable treasure. "Elizur. Wonderful. *Grossartig.* A wonderful Biblical name. Thank you, sir, thank you. Elizur!" He gave me his hand to take his leave and simultaneously invited me to come to the Circumcision. It was a social invitation, made to do his duty, it seemed to me. Nonetheless I decided to be present, for I felt that I had a share in the festivity. I had taught him the blessing and I had found him the name; how could I do other than participate in the celebration?

It was a summer evening, hot, dry, and still. I sat on my balcony to breath a little fresh air. My neighbor sat below me on his balcony. For a long time I heard him murmuring to himself as though he were praying, repeating the blessing,"to mage our zons ender indo de Govenand off Abraham our Fader." For the first time I was aware that we were neighbors.

The following morning I put on my Sabbath suit, took some time off from work and went to the hospital which my neighbor had mentioned to me the day before, in order to be present at the induction of his son into the Covenant of Abraham. I arrived there a bit late, after my neighbor had already said the blessing. I made my way through the crowd till I reached the Seat of Elijah. The circumcised mite was yelling at the first pain he had suffered in his life, and Reb Shlomo Jacob, the circumciser, who is said to have inducted a full myriad of Israelites into the Covenant of our Father Abraham, stood bandaging the child.

Richard Oppenheimer was swathed in a new silk tallis and stood leaning against the godfather's chair. His face was set and strained and pale. I felt sorry that when he had entered my flat the evening before I had thought to myself that he had an Esau face. No, the face was now no longer that of an Esau; he now seemed to be a man overwhelmed by something fateful which could not be avoided. There was a tremendous difference to be seen in his face, and I observed it with wonder. When they reached the naming of the child his face brightened up a little. "Elizur, son of Richard," he proudly told the circumciser. The latter automatically corrected it to "son of Reuven." My neighbor was perplexed for a moment; then his glance met mine. He smiled at me.

It did not take long for the entire ceremony to be completed and the yelling baby to be taken to its mother. The assembly sat down at the tables to enjoy the wine and sweetmeats. They were a noisy lot, congratulating and toasting one another, chattering, rattling their glasses and laughing. Most of them were German immigrants, of whom I hardly knew one. I sat myself down by the oldest of them all, who had been godfather. Both the expression on his face and the fact of his having been godfather attracted me. His white hair rose like a silver diadem on his head. His trim beard and mustache marked his face as though with a capital T. He had the face of a respected man, a man of standing. Had I begun addressing him as *"Herr Hofrat"* he would assuredly have responded; his face told me as much. But since I was not certain, I contented myself by addressing him as *"Herr Doktor"*; nor was I wrong.

"How was the father's blessing, *Herr Doktor?*"

"Very fine, very fine," replied the old man in a measured cultured voice. "Very fine, *grossartig.*"

"I taught it to him," I whispered in his ear, for I suddenly felt like vaunting myself. Or maybe I just wanted to justify my presence there.

"Indeed, indeed...Very fine," murmured the old man politely and poured himself a glass of wine.

"He can't read Hebrew," I continued to talk scandal to him. "I had to write down the blessing for him in Latin characters. He can't even read the prayer-book. Woe to the generation. Eh?"

The old man said nothing but finished his glass.

"I suppose his grandfather was a rabbi in one of the old German communities, and yet he doesn't even know what a Hebrew letter looks like. I'm sorry for the father who brought him up like that."

"His grandfather was not a rabbi, while as for his father—he's sitting right next to you. I am his father ."

It was only now that I noticed that his eyes squinted slightly,

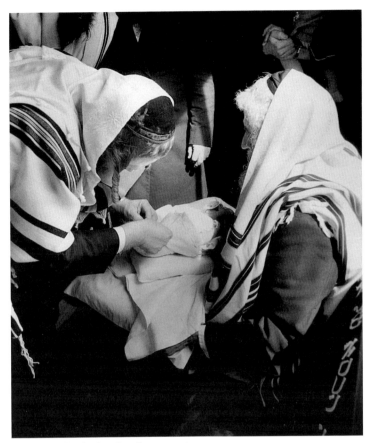

A circumcision in Los Angeles.

and that there was some slight resemblance between him and my neighbor. I flamed crimson with shame and cursed myself at heart for this sudden gush of chatter. It was impossible for me so much as to open my mouth and beg his pardon. He poured himself another glass of wine, drank it slowly to the end, and went on:

"Since you taught my son the blessing, you might as well know the whole story. His grandfather was a doctor, and I, his father am the same. I was converted to Christianity when I was a young man, but I never was a thoroughgoing non-Jew, for I was circumcised, you know...I was always a sort of half-Jew and half-Gentile, a very uncomfortable position. But as for my son Richard, I never had him circumcised, for I didn't want to make his life hard for him. I wanted him to be a complete Gentile, you know...And now a son has been born to my son, and I was honored with the godfatherhood...Do you understand me properly, my dear sir? I sat there on that chair, holding the baby on my knees, and I felt that I was holding two on my knees, that I was supporting my son as well, that I was inducting him as well into the Covenant of our Father Abraham...Do you understand me properly, my dear sir? This was a double Covenant...no, no. A treble Covenant...I too, old man as I am, I entered the Covenant of our Father Abraham together with them...."

The old man laughed in a way that was almost frightening, and wiped a tear from his eyes. That moment his son Richard came up and pressed his hand.

"Mazel tov, Abba."

"Mazel tov," answered the old man as he rose and left me to go with his son and bless the third to enter into the Covenant, the baby who now lay in the next room, forgetting his pain at his mother's breast.

Yehuda Yaari.

"Children's children are the crown of old men." Book of Proverbs.

Jews have always seen themselves as an extended family. Appropriately, the Hebrew word for family, *mishpochah*, also means ancestors or lineage. The following story gives a strong sense of both meanings of the word. It also shows how influential grandparents can be in teaching Jewish tradition to their offspring. As representatives of the past, they illustrate the continuity of Jewish generations to their grandchildren in a very real way.

My Grandfather

His picture is in front of me—a handsome man with a serious face, his thick black hair heavily streaked with gray, his glance stern at first but upon closer investigation sadly meditative. An unusual sadness radiates from those deep eyes.

The old doctor from Miskolc is dressed in a Hungarian festive suit that was popular around 1848. He loved his country passionately. He hid Hungarian *honvéds* in his house after the collapse of the Revolution, and received a stiff jail sentence for it. His great-grandfather too had lived in Miskolc, and because of family tradition, the old gentleman used to say with respectful pride that his family was one of the oldest Hungarian-Jewish families.

He must have been sixty-five when one of his arms became paralyzed. He was a widower. His eyes were afflicted with cataracts and he moved in with his only daughter and son-in-law, my father, the rabbi of Ungvár. There he lived, at the twilight of his life, the old doctor from Miskolc, the respected former *rashekol* of the Jewish community of Miskolc. I remember him from my childhood. He especially liked me, his oldest grandchild. He often took me on his lap and told me unusual, beautiful stories in his somewhat husky, quietly sad voice. Before the High Holy Days, in the small hours of the cool September mornings when the autumn night left behind fine veils of fog above the Carpathian peaks, my grandfather took me by the hand and led me to the *selichos* service in the synagogue, which stood on a slope with its small candlelights flickering in the dark of the night. Although he was supposed to lead me, I walked briskly almost ahead of him, swinging a lamp in my hand on the dark streets while with bleary eyes he walked leaning heavily on my arm.

My grandfather had a meticulously elaborate family tree drawn with primitive artistry. He would often lay the old, faded piece of paper with its pale writing on the table in front of him and explain to me, in a voice half serious half joking, the mysteries of that large many-branched tree, the ancestry of his forefathers. The Hungarian branch reached into the distant times to the Jews who lived in the period of the conquest. His father was a licensed interpreter, his grandfather a famous, pious talmudic scholar. Maria Theresa, Louis the Great, Matthias, contemporary churchmen, dignitaries, merchants, teachers, poor struggling, suffering, and persecuted men followed one another on the branch of his Hungarian ancestors.

There was another branch; it led to German lands. One ancestor had been a relative of the great rabbi of the thirteenth century, Rabbi Meir of Rothenburg. Another branch showed the medieval poet Susskind von Trimberg, and a stern, black-bearded rabbi from Worms, an ascetic, wild-haired chorister, and a fanatical Jewish martyr from Regensburg. There were also pious wigged women, dreamy-eyed mothers who died young.

Then there were the Italians. There was an exegete named Lonzo among them who, according to family legend, had once polemicized with a scholarly bishop about God's religion.

The Russian and Lithuanian branches were made up mainly of ancestors who held communal posts.

The refugee Spanish Jews also played an important role. One of them wandered across the seas on board a ship for long years before he settled in Holland.

With adventurous, mythical turns, the fabulous family tree reached as far as biblical times and then suddenly, jumping from heroes to bards, it came to rest at Mordecai, the son of Kish, the Persian minister. The beautiful eyes of Queen Esther lit up when the tree reached her. Then it climbed to Boaz, the sheaf-binding landowner. It embraced the flowing, scented hair of Naomi and Ruth, and finally came to a halt at the most distant of ancestors, the harp-playing King David.

Outside, the windstorm howled and shook the old runways of the window, and in the kitchen the Slovak servant girl sang a melancholic song. Sitting in his huge armchair, in the long autumn evenings, my grandfather mused over the worn pieces of paper. The dim light of the green-shaded lamp painted shadows on the walls of the small room; the ancestors came to visit. I squatted in front of him and watched the trembling forefinger of his left hand as it slid along the family tree and listened with fascination to his quiet words about the ancestors, the forefathers, as if an old, forgotten song had come to life in the eerie calm.

One day my grandfather became seriously ill. It happened in the autumn, around the Feast of Tabernacles. My grandfather and I had wandered about in the thicket of the Ung gathering branches for *Hoshano Rabbo*. He caught a cold then. He hovered between life and death for weeks. My mother's eyes were red from crying and she devotedly kept vigil at the sickbed of her father, whom she idolized. My father prayed in the synagogue with sad lamentations and with name-changing chants for the gravely ill man, his father-in-law, so that the Angel of Death would not find Akiba, the son of Rachel, whose name he had changed. The *Moloch Hamoves* would never again find the son of Akiba.

I did not hear my grandfather's beautiful tales for a long time. I was concerned and afraid that I would never hear them again. He was running a high fever; his hands and forehead were hot as he lay unconscious on the bed.

Nonetheless, God helped him. He counted my mother's tears—only God could keep count of them—and in His great

Georgian Jewish family in Tel Aviv.

mercy He found that they had filled the chalice of sorrow; and He listened to my father's sad psalms. My grandfather slowly recovered.

On a late autumn afternoon, basking in the fading sunshine, my convalescing grandfather sat in a large armchair in the arbor. The white flowers of the apple tree kept falling on his silvery hair. He unfolded the family tree again and looked at the map of the ancestors with dreamy eyes. He drew me near him with his healthy arm and for the first time since his illness he began to tell a story.

His voice was soft and melodic like the sound of a harp. He stroked my hair and began his story.

* * *

My little boy, I have come home from very far. I almost thought that I would never find the way home, to you whom I love so dearly. I had a dream, a beautiful dream; perhaps it wasn't even a dream...

I was in Heaven, my son. I can't even tell you how beautiful everything is there. The huge antechamber is studded with heavenly garnets and fiery rubies. The multitude of stars that glitter like so many diamonds, the sweet, enchanting song of the angels, and the wondrous, blue celestial roads that are in Heaven are hidden from the people who live on earth. The thousands of enchanted trees are covered with fabulously beautiful flowers that, when the wind hushes through them, play heavenly music. And God's throne! How can I describe to you that enormous brightness or the singing of the *serafim*; the zithers that play by themselves; the stars that glitter like so many diamonds, the sweet enchanting sound of the praising angels' trumpets; the enchanted melodies of hidden violins? No, my son! I cannot describe to you all that beauty.

Just imagine, my little boy, how I cried with happiness when an angel took me by the hand and led me to my mother and father, who had left me an orphan in this world such a long time ago. My dear mother embraced me again and her warm tears fell on my cheeks: "Thank Heaven I can see you again, my dear son! I have waited for you for such a long time!" My father embraced me a hundred times and blessed me as he did when I was a child.

Then they took me by the hand. My mother grasped one, my father took the other.

"Let's go, my son," my father said solemnly. "We are going to visit your ancestors, your grandfathers and great-grandfathers. It is proper that we should introduce you, their distant grandchild, to them."

My heart was beating fast. I would see them at last, the ancestors whose memory is preserved in the family tree.

We walked and walked in Heaven. Miraculously, no one gets tired in Heaven. It is easy to walk there; there are no thorns and prickles like down here on earth.

Then I saw them. I came up to my grandfather, the former licensed interpreter of Miskolc. He was a kind-faced, smiling man. He softly embraced me and kissed me many times. My grandfather and grandmother on my mother's side were also very happy to see me. My grandmother, a pretty, blue-eyed young woman, said, "I remember you. I used to rock your cradle, but I had to depart from earth too soon."

And I saw the long line of great-grandfathers and great-grandmothers—my ancestors who lived in the time of Maria Theresa, Louis the Great, and Matthias, the men who played prominent roles in the community and the synagogue, the poor teachers, the persecuted and long-suffering great-great-grandfathers and great-great-grandmothers. Every one of them embraced me. Naturally, the farther we went visiting, the less familiar my ancestors were to me.

I saw the great Rabbi Meir of Rothenburg, my famous ancestor. There was an unusual turbanlike hat on his head, his gray beard glittered, and his deep eyes sparkled with such brilliance that they looked like precious stones. There were handcuffs on his wrists because he was jailed in his earthly life for his love of the sacred Torah. But in Heaven, the handcuffs on his wrists changed to shining gold. They were no longer tight but soothingly smooth as if they had been made of velvet. When I reached him, the great Rabbi Meir of Rothenburg was bent over the Torah, absorbed in the sacred writing. He put his arm on my shoulder but his eyes rested on me only fleetingly. Small wonder, he must have been visited by numerous grandchildren in the course of time.

I also saw my other famous great-great-grandfather: Susskind, the poet of Trimberg. He was playing a golden harp; in Heaven everyone is allowed to devote himself to his favorite profession. He had just finished a poem when I reached him and kindly told me of the many good things he had heard of the Hungarian branch of his family.

I also saw my martyred ancestor from Worms. He was the stern rabbi with the black beard. I also heard the chanting of my ascetically thin ancestor, the cantor. I stood in front of my stern ancestor from Worms in respectful awe. He merely glanced at me and quickly blessed me. My ancestor from Regensburg was singing a fanatical psalm and praying; he had little time for me. However, my pious, God-fearing great-great-grandmothers welcomed me lovingly. They discovered resemblances between me and some of my ancestors and touched my face with their soft, velvety fingers. They told me that I had a grandson down on

earth and that he—so they heard—especially resembled me. You are that grandson, my little boy.

There was a beautiful but very sad young woman among my ancestors. The other great-great-grandmothers talked about her in whispers. She had had a sad life. She left the parental home against the will of her parents for a poor boy whom she loved very much. Her parents disowned her, but God forgave her and took her into Heaven because of her great capacity for love.

Passing along the long, winding roads, through my Spanish, Russian, and Lithuanian ancestors, I reached Mordecai the son of Jair the son of Shimei the son of Kish. His shoulders were covered with purple and on his chest was a diamond decoration that the king of Persia had given him. There were masked, merry people around him, dancing to sweet music. God himself had decorated him with a beautiful star in his hair, the sparkle of which cast brightness around him.

Mordecai loved his people and was prepared to sacrifice his life for them. There was also the beautiful Queen Esther, his sister, amid respectful admiration. They were celebrating the eternal feast of Purim.

I also saw my ancestor Boaz, the harvester of Bethlehem. His face was cheerful and handsome. Even the usually sad Naomi stood by him smiling. With her flowing hair, the sheaf-binding girl was singing the sweet songs of springtime. All of them kissed me and let me go on.

Finally, I reached the great ancestor who is shining at the top of the highest branch of my family tree: the harp-playing King David. His crown glittered and he played a beautiful sweet song on the harp. I have never seen a handsomer man in my life. He had a large, respectful court. I fell to the ground in front of my most illustrious ancestor and he smiled at me kindly without interrupting his song. And I, too, mingled with the other admirers, grandchildren, and descendants.

My father and mother were the happiest of all. They kissed and hugged me endlessly. I, too, was very, very happy to see them again.

Two weeks passed this way. Yet I became quieter and quieter. I have no idea what kind of sadness got hold of me amid all that happiness.

My father and mother noticed my sadness. They caressed and pampered me and questioned me about my behavior.

Suddenly, tears began rolling down my cheeks and my heart and forehead became hot. In that moment I realized why I was so sad. Then I told my father, crying, "I am longing for my daughter and grandson. I'd like to go home to my family, to Ungvár, where they are waiting and crying for me. Don't be angry with me, my dear parents, because I want to leave you."

My parents loved me very much. They had never denied me anything. They prayed and implored God to let me come home to you. And God permitted me to come home to you for a little longer.

That is how I came home to you, my little son. That is how I recovered and that is what I dreamed about my family tree and that is how I awoke from my miraculous dream.

* * *

That was the end of the story of my grandfather, who has been lying in the cemetery for so long; who had, at one time, rocked me on his knees while explaining his family tree, and to whom, according to my great-grandmother, I bear such an amazing resemblance.

Arnold Kiss.

I Want To Write A Jewish Poem

It will be in the form of an old man
Praying in the Orthodox synagogue
Across the street from the gas station
And kitty-corner from the Yeshivah
Where boys with dangling ribbons of hair
And stern eyes learn the Talmud.
This old man is my grandfather Aaron.
A strong man, a farmer in White Russia
Who lifted heavy bushels of wheat on his back,
He came to America to flee the cossacks.
But my grandfather Aaron was silent in America,
Riding his horse-drawn cart through alleys,
Collecting valuables from garbage cans.
He never spoke English. He seldom spoke Yiddish.
His eyes turned inward to an earlier time
When prophets, poets invoked the words he whispers now.
Standing to the side of the Sacred Ark
Covered by his zebra-striped Tallith,
His yarmulka on his head,
He is one of a tribe of ancient worshippers
Touched by sacred garments, scrolls, words,
Men and women who lift their faces toward the burning bush,
The parting sea, Moses receiving the tablets of The Law on Mt.
    Sinai.
For my grandfather there is a burning light of holiness.
So let the sun go down, so let the darkness come.
Let the other, more worldly Jews,
Some of whom have become rich, leave the synagogue.
There is no place for my grandfather in America
But his synagogue where he stands
Confronting me now with his sad, intense eyes staring through
    his spectacles.
"So Gershon. You think you are a poet.
Yet you have not listened to the poetry of your Fathers.
Come and worship with me now."

                    Gary Pacernick.

PERSONAL FAMILY HISTORY

"We Jews are strange people: we remember Moses, King David and Solomon, but we know little of our own ancestry beyond our parents and occasionally our grandparents."

Vera Weizman.

Perhaps one of the reasons it is so difficult for us to trace our recent family history is because our lives are so radically different from the lives of our grandparents and great-grandparents. We probably live in a different country from theirs, and have few things which connect us with their lives. Because Jews have been wanderers from country to country, it has been difficult to gain access to official records and photographs of past generations. Family heirlooms also have been hard to preserve.

Another reason for the difficulty in finding out more about our recent past has been the encroachment of the Holocaust. Most of us have lost at least some relatives in Europe amongst the six million Jews who were killed by the Nazis, and we may no longer have access to personal sources or photos that could tell us about our family's past.

The following article is a humorous but pointed attempt at illustrating the differences between Jewish and non-Jewish American family histories.

Breeding Will Tell: A Family Treatment

There once appeared in a magazine a photograph of myself taken under obviously youthful circumstances. I assumed that it would be readily apparent to all that this was my high school yearbook picture. I neglected, however, to take into consideration that I number among my acquaintances some people of decidedly lofty background. I was first jarred into awareness of this by a well-born young fashion model who, in reference to said photograph, offered, "I really loved your deb picture, Fran." Had that been the end of it I would undoubtedly have forgotten the incident, but later on that very same evening an almost identical remark was made by a minor member of the Boston aristocracy. As far as I was concerned this constituted a trend. I therefore felt faced with a decision: either snort derisively at the very idea or create an amusing fiction appropriate to such thinking. Being at least peripherally in the amusing fiction business, I chose the latter and thus have prepared the following genealogy.

Margaret Lebovitz, my paternal grandmother, was born in Ghetto Point, Hungary (a restricted community), at the very dawn of the Gay Nineties. An appealing child, she was often left in the care of trusted family retainers (my Aunt Sadie and Uncle Benny), as her father's far-flung business affairs–which were mainly concerned with being conscripted into the army–frequently kept him away from home. Although her mother spent most of her time amusing herself in the cabbage fields, she nevertheless made it a point to visit the nursery every evening and stand guard while little Margaret said her prayers. Margaret's childhood was a happy one–she and her chums exchanged confidences and babushkas as they whiled away the carefree hours picking beets and playing hide and seek with the Cossacks. Tariff, the family estate, where the Lebovitzes wintered (*and* summered) was indeed a wondrous place and it was therefore not surprising when Margaret balked at being sent away to school. Her father, home on a brief desertion, took her into his

straw-lined study–which was affectionately called "Daddy's hide-out"–and explained patiently that unbreakable tradition demanded that girls of Margaret's class acquire the necessary social graces such as fleeing demurely and staying properly alive. Margaret listened respectfully and agreed to begin her freshman year at Miss Belief's.

Immigrants at the Ellis Island Money Exchange in New York harbor.

Margaret was a great success at Miss Belief's, where her taste in footwear quickly won her the nickname Bootsie. Bootsie was an excellent student and demonstrated such a flair for barely audible breathing that she was unanimously elected chairman of the Spring Day Escape Committee. That is not to say that Bootsie was a grind–quite the contrary. An irrepressible madcap, Bootsie got herself into such bad scrapes that the fellow members of her club, the Huddled Masses, were frequently compelled to come to her rescue. Fond of out-door sports, Bootsie longed for summer vacation and happily joined in the girlish cries of "Serf's up!" that greeted the season.

Upon reaching her eighteenth birthday, Bootsie made her debut into society and her beauty, charm, and way with a hoe soon gained her a reputation as the Brenda Frazier of Ghetto Point. All of the young men in her set were smitten with Bootsie and found it absolutely necessary to secure the promise of a waltz days in advance of a party, as her dance pogrom was invariably full. Bootsie's favorite beau was Tibor, a tall, dashing young deserter and two-time winner of the Hungarian Cup Race, which was held yearly in a lavishly irrigated wheat field. Tibor was fond of Bootsie, but he was not unmindful of the fact that she would one day come into her father's great plowshare, and this was his primary interest in her. The discovery that Tibor was a fortune hunter had a devastating effect upon Bootsie and she took to her bed. Bootsie's family, understandably concerned about her condition, held a meeting to discuss the problem. It was concluded that a change of scenery would do her a world of good. A plan of action was decided upon and thus Bootsie Lebovitz was sent steerage to Ellis Island in order that she might forget.

Fran Lebowitz.

(Top) Four generations of Iraqi Jews in Jerusalem after the bar mitzvah of the boy on the right.
(Bottom) A couple in New York holding photographs of parents killed in Russia during the Holocaust.

Pedigrees

Recently at a public banquet I happened to sit next to a lady who tried to impress me by letting me know that one of her ancestors witnessed the signing of the Declaration of Independence. I could not resist replying: "Mine were present at the Giving of the Ten Commandments."

Stephen S. Wise.

(Above) The Fountain of Lions in the Alhambra palace in Granada, Spain, was patterned by its Jewish builder after the 12 oxen of King Solomon's temple—a reminder of Jewish contribution to Spanish culture.

(Preceding pages) Five generations of a German family are grouped around their progenitor (front center) on the occasion of his 90th birthday in 1889. Note that this picture is a composite of several group photos.

The following article is a plea for finding out as much as you can about your personal family history. When you know the recent history of your people through the history of your own family, it becomes more personal and real.

The Family Tree and Circle

We are a nation of wanderers living in a country founded by wanderers in a time of emotional and psychological wandering. To know how to wander is to know how to live in the contemporary world. We have been wandering, off and on, for 4000 years. We have experience.

It has not been easy to live scattered around the world. By every reasonable standard, the Jews should have disappeared long ago. What has held us together? What has bound each successive generation? One component, at least, is clear and can be adopted as a guide in our present day wanderings. We have always remembered where we have been. We always kept records. Historical consciousness has been a cement, binding countless generations of Jews separated from one another in every other way. The future lay as an intangible dream, but the past lay exposed, known, and shared for both its joys and tragedies.

Ideally, we could each trace our own lineage back to one of the 12 tribes of Israel. When tradition says that we all, here and now, left Egypt with Moses or stood at Mt. Sinai to receive the Torah, it means this not only metaphorically, but in the very real sense that a part of *us*, members of our own ancestral family, whose blood still passes through our veins, participated in these events. This is our personal, as well as our ethnic, inheritance.... And we are charged, as individuals and as a people, with inherited responsibility of passing on the tradition....

This consciousness is, perhaps, more important now than ever before. Today, in a society marked by loneliness and alienation, we need to recapture the sense and the purpose of the extended community. As a balance to computerized ID cards, we need to assert our place in time within a context of duration, past and future.

Unfortunately, the handing-down and passing-on is in jeopardy. There have been serious breaks in the links from both external and internal causes. Unless these are reinforced, the entire chain may become nothing more than an illusion. Our prayers invoke the names of "Our fathers Abraham, Isaac, and Jacob," yet we have forgotten the names of our grandparents. How many of us can trace the line back more than one generation? When called to the Torah, how many of us know our parents' Hebrew names let alone our grandparents'? And aside from saying "Somewhere in Russia or Lithuania," how many of us know where we have come from? More important even than losing the traditions which have been handed down from parent to child, we have lost the memory of those who did the handing down. The former we can learn from teachers and books. The latter, once lost, we can never recover.

Richard Siegel.

"As my father planted for me, so do I plant for my children."   *Talmud, Ta'anith, 23a.*

Honi and the Carob Tree

One day Honi happened to be walking along the road and he noticed an elderly man planting a carob tree near the man's home. Honi inquired of the man, "How long does it take for this tree to produce fruit?"

"It takes seventy years for it to bear fruit," answered the old man.

"How foolish," remarked Honi. "You will never live to see the fruits of the tree you are planting."

"Not foolish at all," answered the old man. "See those lovely carob trees bearing fruits in the distance? Those trees were planted by my ancestors. This tree I am planting for my descendants."

Talmud.

Like the carob trees, life continues and families grow. How much do you know about the history of your family? The following pages will help you research your own personal family history. Fill in as much information as you can. Remember no two families are alike, nor do all families have two parents and four grandparents. Adapt the following pages to suit your own unique family. Ask members of your family to provide personal comments or messages to you on the occasion of your Bar Mitzvah.

FACTS ABOUT YOUR FAMILY

Mother: _____ Hebrew Name: _____

Father: _____ Hebrew Name: _____

Maternal Grandmother: _____ Hebrew Name: _____

Maternal Grandfather: _____ Hebrew Name: _____

Paternal Grandmother: _____ Hebrew Name: _____

Paternal Grandfather: _____ Hebrew Name: _____

Brothers and Sisters: _____

Relatives who died in the Holocaust: _____

WHO'S WHO

1.   You
2.   Father
3.   Mother
4.   Paternal grandfather
5.   Paternal grandmother (maiden name)
6.   Maternal grandfather
7.   Maternal grandmother (maiden name)
8-11.   Paternal great-grandparents
12-15. Paternal great-grandparents

2.

Born: Place:

Married: Place:

1.

Born: Place:

3.

Born: Place:

8. _____

Born: _____ Place: _____

Married: _____ Place: _____

Died: _____ Place: _____

4. _____

Born: _____ Place: _____

Married: _____ Place: _____

9. _____

Born: _____ Place: _____

Died: _____ Place: _____

10. _____

Born: _____ Place: _____

Married: _____ Place: _____

5. _____

Born: _____ Place: _____

Died: _____ Place: _____

11. _____

Born: _____ Place: _____

Died: _____ Place: _____

12. _____

Born: _____ Place: _____

Married: _____ Place: _____

6. _____

Born: _____ Place: _____

Married: _____ Place: _____

Died: _____ Place: _____

13. _____

Born: _____ Place: _____

Died: _____ Place: _____

14. _____

Born: _____ Place: _____

Married: _____ Place: _____

7. _____

Born: _____ Place: _____

Died: _____ Place: _____

15. _____

Born: _____ Place: _____

Died: _____ Place: _____

FAMILY MESSAGES

Mother:

Father:

Grandparents:

Siblings:

Other Important Family Members:

PART THREE
THE JEWISH COMMUNITY

"All Jewish people are responsible
for each other."

An Extended Family

The central quality...of being a Jew is the feeling that one is a member of an *extended family*. The components of this feeling are: a sense of solidarity with other Jews; a feeling of mutual responsibility, despite differences of social and economic status and country of residence; and a readiness to recognize other Jews in strange surroundings. It may be described pejoratively as clannishness or honorifically as group loyalty. This quality has the disadvantage that every Jew feels a pang of pain when he reads that another Jew in another part of the world is suffering from anti-Semitic persecution. It has the advantage that wherever a Jew goes in the civilized world he is likely to find welcome and friendship.

Mortimer Ostow.

(Above) A community gathers for the Rosh Hashonah Tashlich ceremony. Crumbs, representing the sins of the previous year, are symbolically thrown into the river.

(Preceding page) Kol Nidre service in Budapest. Built in 1859, this synagogue houses the largest Jewish community in the Eastern Bloc.

Your Bar Mitzvah celebration is a symbolic entry into the Jewish community. You are now a member of your society. Being called up to read from the Torah is your first public act as a participant in your community. Your loyalty to your family is now extended to the Jewish community in which you live.

A Jewish community can be many different things. In a small town or suburb, it can be all the Jewish people in town. In a large urban center, it can mean your neighborhood or the congregation of your synagogue. It might be the members of the religious group to which you belong, be it Hasidic or Reconstructionist. Perhaps it includes members of a Jewish social organization in which you and your family take an active part. If you live in Israel, your community might be the members of the kibbutz to which your family belongs. Alternatively, it can be a circle of friends, or "Havurim," who share Jewish events and holidays, education and ideas together.

These are all examples of local Jewish communities which have several things in common. They are often a center for fellowship and social activity, where events and holidays are celebrated together. The members of such a community may have organized a system for Jewish study, education and recreation. They may have formed a means of helping each other socially and/or financially. They may get together for social or political action and extend support to Jews in need outside their own local community.

The unity of the Jewish people has always been an important aspect of Judaism. Jewish tradition stipulates that no matter how pious, learned, rich or refined an individual may be, he must experience a sense of solidarity and kinship with *all* his fellow Jews, regardless of their status. In fact, before the observant Jew carries out a religious act, he declares in prayer that the act is being carried out in the name of *K'lal Yisroel*, all the Jewish people of the world.

The following is a story of two brothers, both leaders of their respective communities. One brother believes in the superiority of a learned, wealthy "elite." The other believes that all Jews are brothers.

The Two Brothers

In our town there were many groups, organizations, and study circles. But the *Hevrah Shas*, the fellowship which studied the Talmud daily, was the most honored of all. Those who belonged to it were the intellectual aristocracy. All who sought to leave behind their daily toil would gather after the Morning Service at the southern wall in the old synagogue, and experience true spiritual joy.

In my time, the leader of the *Hevrah Shas* was Rabbi Nehemiah. Rabbi Nehemiah was blessed with two "crowns": the crown of learning, and the crown of wealth. When one saw him during business hours in the market place, where he owned a big hardware store, one could not believe that this husky, aggressive merchant was a great scholar. But when one saw him in synagogue, wrapped in a long *tallit* with *tefillin* on forehead and arm, studying the open Gemara, one could not imagine that this studious, pious scholar had any earthly cares at all.

Nehemiah had a younger brother named Akiba. It was said that Akiba was even more learned than Nehemiah, but, unlike his older brother, he was a poor man. However, he was always cheerful and always content with his lot.

No two people could have been more different than these brothers. While Nehemiah was stern, strict, removed from people, Akiba was of a sweet disposition, loving people and enjoying their company. The poor especially would come to him for advice and guidance. He listened to all their troubles with kindness and patience, and gave generously of comfort, advice, and help.

Because they were so different, the townsmen called the older brother "Shammai," and the younger, "Hillel."

Of course, Akiba too was a member of the *Shas* fellowship. Often he would gently chide his older brother for snobbishness, for not associating with anyone outside his special group. Nehemiah, on the other hand, often rebuked his brother for hobnobbing with the poor, the "tailors and cobblers," as he called them.

In those days the number who studied Talmud daily began to dwindle. The older generation was passing and the young did not take its place....

One day the workers of the town, the "tailors and cobblers," decided to organize a Study Fellowship of their own, to study *Haye Adam* daily. They asked Akiba to be their leader.

When the news reached Nehemiah, he confronted his brother: "It is not proper for you to do this."

Whereupon Akiba answered him gently: "The Torah was given to all Israel."

Nehemiah's reply was immediate and stern: "Akiba, you will have to account for this. You are opening a new door...lowering standards. In the past, Jews sacrificed time and strength to learn....A Jew who could not pass the test gave honor to one who acquired learning with blood and sweat....There were standards then....Now, everyone can boast of 'scholarship'.... Every tailor and cobbler will become a Rabbi....The loss will be greater than the gain."

The argument grew more and more heated as Nehemiah's anger swelled. He realized at last that Akiba would not give in,

and he burst out:

"If you persist in doing this, I won't have anything more to do with you!"

From that day the brothers were separated. They did not visit each other, nor talk to one another. When Akiba's daughter was married, Nehemiah did not appear at the wedding. He sent a wedding gift through his wife, and people thought he did not want to mingle with the "tailors and cobblers" whom Akiba had invited.

Akiba's study group grew in numbers and popularity, as Nehemiah's dwindled. And Akiba's influence among the people grew. When he taught, crowds came to hear him. When the month of Elul came, Akiba would preach repentance to his people. Passers-by were amazed and moved to see Akiba's students listen in rapt attention, tears flowing from their eyes.

Akiba watched over his people like a shepherd. And they responded with love and reverence. Especially did they show their affection for their leader on Simhat Torah. Then they would all gather at his home, and carry him to the synagogue with song and hymn. They embraced him, and kissed the hem of his garments.

When Nehemiah saw all this, he remarked disdainfully: "Idol worship!"

One day the news spread: Akiba was ill. The doctor reported that his condition was critical. Akiba's people did everything possible for their beloved Rabbi. . . . They recited Psalms three times a day. Each one offered up private prayers. They made pilgrimages to the graves of saints, and implored their souls to intercede on behalf of their Rabbi. But Akiba grew worse.

A day before Akiba passed away, Nehemiah went to visit his brother. When the haughty, hard Nehemiah saw Akiba on his deathbed, he wept like a child. Akiba opened his eyes, recognized his brother. He wanted to raise his hand to greet him, but couldn't.

Nehemiah came closer and asked gently: "How are you feeling?"

Akiba did not answer. After a long pause, he said weakly: "Nehemiah. . ."

The brother bent over him and heard Akiba whisper: "I am near death."

"While life remains, hope in God's mercy!"

"My end is near," the sick man said. "Who will take care of them? Orphans. . . . With whom shall I leave them?"

Nehemiah forced the tears back: "I'll take care of your family! You need not worry!"

"I don't mean *them*. Nehemiah, I have one request to make of you."

"Anything I can do, I will do."

"I want your promise. Give me your hand on it."

Nehemiah gave him his hand.

"Nehemiah, after I die. . .*you* take my place and teach them '*Haye Adam*'."

Nehemiah hesitated. He hadn't expected such a request. . . . But his brother's eyes were on him.

"Will you?"

Nehemiah nodded his head.

When the week of mourning ended, Nehemiah took his brother's seat at the table of the *Haye Adam* Study Fellowship. As he took his brother's book in hand, his face softened, his voice lost its harsh tone. Indeed, he looked and spoke just as Akiba. And even more strange, when the lesson ended he had become the Nehemiah of old.

Thus he continued, until his dying day. . . .

M. Ben Eliezer.

Bar Mitzvah In The Local Community

"Bar Mitzvah in the shtetl was always a community event; a celebration for and by the people."

In the time of the Temple in Jerusalem, a boy of thirteen was often led by his father to the Temple priest from whom he would receive a blessing, moral counsel and a prayer "that he be granted a portion in the Torah and in the performance of good deeds." This was probably the forerunner of the Bar Mitzvah ceremony.

The earliest reference to a Bar Mitzvah celebration as we know it today appears in a thirteenth century manuscript by a German rabbi. The antisemitic persecutions at that time may have contributed to the emergence of the celebration of Bar Mitzvah. Parents sought divine protection for their children through religious ceremonies, which evoked community blessings. They also sought solace in community celebrations for temporary relief from the dismal realities of everyday life.

Bar Mitzvahs were occasions for community rejoicing and fellowship in the shtetls of Eastern Europe. Members of the community gathered together in the local synagogue, or *shul* as it was called, to hear the Bar Mitzvah boy read from the Torah on the Monday or Thursday following his thirteenth birthday. They were then invited to a *kiddush* of light refreshments in the synagogue or to a larger meal at the home of the young man's family, at which time the assembled community extended good wishes and blessings on the boy.

A detail from the work of folk artist Eliezer Sussman Ben Solomon, an eighteenth-century artist who painted modest wooden synagogues in Germany.

The Derashah— The Bar Mitzvah Speech

If the young man was a prodigy in the study of the *Talmud*, he might deliver a talmudic discourse, called a *derashah*, to his guests. This speech was meant to prove to the assembled community that the young man had been properly educated in Judaism. It was a mark of his intellectual accomplishments, his "thesis" into manhood.

Famous Yiddish storyteller Sholom Aleichem, born Solomon Rabinowitz, writes an autobiographic account of his Bar Mitzvah complete with sketches of his relatives and members of his community. The highlight is, of course, his derashah speech.

A Bar Mitzvah Speech

A Bar Mitzvah was a great and glorious event at the home of Nahum Rabinowitz. Old Minde guided the many preparations.

Clothed in holiday best and wearing her precious kerchief, old Minde ruled the servants with an iron hand. Her slightest bidding was obeyed instantly. No one dared move hand or foot without her consent. She decided on such doubtful matters as who should be invited to the party, who should sit at the head of the table, which courses should be served first, which last. Even the Bar Mitzvah boy did not escape her scolding and bustling. She warned him not to chew his nails, not to giggle, not to act like a clown—in short, not to be his usual mischievous self.

"Since the Lord, blessed be He, has spared us in His abundant mercy and has preserved us and allowed us to see this day of days, the least *you* can do is improve your conduct and behave like a man." Thus she reproached the cause of all the festivities. And while she reprimanded him, she wet her fingers and smoothed his forelocks—the remnant she had saved from Nahum's intentions. For Nahum, her son, had wanted to cut them off entirely, but Minde stopped him.

"When my eyes are closed your sons will be yours," she told him. "Then you may even make them gentiles, if you wish. But while I'm still alive, and as long as I breathe, I want to see God's image on their faces!"

A large crowd of friends accompanied Nahum Rabinowitz home after the synagogue service, with members of the entire family: Aunt Hannah and her sons, Uncle Pini and his sons, other relatives and friends.

Among those present was the teacher, Rabbi Moshe David Ruderman, dressed in his oversized Sabbath caftan and wearing a headgear of worn-out, time-faded plush. Self-effacing and forlorn, the Rabbi tried to curl up in a corner and lose himself. He spoke to no one; he barely touched the wine or the sweets. He sat desolate throughout the festivities, hunched over, inclining his head every now and then, covering his mouth with the folds of his caftan when he coughed.

At last the moment arrived: it was time for the Bar Mitzvah speech. The Bar Mitzvah boy climbed upon the table. Instantly the Rabbi's body straightened; he was awake and alert. His back was as straight as a ramrod, his bushy black eyebrows bristled, his sharp eyes met the eyes of his pupil, piercing them yet steadying

"Bar Mitzvah Speech" by Moritz Oppenheim (1799-1882).

them. His thumb, like the baton of an orchestra conductor, made a grand sweep upward. The sign to begin the speech had been given.

Atop the table, his pupil, the nervous, excited Bar Mitzvah boy, stood above the heads of his audience. Eyes watched him expectantly, waiting for the well-planned words to pour out. He became flustered, almost collapsed. Dark spots danced before his eyes, his knees shook, his tongue dried up, all his senses quivered. He felt as if he were walking on a delicate sheet of ice. In an instant the film would break, plunging him into the depths.

But the fear lasted only a moment. Glancing at the Rabbi and the sturdy sweep of his hand, the boy became calm. He began to speak, and his fear left him. His stage fright disappeared. His mind was crystal clear. His voice swelled and he felt

as if he stood on a broad, unshakeable bridge of iron. He was confident, his excitement grew, a glow penetrated his entire body, warm and sweet, such as he had never before experienced. His words flowed like rich oil, smooth as if poured from a jar.

Throughout the crucial hour that the Bar Mitzvah boy preached from the table, he was given over wholly to the speech. Still, he could not take his eyes from his audience. They sat there, clinging to his words. He watched their faces, their gestures.

Nothing escaped him. Here was Isaac Avigdor, his shoulders twitching, his eyes spreading fear like a robber's. There stood old Joshua, believed to have reached one hundred years of age this very day, his tongue wagging in his toothless mouth like the clapper of a bell. Near him, eyes closed, head turned to one side, stood his son Berka, well advanced in years. Close at hand was Asher Neidis, a well-fleshed man, broad of bone and belly, his silk caftan bursting at the seams.

Over there was Yosi Fruchstein, whose open mouth showed large artificial teeth, whose spectacles reflected the rays of the sun, whose beard was cut short and sparse. People gossiped that he was a "free-thinker." He often played chess with Nahum Rabinowitz, and was known to read forbidden books like *Mysteries of Paris*. At his side stood his younger brother, Michael, shrewd and quicksilver-y, always belittling everyone and everything. It was common knowledge that he permitted his gentile maid to put out the lights on Friday evening, and that he hobnobbed with such "characters" as Moshe Berger and Buni Konover, men known from their very youth to overlook the close trim given to their beards by the barber.

Israel Benditzky was there too. Long ago he had been nicknamed "Israel the Fiddler," though now he owned a fine home and was president of a synagogue. Full-bearded, full-bodied, he was indeed an important man in the community. No one dared call him "Fiddler" any more, not even behind his back, yet to this very day, he would gladly play at weddings.

Even Raphael the sexton was in the audience. Tense and intent, his ears turned to the address like funnels, he sat with his thin face all screwed up, even his nose at attention. Any moment, it seemed, he would slap his hands on the table and cry out his familiar Sabbath singsong: "Ten gulden for Kohen!"

No one escaped the Bar Mitzvah's eyes. Not even his playmates, the mischief-makers who at the beginning had made faces to get him to laugh. Now they were motionless, their mouths open, silent, wondering, envying.

But more than anyone else in the group, there was Uncle Pini. He was dressed in a beautiful silk caftan tied around his full waist by a woven sash, and in blue satin headgear. With one eye closed, Uncle Pini peered upward from his place of honor at the head of the table. His lips wore a wise smile, as if he were chuckling knowingly into his long beard and saying: "This young scoundrel is doing all right—you can't deny the obvious. But does he *daven* every day? Does he wash his hands before meals? Does he say prayers at bedtime? Does he avoid carrying a burden on Sabbath? I doubt it!"

And directly in front of him the Bar Mitzvah boy saw his father's face, bright and shining, as if a new light had been cast on it. He appeared the happiest man alive. He stood erect; he was taller by several inches. His lips moved in rhythm with the lips of his son. His face was radiant, and his eyes moved over the audience, to his brother Pini, to the Rabbi, to the mother of the Bar Mitzvah boy.

And the mother, dear little Haya Esther! There she stood, modest, humble, amid the women. Her head was covered with the Sabbath kerchief. She was nervous, and she sighed softly as she crackled her knuckles. Two tears, shining in the rays of the sun, rolled down her pale white cheeks wrinkled long before their time.

Why the tears? Were they tears of joy, of happiness, of pride? Or were they tears of pain and sorrow for the hardships, the troubles that had come to the Rabinowitz family? Perhaps she hears a still small voice whisper inside her heart—the heart of a mother—that this young son, her Bar Mitzvah boy holding forth so bravely, so clearly, was destined soon to stand over her grave and recite the Kaddish for her departed soul?

Who can penetrate the mysteries of a mother's heart? Who can guess the source of her tears?

Sholom Aleichem.

Later, particularly in Western Europe, the Bar Mitzvah occasion took on an even more festive air by being celebrated during the Sabbath morning service following the boy's thirteenth birthday. It then became customary for the young man to read from the Torah and the Haftorah, the prophetic portion of the day. Sometimes the young man would lead the entire Sabbath morning service.

As intense study of the *Talmud* by the young became less prevalent, the derashah was often replaced by a prayer recited by the Bar Mitzvah boy or a speech of gratitude to parents and community, and allegiance to God and the Jewish people. Though the wording of these speeches has changed through the centuries, the ideas have remained the same.

The following speech was given by Abraham Levy on his Bar Mitzvah, May 2, 1873, at Congregation Beth Jacob, Albany, New York. It is typical of its time, combining moral earnestness and filial devotion.

Bar Mitzvah Speech, 1873

My Beloved Parents, Kind Teacher, Friends All!

I am about to request your kind indulgence for I feel that I must speak and yet the respect, not to say the reverence which a boy like me must feel, when speaking before as worthy and numerous assembly of his seniors—overpowers me. Still I know I have your sympathy and for the same reasons, you will make kindest allowance for my shortcomings.

I know the great importance of this day, I know also what it is to be a Barmitzvah, it is to quit the comforts of careless childhood, and to cross the threshold of manhood, and responsibility. Today I am recognized as a member of the oldest religious community in the world and I have pledged to perform all the duties of an Israelite, and to obey that Law, which I myself have declared: Torath Emeth.—A true law.

Yea! That law is true, and today, as never before in my life have I uttered with more fervor and devotion the passage from our daily prayers:—[Hebrew, followed by English] "Praised be thou O Lord that thou has made me an Israelite."...

After you have heard my convictions, and the confessions of my faith, I now stand forth, to declare to you my determinations and resolutions. And may that Merciful Father in Heaven, who has preserved us unto this day, give me strength of mind, piety of heart, and [about five words missing] with his Brute firmness of will, to carry out truly and fully, all that which my religion requires of me. And you my honored friends, may bear witness to the honesty, and sincerity of purpose that dictate my words.

I declare myself an Israelite, and as my kind Teacher in his address to me truly remarked: "I will cleave to the religion of my fathers, and no worldly advantages, nor disadvantages, nor even persecutions, will be strong enough to induce me to change or forsake it."

And as I feel myself proud to be a descendant of that noble ancestry, Abraham, Isaac, and Jacob, stamped with the Seal of the Covenant, and believing firmly in the Law of Moses, I shall always be happy and ready, to defend that law, which today, I have chosen to be my light, and guide through this life, to a higher existence, and in this world. I shall live and die an Israelite. [Hebrew followed by English] "Hear O Israel, the Lord our God, the Lord is One" is the motto and the banner of our nation. We shall love him with all our hearts, fear him, and walk humbly before Him. He rewards the righteous and punishes the wicked, loves mercy, and commands us to love our neighbors, to love the stranger and to see in every human being, without distinction of creed, or race, our brother, and even to

Bar Mitzvah day in East End London, 1924.

have compassion with his Brute creation. He hates iniquity, and commands us not to endanger, or injure the life, interest or reputation, of our neighbor, for even if the arm of worldly Justice cannot reach us, He knows and sees everything and will reward us accordingly....

Kind Parents! God forbid that I should forget what you have been to me since my birth; in infancy you have nursed me, in sickness you have watched over me and with incessant care, you have protected my helpless childhood. No sacrifice was too hard for you to procure for me a liberal and religious education, so as to enable me to become a useful member of human society. And for all this benevolence and tender love, should I be ungrateful? Oh! No! my dear Parents, and therefore I promise you today, not only to love, to obey, and to honour you, but to strive with all my power to become the pride and pleasure, as well as the staff and support of your old age, which our Heavenly Father may grant you. And you my dear Brothers and Sisters will assist me, and unite your effort with mine, to that holy purpose.

May the Lord, God of Israel, strengthen me, and assist me to fulfill all the promises and pledges which I have vowed today.

And with the prayer of David I will close:–[Hebrew followed by English] "Create in me a pure heart O God! and renew a right spirit within me." Amen.

Abraham Levy.

This prayer was written in the second half of the 1800's by Benjamin Artom, rabbi of the Spanish and Portuguese Synagogue in London, England, to be recited by his Bar Mitzvah students.

Sephardic Bar Mitzvah Prayer, 1800's

O my God, and God of My Fathers:

On this solemn and sacred day, which marks my passage from boyhood to manhood, I humbly raise my eyes to Thee, and declare with sincerity and truth that henceforth I will observe all Thy commandments, and undertake to bear the responsibility of all my actions towards Thee.

In my earliest infancy I was brought within Thy sacred covenant with Israel, and today I again enter as an active, responsible member the pale of Thine elect congregation, in the midst of which I will never cease to glorify Thy holy Name before all nations.

Do Thou, O heavenly Father, hearken unto this my humble prayer, and bestow upon me Thy gracious blessings, so that my earthly life may be sustained and made happy by Thine ineffable mercies.

Teach me the way of Thy statutes, that I may obey them, and faithfully carry out Thy ordinances.

Dispose my heart to love Thee and to fear Thy holy Name, and grant me Thy support and the strength necessary to avoid the worldly dangers which beset the path lying before me.

Save me from temptation, so that I may observe Thy holy Law and those precepts on which human happiness and eternal life depend.

Thus, I will every day of my life trustfully and gladly proclaim:

Hear, O Israel, the Lord Is Our God, The Lord Is One!

Benjamin Artom.

The following tongue-in-cheek excerpt shows a more contemporary humorous attitude towards the Bar Mitzvah speech.

The Most Common Lines from Bar Mitzvah Speeches Today

1 "The first candle will be lit by..."
2 "Today I am a man, no matter *what* my mother says."
3 "If only my Uncle Yitz could be here..."
4 "I'd like to thank my teachers, without whose persistence and tone deafness..."
5 "Today I am an Israeli bond."
6 "If the band could stop playing already, I'd like to thank..."
7 "Unaccustomed as I am to public speaking..."
8 "I'd like to thank Dad for that roasting of his only son. But seriously, folks..."
9 "I'm especially flattered that my Aunt____is here, all the way from ____."
10 "It's a great thrill to finally be Bar Mitzvahed, because now I can finally drop out of Hebrew school and play in the little league like the other kids in the seventh grade."
11 "I can hardly wait to get home and see what's in these envelopes so many of you have handed me."

Allan Gould and Danny Siegel.

THE SEUDAT MITZVAH– THE BAR MITZVAH FEAST

"Two things make the bar mitzvah meal a 'rejoicing of mitzvah': the bar mitzvah's utterance of words of Torah, and his being called to read from the Torah in the synagogue. The joy of the occasion is the joy of Torah, as the bar mitzvah enters into his rightful inheritance, the inheritance of Israel. And all Israel rejoices with him."

Eliyahu Kitor.

The tradition of sharing a meal with the community as a means of celebration is steeped in Jewish tradition. There has always been a connection between food and religious celebration amongst Jews, and generous hospitality has always been a Jewish attribute. The Sabbath, Passover, Rosh Hashonah, Sukkot, and other holidays are celebrated around a festive meal, and much effort is put into the preparation of special foods for these holidays. A community feast usually follows a wedding ceremony and a circumcision, as it does a Bar Mitzvah.

The Bar Mitzvah feast probably began as a modest kiddush in medieval times. In the sixteenth century, however, it was classified a *seudat mitzvah*, a meal celebrating a commandment. The seudat mitzvah is a traditional means of expanding a commandment by celebration to prevent the commandment from being minimized. The importance of the Bar Mitzvah ceremony is in its religious significance; the feast that follows is a joyous way of emphasizing this significance.

The following article expresses the need for jubilant community celebration, especially as a contrast to the more tragic aspects of life. Celebration is part of the Jewish way of life as well as a part of Jewish continuity and survival.

Upstairs / Downstairs

April 12, 1981 was a day of contrasts at Congregation Shaare Tikvah. It seemed as if the synagogue building itself was torn between a tidal wave of solemnity and a strong undertow of exultation. Upstairs, in the main sanctuary, thirteen hundred persons sat spellbound as Elie Wiesel addressed a city-wide Holocaust memorial service. Downstairs, in the social hall, hundreds more had gathered at a luncheon to celebrate the bar mizvah of our synagogue president's youngest son. As rabbi of the congregation, I felt the day's tensions more acutely than most, for I attended both of these concurrent functions.

My afternoon of dissonance began with an appearance at the bar mizvah party. As the clock struck 1:00, I slipped upstairs to take my place on the *bimah* together with the other participants in the memorial. Following the service, I descended the stairs to find myself engulfed for a second time in a sea of music and joy. Only one word can describe my state of mind as I re-entered that bar mizvah party–disoriented.

Upstairs all was silence and outrage, hushed tones and tears. Wiesel spoke movingly of the untold sorrow caused by the loss of the six million. The chairman of the event charged us to remember the atrocities of the Third Reich and to transmit those memories to our children. A more strident note was sounded by the Midwest Counsel General of Israel who bade us to support a militarily strong Jewish homeland so that such horrors would not happen again. We rose–the *hazkarah* was sung, we recited *kaddish*–and then we left.

A group of war survivors dance the hora at the Munich, Germany train station before emigrating to Israel in 1948.

Downstairs, the mood was raucously and radically different. There laughter replaced hushed tones and tears. There trumpets, and not words of outrage, blared out for all to hear. There happy relatives did not stand in silence but instead danced on the table tops and shouted with glee.

Having just left a mournful sanctuary for this hall of celebration, one question formed in my mind: in this thirty-sixth year after Auschwitz, which of these two events was the more appropriate response to the Holocaust–the awesome solemnity upstairs or the sacred joy below? Each was fitting and proper in its own context and yet the question of greater appropriateness doggedly bothered my thoughts. I could find no resolution to this dilemma until I paged through the *haggadah* in preparation for Pesah occurring later that week.

The haggadah graphically recounts the earliest tragedy which befell our people, the enslavement in Egypt. In vivid detail we learn of pharoah's persecutions as he ordered our ancestors to perform bone-crushing labor in compulsory work-camps. We read of the enforced separation of families and the plot to exterminate systematically the male Israelite infants. All types of suffering known to man were visited upon our forebearers, yet somehow the *haggadah* transcends this motif of sorrow with a greater theme, the theme of liberation and divine redemption.

The beauty of the *seder* liturgy is that it neither ignores the first trials of our people in Egypt nor dwells solely upon them. Thus the *haggadah* provides us with a suggested prototype for interpreting other painful chapters in our history: remember the pain but focus on the subsequent redemption. And if we seek a model for responding to tragedy, the *haggadah* provides that too when it quotes the Torah: "and you shall tell your child on that day saying 'I do all of this because of that which God did for me when I went forth from Egypt.'" Our response to attempted

97

annihilation should be to raise generation after generation of Jewish children and to encourage them to ask four and even fourscore questions about our rich heritage. Then we must answer their questions lovingly and thoroughly and join with them in feasting and singing and telling tales during moments like the *seder*, moments of sacred joy.

The Israelites who went forth from Egypt shared both a bond of suffering and a bond of exaltation that came with divine redemption and revelation. From the tone of the *haggadah* it is easy to discern that the latter was the greater of the two ancient bonds. Yet, in our own times, it seems that we have inverted their order of importance. We now link ourselves one to another by invoking the tragedies of our recent past and by enumerating present and future dangers. We do so out of a sense of immediacy and pragmatism, for we have shared more moments of anxiety than of communal rapture in recent memory and because it is easier to rally a people and raise communal funds at times of crisis. By accentuating the bond of suffering we also act out of fear, not merely the justified fear that harm might come to Jews in Israel or in the Diaspora, but the fear that we are not capable of developing redemptive communal bonds based on a positive approach to Jewish life. If we cannot unite ourselves then let the memory of shared horror and the threat of its recurrence achieve this union for us.

The necessary commandment "survive" rings forth from all of our communal forums and we observe this commandment diligently through the activities of our defense and social service agencies. Perhaps it is time to add a second focus to Jewish life, the task of celebrating, attaining and even creating moments of sacred joy. Such an enterprise would involve a massive effort in Jewish education, both cognitive and affective, so that young and old might fully participate in our Sabbaths and festivals and celebrations rather than stand on the periphery as spectators or even as absentises. It would involve the creation of new worship modalities, utilizing music, poetry, religious drama, to augment the traditional liturgy in a way which graphically accents the themes of a given sacred occasion. It also would involve outreach to and support for those who are lonely—the poor, the widowed, the single, the elderly—so that none feels disenfranchised from the warmth of Jewish fellowship. Most importantly, it would involve the articulation of a Jewish life view which goes beyond survivalism and defiance to the formulation of a shared program to highlight and promote the creative religious and social aspirations of Jews in Israel and the Diaspora.

Each Pesah we chant the popular hymn *Dayyenu*. In the first stanza we declare that had God only ensured our physical survival by freeing us from Egypt, "*Dayyenu*", it would have been enough. Yet we know that it would not have been enough, for the song continues and does not cease until we thank God for giving us the Torah, the Sabbath, the land of Israel and the Holy Temple. Physical survival is a prerequisite, but in Jewish history, *lo lanu dai*, it has never been enough. With survival and remembrance must come the commitment to attain the means, the occasions, and the arenas through which our religious culture and social concerns can find full expression.

On Sunday, April 12, a memorial service was convened upstairs while beneath the band played on. Upstairs or down? *'Elyonim 'O tahtonim?* In this thirty-sixth year after Auschwitz which was the more appropriate response? I believe that the answer lay not only in the awesome solemnity above, but also in the sacred joy below.

Rabbi Howard A. Addison.

As the importance of the Bar Mitzvah as a life-cycle event grew, so did the festivities that followed. The meal, which started as a humble kiddush meant to bring joy and togetherness to the family and the community, sometimes became an elaborate banquet for hundreds of people. Fearing loss of religious meaning as well as reprisal from jealous, hostile non-Jewish neighbors, some Jewish communities established sumptuary codes to limit extravagance. As early as 1659, the Jewish Council of the Four Lands in Poland decreed that no more than ten strangers be invited to the Bar Mitzvah feast—and one of the ten had to be a poor man. The Jewish Sumptuary Code of Ancona, Italy in 1766 declared that a festive meal be made only for the immediate family, though coffee and sweetmeats might be served to those who came to the home to extend their congratulations.

In recent times, there has been much concern over the unnecessary extravagance of the Bar Mitzvah feast and party. The fear is that with so much emphasis on the material, the dignity and religious significance of Bar Mitzvah will be lost.

Canadian writer Mordecai Richler takes a satiric view of the cast-of-hundreds Bar Mitzvah. In his novel *The Apprenticeship of Duddy Kravitz*, he creates a Bar Mitzvah script which takes the Bar Mitzvah celebration to the ultimate limit—that of a film extravaganza.

The Screening

DUDLEY KANE ENTERPRISES
with M. Cohen, Inc., Metal Merchants
presents
A Peter John Friar Production
HAPPY BAR-MITZVAH, BERNIE!
executive producer d. kravitz
directed, written, and narrated by
j.p. friar
additional dialogue by
rabbi harvey goldstone, m.a.

'So far so good.'
'Would you mind taking off your hat please, Elsie?'
'Sh.'

1. *A close-shot of an aged finger leading a thirteen year old boy's hand over the Hebrew letters of a prayer book.*
2. *Grandfather Cohen is seated at the dining-room table with Bernard, teaching him the tunes of the Torah.*

NARRATOR: *Older than the banks of the Nile, not so cruel as the circumcision rite of the Zulus, and even more intricate than a snowflake is the bar-mitzvah . . .*

'Hey, what's that he said about niggers being clipped? I thought—'
'—comparative religion. I take it at McGill.'
'Comparative *what*? I'll give you such a *schoss*.'

3. *In the synagogue Bernard stands looking at the Holy Ark. His reaction.*

CHOIR: *Hear O Israel the Lord is Our God the Lord is One.*

4. *Grandfather Cohen, wearing a prayer shawl, hands the Torah to Mr Cohen who passes it to his son.*

NARRATOR: *From generation to generation, for years before the birth of Christ . . .*

'Hssssss . . .'
'O.K., smart guy. Shettup!'

NARRATOR: *. . . the rule of law has been passed from hand to hand among the Chosen People. Something priceless, something cherished . . .*

'Like a Chinchilla.'

'One more crack out of you, Arnie,' Mr. Cohen said, 'and out you go.'

In the darkness Duddy smiled, relieved.

NARRATOR: . . .*a thing of beauty and a joy forever.*

5. *The wrappings come off and Mr. Cohen holds the Torah aloft.*

CHOIR: [RECITES IN HEBREW]*In the beginning God created heaven and earth. . .*

6. *Camera closes in on Torah*

NARRATOR: . . .*In the beginning there was the Word. . .There was Abraham, Isaac, and Jacob. . .There was Moses. . .*

AS CHOIR HUMS IN BACKGROUND
King David. . .Judas Macabee. . .
CHOIR TO CLIMAX
. . .*and, in our own time, Leon Trotsky. . .*

'What's that?'

'His *bar-mitzvah* I would have liked to have seen. Trotsky!'

NARRATOR: . . .*in all those years, the Hebrews, whipped like sand by the cruel winds of oppression, have survived by the word. . .the law. . .*

7. *A close-shot of a baby being circumcised.*

'Lock the doors. Here comes the dirty part.'

'Shame on you.'

'Awright, Sarah. O.K. You've seen one before. You don't have to pretend you're not looking.'

NARRATOR: . . .*and through the centuries the eight-day-old Hebrew babe has been welcomed into the race with blood.*

TOM-TOMS BEAT IN BACKGROUND. HEIGHTENING.

8. [MONTAGE] *Lightning. African tribal dance. Jungle fire. Stukas diving. A jitterbug contest speeded up. Slaughtering of a cow. Fireworks against a night sky. More African dancing. Torrents of rain. An advertisement for Maiden-Form bras upsidedown. Blood splashing against glass. A lion roars.*

'Wow!'

'Are you alright, *Zeyda*?'

DRUMS TO CLIMAX. OUT.

9. *A slow dissolve to close-up of Bernard Cohen's shining morning face.*

NARRATOR: *This is the story of one such Hebrew babe, and how at the age of thirteen he was at last accepted as an adult member of his tribe.*

'If you don't feel well, *Zeyda*, I'll get you a glass of water.'

NARRATOR: *This is the story of the bar-mitzvah of Bernard son of Moses. . . . . .*

10. *A smiling Rabbi Goldstone leads Bernard up the aisle of the Temple. In the background second-cousins and schoolmates wave and smile at the camera.*

'Good,' Duddy said. 'Excellent.' He had asked Mr. Friar to work Rabbi Goldstone into every possible shot.

'Look, there I am! Did you see me, Mommy?'

'You see Harry there picking his nose? If he'd known the camera—'

'A big joke!'

11. *As Bernard and Rabbi Goldstone reach the prayer stand.*

NARRATOR: *As solemn as the Aztec sacrifice, more mysterious than Helen's face, is the pregnant moment, the meeting of time past and time present, when the priest and his initiate each ho'mat.*

Rabbi Goldstone coughed. 'That means priest in the figurative sense.'

'He's gone too far,' Duddy whispered to Yvette. 'Jeez.'

CHOIR: [SINGING IN HEBREW] *Blessed is the Lord our God, Father of Abraham, Isaac, and Jacob. . .*

'There, *Zeyda*, isn't that nice?'

'Oh, leave him alone, Henry.'

'Leave him alone? I think he's had another stroke.'

12. *As Bernard says his blessings over the Torah the camera pans*

around the Temple. Aunt Sadie giggles shyly. Ten-year-old Manny Schwartz crosses his eyes and sticks out his tongue. Grandfather Cohen looks severe. Mr. Cohen wipes what just might be a tear from his eye. Uncle Ernie whispers into a man's ear. The man grins widely.

13. *A close shot of Bernard saying his blessings. The camera moves in slowly on his eyes.*

BRING IN TOM-TOMS AGAIN.

14. *Cut to a close shot of circumcision again.*

'It's not me,' Bernie shouted. 'Honest, guys.'

'Atta boy.'

'Do you think this'll have a bad effect on the children?'

'Never mind the children. I've got such a pain there now you'd think it was me up there.'

15. *Résumé shot of Bernard saying his Haftorah.*

NARRATOR: *The young Hebrew, now a fully accepted member of his tribe, is instructed in the ways of the world by his religious adviser.*

16. *A two-shot of Rabbi Goldstone and Bernard.*

NARRATOR: *'Beginning today,' the Rabbi tells him, 'you are old enough to be responsible for your own sins. Your father no longer takes them on his shoulders.'*

AS CHOIR HUMS ELGAR'S 'POMP AND CIRCUMSTANCE.'

17. *Camera pans round Temple again. Cutting back again and again to Bernard and the Rabbi.*

SUPERIMPOSE KIPLING'S 'IF' OVER THE ABOVE.

NARRATOR: *'Today you are a man, Bernard son of Moses.'*

18. [MONTAGE] *Lightning. Close-shot of head of Michelangelo's statue of David. Cartoon of a Thurber husband. African tribal dance. Close-shot of a venereal disease warning in a public urinal.*

'*Zeyda*, one minute.'

'You'd better go with him, Henry.'

Soldiers marching speeded up. Circumcision close-up again. Upside down shot of a hand on a woman's breast.

'Hey,' Arnie shouted, 'can you use a new casting director, Kravitz?'

'Haven't you any appreciation for the finer things?'

'Hoo-haw.'

Duddy bit his hand. The sweat rolled down his forehead. 'This is meant to be serious, Arnie. Oh, he's such a fool.' *A lion roars. Close-shot of Bernard's left eye. A pair of black panties catch fire. Lightning. African tribal dance.*

NARRATOR: *Today you are a man and your family and friends have come to celebrate.*

GIUSEPPI DI STEFANO SINGS DRINKING SONG FROM
LA TRAVIATA.

19. *Close shot of hands pouring a large scotch.*

20. *Cut to general shots of guests at Temple kiddush.*

'There I am!'

'Look at Sammy, stuffing his big fat face as usual.'

'There I am *again*!'

'What took you so long, Henry?'

'Did I miss anything?'

'Aw. Where's the *Zeyda*?'

'He's sitting outside in the car. Hey, was that me?'

'I'd like to see this part again later, please.'

'Second the motion.'

NARRATOR: *Those who couldn't come sent telegrams.*

21. *Hold a shot of telegrams pinned against green background.*

AS CHOIR HUMS AULD LANG SYNE.

NARRATOR: 'HAPPY BAR-MITZVAH, BERNIE. BEST UNCLE HERBY'... 'MAY YOUR LIFE BE HAPPY AND SUCCESSFUL. THE SHAPIRO BROTHERS AND MYRNA'...'BEST WISHES FOR HEALTH, HAPPINESS, AND SUCCESS FROM THE WINNIPEG BRANCH OF THE COHENS...SURPRISE PARCEL FOLLOWS'...'MY HEART GOES OUT TO YOU AND YOURS TODAY. MYER'....

'You notice Lou sent only a Greetings Telegram? You get a special rate.'

'He's had a bad year, that's all. Lay off, Molly.'

'A bad year! He comes from your side of the family, you mean.'

NARRATOR: *Those who came did not come empty-handed.*

'Try it some time.'

22. *They came with tributes for the boy who had come of age. Camera pans over a table laden with gifts. Revealed are four Parker 51 sets, an electric razor, a portable record player...*

'Murray got the player wholesale through his brother-in-law.'

...three toilet sets, two copies of Tom Sawyer, five subscriptions to the National Geographic Magazine, a movie projector, a fishing rod and other angling equipment, three cameras, a season's ticket to hockey games at the Forum, a set of phylacteries and a prayer shawl, a rubber dinghy, a savings account book open at a first deposit of five hundred dollars, six sport shirts, an elaborate chemistry set, a pile of fifty silver dollars in a velvet-lined box, at least ten credit slips (worth from twenty to a hundred dollars each) for Eaton's and Morgan's, two sets of H.G. Wells's Outline of History.

AS CHOIR SINGS 'HAPPY BIRTHDAY, BERNIE!'

23. *Hold a shot of numerous cheques pinned to a board. Spin it.*

'Dave's cheque is only for twenty-five bucks. Do you know how much business he gets out of Cohen every year?'

'If it had been Lou you would have said he had a bad year. Admit it.'

'Hey, Bernie,' Arnie yelled, 'how many of those cheques bounced? You can tell us.'

'I was grateful for all of them,' Bernie said, 'large or small. It's the thought that counts with me.'

'Isn't he sweet?'

'Sure,' Arnie said, 'but he could have told me that before.'

24. *A shot of Rabbi Goldstone's study. Bernard sits in an enormous leather chair and the Rabbi paces up and down, talking to him.*

NARRATOR: *But that afternoon, in the good Rabbi's study, the young Hebrew learns that there are more exalted things in this world besides material possessions, he is told something of the tragic history of his race, how they were exploited by the ancient Egyptian imperialists, how reactionary dictators from Nehru to Hitler persecuted them in order to divert the working-classes from the true cause of their sorrows, he learns – like Candide – that all is not for the best in the best of all possible worlds.*

AS AL JOLSON SINGS 'ELI, ELI.'

25. *Rabbi Goldstone leads Bernard to the window and stands behind him, his hands resting on the lad's shoulders.*

'Five'll get you ten that right now he's asking Bernie to remind his father that the Temple building campaign is lagging behind schedule.'

Rabbi Goldstone coughed loudly.

NARRATOR (RECITES): *I am a Jew: hath not a Jew eyes? Hath not a Jew hands, organs, dimensions, senses, affections, passions, fed with the same food, hurt with the same weapons, subject to the same diseases, healed by the same oils, warmed and cooled by the same winter and summer as a Christian is? If you prick him does he not bleed?*

26. *Rabbi Goldstone autographs a copy of his book, Why I'm Glad To Be A Jew, and hands it to Bernard.*

27. *Hold a close-shot of the book.*

From there the movie went on to record the merry-making and odd touching interludes at the dinner and dance. Relatives and friends saw themselves eating, drinking, and dancing. Uncles and aunts at the tables waved at the camera, the kids made funny faces, and the old people sat stonily. Cuckoo Kaplan did a soft-shoe dance on the head table. As the camera closed in on the dancers Henry pretended to be seducing Morrie Applebaum's wife. Mr. Cohen had a word with the band leader and the first *kazatchka* was played. Timidly the old people joined hands and began to dance around in a circle. Mr. Cohen and some spirited others joined in the second one. Duddy noticed some intruders at the sandwich table. He did not know them by name or sight, but remembering, he recognized that they were FFHS boys and he smiled a little. The camera panned lovingly about the fish and jugs and animals modelled out of ice. It closed in and swallowed the bursting trumpeter. Guests were picked up again, some reeling and others bad-tempered, waiting for taxis and husbands to come round with the car outside the temple.

And Mr. Cohen, sitting in the first row with his legs open like an inverted nutcracker to accommodate his sunken belly, thought, it's worth it, every last cent or what's money for, it's cheap at any price to have captured my family and friends and foolish rabbi. He reached for Gertie's hand and thought I'd better not kiss Bernie. It would embarrass him.

AS CHOIR SINGS HALLELUJAH CHORUS.

74. *Rear-view long shot. Mr Cohen and Bernard standing before the offices of M. Cohen, Inc., Metal Merchants.*

FADE OUT.

Nobody spoke. Duddy began to bite his fingernails and Yvette pulled his hand away and held it.

'A most edifying experience,' Rabbi Goldstone said. 'A work of art.'

Everybody began to speak at once.

'Thank you very much, indeed,' Mr Friar said. 'Unfortunately the best parts were left on the cutting room floor.'

'Play it again.'

'Yeah!'

Mordecai Richler, from *The Apprenticeship of Duddy Kravitz.*

COMMUNAL RESPONSIBILITY

"When you reap the harvest of your field, you shall not reap your field to its very edge, nor shall you gather the stray ears of corn. Likewise, you shall not pick your vineyard bare, nor gather up the grapes that have fallen. You shall leave these for the poor and the stranger."

Leviticus 19:9-10.

The idea of communal loyalty and responsibility amongst Jews dates back to biblical times. Originally a nation of farmers, Jews were instructed in the Bible to leave part of their harvest for the poor. Another biblical law provides for both the rejuvenation of the land and for the needy. Each seventh year the land was to lie unworked. Whatever grew by itself that year belonged to the poor.

The biblical story of Ruth and Naomi is a fine illustration of this tradition of communal responsibility. When Ruth and Naomi return to Bethlehem, heartbroken and penniless, they are allowed to glean in the fields, according to the age-old Jewish precept of sharing with the poor and the stranger.

The Book of Ruth

In the time when the judges ruled, there was a famine in the land of Judah; so a man named Elimelech from Bethlehem went to live in Moab, he and his wife Naomi and their two sons. Elimelech died, and Naomi was left with her two sons, Mahalon and Kilion, who married Moabite women, one named Orpah, and the other–Ruth. After about ten years, both Mahalon and Kilion died, so that the woman was bereft of her two children as well as her husband.

When she heard that the Lord had remembered his people in Judah and given them food, she left Moab together with her daughters-in-law to return to her own country. But, as they were setting out, Naomi said to her two daughters-in-law: "You go back, each of you to her mother's house. May the Lord treat you as kindly as you have treated the dead and me. May the Lord help each of you find a home in the house of her husband." Then she kissed them. "No," they replied, "we will go back with you to your people."

"Turn back, my daughters," Naomi said, "why should you go with me? Have I any more sons to be husbands to you? No, my daughters, my plight is worse than yours; the hand of the Lord has gone forth against me." Again they wept; Orpah kissed her mother-in-law goodby, but Ruth clung to her.

Naomi said: "Look, your sister-in-law has turned back to her people and to her gods; turn back after her." But Ruth said: "Entreat me not to leave you and to turn back from following you; wherever you go, I will go; wherever you stay, I will stay; your people shall be my people, and your God shall be my God; wherever you die, I will die, and there will I be buried. May the Lord punish me time and again if anything but death parts me from you!" When Naomi saw that she was determined to go with her, she said no more.

The two went on until they came to Bethlehem. Upon their arrival in Bethlehem the whole town was stirred, and the women said: "Is this Naomi?" But she said to them: "Do not call me Naomi; call me Mara, for the Almighty has dealt very bitterly with me. I left here when I was rich, and the Lord has brought me back empty-handed."

The barley harvest was just beginning when Naomi and Ruth reached Bethlehem. So Ruth said to Naomi: "Let me go to the fields and glean ears of corn after one who will be kind to me." "Go, my daughter," Naomi answered. So Ruth went and gleaned in the fields after the harvesters, and she happened to come to the field belonging to Boaz, a kinsman of Naomi's husband. Just then Boaz came out from Bethlehem and said to the harvesters: "May the Lord be with you!" They replied: "May the Lord bless you!"

From the Book of Ruth 2 : 5, an engraving by Gustave Doré (1830-1883).

"Whose girl is this?" Boaz asked the foreman of the harvesters. The foreman replied: "It is the Moabite girl who came back with Naomi. She asked to be allowed to glean among the sheaves after the harvesters, and she has been working ever since morning, without resting even for a moment."

Then Boaz said to Ruth: "Now listen, my daughter. Do not go to glean in another field; do not leave this one, but stay close to my maidservants. Keep your eyes on the field they are reaping and follow them. Whenever you are thirsty, go to the water jars and drink. I have been well informed of all that you have done for your mother-in-law since the death of your husband, of how you left your father and mother and the land of your birth and came to a people who were strange to you. May the Lord reward you for what you have done; may you receive full recompense from the Lord God of Israel, under whose wings you have taken refuge."

She answered: "Thank you, my lord, for speaking kindly to me, even though I am not one of your own servants."

At mealtime Boaz said to her: "Come here and eat some of our bread; dip your slice in the vinegar." So she sat beside the harvesters, and he handed her roasted grains. She ate till she was satisfied, and had some left over. When she got up to glean, Boaz gave orders to his servants: "Let her glean even among the sheaves, and do not be rude to her."

So she gleaned in the field till evening. Then she beat out what she had gleaned and took it away with her to the town. Her mother-in-law asked her: "Where did you glean today? Where did you work? A blessing on the man who was friendly to you!" So she told her mother-in-law that the man's name was Boaz. Then Naomi said: "May he be blessed by the Lord, who has not ceased to be kind to the living and to the dead! The man is a relative of ours; he is one of our near kinsmen."

"Furthermore," said Ruth, "he told me to keep close to his servants till they have finished all his harvesting." But Naomi said: "It is well, my daughter, that you go out with his girls, so as not to be molested in another field." So she kept close to the girls of Boaz as she gleaned until the end of the barley and wheat harvests.

Then Naomi said to her: "Boaz is winnowing barley tonight at the threshing floor. Wash yourself, put on your best clothes, and go down to the threshing floor, but do not reveal your presence to the man until he has finished eating and drinking. Note the place where he lies down; then uncover his feet and lie down there; and he will tell you what to do."

She went down to the threshing floor and did just as her mother-in-law had told her. At midnight the man was startled; he discovered a woman lying at his feet. "Who are you?" he asked. She replied: "I am Ruth; take me in marriage, for you are a close relative." And he said: "May the Lord bless you, my daughter. Have no fear, my daughter, I will do for you all that you ask. It is true that I am a kinsman, but there is a nearer kinsman than myself. If he will do his duty, good and well; if not, I will."

So she lay at his feet until morning, then she went back to the city. "How did you fare, my daughter?" her mother-in-law asked. And she told her all that Boaz had done for her, saying: "He gave me these six measures of barley, for he said that I must not go back empty-handed."

Boaz found the kinsman and asked him if he would buy the parcel of land which belonged to Elimelech. "I will," the man replied. Then Boaz said: "When you buy the field from Naomi, you are also buying Ruth, the widow, so as to carry on the name of her dead husband along with his inheritance." But the kinsman answered: "I cannot, for fear of injuring my own inheritance. Take over my right of redemption yourself, for I cannot redeem the property."

Boaz married Ruth, and she bore a son. Then the women said to Naomi: "Blessed be the Lord who has not left you this day without a kinsman! May the boy's name be renowned in Israel! He will renew your life and nourish your old age, for he is the child of your daughter-in-law, who loves you and is better than seven sons to you." They named the baby Obed. He was the father of Jesse, who in turn was the father of David.

From The Concise Jewish Bible, edited by Philip Birnbaum.

"If a person resides in a town 30 days, he becomes responsible for contributing to the soup kitchen; three months, to the charity box; six months, to the clothing fund; nine months, to the burial fund; and twelve months, for contributing to the repair of the town walls."

Babylonian *Talmud*, tractate *Bava Batra*, 8a.

Because Jews lived in many places where they were denied citizenship, and were segregated into ghettos throughout history, they were always inclined to help themselves and each other, rather than going outside their community.

A tzedakah system was followed that had been used in the days of the Second Temple. Each community had a community chest called a *kuppah*, a charity bowl in which food was kept for the hungry, a clothing fund and a burial fund. Members were taxed according to their means as part of this system. Leaders of the community, called *gabbae tzedakah*, were chosen to be in charge of collecting and distributing communal aid. It was said by the rabbis that a Jewish community with no charity box was not worth living in.

The following story is in the spirit of communal self-help. It is about the poor community of Voinovke in Eastern Europe and how members of the community, after much deliberation and disagreement, learn to compromise and help themselves.

The Poor Community

The little town of Voinovke, which consists of forty houses and thirty-five householders, since five of the houses stand empty, rocked and rumbled and boiled like a steam on the eve of Passover, when the snow begins to melt. But it wasn't the eve of Passover. It was a week before Rosh Hashonoh, and the community had no prayer leader.

In the nearby town of Yachnovke, which is several times larger than Voinovke, one could not only get a prayer leader, but quite a good one—with a neck, a double chin, and in general a cantor's bearing, only he would want to be well paid, and that was the trouble! The town of Voinovke had already disposed of its few public rubles on a cantor whom, through ill luck, the past summer had brought; he had prayed a full Sabbath service with a choir of six. In a way, it had been worth it: since Voinovke had been Voinovke, it had not heard such beautiful singing. The synagogue, which is over two hundred years old, as the older folks tell it, barely survived the cantor and his choir. The windows trembled, the walls shook, and from the ceiling big chunks of plaster fell. In great wonderment the community gave this cantor and his choir all of its public money, and now, a week before Rosh Hashonoh, it suddenly realized that it didn't have a single penny with which to hire a prayer leader. So the townspeople gathered in the synagogue to discuss the problem.

"That was certainly one of the most foolish things in the world!" exclaimed Ariah Leib the tailor, who looks upon himself as a Jew of some standing, since he has a long beard and a little boy who studies in the Yachnovke yeshiva.

"What a thing to do! It could happen only with us," said Chaim the glazier in support of his friend. "In the middle of the year to give a cantor all of our money!"

"Foolishness! Sheer foolishness!" added Chanon the teacher, shrugging his shoulders.

"You know what my decision would be?" said Zorach the shoemaker, stroking his beard in the manner of a rabbi. "I would have those who hired the cantor pay for a prayer leader with their own money. That's my advice," he said gravely, as if

Portrait of Jews in Grodzisk, a town near Warsaw, in the 1930's, by Roman Vishniac.

everything depended on his advice.

"But go find out who hired him! All of us hired him," said Zalmon the smith. "All of us wanted at least once in our lives to hear some religious singing. It's hardly an unworthy desire. But when? When the town is rich! A Yachnovke can afford to spend a few rubles for a cantor in the middle of the year, but not we paupers."

"Well, what shall we do?" asked several voices in the synagogue.

"It's very serious," answered one.

"Chaikel Sheps, you will pray with the Sabbath tune," said Zorach the shoemaker to the leader of the Sabbath prayers.

Chaikel Sheps does have a bit of a voice but doesn't know any prayer tunes other than those of the Sabbath.

"Try, Chaikel, try!" said several of the householders. "Make up your mind!"

Chaikel Sheps got red in the face and weakly replied, "I am afraid."

"Try, try! *Ha-me-lech!*" – Zalmon the smith showed him how.

"Aye, you can do it all by yourself," chimed in Chanon the teacher and went on, "*Yo-shev-el-chi-seh ram-veh-noh-soh-oh-oh! Ai-ai-ai-ai-ai-aai!*"

The whole gathering joined in, and for a few minutes the synagogue rang with the tunes of the High Holidays.

"Now everybody knows it, but when Rosh Hashonoh comes nobody will remember," one householder remarked.

Everybody took this idea seriously, and the gathering settled into deep thought.

"You know, we have no one to blow the *shofar* either," announced the *shammes*, in the middle of everything, from the Torah-reading platform.

The group was startled.

"How come? Where is Nachman?"

It seems we Nachman, a pale thin young man of about twenty, who has "eating days" and is studying by himself, had for two years blown the ram's horn for nothing.

"This year I will blow in the village of Sosnovtchine. They're giving me three rubles–three rubles..." he managed to stammer, fearing for his very skin, which had been clothed by the community.

"You're a cheapskate!" someone called out.

"A ruffian!" another shouted.

"One who always eats without paying," a third said, sneering.

A torrent of words poured down on poor Nachman. He felt as if he were being pricked with needles. "I have to earn something for a winter coat. I cannot–" he pleaded. "Forgive me, but the winter is cold."

"What do people want from him really?" they asked, retreating. "He needs a winter coat. He is going around with nothing on, naked..."

"It really is so," everybody agreed.

"That means we have neither a prayer leader nor a *shofar* blower."

"It seems we have no Torah reader either," admitted the *shammes* from the platform.

"What do you mean?" They were startled. "Where is Old Peshes? Where is he? Where is he?"

"Old Peshes will also read in Sosnovtchine," confessed Nachman, as if he were somehow guilty. "He is getting two rubles."

The group was stricken. Some lowered their heads, as if looking for advice, while others lifted their heads toward the ceiling and stood deep in thought for a few minutes.

"What's there to think about?" asked one. "These High Holidays we'll pray individually. No more congregation."

"A pretty story, and a short one!" said another, laughing bitterly.

"This has to be written down in the permanent record."

"No more Voinovke!"

"Let's all chip in and hire someone with our own money," suggested Chanon the teacher, and was immediately taken aback by his own words.

"All right. Give me a ruble," said Zalmon the smith, extending his hand.

"I have none," said Chanon, shamefaced, "but there are house-holders who do have."

"Who has?"

"Nobody has!"

"The holidays that are coming–they're no trifle!"

The synagogue was in a turmoil. Everybody offered advice, but none of it was good.

Suddenly the old *shammes* banged the table on the platform, and everyone became quiet.

"I have a solution. Keep quiet awhile."

"Really? Really?" they all exclaimed impatiently.

The *shammes* inhaled deeply, took a powerful smell of snuff, wiped his nose, and finally spoke.

"This is the story. During the summer our community did something very foolish. We wasted our few rubles on a triviality. We forgot our poverty, our station, and we yearned to hear a cantor. Who knows really who he is! A cantor who rides from town to town can hardly be such a pious man. A worthy cantor sits home. But the story is–well, it is a thing of the past. The conclusion is: we are left without a prayer leader for the High Holidays, without a Torah reader–absolutely without a thing. And if you want to know something else, the *shofar* itself is not as it should be. Now it will still blow, one way or another; but when Rosh Hashonoh comes, there will have to be so much blowing–a *trooeh, a shvorim, a tekieh gdoleh*–it will surely falter. Even last year it hesitated, if you will recall–I recall very well–and Nachman is a good blower.''

Everybody looked at Nachman, and he blushed.

"Therefore my advice is that this year we should become partners with the Sosnovtchine *minyan*; that is, we should pray there this year. Walking is permitted, and altogether it is three and a half *versts*; it will be a pleasant walk. We shall all save ourselves headaches: where shall we get a prayer leader, a Torah reader, a horn blower and also a horn? Because the horn, I repeat, the horn will give up on Rosh Hashonoh. Surely it won't be able to manage a *trooeh shvorim*–it is too old and already has a few faults. All that remains for us is Sosnovtchine."

After the *shammes*'s talk they all began to grumble.

"From the town to the village, and on Rosh Hashonoh–no!"

"Let those yeshiva students come here!"

"What sort of high-and-mightys have they become?"

"In the past the yeshiva students used to come to us to pray."

"Now that they have learned Hebrew they make a *minyan* at home."

"Never mind the Hebrew, I'm sure they can count money."

"What do they lack? They have the best: bins filled with potatoes, with kraut, with chicken, with eggs–"

"Sour cream, butter and cheese–"

"May all troubles fall on their heads!"

"Sh-sh, don't curse them. It is the month of the High Holidays."

"Who is cursing? Who? Who?"

"Nobody, nobody..."

"Who has any complaints against them?"

"Berke of Sosnovtchine is a fine Jew; it will be a pleasure to pray in his home–a house as big as a field, three times the size of our synagogue."

"A fine Jew!"

"And what's wrong with the other yeshiva students? They're nice people!"

"Of course!"

"So it is settled that this year we'll pray in Sosnovtchine?"

"There is no other solution."

"A fine thing! As I'm a Jew, a mountain has lifted from my back!"

"What a mountain!"

"We must send someone to find out if he'll let us."

"What a question! It will be an honor to him!"

"It's no small thing! Townspeople coming to pray in a village!"

And the meeting ended in peace.

On the morning of the first day of Rosh Hashonoh, when the townspeople, on their way to Sosnovtchine, passed their old, dilapidated synagogue, standing there with cloudy eyes, woebegone and orphaned, their hearts felt sore and tight, and silently, without words, only with their eyes, they begged its forgiveness.

Abraham Reisen.

Early rabbinical authorities outlined seven areas of communal responsibility: (1) giving food and drink to the needy, (2) clothing the naked, (3) visiting the sick, (4) burying the dead and comforting the mourners, (5) redeeming the captive, (6) educating orphans and sheltering the homeless, and (7) providing poor girls with dowries. Raphael Patai, Jewish anthropologist and historian, writes about the history of Jewish communal charity.

The Practice of Communal Responsibility

From the thirteenth century, Jewish charitable societies were organized all over Europe for the practice of these seven charities. The members paid weekly dues and, in addition, were subject to various fees. In some places, these societies proliferated (in Rome, their number reached thirty; in the small Verona community, fifteen) and became highly specialized, and subsequently a tendency for centralization developed. Common to all Jewish communities, even the smallest and poorest ones, was the maintenance of organized charity institutions which made it entirely impossible for any individual Jew to shirk his moral obligations toward his poorer fellow men.

The practice of charity became an almost instinctive Jewish response to such an extent that there was no difference among the Jewish communities, however far removed from one another and however different the surrounding Gentile environment. Nor did it make much difference whether a community was big or small; those who had, even if their means were most limited, gave to those in need, whether local people or transients. The latter, even in the smallest and poorest community, would be invited for a meal and given a place to spend the night....

From the nineteenth century in the Western world, the traditional Jewish charity institutions were gradually replaced by modern social welfare agencies. The very term "charity" fell into opprobrium (except for the continued use of its Hebrew equivalent at traditional burials, where the mourners and their friends are endlessly admonished to give donations because "charity delivereth from death"). However, while the support of the poor, the sick, and the stranger, the orphan and the widow has thus been transformed into modern and largely depersonalized aid and service institutions, the age-old Jewish commitment to the principle that those who have must give to those who have not has in no way diminished.

In the Western world, where after the Emancipation a large Jewish middle and wealthy class developed, the dimensions and variety of Jewish welfare, social service, and other philanthropic institutions rapidly surpassed their Gentile equivalents. The Jewish interest in the welfare of all Jews embraced not only those near home but also those in remote lands; from the middle of the nineteenth century Jewish organizations were set up in the United States, France, England, and Germany, whose purpose was to aid the needy Jews in the less fortunate communities of Eastern Europe and the Muslim world.

In America, the establishment and maintenance of hospitals has become since the 1850's a hallmark of all the sizable Jewish communities, and it has been observed that in virtually all cities with a Jewish population of over 30,000 there are hospitals under Jewish auspices, which in general are among the best such facilities. In addition, there are highly specialized institutions serving the blind, the deaf, the dumb, the tubercular, the insane, the delinquent, the defective, as well as boarding and foster home placement and homemaker services, orphanages, sheltered workshops, recreation programs, etc. Much care was devoted to the new immigrants whose integration in the new country was facilitated by educational, training, and aid institutions, and to the education of the Jewish poor in general. All this resulted in the Jewish community being by far the best-served group as far as institutional support is concerned.

Raphael Patai.

(Right) This relief shows the Assyrian King Sennacherib, enthroned, receiving the surrender of the inhabitants of a town in Judah in 701 B.C.E. This Assyrian attack on Judah is related in the Second Book of Kings.

THE SYNAGOGUE

The Temple

A living being, the Temple was killed
The arms of gold that raised its domes,
Drip with blossoms, now cut, instead of stones.
Scattered over the cemeteries, their pollen
Yet flourishes blue: periwinkles, pansies, violets,
Whispering in the breeze, with a low clear voice,
God's words, Who has abandoned Israel.
From the deserts of sand to the distant salt marshes
A new song of hope with a similar rhythm
Has flowered, a scattering of frail synagogues.

"The Temple's golden vine has cast its shoots
Into the world's vast ocean in which we bathe
(Exiled and pursued, the Rabbis repeat),
And the stubborn hope of rebirth is inscribed
In the sunset's clouds and the fall's golden leaves.

In the agony of life's eve tomorrow's soul
Meditates, preparing itself for prayer
While the ancient stones rise in a new wall."

The Temple is dead, but Israel still lives in the world
Though the barbarian's violent blade now trims
Only men from the branches of the Tree of Life
While everywhere new communities are born
Of the living spirit and of stubborn hope.

From the stones of Zion, a thousand temples are rebuilt.

Gustave Kahn.

The History of the Synagogue

When the Jewish people were exiled from their own land after the destruction of the First Temple (568 B.C.E.) they no longer had the Temple at Jerusalem as the center for their religious observance. In Babylon, we find the synagogue becoming an institution. The word "synagogue" derives from the Greek word meaning "place of assembly." But the synagogue was not only a place of assembly. It was also a house of learning and a house of worship. It was within this institution that a new form of religious observance grew up: prayer.

From these beginnings, religious observances as we know them in Western civilization developed. The forms adopted by the Jewish people became the source from which other religions drew, until today there is not a place in the Western World where a house of worship cannot be found. There men gather together to pray to God.

The synagogue has often meant much more than this to its community. It has been the center of a man's life. Here prayers were said when he was born; here he studied as a child; here he was Bar Mitzvah; here he studied as a man; here he was married; here he celebrated the birth of his children; here he helped the needy; and here too he remembered those who died. All this he did, not alone, but with his family and friends, in his community and in its synagogue.

A synagogue can be formed by any ten men [or today in many congregations by ten men and women]. They can meet in any structure. As we know it today, it is often a large institution, composed of many hundreds of families who have elected a rabbi to serve as their spiritual leader. Whether it is large or small, in it there is an Ark containing the Torah, over which burns steadily the Eternal Light.

Azriel Eisenberg.

Building a synagogue, or a *shul* as it was called in the shtetls of Eastern Europe, was an important achievement. It represented autonomy for the Jewish community and made people feel that they had roots in the town.

Building the Synagogue

At the foot of a high hill in a remote corner of eastern Galicia, not far from the Russian border, lay the village of Yanowitz. Its tiny mud huts with thatched roofs nestled among orchards and forests of great oaks, which formed a shelter from wind and storm. Swift streams rushed noisily from the hill above, watering gardens and ancient willows, feeding the marsh lands and the Nyetchlava River. The villagers, Jews as well as gentiles, prospered and multiplied.

From time to time a new hut would appear, with a *mezzuzah* nailed to the doorpost. The Jews of Yanowitz were rooted in the Galician soil where they had lived for generations, parents bringing up children, marrying them off and helping them settle, children doing the same for their children, an unwearing cycle. Some of the Yanowitz Jews were farmers, and others shared in the prosperity of the region as traders. For the High Holidays they traveled to the city, since the village of Yanowitz could claim no synagogue.

In time the Jews of Yanowitz conceived the idea of building their own synagogue in the garden of the oldest Jewish settler.

"We really need our own synagogue. If we had our own, we wouldn't have to leave our homes to go to the city for the holidays." And there were those who added, "Yes, if we have a synagogue of our own, our children won't fall into the hands of the *goyim*."

With the coming of the warm spring days the Jews of Yanowitz began to build a House of Prayer. They collected straw and bricks, stones and boards. Not only the Yanowitz Jews, but also the Jews from the surrounding villages came, generously giving materials and their own labor as well. The work went forward with great zeal, the women in their bare feet kneading the clay while the men laid bricks and hammered boards. The sweat that ran down the faces of the laborers went unnoticed, and a feeling of closeness grew up: a house was being built where all could come together. From day to day the walls rose higher, and by harvest time supported a roof thatched with straw and decked with flowers and green twigs. By Rosh Hashonoh the synagogue stood completed, reigning on its hillside, bare, with bluish-white tinted walls on a brown brick foundation.

The completion of the synagogue was a great event in the life of the Jews of Yanowitz. Scrubbed clean and dressed in their best clothes, the men in their prayer shawls, they strode out of their homes in the mild Rosh Hashonoh days. Their gentile neighbors greeted them respectfully and wished them a good year. Fields overflowing with wheat, hay, and Indian corn, the beans and hemp laid out in the sun to dry, were left behind with a carefree air. All thought of calves, geese, ducks, hens, and crowing roosters was set aside as they marched toward the synagogue, joyfully shouting to their gentile neighbors that from then on they would never abandon Yanowitz during the High Holidays.

Isaac Metzker.

"Early immigrant congregations often met in basements, tiny apartments, ramshackle stores. God, it was assumed, cared about the authenticity of worship more than the grandeur of architecture."

Irving Howe and Kenneth Libo.

When Jewish immigrants came to North America, the synagogue retained its vital place in Jewish community life. *Landsleit*, Jews who had come from the same towns or villages in Europe, often formed their own synagogues. In large North American cities where Jewish immigration was very high, there existed hundreds of Jewish communities each with its own place of worship. Some might begin as humble *shtieblach*, small storefront or apartment synagogues, but as prosperity spread amongst the congregants more elaborate synagogues were erected. Rich or poor, religious or secular, most Jewish newcomers to America belonged to a community and its shul.

University Settlement Society Report, 1899

An exact estimate of the number of congregations in the district is almost impossible. A canvass of twenty-five streets, made some time ago, at the instance of Dr. Blaustein of the Educational Alliance, showed fully one hundred organizations of sufficient size and permanence to display a sign over the door. It is safe to assert that there are at least as many more which meet in tenement houses. This estimate leaves entirely out of account the host of others which, at holiday time, spring up in lodge rooms, dance halls, and lofts, only to go out of existence when the solemn days of *Rosh Hashanah* and *Yom Kippur* are over.

The first two classes include in their membership not far from forty percent of the adult Jewish population of the district. Of this number at least one-half have no other means of social gratification than that obtained from the synagogue and the streets. Daily–morning, noon, and night–a little company of small shop keepers, peddlers, and "out of works" gather to offer up the prayers of the day. Such rigidity of discipline is possible, however, only to the few. Most must content themselves with one or more services on *Shabbes*. As in most cases, particularly in the smaller synagogues, the members are emigrants from some town in Russia, Poland, or Roumania. These synagogue meetings then serve as a means of keeping them in touch with the old home. A new immigrant coming to the city finds himself immediately included in a little circle of people he has known on the other side. The congregation, anxious to increase the membership, is sure to seek him out, and if he is in need, to assist him with that charity which is the most generous of all, the charity of the tenement house.

Irving Howe and Kenneth Libo.

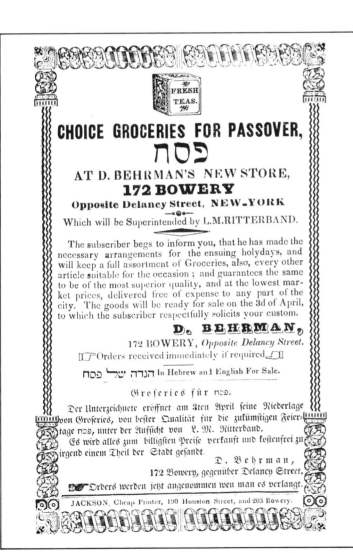

The Jewish neighborhood on the Lower East Side in New York City: a nineteenth century advertisement (left) and Orchard Street (right) today.

How did young Jews, growing up in early twentieth century America, feel about the synagogue life which reflected the past? Alfred Kazin gives an honest account of his ambiguities.

A Walker in the City

Though there was little in the ritual that was ever explained to me, and even less in the atmosphere of the synagogue that in my heart I really liked, I assumed that my feelings in the matter were of no importance; I belonged there before the Ark, with the men, sitting next to an uncle. I felt a loveless intimacy with the place. It was not exclusively a house of "worship," not frigid and formal as we knew all churches were. It had been prayed in and walked through and lived in with such easy familiarity that it never seemed strange to come on young boys droning their lessons under the long twisted yellow flytrap hung from the ceiling, the *shammes*, the sexton, waddling about in his carpet slippers carrying a fly swatter, mumbling old Hebrew tunes to himself—*Ái! Bái! Biddle Bái Dóm!*—as he dashed after a fly, while his wife, whom we mockingly called the *rebbitsin*, the rabbi's wife, red-faced over her pots in the kitchen next door, shrieked curses against the boys playing punchball in the street—*bandits* and *murderers*, she would call the police!—who were always just about to break her windows. The wood in the benches and in the high desk before the Ark had taken in with age and long use such a deep rosy mirror shine that on those afternoons when I strayed in on my way back from school, I would think that if only I bent over it long enough I might see my own face reflect in the wood. I never did. Secretly, I thought the synagogue a mean place, and went only because I was expected to. Whenever I crossed the splintered and creaking porch into that stale air of snuff, of old men and old books, saw the dusty gilt brocade on the prayer shawls, I felt I was being pulled into some mysterious and ancient clan that claimed me as its own simply because I had been born a block away. Whether I agreed with its beliefs or not, I belonged; whether I assented to its rights over me or not, I belonged; whatever I thought of them, no matter how far I might drift from that place, I belonged. This was understood in the very nature of things; I was a Jew. It did not matter how little I knew or understood of the faith, or that I was always reading alien books; I belonged, I had been expected, I was now to take my place in the great tradition.

Alfred Kazin.

COMMUNITY IN NORTH AMERICA

The New Colossus

Not like the brazen giant of Greek fame,
With conquering limbs astride from land to land:
Here at our sea-washed, sunset gates shall stand
A mighty woman with a torch whose flame
Is the imprisoned lightning, and her name
Mother of exiles. From the beacon-hand
Blows world-wide welcome; her mild eyes command
The air-bridged harbor that twin cities frame.
'Keep ancient lands your storied pomp!' cries she
With silent lips. 'Give me your tired, your poor,
Your huddled masses yearning to breathe free,
The wretched refuse of your teeming shore.
Send these, the homeless, tempest-tossed, to me;
I lift up my lamp beside the golden door!'

Emma Lazarus.

Jewish refugees from Russia passing the Statue of Liberty in the 1890's.

Engraved on the Statue of Liberty in New York harbor, this poem by a Jewish poet has become the symbol of American freedom. Jews came to America to escape antisemitism. They came in waves of immigration usually associated with times of heightened persecution of Jews in Europe.

The Jews in America

Although the Jews in America come from many different nations, their religion binds them together as an "ethnic group." Their customs, culture and even religious traditions may vary from country to country, but the synagogue and the Jewish faith are the ties that bind.

There have been three major "waves" of Jewish immigration to the United States. The first Jews, the Sephardim, were descendants of Spanish and Portuguese Jews driven from the Iberian peninsula at the time of Columbus's first voyage to the New World. Given a choice between conversion to Christianity or expulsion, many Spanish and Portuguese chose to resettle in Dutch Brazil rather than convert. When the Portuguese reclaimed the area, some of these Jews fled from Brazil to New Amsterdam in 1654.

Although there had been Jews in America as early as 1492 (Luis de Torres, one of Columbus's crew, was believed to be a "Marrano"–a Jew who outwardly adopted Christianity in order to live peacefully in Iberia), the 23 Sephardic Jews who ventured to New Amsterdam in 1654 formed the backbone of the Jewish community and paved the way for all who followed. The Sephardim won for all Jews the right to serve in the militia, the right to travel and trade freely, and the right to own property. They established North America's first Jewish cemetery and its first congregation, Shearith Israel (Remnant of Israel), still in existence today. (The building no longer stands, but the Jews of New York City have been worshipping continuously as a community since 1655.)

Although the Sephardim were the smallest wave of Jewish immigrants to America, they continued to dominate the religious life of America's Jewish community until the nineteenth century. It wasn't until 1802 that the first Ashkenazic (Eastern European Jewish) congregation was founded, despite the fact that German Jews had outnumbered the Sephardim as early as 1720.

Large numbers of German-Jewish immigrants came to our shores following the Revolution of 1848, and at the time of the Civil War there were almost 150,000 Jews living in America. Some 6,000 or so served the Union cause during the War, and about 1,000 Jews took the side of the Confederacy.

After the pogroms of 1881, Eastern European, Yiddish-speaking Jews began to arrive in record numbers. By 1914, more than 2 million Jewish immigrants had arrived to fill the tenements and sweat shops of major American industrial cities. Altogether some 3 million Ashkenazi came to America between 1880 and 1910. Most were listed by immigration officials not as Jews, but as Germans or Russians, so the exact total will never be known.

Stephanie Bernardo.

JEWS IN EARLY AMERICA

The oldest synagogue that still stands in North America is the Touro Synagogue built in 1763 in Newport, Rhode Island. It was built by the descendants of fifteen Jewish Spanish-Portuguese families who immigrated to the Colony of Rhode Island in 1658 seeking religious freedom. In 1781, this Jewish community and its synagogue were visited by George Washington and the following exchange ensued.

The Touro Synagogue, Rhode Island.

The Hebrew Congregation of Newport, Rhode Island, Message of Welcome to George Washington, August 1790

Sir:

Permit the children of the stock of Abraham to approach you with the most cordial affection and esteem for your person and merits and to join with our fellow-citizens in welcoming you to New Port.

With pleasure we reflect on those days–those days of difficulty and danger–when the God of Israel who delivered David from the peril of the sword shielded your head in the day of battle. And we rejoice to think that the same Spirit, who rested in the bosom of the greatly beloved Daniel, enabling him to preside over the provinces of the Babylonish Empire, rests, and ever will rest upon you, enabling you to discharge the arduous duties of Chief Magistrate in these states.

Deprived as we have hitherto been of the invaluable rights of free citizens, we now, with a deep sense of gratitude to the Almighty Disposer of all events, behold a government, erected by the majesty of the people, a government which to bigotry gives no sanction, to persecution no assistance, but generously affording to all liberty of conscience and immunities of citizenship, deeming every one, of whatever nation, tongue, or language, equal parts of the great governmental machine. This so ample and extensive federal union whose basis is philanthropy, mutual confidence, and public virtue, we cannot but acknowledge to be the work of the Great God, who ruleth in the armies of heaven and among the inhabitants of the earth, doing whatsoever seemeth him good.

For all the blessings of civil and religious liberty which we enjoy under an equal and benign administration, we desire to send up our thanks to the Antient of Days, the great Preserver of Men, beseeching him that the angel who conducted our forefathers through the wilderness into the promised land may graciously conduct you through all the dangers and difficulties of this mortal life. And when like Joshua, full of days and full of honor, you are gathered to your fathers, may you be admitted into the heavenly paradise to partake of the water of life and the tree of immortality.

Done and signed by order of the Hebrew Congregation in New Port, Rhode Island.

Moses Seixas, Warden.

George Washington's Reply

Gentlemen:

While I receive with much satisfaction your address replete with expressions of affection and esteem, I rejoice in the opportunity of assuring you that I shall always retain a grateful remembrance of the cordial welcome experienced in my visit to New Port from all classes of citizens.

The reflection on the days of difficulty and danger which are past is rendered the more sweet from a consciousness that they are succeeded by days of uncommon prosperity and security. If we have wisdom to make the best use of the advantages with which we are now favored, we cannot fail, under the just administration of a good government, to become a great and a happy people.

The citizens of the United States of America have a right to applaud themselves for having given to mankind examples of an enlarged and liberal policy, a policy worthy of imitation.

All possess alike liberty of conscience and immunities of citizenship. It is now no more that toleration is spoken of, as if it was by the indulgence of one class of people that another enjoyed the exercise of their inherent natural rights. For happily the government of the United States, which gives to bigotry no sanction, to persecution no assistance, requires only that they who live under its protection should demean themselves as good citizens, in giving it on all occasions their effectual support.

It would be inconsistent with the frankness of my character not to avow that I am pleased with your favorable opinion of my administration and fervent wishes for my felicity.

May the children of the stock of Abraham who dwell in this land continue to merit and enjoy the good will of the other inhabitants, while every one shall sit in safety under his own vine and fig-tree, and there shall be none to make him afraid.

May the Father of all mercies scatter light and not darkness in our paths, and make us all in our several vocations useful here, and, in his own due time and way, everlastingly happy.

G. Washington.

"For the Jews who came here between the early 1880s and the First World War, one of the main ways they had of keeping the precarious balance between old and new was the landsmanshaft. This...was really the most remarkable institution of the whole immigrant Jewish experience."

Irving Howe and Kenneth Libo.

As the original Jewish communities of America settled in, new waves of Jewish immigration began. These new Jewish immigrants tried to adjust to the American way of life, to "Americanize," while at the same time retaining their old connections. The new immigrants saw themselves as individuals in a free society, far away from the inquisitions and pogroms. Yet life in America was still difficult and frighteningly unfamiliar. They longed for their own language and customs, for a sense of community which linked them with their past. Thus they clung to each other for support–both emotional and financial.

The *landsmanshaft* was based on the age-old tradition of Jewish communal self-help. It provided a constructive way of dealing with hardships in an alien land and became an alternative to charity. People from the same communities banded together for understanding and sociability. The landsmanshaft provided a structure and a purpose for this fellowship. Members pooled their resources, and benefits were provided as circumstances required them. The landsmanshaft was also a credit union. It provided sick benefits and relief to those in need. And it bought land for a community cemetary.

The Inner World of the *Landsmanshaft*

While the Jews had seldom felt much loyalty to Russia or Poland as nations, they brought with them fierce affections for the little places they had lived in, the muddy streets, battered synagogues, remembered fields from which they had fled. The *landsmanshaft*, a lodge made up of persons coming from the same town or district in the old country, was their ambiguous testimony to a past they knew to be wretched yet often felt to be sweet.

The *landsmanshaft* began in the simplest ways. Immigrants, feeling themselves lost in American cities, would seek out old-country neighbors–the phrase *di alte heym*, the old home, keeps reverberating through Yiddish speech, writing, and plays. Coming together, they formed modest little organizations that kept alive memories and helped them fit into the new world.

Many of the *landsmanshaftn* formed during the last few decades of the nineteenth century were also *anshe*, congregations established according to place of origin or by occupation; but by about 1900 the majority of the *landsmanshaftn* were secular in character, some even adorning themselves with English names like the First Kalisher Benevolent Association, signs of a wish to hasten the process of *oysgrinen zikh*, ceasing to be greenhorns.

Why were the *landsmanshaftn* started? A 1938 survey by the Yiddish Writers Group of the Federal Writers Project yields replies by old-timers:

The men here felt miserable, they left their wives or brides back home, so they used to get together in the house of a married *landsman* to drink tea or play cards.

A *landsman* was about to be deported because he was sick, so the *landslayt* realized the importance of having their own organization for self-help.

Immigrants leave Ellis Island by ferry for the mainland and a new life.

A *landsman* died in the factory. People think he is a Greek and bury him in Potter's Field. *Landslayt* hear about it, his body is dug up, and the decision taken to start our organization with a cemetery.

Before the First World War some of these secular *landsmanshaftn* had a semisocialist flavor, bringing together craftsmen from an old-country trade who had lived together in a town or neighborhood. But soon the kinds of immigrants who aspired to political action drifted away, either into the various parties or into the socialistic Workmen's Circle. The *landsmanshaftn* would experience two phases of looking outward, during the First World War, when they would send money to help their people back home, and during the thirties, when they would join the entire Jewish community in trying to help the victims of Nazism. But in the main, the *landsmanshaftn* were jealous of their self-contained character–that impulse to social inwardness which brought a member to the monthly meeting in an East Side hall, away from family quarrels, troubles of livelihood, and the noise of Jewish politics. When the political types dropped away, the remaining members seem to have been relieved, for they preferred not to be bothered by all those orators and intellectuals. What they wanted was the closeness of familiars, the pleasures of smallness regained.

Irving Howe.

(Overleaf) "Einstein and Immigrants" by Ben Shahn (1898-1969).

"General Store in Vancouver Before World War One" by William Kurelek (1927-1977). Collection: The Ontario Heritage Foundation. Courtesy of the Isaacs Gallery, Toronto.

For the second-generation American Jew, life was much easier. And with this new ease, many of the old communal institutions such as the landsmanshaften disappeared. However, the need for Jewish community still remained. Canadian novelist Morley Torgov describes a second-generation Jewish community in a small Ontario town.

A Good Place to Come From

The people of whom I write–the thirty to forty families who made up the local Jewish community–occupied stores and apartments and houses within a relatively small area in the central part of Sault Ste. Marie. The intersection of Queen and Bruce Streets formed the hub of this area, and most of the Jewish business establishments and homes lay no more than a block or two from that point. Despite this apparent concentration, it is impossible to characterize the inhabitants as ghetto-dwellers, nor was this a shtetl environment in the European sense of the term. As you walked along Queen Street, you saw, true enough, signs that read "Himmel's Ladies' Wear," "Friedman's Department Store," "Fishman's Men's Wear. " You heard two neighbouring merchants call to each other on the sidewalk, "Hello, Joe,"

"Hello, Isaac." You heard Mr. Cohen and Mr. Mintz greeting each other in Yiddish outside the Royal Bank. Yet you were not conscious of being in the midst of a Jewish world. It was as if the Jews–even those who owned their own properties–were no more than temporary tenants who borrowed time and space on Queen Street during daylight hours in order to make their living. To the Gentile population, we were a mysterious subterranean breed, a race who surfaced daily from 8:00 A.M. to 6:00 P.M. (midnight on Saturdays) to sell merchandise, and disappeared into the ground after hours to do God-knew-what. There were no Jewish theatres, delicatessens, butcher shops, corner confectionaries; none of the storefront street-level institutions one associates with the ghetto. Until the mid-1940's there was no synagogue.

If there was little resemblance to the big-city ghetto, there was even less resemblance to the shtetl. Having been blown across Europe by a hundred different winds of turmoil, and having vomited their way across seas and oceans to North America, our fathers were far too worldly to live the life of simple villagers. They had shaved off beards and sidelocks, discarded skullcaps, eaten pork when it meant the difference between living or starving, battled with the English language and called down plagues upon its unfamiliar spellings and pronunciations. They worked on the Sabbath, indeed worked harder and longer on the Sabbath than on any other day of the week, for that was the one day of the week when the Gentiles were most often in a spending mood. To nothing–save the inescapable curse of old age–did they resign themselves. Before no one did they bend or cower. The rabbi was always no more than a few minutes away, ready to be consulted when the spirit was low or the conscience was tortured. But somehow he could never be the symbol of rigid, orthodox discipline that his shtetl counterpart had been in Europe; rather, he could only be one of them. Granted he hadn't shed the trappings of his religion as they had done; nevertheless, the same gales that had carried them like pollen from one continent to another, had carried him as well. He and they were comrades, shipmates, fellow-tenants.

Not ghetto Jews, not shtetl Jews. What then were they?

Upside-down weeds…that perhaps is the best way to describe them. Weeds that had planted themselves in strange ground, weeds that grew with their foliage–the fruit of their labours–submerged in the earth and their roots exposed to air and sky. They spent their lives this way, scratching, scraping, building up, tearing down, conniving and surviving. Always there was the struggle to invert themselves, to establish root and leaf in proper order, to become more than mere weeds, to become indigenous plants.

They never entirely succeeded.

Morley Torgov.

JEWS IN SUBURBAN COMMUNITIES

"Jews may no longer be very Jewish, but they are still Jews. And most not only want to remain so but wish their children to remain so, too."

Peter I. Rose.

| The ultimate in the Americanization process was the later trend towards suburban communities which began in the 1950's. After the Second World War, American Jews became more affluent and "socially accepted." They began to move from the cities into the suburbs. Here, they once again formed their own Jewish communities centred around the synagogue–also the place for Jewish education and social activity. In many ways, it was just as it had always been. In the prosperous suburbs, however, there were new dilemmas. |

Moving into the Suburbs

Moving into the suburbs required that people decide whether or not they wanted to declare themselves as Jews. At first everyone seemed amiable and anonymous, young and shiny, not stamped with an encrusted ethnicity. But that was just the trouble, since merely to surrender to the ways of suburbia was in effect a declaration about what one wanted to be.

The inner tone and structure of Jewish life underwent major changes during this shift from city to suburb. Whatever spoke too emphatically of traditional ways in religious practice, or too stridently of traditional ideologies in Yiddish secular life, was left behind. A few Yiddish groups, like the Workmen's Circle, did try to adapt themselves to the new setting, and in

some of the plainer suburbs, like certain towns on Long Island, succeeded in establishing a foothold. But most immigrant institutions held little appeal for the new suburbanites–they were at once too keen in memory and too inharmonious with present desires. Only after life in the suburbs had settled into a measure of stability could they speak openly of their Yiddish origins and memories, giving vent to those feelings of affection they had found it prudent to suppress.

Among Jewish intellectuals and semi-intellectuals, as well as the more sophisticated children of the suburbs, it became a commonplace to disparage the suburban Jews as philistine and vulgar–in books, lectures, and articles there were frequent sneers at "bagel and lox" Jewishness. Of philistinism there was of course plenty in the Jewish suburban communities, though one would be hard put to show there was any more of it than in Yiddish-speaking immigrant neighborhoods or, for that matter, in American society as a whole. Those who loftily dismissed "bagel and lox" Jewishness failed or preferred not to grasp that certain pinched qualities of suburban Jewish life–residual attachments to foods, a few customs, and a garbled Yiddish phrase–might signify not merely self-serving nostalgia but also blocked yearnings for elements of the past that seemed spiritually vital. The suburban Jews had come upon the scene at a moment when Jewish culture in America no longer possessed its earlier assurance and vigor; they lived with whatever remnants of their youthful experience they could salvage; and "bagels and lox" (not to be sneered at in their own right!) were part of what they still had left, tokens of the past to which they clung partly because it reminded them of all that was gone.

Adaptations had to be made to a new order of life: learning how to take care of a lawn and cope with a "garden shop," fixing correctly the tonalities of suburban social life, discovering those softenings of opinion and voice that might be needed at a local school meeting, and finding the kinds of people with whom more could be shared than the accident of proximity. There were pleasures, too, mild but genuine. It was good to bask in a luxury of space, as if all the elements in one's field of vision had been expanded. It was pleasant "to walk on your own earth and feel your own green grass, and plan your own mysteries of birth and bloom and death. Only in our wildest dreams, the ones we didn't tell each other, did we include the ownership of broad acres, half acres, quarter acres."

Irving Howe.

| How do young Jewish people growing up in the suburbs feel about their Jewishness? More specifically how do they feel about becoming a participant in their Jewish community? This article gives some insights. |

Coming of Age in America

Bar Mitzvahs used to be small, at-home affairs until after World War II. Having attained economic power, American Jews felt compelled to display their affluence. The Bar Mitzvah party became a celebration of the parents' position in the community. The bigger the bash the more they could show their immigrant parents and grandparents, as well as the gentiles peeking over the picket fences, that they had *arrived*.

But what about the kids themselves? Why do so many become Bar Mitzvah burnouts who make the ceremony an act of liberation from Hebrew school and a swan song to religious life?

Eddie Freedman, of Wyncote, thinks he won't "be that much involved" in religious life after he becomes a Bar Mitzvah at Beth Sholom Congregation in December. "I've put a lot of time into this," says Eddie. "When it's over, I want more time to myself."

As for the party, Eddie maintains that it's important. "The party has a purpose. It helps a kid get through the training. It gives him something to look forward to."

Eddie remembers one affair at which the name of the Bat Mitzvah girl was written up in lights in the window of the banquet hall. A disc jockey spun records while the rock band took a break. The parents hired breakdancers to add to the excitement. The kids also had a makeup artist to entertain them, an Atlantic City-style Boardwalk T-shirt booth dispensing printed polos of their favorite rock stars, ushers in costumes—was it the Tin Woodsman and the Lion and the other characters from *The Wizard of Oz?* What about the party with the celebrity look-alikes from New York?

"At the moment," Eddie confides, I'm not much into parties. I'm studying to get the service right, because messing up is the worst thing you can do. In other synagogues I've seen people forget what they're doing. I mean the English parts, not just the Hebrew. I've heard rabbis come up behind and whisper the words."

Eddie finds it ironic that the kids who mess up get the same gifts—the money, the stereos, the computers—as the kids who pull off a perfect job.

"It's a lot of time, the studying. I'd say it's worthwhile because going to Hebrew school is the only way you're going to know you're a Jew."

And what of the rite itself?

"It's a performance," smiles Nina Abraham, of Bala Cynwyd, confessing that she wants to be an actress when she grows up.

Matt Silverman, her classmate at Adath Israel of the Main Line, doubts if he'll feel any closer to adulthood on the day he reads from the Torah. "The Bar Mitzvah is the one day when they do everything for *you*," he says. "I'll be an adult after I graduate from college, spend a year as a ski bum in Vail and become a successful real estate developer. I want to build shopping malls."

At 13, Sidney Greenberg didn't burn out. The current rabbi of Temple Sinai in Dresher studied in the yeshiva and became a Bar Mitzvah with flying colors. His reward was pickled herring and kichel at a small family gathering at home.

"The only real difference I find between myself and some of today's kids," says Rabbi Greenberg, "is that it never occured to me that being a Bar Mitzvah would be a *conclusion* to my Jewish involvement."

Still, it happens. In the words of one Bat Mitzvah student, "Being an adult means you don't have to go to Hebrew school anymore."

"Suburbia tends to diffuse the Jewish element," Rabbi Greenberg sighs. "The environment puts less of a premium on Jewish life. Kids don't see Judaism practiced at home. So when they're sent to Hebrew school, they're asked to give more of themselves for something their parents want. A career in Jewish life is not a concern.

Rabbi Greenberg doesn't put the blame on the big parties, as many critics have done. Celebration is central to Jewish life. "I don't inveigh against it because life is too filled with sorrow for us not to celebrate."

There have been times when Rabbi Greenberg has reinterpreted strict Sabbath commandments. "Though we are a Conservative congregation, I permit music—Jewish music—as part of Sabbath functions because I believe this is positive, not negative. We have Psalm 150 to tell us to praise God 'with trumpet sound;

praise Him with lute and harp. . .with tambourine and dance.' At the very least, music helps people remain in the synagogue instead of going to country clubs where more Sabbath violations take place.

"Young people going to Hebrew school must feel that the ceremony is important to them, that it's not a song and dance they're doing to get gifts or impress their friends. They must be encouraged to find their own meaning in being a Bar and Bat Mitzvah."

That meaning, for many 13-year-olds, doesn't extend beyond the performance level. For this reason, modern congregations are including some kind of individual project or activity as part of the Bar Mitzvah ritual. These range from research papers on Jewish life to the creation of works of art and music.

Gary Schechner, a slender, athletic youth who became a Bar Mitzvah at Temple Sinai last year, spent several weeks writing the English translation of his Haftarah in calligraphy. Though he wants to be a professional soccer player when he becomes a "real man," the project was important to him because "calligraphy has been my hobby for a long time."

Gary thinks that the real problem kids have with being Jewish is "that what your parents tell you, and what you study in Hebrew school, and what you feel, are all different things. You hear about what happens in Israel, and you learn the service, but it never seems to be about who you are. Caligraphy is part of my life. By doing my project I had another way of connecting myself with my religion."

Schechner is continuing his Hebrew education, and practicing soccer around it.

Bill Kent.

JEWS WITHOUT COMMUNITY

What about those Jews in America who live outside a Jewish community or in a predominantly Gentile community? How do *they* deal with their needs? Here is a moving story about a young Jewish boy who feels like an "outsider" in his non-Jewish environment. It is also a story about Jewish communal responsibility.

Bond

As a boy I was always haunted by the fear that one of my classmates might accidentally come into Papa's shabby little store and discover my connection with it. I went to the newer of the two schools in our town, and my classmates belonged to the oldest and best families in town, though if I had been completely honest with myself I would have gone to the other school, the one attended by the boys and girls who lived across the tracks in little shacks, which, when the river came up in spring, were washed away. Their parents were Papa's customers.

"Please, Mr. Chazan," they would plead, mispronouncing the name, "is that the best you can do?" And he would peer at them through his thick glasses over the counter piled high with cheap shoes and coarse trousers, muttering dark oaths in Yiddish under his breath; however, in his store their soiled dollar bills stretched further than any other place, for when he grew weary of bargaining with them, he would shrug his shoulders and exclaim, "Take them away—take them out!" and fling the offending articles at his customers. His heavy accent, of which I was forever conscious, never intimidated them.

My father was not an old man, but he acted as though he were. He was not nearly as round-shouldered as he made out to be. Sometimes I was positive he walked that way just to embarrass me. When anyone asked me what his business was I managed to be purposely vague, and if I had been pinned down about his accent, I would have explained it away as being French. When I came to high school, it was necessary to fill out a long questionnaire, which demanded a great deal of information about my parents, such things as place of birth and date of citizenship...I sat before it a long time not daring to bring myself to write in the lie but knowing that unless I did I ran the risk of being found out. Finally in desperation I inked in something, then smeared it over and finally went over the whole mess until nothing was very clear.

That's how it was with everything I did at school...Perhaps my father sensed how little I wanted to do with the store, for he seldom bothered me to help him, except on Saturday mornings, when he had to go to the bank and it was necessary for me to stay. These thirty minutes—for he was never gone much longer—always seemed interminable. In my own mind I had resolved that should anyone from school come in, I would simply seclude myself in the rear behind the tables, which were stacked high with pants and shirts.

One morning in late August, while Papa was at the bank, I was sitting in the cashier's cage reading Alexandre Dumas, when the bell over the front door jingled and a frail old lady, with great hollows under her eyes, who seemed to wobble as she came through the door, stood by the counter. She went through a brief spasm of coughing before she asked for Papa. I noticed she had no trouble with our usually-mispronounced name.

"But it's not important," she said when I explained he was out. "It was only to find out when your holiday comes this year." Her eyes, I noticed, were pale and watery. She looked sick. Perhaps, I speculated, she was one of us, a *landsman*, as Papa would say...but no, in the next moment I recognized her: she

was Dr. Ross' wife. I often saw her name and sometimes her picture in the social columns of the paper. I told her when our holiday *Rosh Hoshanah* fell this year and she thanked me and went out the door as quietly as she had come in. By the time Papa returned from the bank I had forgotten her visit.

About a month later when school had started we saw her again. It was a Friday night and the *Shabbos* candles were burning on the buffet before the window. Papa was already home, for on Friday night he closed the store early and made himself ready for the *Shabbos*. I was sitting in the parlor absorbed as usual in Dumas, when the doorbell rang and my mother called to me to answer it, but by the time I finished the paragraph and marked my place, she had gone to the door herself. I saw her standing before Mrs. Ross, who was talking in a tired, hoarse voice: "I was going by and saw your candles." She peered over my mother's shoulder into our dining room, where the table was set with the special twisted bread loaves covered with a linen napkin and the silver wine cups. Papa, too, the black skull cap perched on the back of his head, was watching Mrs. Ross.

"Maybe," he said slowly with his heavy accent, "Mrs. Ross would like to eat with us."

Raising her pale, sick eyes to him, she nodded, and, as though this were the most ordinary procedure in the world, opened the screen door and stepped inside. She had nothing to say to us during the short time my mother prepared another place at the table for her; not did she speak when we sat down and Papa intoned the *Kiddush*. She did not touch the wine.

In a gentle voice my mother urged her to taste the soup. But she seemed to pay no attention. Her eyes wandered in the direction of the candles and she commenced to cry very softly. Mama and Papa looked at each other in embarrassment. None of us spoke. Finally Papa said to her, "Maybe the soup is too hot—blow a little on it."

"Oh, no," she replied. She had stopped crying now and had picked up the spoon, but after the first mouthful she started to cough. It was a dry, racking cough that never seemed to end. Her wasted, blue-veined hand, with its rings and bracelets, lowered the spoon. "Excuse me," she murmured when the spasm had finally passed, "I shouldn't have bothered you like this," and before any of us could recover from our surprise she had gone out the front door.

"What is to be made of this?" wondered my father.

"So fine a lady," sighed Mama. "Maybe in the head she is not right."

"No," Papa insisted as his nose twitched under thick lenses.

My mother turned questioningly to me. "You think our table was not nice enough?"

I put down my fork and looked at her severely. Mrs. Ross no doubt would tell her friends about our strange customs. All over town people would ridicule us for lighting candles and eating the twisted *challa*. "It'd suit me fine if we had some American food in this house for a change," I said.

"Foolish boy," my father reproved me, "you think that old lady would have come if our food had been like the *goyim* eat?"

"I don't see why we can't have plain white bread instead of *challa*?" I challenged.

"Why all of a sudden white bread?" asked my mother.

"Like other people eat," I bristled.

"Is he crazy?" Mama turned to Papa. "Maybe you are not feeling so good?"

"Aw rats!" As was often the case when I talked to them, I grew angry and finished my meal in silence. I wanted to get back to Dumas....

During the following months we saw nothing of Mrs. Ross.

117

Then one night in early spring I happened to be in the store waiting for Papa to close up. I heard the doorbell jingle and, as was my habit whenever someone came in, beat a hasty retreat to the dimmed interior of the store, hiding myself behind the tables heaped with dusty bargains. When I peered out, I was surprised to see old Dr. Ross.

Papa did not recognize him. "You want something?" he asked in his heavy accent.

Dr. Ross introduced himself. "I have something to ask you." He spoke in that beautifully cultivated voice which I envied so much. "My wife, who is very ill, has sent for you." Papa peered at him without replying. "You see, sir, she was born into your faith..." Dr. Ross was silent a minute. When he spoke, he was facing Papa again. "I am afraid she will not last the night. I would take it as a favor to a dying woman if you'd recite your religious prayers to her."

Papa rubbed his hands over his coat. "Prayers," he repeated, "what have I to do with prayers?"

With sudden horror I realized he was talking in Yiddish! "You're to say *Kiddush* for her," I said.

"But..."Papa faltered, making a broad gesture with his shoulders. "How can I...*doven?*"

"Whatever you say...will ease her last moments," said the doctor.

Papa hesitated, turning the matter over in his mind. After a minute he went back to the cashier's cage, where he kept his prayer book. Slipping it into his pocket, he picked up the skull cap he wore when he prayed. I had followed him. "Don't go, Papa, they won't understand you."

"Understand?" he repeated. "What is there to understand?"

"They'll laugh at you," I cried in exasperation.

"Nu, so they'll laugh," he replied, lapsing into Yiddish. "I must go...she is one of us."

"Aw, Papa, please...you'll only embarrass us."

He put his hand on my arm. "You come too," he said. "Be sensible...the doctor is waiting."

There was nothing to do except follow him out to the car. Within a few minutes we were at Dr. Ross'. The upper hallway was filled with people, friends and relatives of the dying woman—the elite of the town, I noted mentally—who, as we passed into the sick chamber, nodded distantly to us and whispered excitedly among themselves. I could feel my face growing red, and it was only after a few minutes that my eyes grew accustomed to the darkness of the room. Mrs. Ross was lying on the bed under a thin cover. She looked so wasted I hardly recognized her. A low rattling sound came from her.

Dr. Ross motioned Papa to come nearer. From the doorway people watched him remove his hat and fix the skull cap on his head. He opened the prayer book. "Nu," he nudged me, for he counted on my assistance. But conscious of the faces in the doorway, I ignored his summons and pressed myself against the wall. I simply could not face them. Papa, seeing that I would not help him, started the *Kaddush* without me, but the sounds which came from his lips were so blurred that even I, who was familiar with these prayers, could not distinguish one word from another. What must these *goyim*, whispering among themselves, make of us, I wondered, as I fixed my eyes on the maples outside the window and watched them swaying in the night breeze.

Presently someone in the hallway issued a command for silence. Now everything was quiet, for Papa too had paused and, as though this might be the respite he needed to husband his strength, raised his voice. In the next moment the Hebrew prayer on his lips took on a new sound. I could make out the melody. He was himself again, and his voice sounded clear and distinct. I listened as his voice rose above the rustle of the leaves and the rattle of the old lady on the bed. Neither by glance nor gesture did he indicate that he was aware of his surroundings. He might have been at home in the privacy of his room singing his morning praises to God. His shadow moved across the wall above the window. I drank in the sweetness and sorrow of his words. I could not make out his greying temples and the droop of his shoulders. He seemed tremendously sad standing there alone...and also a little splendid. In the secret place of my heart I was proud of him, and all at once I felt ashamed because I wasn't singing. My fingers clutched the skull cap. I saw again the first of the spring's maples swaying outside...and I knew nothing else until I felt his warm touch on my arm.

I stopped. A strange quiet, a kind of uncanny silence, filled the room. We knew Mrs. Ross was dead. Papa closed his book and, as we turned, the waiting, hushed crowd, with one will, parted to let us pass. We walked down the carpeted stairway out the front door. We came to the street. I could smell the grass and honeysuckle. There was something wonderful about this evening. We walked for a short distance. I watched the towers of the town gleaming against the lights and I realized I was holding Papa's hand, just as though I were a little boy again.

It was good being with him. I needed to collect my thoughts and to reason my way back from the enchantment. "Papa," I said, my voice speculative and filled with awe, "why did she want you?"

"What?" he replied after a minute and I was conscious of his voice. In the room of the dying woman it had seemed like poetry. Now it was harsh, foreign.

I looked at the sky of stars and thought of Mrs. Ross who had died with those beautiful melodies singing her to sleep. I burned to know what they were...how had they soothed?

"It is the *Kaddush*," said Papa. "You don't know?"

"Yes, I know, it's the *Kaddush*," I exclaimed impatiently. I wasn't that simple! But I wanted him to explain the magic...and instead he was mumbling about the *Kaddush*, how it was the duty of every faithful son to recite the memorial prayer, to revere the memory of the dead...Suddenly I knew he couldn't make it real. What he was saying now had nothing to do with the radiance which had filled his voice and my own thrill of discovery...I stopped. I was breathing hard. I felt let down. I wanted to cry and then in the next moment I hated myself for having been taken in...

"To where do you go?" he called, seeing that I had started in the opposite direction. I did not reply. His voice was remote... behind me. I was running towards the lights of our town gleaming against the sky...towards the rising moon and the stars that shone a million light years over my head...

Sylvan Karchmer.

LARGER JEWISH COMMUNITIES

Some Jewish communities are based on location. Others are based on consensus of religious belief. Still others are based on religious and cultural traditions that have been passed on from generation to generation. These communities, such as the Sephardic and Ashkenazic communities, may have many locales, but all members are linked by Jewish traditions that are unique to their community and have been practised for hundreds of years.

Over 600 candles light up the interior of the Portuguese synagogue in Amsterdam.

Synagogue in modern Fez, Morocco. The Jewish community numbers 800 today.

Some of the Bar Mitzvah traditions of other communities differ considerably from those described in this book (which are mostly based on Ashkenazic traditions). The Bar Mitzvah customs of the Sephardic Jews of Morocco, for example, are unique and date back to medieval times. Bar Mitzvah was celebrated at age 12 in Morocco. But before the young man was permitted to read from the Torah, he had to memorize an entire Talmudic treatise and pass an examination given by the rabbi and the elders of the community. Once he passed this test, a dinner for the community was given at his home in his honor on the Wednesday night before the Sabbath that he was to be called up to the Torah. On Thursday morning, a service was held in his home, during which the teacher or rabbi and the father put the tefillin on the boy for the first time. The young man then addressed the congregation. Money, collected from the congregation, was thrown in the tefillin bag and given to the teacher of the Bar Mitzvah boy. On the Sabbath of his Bar Mitzvah, the boy was called up to read his portion of the Torah. Almonds, raisins and sweets were thrown at him for good luck, as he recited the final blessings.

To the Marrano Jews of Spain and Portugal, it is believed that Bar Mitzvah developed a whole other significance. These were originally the Jews of Spain and Portugal who, after the first inquisition in 1391, were forced to adopt Christianity, but in fact established a secret community in which they retained their Jewish practices. Jewish scholar Cecil Roth speculates that Marrano parents, unable to teach their younger children about Judaism because its practice was a crime punishable by death, designated the age of Bar Mitzvah as the time when their children were old enough to be told about their Jewish roots. When a Marrano boy reached the age of thirteen, he was not confirmed in, but rather introduced to, the customs and beliefs of traditional Judaism.

A view of the Alhambra palace in Spain. Its older sections were built by Joseph Ibn-Naghdela, Jewish prime minister of the Caliph in the eleventh century.

Bar Mitzvah in Spain

Pierce was only about five years old at the time, but the memory of that dreadful day remains with him always. He remembers his father and mother, pale and trembling with fear, taking him into a dark cave near their home. They begged him not to cry or make a sound, lest evil men, hearing his voice, should come and kill him. They promised him that in a little while, a very little while, their servant, Ferdinand, would come and fetch him from the cave. He remained alone in the darkness, his eyes following his father and mother whom he was seeing for the last time. They called goodbye from the mouth of the cave, standing there hunched over, looking at him.

For many a day, his father's voice rang in his ears: "My son, you will be a Jew—a Jew all your life!"

His mother cried, and pleaded in a broken voice: "My son, will you remember your mother? Tell me, will you remember your mother?"

The dear caressing voices vanished; the dear pale faces disappeared. The opening of the cave was closed. He was alone in the darkness. He lost consciousness.

When he opened his eyes, he found himself in his own room, in Ferdinand's arms. The boy's heart was full of fear. He still saw the blackness of the cave around him.

As the days passed, he enjoyed sitting in the old servant's lap. The world seemed safe from underneath Ferdinand's white beard. But at night—at night darkness covered the land, the world was full of raving evil spirits, ferocious beasts who wanted to kill him. Then the lad would find a warm refuge in Ferdinand's bed. He would listen to the old man's stories of magicians and witches, heroes and villains, heaven and hell. Terrifying stories, but it was nice to hear them with the good old man lying beside him and protecting him with his presence.

Then, it all suddenly ceased, like a dream. Little Pierce didn't know how it happened. One morning he found himself in the monastery. Many boys were there, and young monks and old monks, all in long, black cloaks.

When the boys were by themselves, they would laugh and play. But little Pierce was sad and frightened. He felt the same fear as in the dark cave. At night he would lie in his bed, hide his face in the pillow, and longingly remember Ferdinand. He would hear in his imagination Ferdinand's soothing voice, telling him enchanting stories.

The boy moved among his comrades like a young monk—pale, sad, silent. Every Sunday afternoon the students would assemble in the auditorium, or in the garden among the trees. Antonius, the friar, would tell them about the saints—the many trials they had suffered in their lifetime, the miracles God had wrought for them. Pierce thirstily absorbed all that Antonius said. He thought of all the sorrows that had befallen him, and prayed that God would also work miracles for him.

One day in the garden Pierce saw Antonius speaking to an old monk who had just arrived at the monastery. Pierce passed near them, and heard the old man's voice. He stopped and listened intently. Where had he heard that voice before, he wondered. He knew he had heard it—but where? When?

He looked at the man's face. A strange face, yet it seemed to him he had seen it before. He stood quite still, peering at the old monk's face. He tried to remember—where had he seen him?

The two men noticed the boy, and stopped their conversation.

"Why are you standing here?" called the friar. "Go to your room and memorize the passage I assigned you."

Pierce went to his room, but he could not study a single line. He could not forget the old monk's face and voice. Who was he? He was surer than ever that he had once heard that voice, seen

121

that face. But when? Where?

In the middle of the night he fell asleep. Suddenly he awoke, frightened. The old man stood beside his bed, holding a candle. For a moment Pierce thought he was dreaming, but the old man spoke.

"Get up! The head monk is calling for you."

"Why is he calling? Have I disobeyed in some way?"

"Go to his room. You will find out there."

Who knows what new trouble I'll find there, thought the lad. With trembling hands he dressed, praying for a miracle. The old man opened the door, the boy followed him.

It was very black in the corridor. Pierce began to wonder. He knew that usually there was a light in the hall at night. The darkness heightened the boy's fear. Why no light in the corridor tonight? Where was the old man taking him? What would they do to him?

For a long time he followed the old man through the blackness of many corridors. The old man made no sound, and the poor lad was afraid to ask anything. He followed, weeping silently, swallowing his tears.

At last they came to a room. A small candlestick stood on the table. The old man raised the candlestick to his face, and a glad welcome filled the chamber.

"Who are you?" cried the boy in a quavering voice.

"Look at me, son! Don't you recognize me?"

"I'm sure I've seen you before, but I don't recognize you. Who are you?

The old man caught the boy up in his arms, embraced him lovingly. "I'm Ferdinand–Ferdinand–your faithful servant!"

"Ferdinand!" cried the boy. And tears rolled from his eyes.

That night his old friend revealed to the boy the secret of his past. His parents were Jewish, Ferdinand told him. They had sanctified God's name before the Tribunal of the Inquisition, choosing death rather than give up their faith. Ferdinand told him of his parents' goodbye in the blackness of the cave. Pierce had forgotten the whole terrible incident that had happened to him as a child of five. Now those bitter memories returned, to stand out vividly in his mind.

Ferdinand also told of his own experiences–of trials and dangers he had undergone since they had parted. Now he had come back to Pierce, and he would never leave him. The danger was great–but there was no other choice. Pierce's parents had appeared to Ferdinand in a dream, had commanded him to go to the monastery and bring their son back to the faith of Israel.

"If the spies of the Inquisition discover our secret," said Ferdinand, "we shall be burned at the stake. But there is no other way, Pierce! We have no choice but to walk the way of the Lord God, the God of your fathers. It is a road full of sorrow and danger. But it is also the way to redemption and salvation. Your saintly parents trod that path and died, and you too, my son, must follow it. You must be prepared for anything. The time has not yet come, Pierce, for me to reveal everything to you, but this I can tell you: thousands upon thousands of your brethren are secretly following the road of the Lord, their God. Braving death, they pray for redemption and salvation. They are ready at any time to sanctify the name of God, just as your parents did."

Ferdinand's words were new and wonderful to Pierce. He looked up at the old man with big bewildered eyes. With beating heart he listened to the whispering voice.

From that fateful day on, the boy would get up each night and walk through the dark corridors to Ferdinand's cell. There they would sit together over a Hebrew book, and secretly learn Torah. Thus Ferdinand prepared the boy for the day when he would become Bar Mitzvah. On that day Pierce would enter the sacred covenant of his people. He would become a member of the community of Israel, which, like him, worshiped the God of their fathers in secret. Pierce awaited that day expectantly.

The night before the big day, Ferdinand reviewed all the prayers and blessings of the Bar Mitzvah ceremony. Ferdinand asked Pierce if he was ready to accept the grave responsibility of loyalty to his people and his God.

Pierce, in a firm voice, "*Yes!*"

In the morning, the monastery bells called everyone to prayer. How frightening these bells sounded to Pierce that morning! He accompanied the other boys to the monastery chapel. As they lustily sang the morning prayers, his lips whispered a Hebrew prayer to the God of his fathers–a prayer he had learned by heart at night from Ferdinand's lips.

After breakfast they told him Don Francisco Henriques had come to take him to his house for the day. Pierce was bewildered, frightened. He knew Don Henriques was one of the wealthy men of Lisbon. Pierce had often heard the monks bless him for being one of the faithful followers of the Church. Why had this man suddenly come to take him home? Today of all days! The great, the holy day, for which he had been waiting so long! What would Ferdinand say, and all the people waiting for him in some unknown place?

He was still turning it over in his mind and weeping in his heart when he heard his name called. Anxiously Pierce rose, and approached the monk who called him. Near the monk stood a tall, handsome nobleman. Pierce greeted him, bowing.

"Who are you, boy?" asked the man.

"Diego Pierce–the son of Don Salvador and Dona Angelica Pierce, peace to their souls!"

"Fine, Diego! And I am Don Francisco Henriques. I was a good friend of your parents–may they rest in peace! I have come to take you to my home for a visit."

His face and voice warmed the boy's heart. But how could he go with him, on this, the greatest and holiest day of his life?

"I'll go ask the abbot for permission," said Pierce. A sudden hope flared in his heart that Antonius would not allow him to go.

"I already have Father Antonius' permission," said Don Henriques.

The words fell on the boy's ear like stones.

They left the monastery.

During the whole journey they did not exchange a word. Don Henriques rode as a rich man should, on a beautiful horse. After him rode the boy, in monk's dress, on a little mule.

In a wealthy section of the town, they stopped at a beautiful palace. Frightened and trembling, Pierce followed the big man. The door opened, and they entered a big room. The boy was afraid to raise his eyes. He stood still, head hanging, his body full of misery. Then he felt a gentle hand on his head, and a familiar voice called his name.

The boy looked up and saw Ferdinand standing beside him. Pierce's face glowed with joy. With Ferdinand there, he had nothing to fear! Then he saw people seated around the room, all silent. Why were they quiet? What were they waiting for?

A servant entered the room, whispered something in Don Henriques' ear. Don Henriques gave a signal and everyone rose from his seat. The host led the way, holding Pierce's hand. The rest followed.

They passed through many chambers until they reached a small room with closets lining the walls. Don Henriques opened a closet and entered it with the boy. The closet wall opened, and they were in a big pit.

"Be careful, my son," said Don Henriques. "We have to go down some steps here."

In the darkness they descended many steps. The boy's heart trembled. Where is he leading me? The memory of the dark cave where his parents had taken him swept over him. He wanted to burst out into tears, but suddenly he saw a light. They were in a large cellar, where candles burned in candlesticks and men stood wrapped in white *talleitim*. The boy was filled with joy and fear.

They gave him a prayer shawl, in which he wrapped himself. He felt a great gladness. This, indeed, was the big day about which Ferdinand had told him. His day!

A deep, strong voice filled the room.

"Praise the Lord and let us exalt His name!"

Pierce recognized the voice and grew faint. Antonius—the head of the monastery! He had fallen into a trap! Ferdinand and Don Henriques had plotted against him! They would burn him at the stake! But after a moment, he grew calm. He saw Antonius, wrapped in a *tallit*, standing on the platform, and in his arms a Torah. Antonius put the Torah on the table, opened it, began to read from it.

"And it shall come to pass, if you listen to the voice of the Lord, thy God, and keep and obey all His commandments..."

He chanted the words with great feeling and in beautiful melody. The sound entered deep into the boy's soul, like a bright holy light.

Pierce closed his eyes. It seemed to him he was dreaming a sweet dream. He could not believe that Antonius and Don Henriques were Jews too.

He looked at the congregation sitting here in the cellar, listening, with a holy glow on their faces, to the words of the Torah. They were all his people—Jews. Brave Jews, daring death and disaster to be true to their faith.

He remembered what Ferdinand had said about the path to the God of Israel—a path of sorrow and danger, but also a path to redemption and salvation. Here they were, treading this path, and he, Pierce, was one of them.

There was sudden silence in the cellar. Pierce sat erect. Everyone was looking at him.

Antonius called, "Rise, Solomon, son of Meshulam Molkho!"

His heart said to him—"that's your name, Pierce; that and no other. They are calling you to the Torah. Go up!" Head high he went up—in the path of the God of Israel.

Later Antonius spoke to him, his voice sounding like a song, like a prayer. "Today you have joined the covenant of God and our people. You are taking upon yourself the holy duty of keeping the words of this Torah and walking in the path of your parents and forefathers. You have chosen it willingly. May you follow it all the days of your life!"

The picture of his childhood came to him vividly. He saw his father and mother standing in the mouth of the cave, he heard their voices.

"My son—you will remain a Jew—a Jew all your life. What did your father tell you? Who are you?"

"A Jew, Mother."

"Tell me again, my dear one."

"A Jew, Mother."

"Again, my beloved!"

"A Jew, Mother!"

The boy placed his hand on the Torah. "I swear it!" he cried in a strong, firm voice. "Amen, amen!"

A.A. Kabak.

THE SEPHARDIC AND THE ASHKENAZIC COMMUNITIES

How are the Sephardic Jews different from their counterpart group, the Ashkenazim? The following essay by the well-respected theologian Abraham Johsua Heschel gives some insight into these two important Jewish communities.

The Two Great Traditions

In the past thousand years, two major traditions flowered in Jewish life, corresponding to the two groups that have successively held the spiritual hegemony: first the Spanish Sephardic, and in the later period, the Ashkenazic.

The Sephardic group is composed of the descendants of Jews who settled in the Iberian Peninsula during the Mohammedan period. Spain is called in Hebrew *Sephard*, and these Jews therefore are known as Sephardim. Compelled to migrate and later expelled from Spain and Portugal in the fifteenth century, these Jews settled largely along the Mediterranean coast and in Holland, England, and their dependencies.

The Ashkenazic community includes the descendants of Jews who came from Babylon and Palestine to the Balkans and Central and Eastern Europe, and who since the later Middle Ages have spoken German or Yiddish. They are called Ashkenazic Jews, from the Hebrew word *Ashkenaz*, which means Germany.

Up to the nineteenth century, all Ashkenazic Jews who lived in the area bounded by the Rhine and the Dnieper and by the Baltic and the Black Sea, and in some neighboring regions as well, presented a culturally uniform group. At the center of this cultural period stood Rashi, the greatest commentator on the Bible and the Talmud, as well as Rabbi Jehudah the Pious and his circle. The spiritual development of the Ashkenazic period reached its climax in Eastern Europe, particularly with the spread of the Hasidic movement. Today the Ashkenazim form the preponderant majority of our people.

The Jews of the Iberian Peninsula were responsible for the earlier brilliant epoch in Jewish history, distinguished not only by monumental scientific achievements, but also by a universality of spirit. Their accomplishment was in some respects a synthesis of Jewish tradition and Moslem civilization.

The intellectual life of the Jews in Spain was deeply influenced by the surrounding world. Literary forms, scientific methods, philosophical categories, and even theological principles were often adopted from the Arabs. Stimulated and enriched in their writing and thinking by foreign patterns, Jewish authors were inclined to stress the basic agreements between the doctrines of their faith and the theories of great non-Jewish thinkers. Indeed, they often seemed to emphasize the elements Judaism had in common with classical philosophy to the neglect of pointing out its own specific features. They were under constant challenge and attack by members of other creeds, and felt compelled to debate and to defend the principles of their faith.

In the Ashkenazic period, the spiritual life of the Jews was lived in isolation. Accordingly, it grew out of its own ancient roots and developed in an indigenous environment, independent of the trends and conventions of the surrounding world. Intellectually more advanced than their average Germanic or Slavic neighbors, the Jews unfolded unique cultural patterns in thinking and writing, in their communal and individual ways of

Part of a mural showing a gathering of scholars in a Jewish street in Toledo, Spain in the thirteenth century.

life. Tenaciously adhering to their own traditions, they concentrated upon the cultivation of what was most their own, what was most specific and personal. They borrowed from other cultures neither substance nor form. What they wrote was literature created by Jews, about Jews, and for Jews. They apologized to no one, neither to philosophers nor theologians, nor did they ask the commendation of either prince or penman. They felt no need to compare themselves with anyone else, and they wasted no energy in refuting hostile opinions.

There, in Eastern Europe, the Jewish people came into its own. It did not live like a guest in somebody else's house, who must constantly keep in mind the ways and customs of the host. There Jews lived without reservation and without disguise, outside their homes no less than within them. When they used the phrase "the world asks" in their commentaries on the Talmud, they did not refer to a problem raised by Aristotle or Averroes. Their fellow students of Torah were to them the "world.". . .

The dualism of Sephardic and Ashkenazic culture did not disappear with the tragic expulsion from Spain in 1492. The Sephardic strain, striving after measure, order, and harmony, and the Ashkenazic strain, with its preference for the spontaneous and dynamic, can both be traced down to the modern period. The Sephardim retained their independent ways in custom and thought and refused to amalgamate. In their seclusion, a severe loyalty to their heritage was combined with a feeling of pride in the splendor of their past. Their synagogue services were like silent mirrors of the ancient rite. The spontaneous was tamed, the unbecoming eliminated. But the continual trimming of the offshoots often tended to suppress any unexpected drive in the roots. . . .

The culture of Spanish Sephardic Jews was shaped by an elite; it was derived from above and was hardly touched by the archaic simplicity, imaginative naïveté, and unaffected naturalness of the humble mass. . . .

Because the ideals of the Ashkenazic Jews were shared by all, the relations between the various parts of the community—between the scholarly and the ignorant, the Yeshiva student and the trader—had an intimate organic character. The earthiness of the villagers, the warmth of plain people, and the spiritual simplicity of the *maggidim* or lay preachers penetrated into the *beth ha-midrash*, the house of prayer that was also a house of study and learning. Laborers, peasants, porters, artisans, storekeepers, all were partners in the Torah. The *maggidim*—the term presumably originated in Eastern Europe—did not apply for diplomas to anyone. They felt authorized by God to be preachers of morals.

Here, in the Ashkenazic realm, the amalgamation of Torah and Israel was accomplished. Ideals became folkways, divine imperatives a human concern; the people itself became a source of Judaism, a source of spirit. The most distant became very intimate, very near. . . .

Much of what the Sephardim created was adopted by the Ashkenazim and transformed. Under the spell of the Hasidim, the rich and ponderous speculations of the Sephardic mystics were stripped of their tense and stern features without any loss of profundity or earnestness. The lofty and elaborate doctrines of the [Sephardic] Kabbalah were melted into thoughts understandable by the heart.

Abraham Joshua Heschel.

(Opposite page) The house of Moses Maimonides (1135-1204) in Fez, Morocco. Philosopher, medical writer, rabbi, and Talmudic scholar, Maimonides urged the reconciliation of reason and religious faith through logic.

THE FOUR BRANCHES OF JUDAISM

There are four branches in Judaism–Orthodox, Conservative, Reform, and, more recently, Reconstructionist. Each makes up a kind of community. Each is a large group of people with similar religious and cultural affiliations. These communities are broken up into smaller congregations, with their own respective synagogue and rabbi, but adhering to the beliefs and religious practices of the larger community.

Why Are There Divisions in Judaism?

Everyone knows that Orthodox Jews wear hats in the synagogue and conduct their services in Hebrew. They eat only kosher food, and will neither ride nor light fires on the Sabbath. Reform Jews, on the other hand, do not wear hats in the temple, and they conduct their services mostly in English. Few of them observe the kosher food laws, and none of them refrain from riding or lighting fires on the Sabbath. The behavior of Conservative Jews resembles that of the Orthodox while they are in the synagogue, but in daily life they act more like Reform Jews.

Part of the Reform argument for abolishing the old laws is that they are out of date. For instance, thousands of years ago, when the laws were made, you had to work to light a fire, and you had to make a horse work if you wanted to ride. But today there is no labor involved for man or animal in turning on an electric switch or in driving a car. Also, they say the laws against eating pork were sensible when the Bible was written, because at that time pork often caused trichinosis. But with today's hygienic farming, plus governmental inspection, pork can be as safe and healthful as any other meat.

If this is so, then why do people stay Orthodox? What does an intelligent and enlightened Orthodox Jew say to the Reform arguments? The Orthodox Jew would say that the Torah was given to us by God. God knew that conditions would change. Nevertheless, He gave the Torah for all time. And the Orthodox Jew says that because the Torah comes from God, we must always obey it, even when we don't understand its purpose. But this basic Orthodox belief cannot be proved. It is said many times in the Torah that the Torah is God-given. But this is a proof only to someone who believes that every word in the Torah is literally true....

The central purpose of the Torah is to teach us how to lead the good life. And for the Orthodox Jew, the only way to do this is to obey the 613 God-given commandments. But for the non-Orthodox, the path is not so simple. He must first ask if these laws still serve the central purpose. And if they don't, then he must change these laws or stop observing them.

The non-Orthodox Jew has found that a whole group of laws are not concerned with the good life, with morality. There is nothing moral (or immoral) about not eating pork, or wearing a hat in synagogue, or conducting services in Hebrew. We call this kind of law "ritual" or "ceremonial."

At one time, a radical wing of Reform Judaism dropped this whole class of laws. These extremist Reform Jews believed that ritual is a holdover from the past and has no useful function today. They felt that if they got rid of these external ceremonies they would be left with the pure essence of Judaism–ethical monotheism.

There are still Reform Jews today who take this radical view, but far fewer than fifty years ago. In recent years, even in Reform, there has been a growing emphasis on tradition. Reform services tend more and more to be conducted partly in Hebrew. And many Reform Jews are returning to ancient practices, such as lighting candles on Friday night.

One reason for this turning back to ritual is the feeling that it is a powerful help toward living the good life. The good life itself consists in living by the moral laws, but ceremonies can lead us in the right direction. We cannot behave morally without self-discipline, and traditional laws concerning fasting or praying in Hebrew at fixed periods help achieve self-discipline. It is all very well for a person to say he will pray whenever the spirit moves him; but we know from experience that unless he sets fixed times, the spirit may never move him.

Of course, this is not the whole story. There are more complicated cases in which the observance of a law may hurt the good life instead of helping it. If a man studies Hebrew with love and patience, his religious life will be greatly enriched if he prays in Hebrew. But if someone does not understand the language, his Hebrew prayer may be completely empty of meaning. Or one man may attain a deep sense of the sanctity of Yom Kippur by fasting. But the man who spends all that day thinking only of food should not have fasted in the first place.

Shall we keep Hebrew in the services, or drop it? Shall we fast on Yom Kippur, or eat? It is difficult, if not impossible, to arrive at "correct" answers, and Conservative and Reform Jews (even among themselves) frequently disagree on these questions. And so we see that even when we try to change the laws to guide us in the good life today, there is no one way of changing them.

But keeping the ceremonial laws has still another purpose. It not only serves moral ends, but it also keeps the Jews together as a people. We know that it is necessary for the Jews to remain a separate entity if they are to fulfill the mission of Israel. The radical Reform Jews believe that the Jews can maintain their identity simply by remaining faithful to their beliefs. But all other Jews believe that ritual is necessary, too. They believe that the Jews never would have survived through all these centuries if they had not had a way of living–of eating and dressing and speaking and praying–which was different from all others, and distinctively Jewish....

There is a sharp difference between Orthodoxy and non-Orthodoxy; but between Conservatism and Reform there is only a variation in emphasis. Reform Judaism has always stressed that the one God of Judaism is the God of all mankind. The moral laws of Judaism are valid for all nations, and Israel's mission is in behalf of the whole human race. This philosophy is called *universalism*. The universalist elements have of course always been an essential part of Judaism. But during the centuries of ghetto life, when the Jews were cut off from other people, the universalist ideas were sometimes understressed, or even forgotten. When the Jew emerged from the medieval ghetto in the nineteenth century, the universalist ideas came to life again in Reform Judaism.

Conservative Judaism stresses the element of historical continuity. Conservatism stresses that traditions have helped hold the Jews together. It believes that strict following of old customs is not good, but it believes in a living tradition which changes according to the needs of the time. Therefore Conservative Judaism has concentrated on keeping alive much of the Jewish religious tradition, including its customs, ceremonies and folklore.

But it must not be thought that this difference between Reform and Conservative Judaism is more than a difference in emphasis. On the one hand, even the most radical wing in Reform Judaism has never wholly denied that Judaism must have a living tradition if it is to continue to exist. On the other hand, Conservative Judaism has always affirmed that the Jewish reli-

Simchat Torah in the Lower East Side, New York City.

gion has a universal message for all men. . . .

Each division fulfills a function essential to the preservation of Judaism. Each Jew must decide for himself his branch of Judaism. But whichever he chooses, he should be glad that the others exist.

Emile L. Fackenheim.

Reconstructionism is the smallest and youngest of the four branches of Judaism. According to sociologist and political scientist Leonard Fein, "Reconstructionism is probably the dominant belief system of American Jews," though many Jews may not identify themselves as being part of this community. With its strong emphasis on Jewish culture, Jewish community and "havurot" (groups of friends who study and celebrate together) and egalitarianism, the Reconstructionist community is very much in the spirit of Judaism.

How Reconstructionism Differs

Unlike Orthodoxy, Reconstructionism does not believe the Jewish religion to be supernaturally revealed to Moses, never to be changed. Nor do we accept as final the authority of the Talmud or rabbinic interpretations of talmudic law. Reconstructionists believe that every generation has the responsibility–the right and the duty–to fashion its beliefs and practices in the light of its own highest ideals and authentic knowledge. . . .

Unlike classical Reform, which sought to free the universal ideals of Judaism from every ethnic and particularist expression and which denied the importance of Jewish peoplehood, Reconstructionism holds that religion is a function of our peoplehood. It is a consequence of the people's response to history. Great Jewish ideals will be lost if they are not rooted in the unique experiences of the Jewish people. They become cold if not communicated through the particular rites and ceremonies of our people's historically developed pageantry. . . .

Hence Reconstructionism places greater emphasis than does Reform upon traditional rites and practices, upon Zion, upon a knowledge of Hebrew, upon the structures of corporate Jewish living, upon the so-called secular aspects of Jewish existence such as art, music, dance, literature and social action. . . .

Unlike Conservative Judaism, which holds Jewish Law to be authoritative and delimits to a small group of legal experts the right to change the law, Reconstructionists insist that the law itself must be judged by the standards of feasibility, morality and justice, which committed Jews feel to be relevant for life. Thus, while respecting tradition, Reconstructionists have been more willing than Conservative Jews to bring changes to the law and practice of religion. While respecting talmudic law as a guide and as a sign of past convictions and value judgments, Reconstructionists are prepared to have the law changed by the Jews themselves, by rabbis and laypeople acting in responsible concert.

Reconstructionists believe that godliness is achieved through human devotion to truth and justice, through compassion and understanding. We are confident that all people are given the capacity to redeem their lives. We believe that there is a power that works through us, presses us, drives us onward toward a just human community. We do not believe in a personal Messiah but we are Messianic in our hopes for the future. It is this profound respect for the givenness of human dignity and this faith in man's ultimate capacity to achieve salvation together that marks Reconstructionism as a philosophy of religious naturalism.

From "The Reconstructionist Movement: Theory and Practice."

"You shall not separate yourself from the community."   Ethics of the Father, 2:5.

Jewish Community

Jews must gather, not because they are friends or even because they agree, but simply because they need each other to go on being Jews. Hermits are noticeably absent from our history. What is more, tzaddikim—the pious ones, the ego models for the Jews—who could probably live their Jewish lives without the support of a group, don't want to. They teach us by their example that there is intrinsic value in performing mitzvot—commandments—as a group. The very act of working with the congregation for the sake of heaven is a mitzvah in itself. And so it has been until our own era.

Sharon and Michael Strassfeld.

The setting of your Bar Mitzvah celebration and the guests with whom you share it are two very important elements of your Bar Mitzvah. They represent the Jewish community to which you and your family belong. You may not remain in the same community all your life, but the community that has embraced you into Jewish adulthood is certainly worth remembering. The following pages will help you to document your Bar Mitzvah in its community context. Be sure to ask your rabbi, your Bar Mitzvah teacher and your other guests to add their comments to your book. After all, it is people that make up a community.

FACTS ABOUT YOUR COMMUNITY

Description of your Bar Mitzvah setting and why you chose it:

_____

Your Synagogue: _____

Your Rabbi: _____

Your Bar Mitzvah Teacher: _____

Jewish organizations to which you and your family belong:

PERSONAL COMMENTS FROM YOUR GUESTS

Rabbi:

Bar Mitzvah Teacher:

Other Guests:

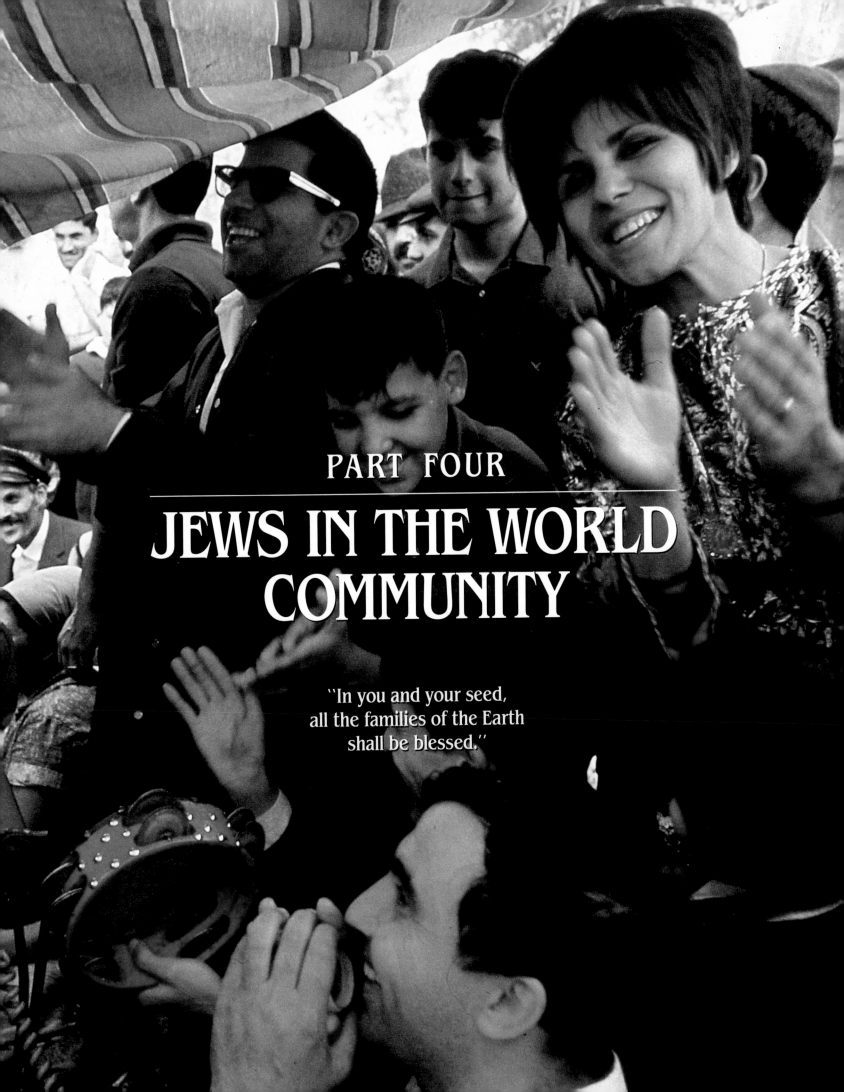

PART FOUR

JEWS IN THE WORLD COMMUNITY

"In you and your seed,
all the families of the Earth
shall be blessed."

Out of the Strong, Sweetness

Out of the strong, sweetness;
and out of the dead body of the lion of Judah,
the prophecies and psalms;
out of the slaves in Egypt,
out of the wandering tribesmen of the deserts
and the peasants of Palestine,
out of the slaves of Babylon and Rome,
out of the ghettos of Spain and Portugal, Germany and Poland
the Torah and the prophecies,
the Talmud and the sacred studies, the hymns and songs of the
  Jews;
and out of the Jewish dead
of Belgium and Holland, of Rumania, Hungary, and Bulgaria,
of France and Italy and Yugoslavia,
of Lithuania and Latvia, White Russia and Ukrainia,
of Czechoslovakia and Austria,
Poland and Germany,
out of the greatly wronged
a people teaching and doing justice;
out of the plundered
a generous people;
out of the wounded a people of physicians;
and out of those who met only with hate,
a people of love, a compassionate people.

Charles Reznikoff.

(Above) A Sabra cactus is sweet inside and thorny outside. Those born in Israel are called Sabras.

(Preceding page) Israelis of Moroccan Jewish descent celebrate the birthday of Maimonides.

Becoming a member of the greater Jewish community entails a sense of responsibility as a citizen of the world. This doesn't mean that you must assume all the burdens of the world. What it does mean is that it is time to look outside yourself, to be more aware of the people around you, as well as those in the world at large. Judaism is based on a strong moral tradition. It is important to be generous, fair, and compassionate to the people with whom you have close contact—your family, your friends, your neighbors. It is also essential to understand and be respectful of those who are different from you.

Universalism has been in the nature of the Jewish people for thousands of years. Since the destruction of the First Temple in Jerusalem, the Jewish people have been dispersed throughout the world and have been forced into a very conscious awareness of other peoples. Though it has been important for Jews to group together and to practise their own customs in order not to lose their identity, they have always been painfully conscious of the need for universal tolerance. Judaism teaches that God is not only the God of the Jews but equally the God of all people. Judaism's prophetic visions encompass all humanity. In the future, said the prophet Isaiah, all the nations will learn to live in peace with each other.

Abraham became the first Jew when he accepted a contract with God in which he promised to be God's partner in the job of caring for all humanity, "all the families of the earth." He and his descendants, the Jewish people, took on the responsibility of teaching the concept of one God and of universal morality. Abraham introduced ethical monotheism, and his descendants were to provide a moral model to improve the world. Judaism was in fact the basis for the other two great ethical cultures of our time, Christianity and Islam.

The special covenant with God, and the label of the "chosen people" which accompanied it, has been a mixed blessing for the Jews. Traditionally, it is in the sense of moral commitment that Jews considered themselves the chosen people. The devout Jew accepted the status with humility and thanksgiving, seeing it as a yoke and a burden as well as a distinction. Being "chosen" did not mean being privileged. Instead, it often meant increased responsibility, hardships, and persecution. The exclusivity of calling themselves the chosen people may also have brought additional hostility onto the Jews. In the words of Sholom Aleichem: "Dear God, I know we are the chosen people, but couldn't you choose some other people for a change?"

On the other hand, the unwavering moral commitment and steadfast sense of identity based on the covenant have given Jews the motive and the courage to survive many catastrophes over the last 4,000 years. They have persevered through a multitude of persecutions and resisted conversion, from the time of the Babylonian exile to the tragic Holocaust in recent times. Jewish exclusivity may have served a purpose: to keep the Jewish heritage intact—but not the expense of others. Jewish identity has always been accompanied by a strong sense of respect for humanity.

We Alone Survived

Of the whole welter of ancient peoples we alone survived... Dispersed, broken into fragments...multi-colored and diversified, black and yellow and white, occidental and oriental but withal one people.

We survived, I should like to believe, because we were inveterate optimists. No obstacle stopped us, no crisis dismayed us, no catastrophe crushed us. We swallowed the bitterness of life and pursued the sweet thereof. Aye, we loved life—this very thing of living. "Be fruitful and multiply," we urged unashamed, unapologetic..."Remember us unto life, O King, that delightest in life."...Israel wanted life abundantly, clung to it and lived.

We survived because of Torah. We loved life and our sages knew that life needs direction, norms, discipline. We denied

A soldier of the Israeli army blows the ram's horn during the Hakkel ceremony in Jerusalem, October, 1962. Hakkel commemorates the ancient ritual of reading a portion of the Torah.

ourselves that we might live. We placed ourselves under the yoke of the Torah and rejoiced that we had *Mitzvot*. The Prophets, the Scribes, the Pharisees fashioned Torah—the blending of thought with resolution—thought that leads to action. The Torah is teaching and living. Our greatest intellects concerned themselves with "everyday things." Even the trifles that "man treads under his heel" were the concern of a Hillel, an Akiba, a Rashi, or a Maimonides.

We survived because ours was a genuine democracy. No caste system was permitted to develop, no autocrat went unchallenged. The lowly and the mighty were the children of Abraham, Isaac and Jacob. Smiths, peddlers, shoemakers could become great teachers and be hearkened to by the whole people. The son of a carpenter could believe himself a Messiah and humble fishermen might become the founders of a new religion.

At the end of the eighteenth century it could be maintained in civilized England that "everyone but an idiot knows that the lower classes must be kept poor," and that it were folly to educate the poor for they might become "insolent to their superiors." In Israel it was hoped in the remotest past, "Would God that all the Lord's people become prophets." We could say to every man, "*Bishvilkha Nivra Ha-Olam*," for thy sake the world was created. . . .

We survived, I believe, above all, because of the prophetic voices that broke out in Israel from time to time. We were blessed with men that never made peace with the foibles of the people or the whims of the rulers. We were compelled to listen to denunciations that "cried aloud like a trumpet." We could not allow ourselves to sink into the sweet lassitude of dissipation and degeneracy which led so many peoples to despair and death. We were shaken by a mighty hand and outstretched arm. Israel, we were warned, . . . "Wash ye, make you clean. . . cease to do evil; learn to do well; seek judgment, relieve the oppressed, judge the fatherless, plead for the widow."

Solomon Goldman.

The following contemporary story shows how Jews have learned to survive by adjusting to other cultures without losing their self-respect or their respect for others—and, also important, without losing their sense of humor.

The Loudest Voice

There is a certain place where dumb-waiters boom, doors slam, dishes crash; every window is a mother's mouth bidding the street shut up, go skate somewhere else, come home. My voice is the loudest.

There, my own mother is still as full of breathing as me and the grocer stands up to speak to her. "Mrs. Abramowitz," he says, "people should not be afraid of their children."

"Ah, Mr. Bialik," my mother replies, "if you say to her or her father 'Ssh,' they say, 'In the grave it will be quiet.'"

"From Coney Island to the cemetery," says my papa. "It's the same subway; it's the same fare."

I am right next to the pickle barrel. My pinky is making tiny whirl-pools in the brine. I stop a moment to announce: "Campbell's Tomato Soup. Campbell's Vegetable Beef Soup. Campbell's S-c-otch Broth. . ."

"Be quiet," the grocer says, "the labels are coming off."

"Please, Shirley, be a little quiet," my mother begs me.

In that place the whole street groans: Be quiet! Be quiet! but steals from the happy chorus of my inside self not a tittle or a jot.

There, too, but just around the corner, is a red brick building that has been old for many years. Every morning the children stand before it in double lines which must be straight. They are not insulted. They are waiting anyway.

I am usually among them. I am, in fact the first, since I begin with "A."

One cold morning the monitor tapped me on the shoulder. "Go to Room 409, Shirley Abramowitz," he said. I did as I was told. I went in a hurry up a down staircase to Room 409, which contained sixth-graders. I had to wait at the desk without wiggling until Mr. Hilton, their teacher, had time to speak.

After five minutes he said, "Shirley?"

"What?" I whispered.

He said, "My! My! Shirley Abramowitz! They told me you had a particularly loud, clear voice and read with lots of expression. Could that be true?"

"Oh yes," I whispered.

"In that case, don't be silly; I might very well be your teacher someday. Speak up, speak up."

"Yes," I shouted.

"More like it," he said. "Now, Shirley, can you put a ribbon in your hair or a bobby pin? It's too messy."

"Yes!" I bawled.

"Now, now, calm down." He turned to the class. "Children, not a sound. Open at page 39. Read till 52. When you finish, start again." He looked me over once more. "Now, Shirley, you know, I suppose, that Christmas is coming. We are preparing a beautiful play. Most of the parts have been given out. But I still need a child with a strong voice, lots of stamina. Do you know what stamina is? You do? Smart kid. You know, I heard you read 'The Lord is my shepherd' in Assembly yesterday. I was very impressed. Wonderful delivery. Mrs. Jordan, your teacher, speaks highly of you. Now listen to me, Shirley Abramowitz, if you want to take the part and be in the play, repeat after me, 'I swear to work harder than I ever did before.'"

I looked to heaven and said at once, "Oh, I swear." I kissed my pinky and looked at God.

"That is an actor's life, my dear," he explained. "Like a

soldier's, never tardy or disobedient to his general, the director. Everything," he said, "absolutely everything will depend on you."

That afternoon, all over the building, children scraped and scrubbed the turkeys and the sheaves of corn off the schoolroom windows. Goodbye Thanksgiving. The next morning a monitor brought red paper and green paper from the office. We made new shapes and hung them on the walls and glued them to the doors.

The teachers became happier and happier. Their heads were ringing like the bells of childhood. My best friend Evie was prone to evil, but she did not get a single demerit for whispering. We learned "Holy Night" without an error. "How wonderful!" said Miss Glacé, the student teacher. "To think that some of you don't even speak the language!" We learned "Deck the Halls" and "Hark! The Herald Angels". . . .They weren't ashamed and we weren't embarrassed.

Oh, but when my mother heard about it all, she said to my father: "Misha, you don't know what's going on there. Cramer is the head of the Tickets Committee."

"Who?" asked my father. "Cramer? Oh yes, an active woman."

"Active? Active has to have a reason. Listen," she said sadly, "I'm surprised to see my neighbors making tra-la-la for Christmas."

My father couldn't think of what to say to that. Then he decided: "You're in America! Clara, you wanted to come here. In Palestine the Arabs would be eating you alive. Europe you had pogroms. Argentina is full of Indians. Here you got Christmas. . . .Some joke, ha?"

"Very funny, Misha. What is becoming of you? If we came to a new country a long time ago to run away from tyrants, and instead we fall into a creeping pogrom, that our children learn a lot of lies, so what's the joke? Ach, Misha, your idealism is going away."

"So is your sense of humor."

"That I never had, but idealism you had a lot of."

"I'm the same Misha Abramovitch, I didn't change an iota. Ask anyone."

"Only ask me," says my mama, may she rest in peace. "I got the answer."

Meanwhile the neighbors had to think of what to say too. Marty's father said: "You know, he has a very important part, my boy."

"Mine also," said Mr. Sauerfeld.

"Not my boy!" said Mrs. Klieg. "I said to him no. The answer is no. When I say no! I mean no!"

The rabbi's wife said, "It's disgusting!" But no one listened to her. Under the narrow sky of God's great wisdom she wore a strawberry-blond wig.

Every day was noisy and full of experience. I was Right-hand Man. Mr. Hilton said: "How could I get along without you, Shirley?"

He said: "Your mother and father ought to get down on their knees every night and thank God for giving them a child like you."

He also said: "You're absolutely a pleasure to work with, my dear, dear child."

Sometimes he said: "For God's sakes, what did I do with the script? Shirley! Shirley! Find it."

Then I answered quietly: "Here it is, Mr. Hilton."

Once in a while, when he was very tired, he would cry out: "Shirley, I'm just tired of screaming at those kids. Will you tell Ira Pushkov not to come in till Lester points to that star the second time?"

Then I roared: "Ira Pushkov, what's the matter with you? Dope! Mr. Hilton told you five times already, don't come in till Lester points to that star the second time."

"Ach, Clara," my father asked, "what does she do there till six o'clock she can't even put the plates on the table?"

"Christmas," said my mother coldly.

"Ho! Ho!" my father said. "Christmas. What's the harm? After all, history teaches everyone. We learn from reading this is a holiday from pagan times also, candles, lights, even Chanukah. So we learn it's not altogether Christian. So if they think it's a private holiday, they're only ignorant, not patriotic. What belongs to history, belongs to all men. You want to go back to the Middle Ages? Is it better to shave your head with a secondhand razor? Does it hurt Shirley to learn to speak up? It does not. So maybe someday she won't live between the kitchen and the shop. She's not a fool."

I thank you, Papa, for your kindness. It is true about me to this day. I am foolish but I am not a fool.

That night my father kissed me and said with great interest in my career, "Shirley, tomorrow's your big day. Congrats."

"Save it," my mother said. Then she shut all the windows in order to prevent tonsillitis.

In the morning it snowed. On the street corner a tree had been decorated for us by a kind city administration. In order to miss its chilly shadow our neighbors walked three blocks east to buy a loaf of bread. The butcher pulled down black window shades to keep the colored lights from shining on his chickens. Oh, not me. On the way to school, with both my hands I tossed it a kiss of tolerance. Poor thing, it was a stranger in Egypt.

I walked straight into the auditorium past the staring children. "Go ahead, Shirley!" said the monitors. Four boys, big for their age, had already started work as propmen and stagehands.

Mr. Hilton was very nervous. He was not even happy. Whatever he started to say ended in a sideward look of sadness. He sat slumped in the middle of the front row and asked me to help Miss Glacé. I did this, although she thought my voice too resonant and said, "Show-off!"

Parents began to arrive long before we were ready. They wanted to make a good impression. From among the yards of drapes I peeked out at the audience. I saw my embarrassed mother.

Ira, Lester, and Meyer were pasted to their beards by Miss Glacé. She almost forgot to thread the star on its wire, but I reminded her. I coughed a few times to clear my throat. Miss Glacé looked around and saw that everyone was in costume and on line waiting to play his part. She whispered, "All right. . ." Then:

Jackie Sauerfeld, the prettiest boy in first grade, parted the curtains with his skinny elbow and in a high voice sang out:

"Parents dear
We are here
To make a Christmas play in time.
It we give
In narrative
And illustrate with pantomime."

He disappeared.

My voice burst immediately from the wings to the great shock of Ira, Lester, and Meyer, who were waiting for it but were surprised all the same.

"I remember, I remember, the house where I was born. . ."

Miss Glacé yanked the curtain open and there it was, the house—an old hayloft, where Celia Kornbluh lay in the straw with Cindy Lou, her favorite doll. Ira, Lester, and Meyer moved

slowly from the wings toward her, sometimes pointing to a moving star and sometimes ahead to Cindy Lou.

It was a long story and it was a sad story. I carefully pronounced all the words about my lonesome childhood, while little Eddie Braunstein wandered upstage and down with his shepherd's stick, looking for sheep. I brought up lonesomeness again, and not being understood at all except by some women everybody hated. Eddie was too small for that and Marty Groff took his place, wearing his father's prayer shawl. I announced twelve friends, and half the boys in the fourth grade gathered round Marty, who stood on an orange crate while my voice harangued. Sorrowful and loud, I declaimed about love and God and Man, but because of the terrible deceit of Abie Stock we came suddenly to a famous moment. Marty, whose remembering tongue I was, waited at the foot of the cross. He stared desperately at the audience. I groaned, "My God, my God, why hast thou forsaken me?" The soldiers who were sheiks grabbed poor Marty to pin him up to die, but he wrenched free, turned again to the audience, and spread his arms aloft to show despair and the end. I murmured at the top of my voice, "The rest is silence, but as everyone in this room, in this city—in this world—now knows, I shall have life eternal."

That night Mrs. Kornbluh visited our kitchen for a glass of tea.

"How's the virgin?" asked my father with a look of concern.

"For a man with a daughter, you got a fresh mouth, Abramovitch."

"Here," said my father kindly, "have some lemon, it'll sweeten your disposition."

They debated a little in Yiddish, then fell in a puddle of Russian and Polish. What I understood next was my father, who said, "Still and all, it was certainly a beautiful affair, you have to admit, introducing us to the beliefs of a different culture."

"Well, yes," said Mrs. Kornbluh. "The only thing...you know Charlie Turner—that cute boy in Celia's class—a couple others? They got very small parts or no part at all. In very bad taste, it seemed to me. After all, it's their religion."

"Ach," explained my mother, "what could Mr. Hilton do? They got very small voices; after all, why should they holler? The English language they know from the beginning by heart. They're blond like angels. You think it's so important they should get in the play? Christmas...the whole piece of goods... they own it."

I listened and listened until I couldn't listen any more. Too sleepy, I climbed out of bed and kneeled. I made a little church of my hands and said, "Hear, O Israel..." Then I called out in Yiddish, "Please, good night, good night. Ssh." My father said, "Ssh yourself," and slammed the kitchen door.

I was happy. I fell asleep at once. I had prayed for everybody: my talking family, cousins far away, passers-by, and all the lonesome Christians. I expected to be heard. My voice was certainly the loudest.

Grace Paley.

THE DIASPORA

A detail from the Titus Arch in Rome showing the conquest of Jerusalem, 70 C.E.

"No matter how foreign the soil, the Jewish people lived to flower and renew itself from generation to generation. Part of the answer to this enigma may lie in the dispersal itself– the scattering of the Jewish people which is called in a single word diaspora."

Abba Eban.

Diaspora originates from the Greek word *diaspore*, a milkweed pod containing many seeds which are scattered by the wind. It has come to mean the dispersion of the Jewish people around the world, either by exile or by their own choice.

Different attitudes are taken towards the diaspora. On one hand the diaspora connotes the state of captivity, homelessness, and alienation for Jews. It is often associated with antisemitism and world persecution of the Jewish people. For centuries, the Jews have mourned the loss of their homeland and have been vulnerable to the whims of the leaders of their host countries.

Diaspora, however, also signifies the voluntary settlement in environments where Jews and Judaism have been able to flourish. Today, in spite of the establishment of the State of Israel, there are ten million Jews living in the diaspora, mostly by choice. From their diaspora experiences Jews have learned from many

sources and have grown and adapted more freely than many other cultures. They have also had more opportunities to contribute and influence the reigning cultures of their time. In the following article, Abba Eban talks about the advantages of the diaspora.

The Uses of Adversity

The date is 586 before the Christian Era. The Temple of Solomon is burned to the ground. The Land of Judah is ravaged. Thousands of its people are carried off into Babylonian exile by the armies of Nebuchadnezzar. The Jewish memory would never lose the anguish of that hour. And from year to year, from generation to generation, on the ninth day of Av, the descendants of the Jewish exiles would recite the lamentation for the departed glory of their kingdom.

By all logic, the Jews should now have sunk into oblivion. But history does not always follow the voice of logic, and the Jews did not disappear, although for the next five centuries they roamed far and wide over the earth. They had learned what no other people had ever learned before–how to maintain their faith and identity away from home. They were autonomous,

"The Lamentation Over Jerusalem" by L. Horowitz (1838-1917).

mobile, unfettered by territorial roots. For this very reason, exile now set the Jewish mind and spirit freer than ever before to make contact with other civilizations. Temple sacrifices could be made only in Jerusalem, but synagogues could be built anywhere, and prayer was not restricted to any single place. Exile was also a liberation in the purely religious sense. . . .

The Jews with their new freedom were able to diffuse their culture and to transmit their ideas into history. Their identity no longer depended on a particular place. It could take expression in the power of principles and ideas; it could be expressed in synagogues and academies and in literature.

The Jews had very little influence on the civilizations of Babylonia and of Persia. But with Greece it was another matter. We find the great philosopher Philo of Alexandria, a contemporary of Jesus of Nazareth, engaging in discussion on the possibility of harmonizing Hebrew prophecy with Greek philosophy. Rabbinic Judaism also was to have a far greater influence than Titus could ever have imagined. Not directly: the Jews had little talent and little instinct, indeed, no power for conversion. They could not impose their ideas upon others. But who could have

predicted. . .what a powerful influence the Jewish captives were going to have through the penetration of universal culture in the rise and expansion of Christianity?

Abba Eban.

Diaspora Jews

When the Druzes come together
they sing.
When the gypsies come together
they dance.
When Englishmen come together
they are silent.
When Frenchmen come together
they laugh.
And what about the Jews?
Alas, when Jews get together
they sigh.

Rachel Boimwall.

139

*"There is a people scattered abroad
And dispersed among the nations."*

Book of Esther, 3:8.

The Jewish dispersion began when the Jewish State of Judea was conquered by the Babylonians and large numbers of its people were shipped to Babylonia. During their exile, the Jews struggled to keep their own culture and national heritage. They stayed together and continued to feel a strong affiliation with remaining kin back in the homeland.

When the Persians captured Babylonia, the Jews were permitted to return and rebuild their temple in Jerusalem, beginning the Second Jewish Commonwealth. But not all returned. Many Jews who had acquired wealth, position, and a better life remained in the Persian Empire by choice where they formed the first diaspora community.

The Book of Esther, found in the third division of the Bible, tells the story of one diaspora community in Persia. It is an allegory of Jewish life, Jewish bonds, and Jewish deliverance which represents not only the Persian period but many periods in Jewish history.

The Book of Esther

King Ahasuerus, who reigned over a hundred and twenty-seven provinces from India to Ethiopia, gave a banquet to the nobles and officers of the army and displayed his royal treasures. The banquet lasted one hundred and eighty days, and was followed by a seven-day banquet for all the people in Shushan, the capital. Queen Vashti also gave a banquet for the women. On the seventh day, when the king's heart was merry with wine, he commanded Queen Vashti to appear in order to show off her beauty, but Queen Vashti refused to go before the court. Enraged, the king asked his wise men what should be done with her. "Let the king assign her royal position to a better woman," Memucan advised, and the king acted accordingly. He also sent letters to every province directing that every man should be lord in his own house.

There was a Jew in Shushan by the name of Mordecai. He had adopted his orphaned cousin Esther and brought her up as his own daughter. Beautiful and lovely, she was taken into the royal house where she became a favorite. She said nothing about her people or her descent, for Mordecai had told her not to reveal it. The king loved Esther more than all his wives and he made her queen instead of Vashti.

After these events, King Ahasuerus promoted Haman and advanced him above all his officers. All bowed low before Haman, but Mordecai would not bow to him. This infuriated Haman so much that he decided to destroy all the Jews throughout the empire of Ahasuerus. He said to the king: "There is a certain people dispersed in every province of your kingdom whose laws are different from those of other people and they do not obey the king's laws. The king should not tolerate them in the land. If it please the king, let it be decreed that they be destroyed, and I will pay ten thousand talents of silver into the royal treasury."

"Keep your money," the king said to Haman, "and do what you like with the people." Then instructions were sent to all the king's provinces to massacre and destroy all the Jews, young and old, women and children in one day, the thirteenth day of the month of Adar. The king and Haman sat down to drink, but the city of Shushan was perplexed.

When Mordecai learned all that had been done, he rent his garments, put on sackcloth and went about the city, crying bitterly. There was great mourning among the Jews in every province, wherever the king's command was heard. Esther ordered Hathach to go and find out from Mordecai what was the meaning of it all. Mordecai told him all that had happened and gave him a copy of the decree, which he was to show to Esther, charging her to intercede with the king on behalf of her people.

When Hathach told Esther what Mordecai had said, she gave him this message for Mordecai: "Everybody knows that there is one penalty for any person who goes to the king without being summoned; it is death. I have not been summoned for thirty days." Whereupon Mordecai replied: "Do not imagine you will escape inside the royal palace any more than the rest of the Jews on the outside. If you keep silent at a time like this, relief and deliverance will arise from another quarter; but you will perish, you and your father's house. Who knows whether it was not for a time like this that you have been raised to royalty."

Then Esther sent this reply to Mordecai: "Go gather all the Jews of Shushan and fast on my behalf; eat and drink nothing for three days and three nights; I and my maids will fast likewise. Then I will go to the king, though it is against the law; and if I perish, I perish." Mordecai did as Esther ordered him.

On the third day Esther stood in the inner court of the royal palace. When the king saw Esther standing in the court, he held out the golden scepter to her; Esther approached and touched it. "What is your wish, Queen Esther," the king asked, "what is your request? It shall be given you were it even half of my kingdom." Esther said: "If it please the king, let the king and Haman come today to a banquet which I have prepared for the king."

"Bring Haman at once," the king ordered, "that we may do as Esther desires." So the king and Haman came to the banquet that Esther had prepared. As they were drinking wine, the king said to Esther: "What is your petition? It shall be granted; were it even half of my kingdom, it shall be fulfilled." But Esther replied: "My petition and my request—well, if it please the king, let the king and Haman come tomorrow to the banquet which I will prepare for them; tomorrow I will do as the king has said."

That day Haman was joyful and glad of heart. He told his friends and his wife Zeresh: "Queen Esther invited no one except myself along with the king to the banquet she had prepared, and she had invited me again tomorrow together with the king. But all this does me no good as long as I see Mordecai the Jew sitting at the king's gate." Then his wife and all his friends said to him: "Let a gallows be made, and in the morning tell the king to have Mordecai hanged upon it; then go merrily with the king to the banquet." This pleased Haman, and he had the gallows made.

On that night the king could not sleep, so he had the book of records brought and read in his presence. It was found that Mordecai had saved the king's life. The king asked: "What honor, what dignity has been bestowed on Mordecai for this?" "Nothing has been done for him," the king's attendants replied. Then the king asked: "Who is in the court?" Haman had just entered the outer court to speak to the king about hanging Mordecai. So the king's attendants said: "Haman is standing in the court." And the king said: "Let him come in."

Haman came in, and the king asked him: "What should be done to the man whom the king delights to honor?" Haman said to himself: "Whom would the king delight to honor more than me?" So he said to the king: "For the man whom the king delights to honor, let a royal robe be brought which the king has worn, and a horse on which the king has ridden, with a royal crown upon its head; let the robe and the horse be entrusted to

Details from a Scroll of Esther written on parchment and illuminated in China. Circa eighteenth century.

one of the king's noblest officials. He shall see that the man whom the king delights to honor is arrayed and led on horseback through the streets of the city, proclaiming: 'This is done for the man whom the king delights to honor.'"

The king said to Haman: "Make haste, take the robe and the horse, as you have said, and do all this to Mordecai the Jew; leave out nothing of what you have spoken." So Haman took the robe and the horse and arrayed Mordecai and led him on horseback through the streets of the city proclaiming: "This is done for the man whom the king delights to honor."

Then Haman hurried home lamenting, and told his wife Zeresh and all his friends everything that had befallen him. They said to him: "If Mordecai, before whom you have begun to fall, is of the Jewish people, you will never defeat him, but you will keep falling before him." Just as they were talking, the king's attendants arrived and hurried Haman to the banquet that Esther had prepared.

So the king and Haman came to feast with Queen Esther. On the second day of the banquet, the king again asked Esther: "What is your petition, Queen Esther? It shall be granted you. What is your request? Were it half my kingdom, it shall be fulfilled." Queen Esther replied: "If I have found favor in your sight, O king, and if it pleases the king, let my life be given me—that is my petition! Grant me my people—that is my request! I and my people are to be destroyed, to be slain, to be annihilated." King Ahasuerus asked Esther: "Who is it? Where is the man who has dared to do this?" Esther replied: "A foe, an enemy, this wicked Haman!"

Haman trembled before the king and the queen. The king rose in fury from the feast and went into the palace garden. Haman came forward to beg Queen Esther for his life, for he saw that the king had determined evil against him. When the king came back from the palace garden, Haman had fallen on the couch where Esther sat! "Will he even violate the queen in my presence, in my own house?" said the king. One of the royal attendants, Harbonah, said: "At Haman's house a gallows is standing, which he prepared for Mordecai who saved the king's life." "Hang him on that!" the king ordered. So they hanged Haman on the gallows which he had prepared for Mordecai.

Then Esther spoke again to the king; she fell at his feet and begged him with tears to avert the evil design of Haman against the Jews. She said: "If it please the king, let an order be written to revoke the letters sent out by Haman, in which he commanded the destruction of the Jews throughout the king's empire. How can I bear to witness the calamity that befalls my people? How can I endure the destruction of my kindred?" Thereupon King Ahasuerus said to Esther and Mordecai: "Write as you please about the Jews, write it in the name of the king and seal it with the signet of the king."

The king's secretaries were summoned, and an edict was written to the governors and officials of the provinces, from India to Ethiopia, to every province in its own script and to every people in its own language, and also to the Jews in their script and their language. The writing was in the name of King Ahasuerus and sealed with the king's signet ring. Letters were sent by mounted couriers riding on swift horses. By these the king gave the Jews permission to gather and defend their lives on the thirteenth day of the twelfth month, which is the month of Adar.

The couriers rode out in haste, and the decree was issued in Shushan. The Jews had light and joy and gladness and honor. In every province and in every city, wherever the king's edict arrived, there was gladness and joy among the Jews. Indeed, many pagans became Jews.

Mordecai sent despatches, giving to the Jews in every city the king's permission to defend their lives and destroy any armed forces that might attack them. On the thirteenth day of Adar, the Jews triumphed over their adversaries. In Shushan they fought for their lives on the thirteenth and the fourteenth, resting on the fifteenth and making that a day of feasting and rejoicing and sending gifts to one another.

Mordecai charged all the Jews to keep both the fourteenth and the fifteenth of the month of Adar, every year, as days of feasting and rejoicing. These days are called *Purim* after *pur*, lot, for Haman had cast the lot to destroy and annihilate the Jews, but his wicked plot recoiled upon his own head. Mordecai was great and popular among the Jews, for he sought their welfare and peace.

JEWS AROUND THE WORLD

"Jewish history is interlaced with that of every other nation and empire."

The conquest of the Jews by Babylonia was followed by the Greek conquest in 333 B.C.E., and finally the Roman conquest in 70 C.E.–which resulted in the destruction of the Second Jewish Commonwealth. From this time, until the formation of the State of Israel in 1948, the Jewish people lived without a homeland in the lands of their dispersion, where they were alternately welcomed and expelled.

By the end of the second century, there were diaspora communities throughout the Roman Empire. Jewish communities spread from a small area bordering the Mediterranean Sea to all parts of the Old World–Greece, Italy, Spain, North Africa, France, Germany, England, Holland, Russia, Poland, Lithuania, etc.–and years later to the North and South American continents.

Some diaspora communities blended in with their host cultures. Others kept more to themselves. But always there were mutual influences between host culture and Jewish "guest." The result was that Jewish communities throughout the world developed diverse characteristics. The main precepts of Judaism remained the same, but Jewish prayers and rituals differed from place to place. Though Hebrew remained the holy language of the Jews, different pronunciations developed, while the indigenous languages of the host countries were usually spoken in everyday life. Jewish occupations varied, according to the environment. Even physical characteristics amongst groups of Jews began to differ with time. But what remained as a bond among all diaspora communities around the world was a common history and a common belief in Jewish roots and values.

Bonds of Kinship

The universalism that permeates the faith of Israel is reflected not only in its theological formulations and in its visions of the future, but in the very composition of its people. This seemingly "exclusive" people includes those whose skins range from the lightest to the darkest in colors, and within it a broad range of cultural diversity is represented. Yet despite the diversity that exists among them and the multitude of languages they speak, Jews regard themselves as related, as true brethren stemming from a common Semitic family. Although it is religion which unites them and it is only on the basis of religion that newcomers are admitted into fellowship, this feeling of kinship is very strong–and the mystery deepens when we realize that even Jews who rebel against the faith and discard its religious beliefs and practices are still regarded as Jews, and generally themselves still feel the bonds of kinship.

Rabbi Hayim Halevy Donin.

A young immigrant from Ethiopia studies in school with his Sabra friend.

Amongst the oldest diaspora communities are those which developed in the Middle East and in North Africa. Though these Jews identified themselves as Jews first and foremost, they were greatly influenced by the surrounding Muslim culture. Elias Canetti, winner of the 1981 Nobel Prize for Literature, describes his visit to the Jewish district of Marrakesh in Morocco. Though this trip took place during the mid-twentieth century, the distinctly oriental way of life of this community takes us back to another era in history.

A Visit to the Mellah

On the third morning, as soon as I was alone, I found my way to the Mellah. I came to a cross-roads where there were a great many Jews standing about. The traffic streamed past them and round a corner. I saw people going through an arch that looked as if it had been let into a wall, and I followed them. Inside the wall, enclosed by it on all four sides, lay the Mellah, the Jewish quarter.

I found myself in a small, open bazaar. Men squatted among their wares in little low booths; others, dressed European style, sat or stood. The majority had on their heads the black skull-cap with which the Jews here mark themselves out, and a great many wore beards. The first shops I came to sold material. One man was measuring off silk. Another bent thoughtfully over his swiftly-moving pencil, reckoning. Even the more richly-appointed shops seemed very small. Many had callers; in one of the booths two very fat men were carelessly ensconced about a third, lean man–the proprietor–and were holding a lively yet dignified discussion with him.

I walked past as slowly as possible and looked at the faces. Their heterogeneity was astonishing. There were faces that in other clothing I would have taken for Arab. There were luminous old Rembrandt Jews. There were Catholic priests of wily quietness and humility. There were Wandering Jews whose restlessness was written in every lineament. There were Frenchmen. There were Spaniards. There were ruddy-complexioned Russians. There was one you felt like hailing as the patriarch. Abraham; he was haughtily addressing Napoleon, and a hot-tempered knowall who looked like Goebbels was trying to butt in. I thought of the transmigration of souls. Perhaps, I wondered, every human soul has to be a Jew once, and here they all are: none remembers what he was before, and even when this is so clearly revealed in his features that I, a foreigner, can recognize it, every one of these people still firmly believes he stands in direct line of descent from the people of the Bible.

But there was something that they all had in common, and as soon as I had accustomed myself to the rich variety of their faces and their expressions I tried to find out what it was. They had a way of swiftly glancing up and forming an opinion of the person going past. Not *once* did I pass unnoticed. When I stopped they would scent a purchaser and examine me accordingly. But mostly I caught the swift, intelligent look long before I stopped, and I even caught it when I was walking on the other side of the street. Even in the case of the few who lay there with Arab indolence, the look was never indolent: it came, a practised scout, and swiftly moved on. There were hostile looks among them; cold, indifferent, disapproving, and infinitely wise looks. But none of them struck me as stupid. They were the looks of people who are always on their guard but who, expecting hostility, do not wish to evoke it: no trace of a challenge; and a fear that is careful to keep itself hidden. . . .

I noticed how, the deeper I penetrated into the Mellah, the poorer everything became. The beautiful woollens and silks were

View of the Jewish bazaar in Tetuan, Morocco. Circa 1860.

behind me. No one looked wealthy and princely like Abraham. The bazaar by the entrance gate had been a kind of posh quarter; the actual life of the Mellah, the life of the simple people, went on here. I came into a small square that struck me as being the heart of the Mellah. Men and women stood together around an oblong fountain. The women carried pitchers that they filled with water. The men were filling their leather water-containers. Their donkeys stood beside them, waiting to be watered. A few open-air cooks squatted in the middle of the square. Some were frying meat, others little doughnuts. They had their families with them, their wives and children; it was as if they had moved house out into the square and were living and cooking their meals here now. . . .

I had the feeling that I was really somewhere else now, that I had reached the goal of my journey. I did not want to leave; I had been here hundreds of years ago but I had forgotten and now it was all coming back to me. I found exhibited the same density and warmth of life as I feel in myself. I *was* the square as I stood in it. I believe I am it always.

I found parting from it so difficult that every five or ten minutes I would come back. Wherever I went from then on, whatever else I explored in the Mellah, I kept breaking off to return to the little square and cross it in one direction or another in order to assure myself that it was still there.

I turned first into one of the quiet streets in which there were no shops, only dwelling-houses. Everywhere, on the walls, beside doors, some way up from the ground, large hands had been painted, each finger clearly outlined, mostly in blue: they were for warding off the evil eye. It was the sign I found used most commonly, and people painted it up for preference on the place where they lived. Through open doors I had glimpses of courtyards; they were cleaner than the streets. Peace flowed out of them over me. I would have loved to step inside but did not dare, seeing no one. I would not have known what to say if I had suddenly come across a woman in such a house. I was myself alarmed at the thought of perhaps alarming someone. The silence of the houses communicated itself as a kind of wariness. But it did not last long. A high, thin noise that sounded at first like crickets grew gradually louder until I thought of an aviary full of birds. 'What can it be? There's no aviary here with hundreds of birds! Children! A school!' Soon there was no doubt about it: the deafening hubbub came from a school.

Through an open gateway I could see into a large courtyard. Perhaps two hundred tiny little children sat crammed together on benches; others were running about or playing on the ground. Most of those on the benches had primers in their

A view of Fez, the Imperial capital of Morocco, with the Jewish cemetery in the foreground.

hands. In groups of three or four they rocked violently backwards and forwards, reciting in high-pitched voices: 'Aleph. Beth. Gimel.' The little black heads darted rhythmically to and fro; one of them was always the most zealous, his movements the most vehement; and in his mouth the sounds of the Hebrew alphabet rang out like a decalogue in the making.

I had stepped inside and was trying to unravel the tangle of activity. The smallest children were playing on the floor. Among them stood a teacher, very shabbily dressed; in his right hand he held a leather belt, for beating. He came up to me obsequiously. His long face was flat and expressionless, its lifeless rigidity in

marked contrast to the liveliness of the children. He gave the impression that he would never be able to master them, that he was too badly paid. He was a young man, but *their* youth made him old. He spoke no French, and I expected nothing of him. It was enough for me that I could stand there in the middle of the deafening noise and look around a bit. But I had underestimated him. Beneath his rigor mortis there lurked something like ambition: he wanted to show me what his children could do.

He called a little boy over, held a page of the primer up in front of him in such a way that I could see it too, and pointed to Hebraic syllables in quick succession. He switched from line to

two more children. Throughout this proceeding the din continued unabated, and the Hebraic syllables fell like raindrops in the raging sea of the school.

Meanwhile other children came up to me and stared at me inquisitively, some cheeky, some shy, some flirtatious. The teacher, in his impenetrable wisdom, ruthlessly drove off the shy ones while letting the cheeky ones do as they liked. He was the poor and unhappy overlord of this part of the school; when the performance was over the meagre traces of satisified pride disappeared from his face. I thanked him very politely and, to give him a lift, somewhat condescendingly, as if I were an important visitor. His satisfaction must have been obvious; with the clumsiness of touch that dogged me in the Mellah I determined to return next day and only then give him some money. I stayed a moment longer, watching the boys at their reciting. Their rocking to and fro appealed to me; I like them best of all. Then I left, but the din I took with me. It accompanied me all the way to the end of the street.

This now started to become busier, as if it led to some important public place. Some way in front of me I could see a wall and a large gateway. I did not know where it led to, but the closer I got to it the more beggars I saw, sitting on either side of the street. I was puzzled by them, not having seen any Jewish beggars before. When I reached the gateway I saw ten or fifteen of them, men and women, mostly old people, squatting in a row. I stood rather self-consciously in the middle of the street and pretended to be examining the gate, whereas in reality I was studying the faces of the beggars

A young man came over to me, pointed to the wall, said 'le cimetière israélite', and offered to take me in. They were the only words of French he spoke. I followed him quickly through the gate. He moved fast, and there was nothing to say. I found myself in a very bare, open space where not a blade of grass grew. The gravestones were so low that you hardly noticed them; you tripped over them as if they had been ordinary stones. The cemetery looked like a vast heap of rubble; perhaps that was what it had been once, only later being assigned its more serious purpose. Nothing in it stood up to any height. The stones you could see and the bones you could imagine were all *lying*. It was not a pleasant thing to walk erect; you could take no pride in doing so, you only felt ridiculous.

Cemeteries in other parts of the world are designed in such a way as to give joy to the living. They are full of things that are alive, plants and birds, and the visitor, the only person among so many dead, feels buoyed up and strengthened. His own condition strikes him as enviable. He reads people's names on the gravestones; he has survived them all. Without admitting it to himself, he has something of the feeling of having defeated each one of them in single combat. He is sad too, of course, that so many are no more, but at the same time this makes him invincible. Where else can he feel that? On what battlefield of the world is he the sole survivor? Amid the supine he stands erect. But so do the trees and gravestones. They are planted and set up there and surround him like a kind of bequest that is there to please him.

But in that desolate cemetery of the Jews there is nothing. It is truth itself, a lunar landscape of death. Looking at it, you could not care less who lies where. You do not stoop down, you make no attempt to puzzle it out. There they all lie like rubble and you feel like scurrying over them, quick as a jackal. It is a wilderness of dead in which nothing grows any more, the last wilderness, the very last wilderness of all.

Elias Canetti.

line, backwards and forwards across the page at random; I was not to think the boy had learned it by heart and was reciting blind, without reading. The little fellow's eyes flashed as he read out: 'La-lo-ma-nushe-ti-ba-bu.' He did not make a single mistake and did not falter once. He was his teacher's pride, and he read faster and faster. When he had finished and the teacher had taken the primer away I patted him on the head and praised him—in French, but *that* he understood. He retired to his bench and made as if he could no longer see me, while the next boy took his turn. This one was much shyer and made mistakes; the teacher released him with a gentle spank and fetched out one or

Language was an important factor in the diaspora communities. Hebrew was taught in most communities, but was reserved for prayer and study. It was the language of the host country that was more often used for everyday use. However, in several of the larger diaspora cultures, new folk languages were developed for everyday life. These languages were often a cross between Hebrew and the language of the region.

After the Roman conquest, Jews settled in the Iberian peninsula and flourished during what is called the "Jewish Golden Age of Spain." Before 1492, one out of every ten Spaniards was Jewish, or descended from Jews. Jews were prominent in commerce, medicine, literature and the arts. As Sephardic culture bloomed, so did the Sephardic vernacular *Ladino*, a mixture of medieval Spanish and Hebrew, written in the Hebrew alphabet. Expelled from Spain in 1391 and again in 1492, Sephardic Jews migrated to Portugal, Turkey, North Africa, Holland and England, bringing with them the Sephardic culture and the Ladino language. Today Ladino is still used by Sephardic Jews throughout the world.

The early Ashkenazic Jews who first settled in the land along the Rhine River used French, not German, as their language. From the eleventh century, the Jews in the Rhine provinces began to speak German which, combined with Hebrew, developed into the *Yiddish* language. When Jews were expelled from Germany several centuries later, they took their Yiddish language with them to Poland, Galicia, Lithuania, Hungary, Rumania, Russia, etc.

Yiddish became a cultural bond amongst Jews throughout the European continent, and later in America. Before the Second World War, Yiddish was the language of 11 million Jews. By the 1920's, two-thirds of all Jews in the world understood Yiddish. In its heyday, Yiddish became the language used by Jewish writers to create the rich Jewish literature, folksongs and theater of the nineteenth and early twentieth centuries.

Today, Yiddish is considered by some to be a dying language, due to the destruction of Eastern European Jewish culture during the Holocaust. However, some estimate that there are still four million people who speak Yiddish, and there is a growing interest in the revival of the Yiddish culture. Amongst today's greatest champions of the Yiddish language and culture is Isaac Bashevis Singer, Yiddish writer, scholar and winner of the 1978 Nobel Prize for Literature.

From I. B. Singer's 1978 Nobel Lecture

NOBEL PRIZE CITATION:
"The Nobel Prize for Literature to
ISAAC BASHEVIS SINGER
for his impassioned narrative art
which, with roots in a Polish-Jewish
cultural tradition, brings universal
human conditions to life."

Mr. Singer read the following in Yiddish, at the start of the lecture:

The high honor bestowed upon me by the Swedish Academy is also a recognition of the Yiddish language–a language of exile, without a land, without frontiers, not supported by any government, a language which possesses no words for weapons, ammunition, military exercises, war tactics; a language that was despised by both gentiles and emancipated Jews. The truth is that what the great religions preached, the Yiddish-speaking people of the ghettos practiced day in and day out. They were the people of the Book in the truest sense of the word. They knew of no greater joy than the study of man and human relations, which they called Torah, Talmud, Musar, Kabbalah. The ghetto was not only a place of refuge for a persecuted minority but a great

experiment in peace, in self-discipline, and in humanism. As such, a residue still exists and refuses to give up in spite of all the brutality that surrounds it.

I was brought up among those people. My father's home on Krochmalna Street in Warsaw was a study house, a court of justice, a house of prayer, of storytelling, as well as a place for weddings and Hasidic banquets. As a child I had heard from my older brother and master, I. J. Singer, who later wrote *The Brothers Ashkenazi*, all the arguments that the rationalists from

Isaac Bashevis Singer, the reknowned American Yiddish writer. Born in Poland, he emigrated to the U.S.A. in 1935.

Spinoza to Max Nordau brought out against religion. I have heard from my father and my mother all the answers that faith in God could offer to those who doubt and search for the truth. In our home and in many other homes the eternal questions were more actual than the latest news in the Yiddish newspaper. In spite of all the disenchantments and all my skepticism, I believe that the nations can learn much from those Jews, their way of thinking, their way of bringing up children, their finding happiness where others see nothing but misery and humiliation.

To me the Yiddish language and the conduct of those who spoke it are identical. One can find in the Yiddish tongue and in the Yiddish style expressions of pious joy, lust for life, longing for the Messiah, patience, and deep appreciation of human individuality. There is a quiet humor in Yiddish and a gratitude for every day of life, every crumb of success, each encounter of love. The Yiddish mentality is not haughty. It does not take victory for granted. It does not demand and command but it muddles through, sneaks by, smuggles itself amid the powers of destruction, knowing somewhere that God's plan for Creation is still at the very beginning.

There are some who call Yiddish a dead language, but so was Hebrew called for two thousand years. It has been revised in our time in a most remarkable, almost miraculous way. Aramaic was certainly a dead language for centuries, but then it brought to light the Zohar, a work of mysticism of sublime value. It is a fact that the classics of Yiddish literature are also the classics of modern Hebrew literature. Yiddish has not yet said its last word. It contains treasures that have not been revealed to the eyes of the world. It was the tongue of martyrs and saints, of dreamers and kabbalists—rich in humor and in memories that mankind may never forget. In a figurative way, Yiddish is the wise and humble language of us all, the idiom of frightened and hopeful humanity.

THE HOLOCAUST

"In every generation there are those who seek to annihilate us."

From the Passover Hagaddah.

The Jewish people have survived slavery, crusades, inquisitions, pogroms and many other forms of persecution. But the most devastating Jewish tragedy occurred within the last fifty years. Hitler's "Final Solution" to the "Jewish problem," his demonic plan to kill all the Jews of the world, was the most systematic genocide the world has ever seen. Approximately six million Jews were murdered in the Holocaust.

The following selection is taken from a speech by Gideon Hausner, Chief Prosecutor at the 1962 trial of Adolf Eichmann in Israel. Eichmann had been the Nazi official in charge of the deportation of Jews to the death camps.

Six Million Accusers

When I stand before you here, Judges of Israel, to lead the Prosecution of Adolf Eichmann, I am not standing alone. With me are six million accusers. But they cannot rise to their feet and point an accusing finger towards him who sits in the dock and cry: "I accuse." For their ashes are piled up on the hills of Auschwitz and the fields of Treblinka, and are strewn in the forests of Poland. Their graves are scattered throughout the length and breadth of Europe. Their blood cries out, but their voice is not heard. Therefore I will be their spokesman and in their name I will unfold the awesome indictment.

The history of the Jewish people is steeped in suffering and tears....Yet never, down the entire blood-stained road travelled by this people, never since the first days of its nationhood, has any man arisen who succeeded in dealing it such grievous blows as did Hitler's iniquitous regime, and Adolf Eichmann as its executive arm for the extermination of the Jewish people. In all human history there is no other example of a man against whom it would be possible to draw up such a bill of indictment as has been read here....Murder has been with the human race since the days when Cain killed Abel; it is no novel phenomenon. But we have had to wait till this twentieth century to witness with our own eyes a new kind of murder: not the result of the momentary surge of passion or mental black-out, but of calculated decision and painstaking planning....

This murderous decision, taken deliberately and in cold blood, to annihilate a nation and blot it out from the face of the earth, is so shocking that one is at a loss for words to describe it. Words exist to express what man's reason can conceive and his heart contain, [but] here we are dealing with actions that transcend our human grasp. Yet this is what did happen: millions were condemned to death, not for any crime, not for anything they had done, but only because they belonged to the Jewish people. The development of technology placed at the disposal of the destroyers efficient equipment for the execution of their appalling designs. This unprecedented crime, carried out by Europeans in the twentieth century, led to the definition of a criminal concept unknown to human annals even during the darkest ages—the crime of Genocide.

Gideon Hausner.

This cynical Nazi slogan "Work Makes One Free" has been preserved as a reminder of the horrors of genocide over one of the gates in the infamous Dachau concentration camp.

Survivors of Auschwitz, Bergen-Belsen, Treblinka, Maidanek, Dachau, Chelmno, Buchenwald, Sobibor, and many other death camps have told devastating stories of what happened in these camps. Today, all survivors are over 40 years of age; most are over 60. Many survivors have lived as "normal" lives as they could after the Holocaust, raising new families, starting new livelihoods, forming new relationships. Most have valiantly struggled with their pasts and resumed lives as productive members of society. Yet within each survivor lie painful memories, haunting nightmares, heartbreaking losses.

The Non-believer

Facing the inmates assembled on the *Appel Platz*, the two men seem to be acting out an unreal scene.

"Deny your faith and you will eat for an entire week," the officer is yelling.

"No," says the Jew quietly.

"Curse your God, wretch! Curse Him and you will have an easy job!"

"No," says the Jew quietly.

"Repudiate Him and I will protect you."

"Never," says the Jew quietly.

"Never? What does that mean? A minute? In a minute you will die. So then, you dog, will you finally obey me?"

The inmates hold their breath. Some watch the officer; others have eyes only for their comrade.

"God means more to you than life? More than I? You asked for it, you fool!"

He draws his gun, raises his hand, takes aim. And shoots. The bullet enters the inmate's shoulder. He sways, and his comrades in the first row see his face twist. And they hear him whisper the ancient call of the martyrs of the faith: "*Adoshem hu haelokim, adoshem hu haelokim*–God is God, God alone is God."

"You swine, you dirty Jew," screams the officer. "Can't you see I am more powerful than your God! Your life is in my hands, not in His! You need me more than Him! Choose me and you'll go to the hospital and you'll recover, and you'll eat, and you'll be happy!"

"Never," says the Jew, gasping.

The officer examines him at length. He suddenly seems fearful. Then he shoots a second bullet into the man's other shoulder. And a third. And a fourth. And the Jew goes on whispering, "God is God, God is. . ." The last bullet strikes him in the mouth.

"I was there," his son tells me. "I was there, and the scene seems unbelievable to me. You see, my father. . .my father was a hero. . .But he was not a believer."

Elie Wiesel.

The Child Who Survived

Joel the Redhead was five years old and he knew that he must not shout; to shout was dangerous.

An unusually clever hiding place had been found for him: under the cave whose entrance, according to the experts, could not be found. Joel was not alone there. With him were his father, his mother, his older brother Yekutiel and his Uncle Zanvel, whom he loved because he told him stories.

Joel knew many things, but not whether it was day or night outside. In his cave under the cave it was always dark, which increased it value and price, according to the ghetto's engineers.

During the raids the subterranean inhabitants had learned to communicate silently. Uncle Zanvel told his funny stories without a sound.

Joel's father was the first to go, having ventured out to look for water one night. A rifle shot cut him down. A scream was heard. That was all. And in the shelter Joel succeeded in crying without crying.

His mother placed her hand over his mouth when a few days later Yekutiel was arrested. That same evening she, too, was taken. Joel the Redhead knew that he was going to burst with pain, but his Uncle Zanvel's hand was on his mouth.

Zanvel, too, disappeared. And Joel was left alone in the darkness. His hand covering his mouth, he began to sob without a sound, scream without a sound, survive without a sound.

Elie Wiesel.

Approximately two million children died in the Holocaust. Half were murdered and half died of illness and starvation. Parents, knowing what their children faced in concentration camps, often sent their children away, hoping that they might have a better chance at survival on their own. Thousands of Jewish children wandered throughout Europe alone looking for food and shelter, terrified and helpless. The following are writings by young Jewish children who did not survive the Holocaust.

Fear

Today the ghetto knows a different fear
Close in its grip, death wields an icy scythe.
An evil sickness spreads a terror in its wake,
The victims of its shadow weep and writhe.

Today a father's heartbeat tells his fright
And mothers bend their heads into their hands.
Now children choke and die with typhus here,
A bitter tax is taken from their banks.

My heart still beats inside my breast
While friends depart for other worlds.
Perhaps it's better–who can say?
Than watching this, to die today?

No, no my God, we want to live!
Not watch our numbers melt away.
We want to have a better world,
We want to work–we must not die!

Eva Pickova.
Died in Auschwitz on December 18, 1943.

Diary of a Young Girl

In spite of everything I still believe that people are really good at heart. I simply can't build up my hopes on a foundation consisting of confusion, misery, and death. I see the world gradually being turned into a wilderness, I hear the ever-approaching thunder, which will destroy us too. I can feel the sufferings of millions and yet, if I look up into the heavens, I think that it will all come right, that this cruelty too will end, and that peace and tranquility will return again.

In the meantime, I must uphold my ideals, for perhaps the time will come when I shall be able to carry them out.

Anne Frank, *Diary of a Young Girl*, entry for Saturday, July 15, 1944. The last entry in this diary was made on August 1, 1944.

The Butterfly

The last, the very last,
So richly, brightly, dazzlingly yellow.
Perhaps if the sun's tears would sing.
against a white stone. . .
Such, such a yellow
Is carried lightly, way up high.
It went away I'm sure because it wished to
kiss the world goodbye.
For seven weeks I've lived here.
Penned up inside this ghetto
But I have found my people here.
The dandelions call to me
And the white chestnut candles in the court.
Only I never saw another butterfly.

That butterfly was the last one.
Butterflies don't live in here,
in the ghetto.

Pavel Friedman.
Died in Auschwitz on September 29,1944.

(Right) "Fear", a sketch from the collection of children's art drawn in the Theresienstadt concentration camp.

Jewish resistance to the Nazis and their collaborators took many forms. The valiant Warsaw Ghetto freedom fighters, for example, fought with knives, smuggled pistols and homemade grenades against Nazi tanks and artillery. Other Jews fled to the forests where they became guerilla partisans. But Jews were not equipped to fight a war. Firstly, they were a peace-loving people. Secondly, they had no central government to organize their resistance and supply them with arms.

The most successful Jewish resistance was in fact the spiritual resistance that had been a part of Jewish history for 4,000 years. Jews resisted by continuing to educate their children whenever they could, by celebrating Jewish occasions in ghettos, forests and concentration camps.

The following is an account of the Bar Mitzvah of Ralph Blume held in 1944 in the "model" camp of Theresienstadt, and presided over by Rabbi Leo Baeck, leader of the pre-war Reform Jewish community in Berlin, Germany before its demise. Note that conditions at Theresienstadt were much better than in all other camps. Theresienstadt was a showplace for the Nazis, the camp where neutral parties, such as visiting Red Cross dignitaries, were allowed to visit, to see for themselves that conditions for Jewish prisoners were "humane."

Young survivors of the Buchenwald concentration camp, liberated by the U.S. Third Army, 1945.

Bar Mitzvah in Theresienstadt

My Bar Mitzvah took place in one of the barracks in which one of the smaller rooms had been converted into a synagogue. We had a Torah...Eight people were called up and Leo Baeck called me for my Torah portion. He had no singing voice although a beautiful speaking voice, deep and impressive...

In his address to me on this day, Leo Baeck mentioned how sad this occasion was and also how far away we were from our "Heimatland." Yet, Baeck continued, we should rejoice for after all it is a happy occasion and how fortunate I am to celebrate this together with my mother. The white shirt which I wore then was made from a set of shrouds normally used for the dead.

Rabbi Baeck said further that despite the terrible circumstances, I was still brought up as a Jew...I think the point Leo Baeck made which, in my opinion, was the most important, was that, despite all I had gone through so far, I should never change my religious beliefs.

By the way, we "celebrated" the occasion by having a special treat; we had dry bread and mustard.

Ralph Blume.

AFTER THE HOLOCAUST

The Holocaust has had a profound effect on Jews all over the world, whether or not they have experienced it themselves. Even "assimilated" Jews have been profoundly affected by the Holocaust and have felt its significance in their own lives.

In Germany: The End of Assimilation

I think of myself as an assimilated Jew. I say that without any particular pride or passion, but merely to provide a perspective for what follows. It was because I consider myself assimilated that I was able to plan a business trip to West Germany last fall without ever thinking twice. It was a trip of more than 2,000 miles through much of the country and I can honestly say that I regarded it as just another job. I left New York on the first night of Rosh Hashanah, 5732.

A flight that leaves New York in the early evening lands in Frankfurt am Main at dawn. Dulled though one's senses might be so early in the day, the impression the Frankfurt airport makes is strong and irresistible. Miles of rubber-clad corridors, with large windows and chrome and aluminum walls and railings, present a strikingly austere and sterile appearance, like something out of Stanley Kubrick's "2001." The poured concrete buildings are starkly simple, and at dawn there are few signs of activity.

I was surprised by the informality of German immigration and customs procedures, which were, I thought, rather atypical for a country known for strict adherence to rules and discipline. Passports weren't checked or stamped; luggage wasn't inspected. This struck me as odd, but not quite as odd as the fact that I was entering Germany on the second day of the Jewish New Year.

At the exit gate a West German corporate executive who would serve as my driver and guide throughout my stay in Germany was waiting. We would be together constantly for the next 10 days. He was tall and erect, an imposing figure of about 60. Subtract 32, I suddenly thought, and that would make him about 28 at the start of World War II. I found myself wondering what military unit he'd been a part of, and my attitude became hostile. It was an automatic and unreasoning response, yet one I wouldn't shake for most of my stay in Germany. For whatever reason, I perceived my guide-to-be as an instant enemy, and my reaction to him surprised me. After all, I'm a thoughtful and reasonable man. I don't judge people irrationally, and besides, I'm a totally assimilated Jew.

The guide–I'll call him Hans–didn't help things much with his greeting. "Birnbaum," he said, "that's a German name, isn't it? Means pear tree. Tell me, do your people come from Germany?"

It didn't seem worthwhile to explain that while my father's roots were undeniably German, my ancestors had joined a 13th-century Jewish migration to Poland. After all, the move, though made seven centuries before, hadn't saved my father's parents and five sisters from Hitler. So I replied, "Yes, they came from Germany."

"It must have been *difficult* for them during the war," said Hans in clipped, crisp tones.

I nodded, at a loss for an answer. Suddenly my grandparents, my aunts and their husbands, their unknown numbers of children, were real to me. I had been about 6 years old when my parents learned of their deaths and I had never seen any of them. I had never even thought about them before but now I was trying to imagine what they had been like. It had taken two steps onto German soil and just a few words from the first German I had met to evoke this reaction. Talk about consciousness raising…

My musings were interrupted by Hans. "But that is all over now," he said, "it is all forgotten. It is all in the past, and we must live for today. Let us now concentrate on enjoying the beauty of today's Germany."

My ears heard and my mind actually agreed. This was, after all, supposed to be a rather pleasant business trip. But there was something rumbling in the pit of my stomach, something I couldn't control.

The uneasiness I experienced in that first conversation with Hans was shunted to the back of my mind once I got involved in my work, for business in West Germany is conducted in much the same way as in Akron or Atlanta. And in Frankfurt, a totally rebuilt, modern city, generally indistinguishable from most major American cities, everyone I met spoke English.

From Frankfurt my schedule took Hans and me through the beautiful Rhine valley. Medieval castles, high above steep vineyards and the bustling river, made the stretch of road from Mainz to Cologne a more than pleasant interlude.

Once in Cologne, I was off to the mammoth ANUGA Fair, a biannual event that caters to West Germany's thriving hotel and restaurant business. For nine days the good burghers of Hamburg and the beer barons of Bavaria inspect every conceivable type of sausage, strudel and sauerkraut. For me the fair was a long series of meetings.

The meetings were fine but my local interpreter gave me a bit of a jolt. He resembled nothing so much as a character from the cast of an English drawing room comedy, the one who bounds in from stage left, handsome and blond, wearing impeccable whites, racquet in hand, and asks, "Tennis anyone?" The interpreter was blond and wore a perfectly pressed white suit and though a little past the age of male ingenue, was no less enthusiastic. "I am Guntar," he exclaimed. "I speak perfect English. I learned it in a prisoner of war camp." His smile was dazzling.

I shook my head in disbelief. How is it possible to make that statement out loud, I wondered, much less with obvious pride? He actually seemed proud to have been a prisoner; after all,

hadn't he learned English? Why wasn't he even a little bit ashamed or self-conscious? I didn't expect breast beating and the rendings of his garments, but did he have to come on this way? I ended up being embarrassed, and I didn't understand the feeling at all.

From Cologne we rode through the Ruhr valley with its huge factories and mills whose predecessors had once fueled the German war machine. From there we traveled along the rolling plains of Westphalia, passing an endless succession of spotless farms, all with austere red brick farmhouses. Then north to Emsland, to a small village not far from the cold North Sea coast, where I was invited for my first meal in a German home.

The home could hardly have been called typical. Though very much in the regional style of architecture, it was more than 500 years old. It was, however, fully restored, for restoration was a great hobby of my host. Long hallways led to large, drafty chambers, and if I had heard the cry of "Off with his head!" it would not have seemed the least incongruous. Dinner was formal and restrained, with somber servants bringing course after course. Cigars and lethally strong brandy followed, and they in turn were followed by a tour of the house.

As we walked along, old suits of armor stood rigidly at attention. Coats of arms and ancient standards hung forlornly from the walls and ceilings. We made our way through a narrow passageway and finally entered a long hall hung with large oil paintings."This was my great-great-grandfather," said my host, pointing to a portrait of an archduke of somewhere or other. Next came a couple of counts, a baron or two and some miscellaneous civil dignitaries of apparently unquestioned importance. Then he pointed over my shoulder. "And that," he said, with obvious pride, "is my father."

The portrait was not as large as some of the others but it was no less impressive. The father stared out at his son with steely blue eyes and a fiercely determined jaw. His resoluteness was what the artist had primarily attempted to capture, and he had succeeded. Here was a man of bearing and purpose. The artist had missed nothing, right down to the highlights on the lacquered brim of the black military cap and the shining silver SS initials on the collar.

I felt my dinner rising and uttered silent, grateful thanks that I was able to keep it down. I was speechless. What am I doing here? I thought. What am I doing calmly breaking bread with the son of a Gestapo officer and then casually taking a tour of the "family album?" I found it absolutely impossible to remain in the house a moment longer.

My exit was clumsy and confusing. I'm sure my host still thinks that all Americans are quite mad, but my need for air was such that I gave no thought to good manners. Once out of the house, I shook with anger. It was uncontrollable. Five days in Germany had uncovered an identity I had labored a lifetime to minimize. I was a Jew; there was no getting away from it. And I felt a Jew's anger, a Jew's frustration. Assimilation or not, I was in a rage.

Until that night I had been focusing all my undefined belligerence on Hans. A nice man by any objective standard, he nevertheless evoked my initial uneasiness at the airport, and so I had directed my hostility at him. Nothing downright mean, mind you, but I just was not very friendly. Fortunately our driving sessions between stops were relatively short, and conversational necessities were few. But he tended to aggravate the strained atmosphere by laughingly referring to himself every so often as an "old militarist."

I felt so disquieted after the painting episode that I decided to eliminate scheduled visits to Hamburg and Berlin. They were stops that were not essential to my trip and I had neither the heart nor the stomach for them. But passing them up meant a 375-mile drive from the northwesternmost area of West Germany to Regensburg in the southeast, and a full day in the car with Hans.

The trip itself was pleasant enough; the West German autobahns are among the best roads in Europe. And the conversation, surprisingly, was equally pleasant. Hans was something of a local historian, and he spoke knowledgeably about the towns and cities through which we passed. He also spoke happily about his job and proudly about his wife and children.

After a while our conversation shifted to politics and suddenly Hans did not sound quite so much like an "old militarist." Though Eastern European Communism seemed a real threat to him, he turned out to be not the least interested in having West Germany raise a larger army. In fact, the notion of a larger German Army seemed to worry him more than the Communists.

"Have you read Albert Speer's book about the war?" I asked, apropos of nothing. He hadn't. He had, however, heard of the book, written by Hitler's personal architect and later Minister of Armaments, and was anxious to read it. "I knew Speer," he said pensively, "and I liked him very much. He was a very able man." Then he paused a moment, reflected, and added, "He saved my life."

Hans had been working in a factory during *Kristallnacht*, in November, 1938, when an orgy of window smashing, arson, property destruction and murder victimized Jews all over Germany. Hans's maternal grandmother was Jewish, and under German law Hans was, therefore, a Jew. He was among thousands arrested that night, and was slated to go to a labor camp, and probably a concentration camp and gas chamber later on. Speer personally intervened and undoubtedly saved his life, not out of any particular compassion for Jews but because Hans's technological expertise was too valuable for the fatherland to lose. Speer protected Hans all through the war by destroying the evidence of his Semitic forbears.

Some "old militarist!" My surprise was total. Suddenly I had what almost seemed like a coreligionist riding next to me, and the saying about feeling more comfortable with your "own" proved to be quite accurate. Hans had probably never seen a Jewish service in his life, or spoken to more than two Jews, but to me he was now a kindred soul. In the space of three minutes my whole attitude had changed. I now felt I could ask him to help me with a project I'd been considering since early morning.

"Tomorrow we'll be in Regensburg," I said, "and it is Yom Kippur." He nodded, and apparently I didn't need to explain the meaning of the holiday to him—that it was the Day of Atonement. "There is a temple in Regensburg," he said, anticipating my next question. "Do you wish to go?"

"Yes," I said. "Can you arrange it for me?" He nodded, then fell silent until we reached Regensburg some hours later.

We arrived in the city shortly before sundown, and Hans barely had time to call and ask permission to attend the services and to get directions. They were more than happy to have me. Regensburg is old, with ruins dating back more than 2,000 years, and its position at the point where the Danube River becomes navigable has made it a center of commerce for centuries. The streets are narrow and winding, and there are many dark alleyways. We decided to try to find the temple before going to bed that night, anticipating some difficulty. But we found it barely a block from the city's main commercial thoroughfare.

I hadn't been in a synagogue for more than 18 years, and in the morning, with the services scheduled for 9.30, I presented myself promptly at 9.25. The only other person in the synagogue was the cleaning woman. She looked at me and I returned her stare. We said nothing. After a few moments she tucked her dust cloth into an apron pocket, lifted her broom and left the room. Now I was totally alone.

The synagogue was very small and appeared to be fairly new. It was simplicity itself, its clear rectangular lines broken only by a raised platform at the front. On the front wall was the enclosure that held the rolled scriptures. The only decorations in the room were two velvet and brocade cloths on the side walls, rescued from the ruins of synagogues built over a century ago. Beside each were small cards attesting to their origin. There were perhaps a hundred folding chairs arranged neatly in rows, with a small section at the back of the room separated from the rest by a low, movable screen. Apparently the Jewish Orthodox tradition of separating the sexes was still being observed in spirit.

For about 15 minutes I remained alone. Then two old men entered and nodded to me. Between their halting English and my nearly nonexistent German I was able to determine that one of them had taken Hans's call the night before, and that they were expecting me. They seemed unusually glad that I had come. Their happiness, however, did not preclude a reproving look as they handed me a black paper skullcap and indicated the top of my head. I put it on a little ashamedly.

The two men moved to the front row and each put down a paper parcel he had been carrying. Each parcel contained slippers and an embroidered velvet bag. The men unlaced their shoes, placed them neatly under their chairs and put on the slippers. Then they placed the small velvet bags on their laps. I knew those bags well, and for an instant I was an 8-year-old boy again, sitting beside my father in temple.

One of the old men was looking at me. Without warning or comment, he pushed up his left sleeve. There, on his forearm, was a concentration camp tattoo consisting of indelible blue numbers, a mark of horrors seen and survived. His companion also rolled up a sleeve, revealing his own tragic souvenir. When they were sure I had seen, they let their sleeves fall back into place, and in the same matter-of-fact manner unzipped their velvet bags and took out their prayer shawls.

Now a bent old man shuffled slowly into the room, much older even than the two who had preceded him. They all exchanged holiday greetings, and then the old man was introduced to me. He, too, rolled up his sleeve to reveal his own blue numbers, then moved to the other side of the hall where he took a long white cotton caftan from a paper parcel and slipped it over his worn blue suit. He also changed from street shoes to slippers.

It was now 10 o'clock, and there were but four of us in the temple. Then an old woman arrived, followed by another. They exchanged greetings and retired to their prescribed section at the back of the hall. Neither of them greeted any of the men, and the men did not acknowledge them.

Ten minutes later a single man arrived, followed by another with his teen-age son. The son and I were the only persons in the room under the age of 60. Each new arrival was introduced to me, and every one (with the exception of the teen-age boy) went through the sleeve-rolling ritual. The tattoos seemed to be a bond between them, a symbol of tragedy shared.

At 10:25 two more men arrived, one of whom was introduced as the rabbi. He was a shopkeeper in the city. Conversation had switched from German to Yiddish, becoming animated with the entrance of each new arrival. But after a while the talk ceased and the old men stood around toeing the carpet. It was an hour after the services had been scheduled to begin. Then something suddenly dawned on me: They didn't have a *minyan*,

Yom Kippur before the battle at Metz, as observed by the Jewish soldiers in the German Army, 1870.

the quorum of 10 men needed to hold a Jewish service. On Yom Kippur morning, the holiest day in the Jewish calendar, they couldn't find 10 men for a service. No wonder they had been glad to hear from Hans that I would be coming.

Names were mentioned as those assembled searched their minds for someone to summon so the service could be held. Then came a collective sigh of relief as a figure appeared in the doorway. Enter the 10th man.

Unlike the others, who wore navy blue suits, the new arrival was dressed in brown. His suit was of British cut, with a nipped-

in-waist and flared trousers. He must have been the same age as the rest, but his deep tan contrasted sharply with their sallow complexions. He wore highly polished brown boots, a pink shirt and a wide red tie. Large gold links shone at his cuffs, and a star sapphire sparkled on his pinky. The rabbi rushed to greet him warmly. They were obviously not strangers. After they had exchanged greetings in Yiddish, the rabbi brought him over to me. "From America," said the rabbi, pointing first to one of us, then the other. The new arrival sat down beside me.

The rabbi reached over to one of the chairs and picked up a

153

prayer book. Already the bent old man in the caftan had gone to the lectern and was beginning to pray. The rabbi opened the prayer book to the proper page, pointed to a passage, then handed the book to me. He then moved onto the raised platform at the front of the room.

"Ben Mandel, Plainfield, New Jersey," said the man sitting beside me. We shook hands. As the service droned on around us, we spoke and it seemed that Ben, like myself, was there more to be present than to pray. He told me about his new home in Plainfield, his business, and about the hotel he owned not far from where I once lived on the West Side of Manhattan. We talked about why he had left Manhattan for the suburbs: the dirt, the violence, Mayor Lindsay. Then I asked, "How do you happen to be in Regensburg?"

"I was liberated here," he replied. Then he rolled up his suit and shirt sleeve to reveal his own set of numbers on his left arm. They stood out starkly despite his tan. "I come from a small town not far from here," he said. "First my brother and I were sent to a labor camp. That was in the late thirties. When Hitler decided that he didn't even want Jews as laborers in his precious Germany, we were shipped to Auschwitz. The two of us were sent there with our sister. She died in the camp."

He paused for a moment. It appeared he hadn't told this story in a long time and it was hard for him.

"We were just lucky. If the Allies had arrived a few days later, I would be fertilizing the fields. They liberated us in Regensburg, and we lived here for a while. Then my brother decided to go to Israel, and I went to America. I can't complain. I've done very well. So every year I visit my brother in Tel Aviv for Rosh Hashanah and spend a week there with him and his family. Then I come here for Yom Kippur.

"It helps me remember how lucky I've been. It makes me remember how it was. Besides, there aren't many Jews left here, just these few old men. Once 10,000 Jews lived in the area, now they can hardly make a minyan on Yom Kippur. Imagine."

The bent old man held firmly to his lectern as he rocked back and forth. The other members of the congregation, all wrapped in silk prayer shawls with long fringes, rocked with him, reciting the ancient prayers.

I closed my prayer book, sat back and cried.

Germany is not the place for an assimilated Jew to visit if he expects to stay assimilated.

Stephen Birnbaum.

How can we come to terms with the Holocaust today—we Jewish people who have not experienced the horrors firsthand? We are the children of the survivors, the Jews of today, who must carry with us the memory of our six million murdered people. Just as the Passover Haggadah instructs us that in each generation we Jews must see ourselves as if we too were slaves in Egypt, so as Jews of this generation we must imagine ourselves as survivors of Auschwitz and never forget. . . .

Lest We Forget

On this night of the Seder we remember with reverence and love the six millions of our people of the European exile who perished at the hands of a tyrant more wicked than the Pharaoh who enslaved our fathers in Egypt. Come, said he to his minions, let us cut them off from being a people, that the name of Israel may be remembered no more. And they slew the blameless and pure, men and women and little ones, with vapors of poison and burned them with fire. But we abstain from dwelling on the deeds of the evil ones lest we defame the image of God in which man was created.

Now, the remnants of our people who were left in the ghettos and camps of annihilation rose up against the wicked ones for the sanctification of the Name, and slew many of them before they died. On the first day of Passover the remnants in the Ghetto of Warsaw rose up against the adversary, even as in the days of Judah the Maccabee. They were lovely and pleasant in their lives, and in their death they were not divided, and they brought redemption to the name of Israel through all the world.

And from the depths of their affliction the martyrs lifted their voices in a song of faith in the coming of the Messiah.

Rufus Learsi.

Survivors blow the Shofar during ceremonies commemorating the tragedy of the Holocaust. Washington, 1983.

The Voice of Auschwitz

What does the Voice of Auschwitz command?

Jews are forbidden to hand Hitler posthumous victories. They are commanded to survive as Jews, lest the Jewish people perish. They are commanded to remember the victims of Auschwitz, lest their memory perish. They are forbidden to despair of man and his world, and to escape into either cynicism or otherworldliness, lest they cooperate in delivering the world over to the forces of Auschwitz. Finally, they are forbidden to despair of the God of Israel, lest Judaism perish. A secularist Jew cannot make himself believe by a mere act of will, nor can he be commanded to do so....And a religious Jew who has stayed with his God may be forced into new, possibly revolutionary relationships with Him. One possibility, however, is wholly unthinkable. A Jew may not respond to Hitler's attempt to destroy Judaism by himself cooperating in its destruction. In ancient times, the unthinkable Jewish sin was idolatry. Today, it is to respond to Hitler by doing his work.

Emile L. Fackenheim.

Alexander Donat Writes to His Grandson, June 1970

My dear grandson, my son's firstborn:

Your father, and my son, was exactly your age on that spring of 1945 when returning from a long journey through Hitler's night via the Warsaw ghetto, Maidanek, Dachau, Ravensbrück, Natzweiler, Auschwitz, we found him emaciated and covered with sores, but miraculously alive, in a Catholic orphanage near Warsaw....In April, 1943 we handed our only son, Wlodek, to our Christian friends over the Warsaw ghetto wall. This was the only way we could hope to save his life. He was then five years and four months old....

Should I try to describe our last night? Could I? In the morning Maria (a Christian friend) took Wlodek's hand and walked briskly away. His mother did not shed a tear, this was the time of the assassin and the time of the hero. It was April 5, 1943, two weeks before the end of the ghetto. We gave away our son, for agony and for survival....

We survived, against hope and against the rules. It was an incredible miracle of survival. We left behind a graveyard of our people. And your father Wlodek, now William, at present thirty-two years old, is father of three children, of whom you are the first-born. You are now seven years old, exactly the age your father was when we found him at the end of the war.

You may ask: Aren't twenty-five years sufficient to dull the pain? Why not forget the past and enjoy life now?

The answer is very simple: Those things are unforgettable. The scars can never be erased. There is no escape from the past except into the future. The guilt of having survived would be unbearable were it not for the mission to convey a message.

The most dreadful aspect of the Holocaust was that it turned what we regarded as impossible into a commonplace.... Nobody can delude himself any longer that "it cannot happen here." It can happen here and any place, now and at any time, against Jews, Biafrans, Vietnamese, Russians, or Americans....

Had I considered our Holocaust a tragic but closed episode, I would have recommended that it be consigned to oblivion, as one of the many cyclical catastrophes in our history. But it is my firm conviction that the Holocaust was the beginning of an era, not its end–an era of turmoil and upheaval, of irrationality and

(Above) This monument to the valiant freedom fighters of the Warsaw Ghetto, who rose up against Nazi oppression in 1943, is all that remains of the ghetto.

(Overleaf) Memorial to the victims of the Holocaust at Yad Vashem Museum of the Holocaust in Jerusalem.

madness, an era of Auschwitz. We are now in the 29th year of this era, and it may last for centuries if the Bomb will let mankind live that long. A new apocalyptic calendar may well start with a new Genesis: "In the beginning there was Auschwitz...."

In a world haunted by the memory of six million unvindicated victims behind us, and a cataclysmic perspective of an atomic doom ahead, with youth devoid of any ideal worth living for and wallowing in the satiated sterility of our affluent futility, what legacy do we leave you? Can I offer you the soothing belief in a good God watching and protecting us? I cannot even tell you that crime doesn't pay for it does. I am ashamed of the world our generation is leaving to you. I cannot assure you that there will be no more Anne Franks, as her father wishfully thinks. I cannot assure you that Auschwitz's chimneys will never smoke again.

What then can I say to you now? Only that I love you. You are my promised immortality.

ISRAEL

Crowds gather to worship at the Western Wall in Jerusalem.

"I give the land you sojourn in to you and your offspring to come, all the land of Canaan, as an everlasting possession."

Genesis, 17:8.

Israel was a concept in the minds of Jews long before it became an independent state in 1948. According to the Bible, *Eretz Yisroel* was the land promised by God to the Jewish people, first through Abraham, Isaac, and Jacob, and then through Moses. To Jews, it also meant the unification of the Jewish people, dispersed throughout the world, but connected through history, traditions, and beliefs. It represented an end to thousands of years of Jewish persecution.

In their dispersion, Jews kept alive an almost mystical yearning for their homeland of long ago and the hope that they would one day return. "Next year in Jerusalem" has been a Jewish incantation for 2,000 years.

The medieval Sephardic poet Yehuda HaLevi expressed his longing for Zion, the ancient name for Jerusalem, in these words.

My Heart is in the East

My heart is in the East and I
at the rim of the West
How can I taste what I eat
much less savor it
How can I fulfill my vows and oaths
while Zion is in Edom's bounds
and I in Arab bonds?
How easy it would be to leave
all the comforts of Spain
To see the precious dust
of the destroyed Sanctuary.

Yehuda HaLevi.

"Today I have founded the Jewish State. Today many would laugh at these words, but in five years more–certainly in 50 years–everyone will understand this."

Theodor Herzl.

Jews longed for a Jewish nation for thousands of years, but it wasn't until Theodor Herzl initiated the Zionist Movement that Jews began to rally together. Inspired by Herzl's words, many Jews from all over the world emigrated to Palestine as *chalutzim*, pioneer settlers, while others lobbied for world support of a Jewish homeland.

The need for a Jewish homeland was finally accepted by a guilt-ridden world, but only after six million Jews had been murdered in the Holocaust. Israel became a state in May 1948 and Jews from all over the world flocked from the countries of their dispersion, and in many cases their persecution, to their homeland. Jewish refugees from Europe, Jewish American Zionists, Jews from Middle-Eastern countries, Jews from North Africa all joined the Jewish chalutzim in building a new *Eretz Yisroel* together.

The Rebirth of Israel

Few events in human history have seemed so startlingly improbable as the rebirth of Israel. On a patch of land no more than 200 miles (320 km) long and 100 miles (160 km) wide at its broadest point, a people now numbering only a few million out of all the world's billions has, 3,000 years after the Kingdom of David, nineteen centuries after the devastation of Jerusalem by Rome, reestablished its home in the land where it was born and from which it was largely separated for thousands of years. This was achieved against every calculation of chance. The land was barren, despoiled of its ancient fertility, the people dispersed and enfeebled by the recent Holocaust, its national aims resisted with fierce obduracy by the Arab world and cruelly frustrated by British antagonism. This was the lowest point in the modern history of the Jewish people, when many must have wondered if an end had come to its time on history's stage. How could it summon the energies and hope necessary for its own recovery? Yet within a few years of its darkest days, the Jewish people would see its flag planted in the family of nations from which it had been absent for so many tragic epochs. Warm waves of pride would flow in every home across the world in which the traditions of the Jewish people were cherished. Never was this people stronger than in its moment of weakness, never more hopeful than in its moment of despair.

Abba Eban.

One of Israel's first laws proclaimed the right of all Jews to "return" to their homeland. The Law of Return passed by the Knesset, the Israeli parliament, promised immediate citizenship to Jews from all over the world.

Address to the Knesset on the Law of Return

The Law of Return and the Law of Citizenship that you have in front of you are connected by a mutual bond and share of common conceptual origin, deriving from the historical uniqueness of the State of Israel, a uniqueness vis-à-vis the past and the future, directed internally and externally. These two laws determine the special character and destiny of the State of Israel as the state bearing the vision of the redemption of Israel.

The State of Israel is a state like all the other states. All the general indications [of statehood] common to the other states are also to be found in the State of Israel. It rests on a specific territory and a population existing within this territory, it possesses sovereignty in internal and external affairs, and its authority does not extend beyond its borders. The State of Israel rules only over its own inhabitants. The Jews in the Diaspora, who are citizens of their countries and who want to remain there, have no legal or civil connection to the State of Israel and the State of Israel does not represent them from any legal standpoint.

Nevertheless, the State of Israel differs from the other states both with regard to the factors involved in its establishment and to the aims of its existence. It was established merely two years ago, but its roots are grounded in the far past and it is nourished by ancient springs. Its authority is limited to the area in which its residents dwell, but its gates are open to every Jew wherever he may be. The State of Israel is not a Jewish state merely because the majority of its inhabitants are Jews. It is a state for all the Jews wherever they may be and for every Jew who so desires.

On the fourteenth of May, 1948 a new state was not founded *ex nihilo*. Rather, the crown was restored to its pristine splendor 1,813 years after the independence of Israel was destroyed, during the days of Bar Kochba and Rabbi Akiba....

David Ben-Gurion.

"A State is not created by a declaration. It is built day after day, by endless toil and the labor of years, even of generations."

David Ben-Gurion.

Life in Israel has been the fulfillment of a great Jewish dream. However, in reality, life in Israel has not been easy. Building a country out of a desert, continuous warring with hostile neighbors, economic and diplomatic problems–all these have been a part of the Israeli experience. Those Jews who have chosen to become Israelis and those who have been born in Israel make up a special Jewish community–a community of strong, tenacious, sometimes aggressive people.

Here are some observations made by American novelist Saul Bellow on this special breed of people.

The Israelis

Certain oddities about Israel: Because people think so hard here, and so much, and because of the length and depth of their history, this sliver of a country sometimes seems quite large. Some dimension of mind seems to extend into space.

To live again in Jerusalem–that is almost like the restoration of the Temple. But no one is at ease in Zion. No one can be. The world crisis is added to the crisis of the state, and both are added to the problems of domestic life. It is increasingly difficult to earn adequate wages, since from the first Israel adopted the living standards of the West. Taxes are steep and still rising, the Israeli pound is dropping. The government has begun to impose austerity measures. We meet people who work at two jobs and even this moonlighting is insufficient. The Israelis complain but they will accept the austerity measures. They know that they must, they are at bottom common-sensical. Yet everyone looks much shabbier and more harassed than in 1970....

In almost ever apartment house the neighbors tell you of a war widow who is trying to bring up her children. The treatment of young widows and of parents who have lost their sons is, I am told, a new psychiatric specialty. Israel is pressed, it is a suffering country. People feel the pressures of enemies as perhaps the psalmists felt them, and sometimes seem ready to cry out, "Break their teeth, O God, in their mouth." Still, almost everyone is reasonable and tolerant, and rancor against the Arabs is rare. These are not weak, melting people....

No people has to work so hard on so many levels as this one. In less than thirty years the Israelis have produced a modern country—doorknobs and hinges, plumbing fixtures, electrical supplies, chamber music, airplanes, teacups. It is both a garrison state and a cultivated society, both Spartan and Athenian. It tries to do everything, to understand everything, to make provision for everything. All resources, all faculties are strained. Unremitting thought about the world situation parallels the defense effort. These people are actively, individually involved in universal history. I don't see how they can bear it.

Saul Bellow.

> The following Bar Mitzvah story relates a sense of the history of modern-day Israel, as well as the importance of standing up for oneself and one's own people.

An Israeli Bar Mitzvah Story

In the theater of this night—a darkly-quiet night, lit by an orange moon that hangs like a jewel above our watchmen in their ambushes, as well as above the mosque on the other side—I want to make you this record, my son. Tomorrow, the village will celebrate your birthday, the glorious thirteenth, when you will be the Bar Mitzvah boy, the "son of the commandment" who now becomes a man.

For this night, Joshua, I would spend it close to you. I think the old scribes who handed down the Bible's legends probably feel as I do tonight—as I put down the story of why you sleep in peace and safety in the children's building, though thirteen years ago this night all in this kibbutz had been destroyed.

As I write, I hear the prayerful chants of those who call themselves our enemy coming from a few yards to the west in the desert—floating down from the mosque with the same mournful, shrill importunings as our own prayers, theirs to Allah and ours to God. I wonder that "the whole earth is full of His glory"—their earth as well as our earth.

Our land now throbs with the music of new creation. The orange moon hangs over nearly 10,000 dunams here planted to wheat and barley, apple and pear orchards and a good banana crop. We have 700 hives of bees, 60 milking cows and 150 cows for meat, 8,000 laying chickens and incubators for 40,000 eggs that produce 400,000 chicks a year—a prosperous kibbutz, we are called. Thirteen years ago there was nothing left alive in these fields and no person left behind to write or ponder anything; all that remained were the twenty-six men and one woman who lay dead in these fields.

But I am going ahead of the story, and I want to tell it carefully, for many people were involved. Our friends popped up in the strangest places.

This is how it happened.

Our kibbutz, as you know, was named after a leader of the Warsaw Ghetto uprising. I have often wondered what the word ghetto conjures up in your mind—you who have only known freedom! Do you see a great wall damming in old Jews with flowing beards and earlocks, weighed down under their prayer-shawls with the grief of the ages? That would be partly true. More true would be the picture and spirit of the younger men,

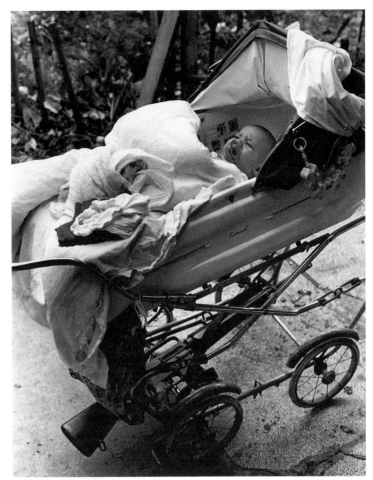

Two aspects of life in Israel.

like your namesake, Joshua of Warsaw, who knew that they would have to die—there was no other way—but who refused to be stepped on like vegetables. Joshua had a very great idea, and though he and his little band of men had few guns and were quickly, even lazily, killed by the keepers of the ghetto, his idea never perished. It was that Jews must not tremble before those who would harm them. Even in the twentieth century, that is a new idea for the world.

We named the kibbutz for him because we believed in his idea. We had just started our kibbutz that year of 1943, the year of the Warsaw Ghetto uprising, and all our members had lost their families in Poland or the ghettos of other countries. We had to maneuver fast in order to get it built. The British, who held the Mandate over Palestine then, had forbidden the Jews to build here in the desert. We came at night, sometimes in terror—not of the British but of the jackals which infested the Arab fields nearby.

We threw up houses in a few hours and, most important, got roofs on them; the British had a law that when you built a house with a roof on, it could not be destroyed. In this way, our village—and any more like ours—got started on "forbidden land."

Some have compared our land, so strangely shaped, to an hour-glass where the sands of green and lovely Galilee in the north spill down to the Negev wilderness in the south. That description is poetic but incomplete. This land is a great heart that beat faintly for a long time, for thousands of years, so faintly that it seemed to be stopping altogether. But suddenly, not long ago, it began to pound with new health inside the old and frail body. The desert shall rejoice and blossom as the rose, said

Isaiah, and that is what we set about doing here.

We put up our watch-tower, which also became our water-tower. From Tel Aviv and Haifa and far-off America there came tractors and live stock and seed to help us begin on the land. Technicians and water experts came to show us–shop-keepers, tailors, doctors, clerks–how to be farmers. Above all, though we did not need to be told this, they wanted us to make friends with our neighbors. The last was the easiest task to fulfil.

We were surrounded by Arab villages, so we had to be friends in order to develop. We wanted to in any case because–how can this be forgotten?–we are cousins. We felt the family ties very strongly.

Some Arabs were afraid at seeing a Jewish settlement so near to their villages in Migdal and Gaza. But before long they started to come. One very large village of more than 2,000 souls sent some of its members to us. In their flowing white robes and headdresses of many colors they might have stepped out of your Bible.

"We have watched your men in the field," they told us, "and we are curious. We must use sticks to scratch the earth. We like your tractor and would like to try it."

We let them borrow it. They brought us meat from Gaza, since Tel Aviv was too far off for us; we sold them guavas that were growing nicely, and gave them manure for their fields. They learned about our doctor and came to him. Their women were too bashful to come into the settlement; we built a wooden hut at the gate, and the doctor treated them there.

One of our members, Simeon, was an Iraqi Jew who taught us Arabic to help us understand our friends better. Whenever he met us in the fields or in the dining-room or library, he would insist on talking to us in Arabic. He was one of our shepherds, a rough, kindly man, not more than twenty-two, who hoped one day to be able to bring in his huge family who remained in Bagdad.

Simeon was happiest when he was out at the crack of dawn with the sheep, leading them to the hills, watching the day slowly ripen–that is, until Deborah came back from her studies at the University. She was the loveliest of our girls, as fair and blue-eyed as Simeon was dark and black-eyed. Soon he was teaching her Arabic so that she could be of help to the Moslem women in the medical hut.

All the *haverim*, the villagers, soon saw that nothing could separate these two, and they began to tease Simeon for teaching the teacher, instead of tending the sheep. He never minded the teasing; in fact, Deborah's presence seemed to make him work with the strength of a dozen men in the fields.

Amos was the secretary then–the *mukhtar*, the Arabs used to call him as they called their own village mayor–and some of us would go with Amos to visit our Arab neighbors in their villages, drink coffee together, and talk over farm problems.

In the spring, in just this time of year when the rain is over and gone, Simeon and Deborah were married by a rabbi who came from Tel Aviv. The mukhtars and their families came with many presents of sheep and fruit and a marvelous old coffee pot for the bride and groom. It was a big occasion, and we sang the songs of joy and of harvests.

For many years we were friends.

Then, in the fall of 1947 the United Nations wanted to divide Palestine and make it into two states–one for the Jews, one for the Arabs–and almost at once trouble broke out in our part of the country. It did not come from our friends, but from further west, from Arabs who did not know us or live among us. As a precaution, the Army sent up a few young soldiers from Tel Aviv. Some Arabs opened fire on them, which they returned.

There were no casualties–but, though we did not realize it at once, the incident seemed to close a period of history.

Amos and another went on their horses next day to a neighboring village to talk it over, but the mukhtar refused to see them. When he returned, Amos told us quietly, "No one welcomed us or recognized us any more. Relations are finished."

He did not come to dinner that evening, but he doubled the watch at the fences, and stayed down at the gate with the soldiers.

There began a strange period of isolation and harassment. It could not have been created by our simple farm friends. It was ordered, or forced upon them, by some faceless higher ups who knew nothing of us.

We were one Jewish village surrounded by many Arab villages. They put mines on the main road and in our fields. The haverim had to find ways to work the fields, while trying at the same time to cut the wires of the mines. Two members were killed while cutting the wires.

There was no question about our staying. We were Zionists who loved our homeland–so it was understood by New York and London as well as Tel Aviv that we would remain and we did not need instructions about this. We went on working our orchards and grazing our cattle and more men were killed by mines, but no one thought of leaving.

British officers who used to come through would ask in a not unfriendly way, "Why do you stay here? It is dangerous."

But they understood that we would not leave. Many of us had fought in the British Army against a common enemy during the war; we admired them for their pluck and stubborn resistance, and they knew that our people could be as stubborn. Some of the British wept when they came in to search for our arms; they told us that they were required to do this.

Just before you were born it was becoming clear that the British were really leaving the country, and that there might be war. The uppermost longing was to get the children out. There were seventy-five children here.

The doctor said that your mother must go to a hospital at once, but the way over the main road would be dangerous, and the way over the sands too difficult.

I had a friend in the British Army, a major stationed at Gaza, who had come to the kibbutz in the old days to talk and listen to the music. I went to the main road one day, stopped a British car and gave its driver a message to the major: "Please come at once. I need your help."

After an hour he came, and I told him that I wanted to take my wife to the hospital at Rehovoth. He said to hold on, he would ask permission of Cairo. As good as his word, he came back quickly with the answer–this time driving a Sherman tank for the journey! He was escorted by three other tanks. Your mother got into the major's tank and the convoy took off for Rehovoth. For ten tortuous days I did not know anything–until the good major returned with the word that we had a son.

When the Egyptians encircled the camp that spring, our local commander came himself for the children. He drove in with his soldiers in armored cars, breaking through the line. They scooped up all the children, put them in cars, and drove them out. From the water-tower, we could see that the children had penetrated the line in peace. When we saw that, everything seemed possible again.

By Passover, 1948, it was very tense. But some Arabs secretly remained our friends.

The mukhtar of one village helped to cut the wires of the mines to help the Israeli convoys go through. Another young Arab used to buy bullets in Gaza and bring them to us in a basket.

Masada, near the Dead Sea, is a symbol of Jewish perseverance and determination. Here, in 73 C.E., the last group of Jewish Zealots killed themselves after a long siege rather than give in to the Roman conquerors.

He charged us high prices, but it was dangerous for him and we were willing to pay any price for them. We had no supplies.

The first night of Passover, we sat in the old dining-room, singing *Hatikvah*, with our soup and fruit and wine on the table. We kept on singing though the Arab village next to ours opened fire on us for the first time. We had guards outside and knew that the Arabs would not try to come in, but the machine-gun fire made a strange obbligato.

Later, at our radio, we heard that independence had been declared in the Museum of Tel Aviv, and that excitement in the streets and cafes was high. We could hear the Old Man's voice–and visualized him with his foaming white hair telling that distinguished gathering and the United Nations and the whole world the words that became engraved on our memory: "We,... assembled on the day of the termination of the British Mandate for Palestine...do hereby proclaim the establishment of a Jewish state in the Land of Israel."

There was no time for us to think about independence then or to drink to it. For two weeks we had been sleeping in our clothes. The others were worrying about their children. We had no water. We had a few arms and bullets. We could see the preparations for war around us.

When it was just breaking dawn, the Egyptian planes came over. They dropped their bombs and had an easy time of it. We had nothing to use back. At six o'clock the following morning, the Egyptian land forces started firing. They came with big guns, heavy artillery, tanks and machine guns. There was no heavy artillery at the kibbutz.

For eight days they fired over from the hills. It was not hard for them to shoot down everything that we had built for five years. Many of ours were killed.

I will tell only of one–Simeon.

He had been badly shattered with a grenade, his belly smashed to pieces. Deborah kept asking for him, and at last we told her and took her to Amos' house where he had been laid out. She looked at him without moving or crying, like a block of stone. Very quietly she took off his wrist watch. He was so drenched with blood that we had not had the heart to take off his belt of bullets. She reached over and loosened the belt for us, took it off herself, and handed it to us. Not until she left the room did she begin to shiver and break.

By the end of the eighth day we had orders from the Army to leave the kibbutz. We buried our dead in a common grave, and left everything behind except our rifles and signal wireless.

We were a silent group that left the settlement. But we did not feel the awful desperation that Joshua must have known in the Warsaw Ghetto—for there was no way that he could break out of the wall, while we were sure we were only withdrawing temporarily. He had been behind a wall; we were in our own country. There had to be a difference. This could only be an interlude. We had not waited for this moment for two thousand years, only to give in because a round had been lost. Those were our thoughts, and our faith was justified.

The members spread around in various settlements. A few months later, the commander of the Northern Negev sent word by bicycle messenger that our kibbutz had been liberated. It was on the newscast from Jerusalem. Then everyone who had been in the kibbutz, for miles around, simply left their work and went to the road and hitched rides. They came back without even having to communicate with one another. Deborah came back, too.

"This is my only home," she said.

The destruction of the kibbutz was complete. We went first to stand at the grave of our comrades. Then we tried to find our rooms. Nothing was left. It was sad to see how people went looking for some belonging, a picture, a letter.

Everything in the music corner had been hacked to bits. This seemed hardest to believe. We had a rather large collection of records, all the good stuff—Beethoven, Chopin, Mozart—no dances. Every record had been broken and the bits piled in pails. The piano was smashed into small pieces. I remember feeling a strange anger at this senselessness. Why hadn't they taken the records with them instead of smashing everything?

Soon we were all reunited again—to start to build again, but this time ringed in by neighbors who now called themselves our enemy. Yet they are the same neighbors.

You asked me to look over your homework, my son, and I find that it makes a matchless postscript to what I have been writing.

Your teacher, Deborah, asks how you feel about living on the spot where history has been made, and whether you are afraid.

"*Lo*—no," you answer. "I am not afraid. This kibbutz is my country. All the years that we are living we are educated to live in such a place as this village, and I am not afraid. And the Arabs must not be afraid. We have to live with them in peace, because with war life can never be served here.

"We are Zionists and Socialists. We believe and we know that the poor people and the workers have no reason to fight, because the man working his fields must have peace to work to get his corn in and his milk in. I am sorry about the death of the Israeli soldiers and of the Arab soldiers, too. After all they are all sons of mothers who loved them and lost them forever."

My blessing for your Bar Mitzvah, my son, is that you retain this idealism and wisdom all the days of your life.

Gertrude Samuels.

162

Isaac

It was my father forced him into the desert—
My father, the patriarch, fearing for my inheritance,
And my mother, jealous of the strength of a concubine's child.

And I vaguely remember the mocking, knowing boy
Who played his secret games around our tents
And crept in at night to his mother the slave woman's pillow.

He could do marvellous things: whistle wild songs,
Climb trees I couldn't, find unknown caves and streams;
His exploits were legend among our lesser household.

But there was that day my father, a man perplexed,
Rejected his furtively proud, unorthodox son:
His God wanted me and my father always listened.

I hear now my brother is a chief of a tribe in the desert;
He lives by conquest and has many enemies.
His children plot and starve when he is defeated.

I hear rumours he dreams of marching against me.
To seize his inheritance. What shall I do against God and my
    father?
I, too, believe in the destiny of my children.

I, too, have suffered, perhaps more than he:
I have had a sacrificial knife laid at my throat.
These lands are a small exchange for that terrifying moment.

I would like to help my brother, but he is still proud.
There will be no discussion of peace between us;
And our father, the old God-fearing man, has been dead many
    years.

A.C. Jacobs.

Israel Independence Day parade in New York City.

How does the Diaspora Jew, the Jew who has chosen to live outside the "homeland," feel about the State of Israel? Most Jews who have not emigrated to Israel are deeply committed to its existence. Since its inception, Jews from all over the world have unfalteringly supported Israel with financial and political aid. Whenever there has been a crisis in Israel, the support has escalated. Today, every Jew, regardless of where he or she lives, feels a special connection to Israel. Most Jews feel that Israel is their second, if not their first, home. Elie Wiesel writes about his feelings towards Israel from the point of view of a Diaspora Jew.

A Diaspora Jew Looks at Israel

Face to face with Israelis, it is normal that we should often feel at fault, ill-at-ease. How can we, day after day, implore God in our prayers to "bring us back to Zion," and yet not go there when the opportunity is offered us? We are anchored in Israel's history, yet we do not take part in its experiments. After waiting for a state for two thousand years, how can one explain the Diaspora's refusal to heed its call?

There are two possibilities: either Israel belongs to the entire Jewish people, or else the Diaspora has nothing to do with it. For us, only the first hypothesis is valid. What is Israel? The sum of age-old struggles, aspirations, undertakings. A place where military bravura and literary creation are almost as essential as religious faith and metaphysical thought. Rabbi Yohanan Ben-Zakkai and Bar Kochba, Yehuda Halevy and Isaac Luria have contributed as much to it as Theodor Herzl and Vladimir Jabotinsky. If Israel's rebirth had been accomplished solely by its citizens, its impact would hardly be felt beyond its borders.

For Israel to reemerge, it was necessary that a long procession get under way. The mystics of medieval Spain, the wandering Just Men of Poland, the sages of Slobodka and the visionaries of Morocco—it is thanks to them, the known and unknown heroes of Jewish legend that Israel lives and relives. Israel is protected not only by its visible forces but also by its invisible, clandestine defenders, who lived and fought far removed from it in territory and time. . . .

As a Diaspora Jew, I live the life and the destiny of Jerusalem. And I should like you [my Israeli brother,] to understand us. We are responsible for one another; you do not deny it. If the principal task of the Diaspora is to protect Israel, yours should be to become a new source of life to the Diaspora. Let us assume the dialectics of our so singularly Jewish and so Jewishly singular condition: that we both live on two levels simultaneously, that we both lead a double life, that we be one another's heart and conscience, constantly questioning and enriching one another. Without the Diaspora, Israel would have no one to question and no one to be questioned by. Without Israel, the Diaspora would know nothing of victory but the anguish that precedes it.

In these extraordinary times our generation is at once the most blessed and the most cursed of all. Some thirty years ago Jewish heroes wept every time a courier brought them a weapon; today strategists marvel at the Jewish army's military genius. Fifty years ago nobody imagined that Russian Judaism could survive Communist dictatorship; today we are witnessing its rebirth. A generation ago we discovered the ruins of the world and the dark side of God; today it is on them that we are building future Jewish history.

Elie Wiesel.

ENDANGERED JEWISH COMMUNITIES

Israel has been a place of refuge for endangered Jewish people from all over the world, even before its inception as a Jewish State. Before 1933, European Jews came to Palestine, as it was called before 1948, mostly for idealistic reasons. After 1933, they came in search of safety.

Access to Palestine at that time was not easy. Palestine was then under British mandate and the British limited Jewish immigration. But thousands of young Jewish children were rescued from Germany and other Nazi-occupied countries through Youth Aliyah. Other desperate Jews escaping Hitler managed to smuggle themselves in through such illegal Jewish immigration organizations as *Mossad*. After the war, Jewish survivors from displaced persons' camps boarded illegal ships which ran the British blockade to get into Palestine.

Since its statehood, Israel has been a haven for threatened Jewish Middle-Eastern and North African communities, who have suffered from poverty and prejudice. An estimated 120,000 Iraqi Jews resettled in Israel after 1947. Forty-six thousand Yemenite Jews were airlifted to Israel through "Operation Magic Carpet." Thousands of Jews from Egypt, Iran, Libya, Tunisia, and Morocco also resettled in Israel.

Today, whenever there is a Jew in the world who requires shelter, there is a Jewish place of refuge. Jews from Soviet Russia and from Ethiopia are the most recent beneficiaries of Israeli rescue efforts. In Soviet Russia, however, Jews are generally refused the right to emigrate.

(Above) Illegal Jewish immigrants landing on the coast of Palestine in 1947.

(Top) An ancient Jewish community still exists on the island of Jerba, Tunisia. Numbering only some 300 today, here they celebrate the holiday of Sukhot in their synagogue.

JEWS OF SOVIET RUSSIA

"We, Jews, are a community based on memory. By denying us the right and ability to transmit our heritage to our children, Soviet authorities are bringing about the destruction of our precious possession."

Ephraim Rosenshtein, Moscow.

"I often talk man-to-man with my son about our situation. I try to be constructive. When on the eighth anniversary of our first refusal, he asked me, 'Well, how long are we supposed to wait?' I felt ashamed. I had no answer to give him."

Michail Kosharovsky, Moscow.

The son of Michail Kosharovsky, refusenik.

Russian history is filled with oppression towards its large Jewish population. Escaping pogroms was a way of life for Russian Jews for hundreds of years. When the czar was overthrown and revolution came to Russia in 1917, many Jews who had fought for the Revolution thought that their lives would be better and safer. This was not to be the case. Russian citizens had been so inured with antisemitism for so long that even in their revolutionary quest for equality Jews were still the scapegoat.

After the Revolution

Together with a number of families, my wife and children and I are cowering under a storm of bullets over our heads. We remain powerless, useless, paralyzed.

On the seventeenth we were "presented" with the constitution for which our brothers spilled their blood like water. On the same day a rumor was spread abroad that orders had been given to attack the Jews—and the attack began from all sides. Simultaneously, an order was issued that we should not shoot from the windows, and not throw stones. If we should do that, the soldiers would fire back and destroy our houses. Seeing soldiers on the street—and cossacks—we felt reassured; and they did help, but not us. They helped to rob, to beat, to ravish, to despoil. Before our eyes and in the eyes of the whole world, they helped to smash windows, break down doors, break locks and to put booty in their pockets. Before our eyes and in the eyes of our children, they beat Jews grievously—men, women and children—and they shouted, "Money, give us your money." Before our eyes women were hurled from windows and children thrown to the cobblestones.

The local newspapers publish only one hundredth part of the frightful details of the happenings in Kiev. Now, imagine what is happening in hundreds of Jewish towns and villages. Too dear will our freedom cost, and God only knows whether we will live to enjoy it. The tyrant will not surrender his rod, the swords are being sharpened. . . . In God's name, brethren, help. To act, to help, to resist, that we are not permitted. For the life of one drunken brute that we take when he attacks our wives and our children we pay with hundreds of innocent lives.

What shall we do? No place to hide. Gentiles will not give shelter to Jews.

Brother, do something. Publish this in English as well as in the Jewish press.

Well then, if I cannot be saved, if I must die, I am ready. Perhaps it is better that I shall fall a sacrifice with the rest. My people are being consumed. The whole of Russian Jewry is in danger.

Sholom Aleichem.

The modern government of Soviet Russia has made few improvements in its treatment of its two and a half million Jewish citizens. Both the religious and cultural practices of Judaism are strongly discouraged. Jewish books and religious objects are not allowed to be manufactured or imported and are often confiscated. It is illegal to teach Hebrew, Jewish history or Jewish culture. No Jewish organizations are allowed.

Many Russian Jews have applied for emigration to Israel or North America, only to be refused by the Soviet government. These "refuseniks," as they are called, have been fired, demoted or prosecuted for their efforts. Their families have often lived with constant police harassment.

For several decades, young Jewish people in Soviet Russia have received no formal Jewish education. Many know of their Jewish roots, but are ignorant of Jewish traditions and religion. There are those who, like the Marranos in Spain, are secretly taught about their Jewish heritage, either in their home or by some underground means.

In a repressive society, as in fifteenth-century Spain or in modern-day Soviet Russia, where it is forbidden to practise Judaism, the significance of Bar Mitzvah becomes even more poignant and meaningful. On the next page, Greville Janner, Member of British Parliament and a Jew who has led worldwide campaigns on behalf of Soviet Jews, tells about a Jewish family in Moscow, who were brave enough to celebrate their son's Bar Mitzvah and take the consequences.

Bar Mitzvah in Moscow

My closest attachment was, and remains, to the latter-day, bearded, steadfast and genial saint, Vladimir Slepak and to his family–his wife, Masha; his elder son Alexander (married to Helen), and his younger lad, Leonid.

I will never forget the "*bar mitzvah* episode" in 1972 and all that followed. I was able to talk with Vladimir (or Valodya, as he is called) on the telephone. (We could talk rather freely in those days.) "When will Leonid be 13?" I asked.

"In a few months."

"Will he be *bar mitzvah*?"

There was a pause. "We have never had a *bar mitzvah* in the Moscow Synagogue," Valodya replied.

"Well, why not create a precedent?"

I knew that the Slepaks went to the Moscow Synagogue on Archipova Street every Shabbat–to the synagogue but not inside it. Together with fellow activists, they exchanged news and views, met visitors and enjoyed each other's company. At that time the narrow street was faced with an open lot which provided plenty of room for the Jews to circulate. Only later was the lot blocked off by a wooden barrier and traffic directed into that street, to make the lives of the Jewish activists even more unpleasant.

Leonid's *bar mitzvah* was organized in Moscow and London. The Committee [for Soviet Jewry] bought an ordinary *siddur* and arranged for it to be signed by Edward Heath, then Prime Minister; by most of the Cabinet; by Harold Wilson, then leader of the Opposition, and by most of his Shadow Cabinet–in all, by some 250 MPs. We then shipped this unique book off to Leonid, with love. Father and son went to the airport to collect it. They were allowed to see and examine it. Then it was impounded–and disappeared.

Next step: Parliamentary questions. "Where is the prayer book?" "Will Her Majesty's Government intervene to secure the release of the prayer book?" The Slepak file in the Foreign Office grew bulkier. The Russians protested this "interference" in the internal affairs of the country.

Suddenly the prayer book turned up again. It was returned to British Airways, which brought it back to London, where it received a royal reception. It went on display at exhibitions throughout the United Kingdom and was shown at the Soviet Jewry Exhibition in Brussels last February–a symbol of the Soviet Union's refusal to grant even the most basic religious rights to its Jewish minority.

The *bar mitzvah*, the first to be held in the Moscow Synagogue in two decades, was celebrated without undue incident. Scores of "refuseniks"–Jews denied visas for emigration to Israel–joined the family and the congregation for the service. But then Valodya, who had been arrested several times before, was again imprisoned for protesting the continued refusal of visas to himself and to his family. When he was released fourteen days later I spoke to him by telephone and he told me that he had been kept for eighteen hours in a cell half a metre by one metre in size, its walls covered with "thorns." To make sure that I had understood him properly, I asked Esther Markish (widow of the great Yiddish poet, murdered by Stalin), who was then with him, to translate his explanation into French. Yes, he had been kept in this tiny "iron maiden," unable to sit or even lean. It was torture.

At once we protested loudly and publicly in many ways–in Parliament, in the press and on the radio, in letters and delegations addressed to the Soviet Embassy. Our protest was echoed by newspapers throughout most of the Western world. And as if to prove that our protest had reached its target, the Soviet journals counterattacked, claiming that the account was a malicious invention.

Still, other Jews who were later imprisoned thanked us. The iron maiden had gone out of service.

But as of this writing the Slepak family has not been released. They remain harassed and persecuted in their Moscow home. On the other hand, many of their friends who have been saved have told us that the public outcry at the time of the *bar mitzvah* and thereafter at least kept the Slepaks from an even worse fate. For the Soviets know that if they lay hands on this family, there will be an immediate outraged reaction, not only from the British Parliament but in many other countries.

Greville Janner.

We were moved that David has chosen to share his Bar Mitzvah ceremony with Seva Genis, son of Anatoly and Galia, Refusniks from Moscow. Seva is soon to reach his thirteenth birthday and is unable to celebrate a Bar Mitzvah of his own. At David's request, and to symbolize the occassion, David has twinned himself to Seva and invites him to share in his Simcha.

Many Bar Mitzvah boys in North America symbolically include a Soviet Jewish boy of similar age in their ceremony. This is being done in support of those unable to have celebrations of their own due to Soviet oppression of Jews.

In 1917, there were 5,000 synagogues in Russia; today there are 50. Those that remain open are poorly attended, since Jews fear reprisals in their personal lives. In Moscow, where there is one synagogue in use on Archipova Street, Jews gather together on the holiday of Simchat Torah to talk, sing, and dance late into the night. Once a year, about 20,000 Jews pack Archipova Street; many of them come in secret.

Simchat Torah on Archipova Street

Simchat Torah was an unforgettable experience. We arrived early and already there were some 5,000 people in the street. We pushed our way into the synagogue with some difficulty, and remained there for the first part of the service. When we made our way back outside, we found about 20,000 Jews packed into Archipova Street, lining it from one end to the other.

Later that evening, the meaning of this mass experience became clear to me. "I have been secretly coming to Archipova Street on Simchat Torah for the last five years," said Boris, a middle-aged man we met. "It has been the one public way I have allowed myself to identify with the Jewish people. I never told the other members of my family where I was going or what I was doing. I wanted no harm to befall them. This evening, as I made my way through the crowd, I came face to face with my 18-year-old son. Our eyes met in recognition. He has secretly been coming to Archipova Street on Simchat Torah for the last three years."

From the notes of Ahavia Scheindlin.

The crowd gathers on Archipova Street in front of the Moscow synagogue on Simchat Torah evening.

There are Soviet Jews who never apply for emigration. They have resigned themselves to live in Soviet Russia and experience their Jewishness as best they can. Photographer Nodar Djindjihashvili, a Soviet Jew himself, travelled throughout the Soviet Union interviewing Jews in remote areas who are trying to save their culture within the confines of Soviet Russia.

The Vanishing Jews of Russia

"In Hebrew my name is Meir, the same as my grandfather's, Rabbi Meir," says photographer Nodar Djindjihashvili. "On the day of my bar mitzvah my grandfather revealed to me a secret dream." Rabbi Meir claimed to believe that when the sky-blue Jerusalem Temple was destroyed nearly 2,000 years ago, its bricks were scattered over the face of the earth. "Not until those bricks were gathered up," Nodar says, "would the Temple be rebuilt and the Messiah come to earth. My grandfather's dream was to gather those bricks." Two weeks after Rabbi Meir told him this story, the old man died. "Soon I began dreaming of the blue bricks every night. His dream became my own. And I began to realize that I had a mission: to go all over Russia–even to the ends of the earth–searching for the lost bricks of the Temple."

As a younger man, Nodar...had sought to establish his own Jewish identity. He spent 14 years compiling an anthology, *The Jewish Spirit from Moses to Marx* ("By Marx," he says, "I meant Groucho, not just Karl"). In 1977 Nodar published a book of philosophy that upset Soviet officials. Not only were his views unorthodox, but the book contained quotations from Jewish sages, and its cover, with the title in Hebrew-style lettering was colored blue and white, like the Israeli flag. Such achievements

are rare for a man who spent his boyhood in the backyard of the Tbilisi synagogue in Soviet Georgia. A filmmaker and author (recently awarded a Rockefeller Foundation Humanities Fellowship), he was the youngest, at 34, in the history of the Soviet academies to earn the distinction of Doctor of Sciences in philosophy.

But in 1978 the dream of the blue bricks returned to haunt him, and Nodar says he could no longer spare himself the danger and mysticism of his "mission." He decided to take his camera and record Jewish life in the Soviet Union. Somehow the photographs would be his bricks. Using as a cover his memberships in both the journalists and filmmakers unions, he crossed 20,000 miles of the Soviet terrain....Most Jews were reluctant to be photographed, fearing reprisals. On 15 occasions, Jews informed on him to local KGB officials. When questioned, he would explain that he was doing a photo essay on old architecture for a Moscow publisher. Later, after developing the color slides in his bathtub, he sent out his more than 3,000 photographs with the help of 13 foreigners who had diplomatic status and whose luggage was exempt from inspection.

"Part of the journey was mystically motivated by my grandfather," he says, "but part was purely philosophical. I became preoccupied with finding the essence of the Jewish spirit." Nodar, who now lives in the Corona section of New York City with his wife, mother and daughter, says that he was seeking explanations for the persecution of Jews in Russia. Many Western experts contend that there has been a resurgence of anti-Semitism there. Nodar rules this out. "All rites of religion are considered taboo. But what makes the authorities nervous about

Jews in particular is the backbone of their spirit—the tendency toward critical thinking, the passion for doubting. At the core of Judaism is the critical study of man and the universe—the Bible. In no other religion or culture are great men so openly and welcomely criticized. Moses, David, Solomon—all important Jewish leaders—are open to criticism. This Jewish spirit of criticism is precisely what the Kremlin finds threatening.

"It is no surprise," Nodar continues, "that this same criticism founded the Soviet state. The October Revolution of 1917 was prepared and fashioned by many Jews. Both of Karl Marx's grandfathers were rabbis. Lenin's grandfather was allegedly Jewish. Sverdlov, the first chief of state, was a Jew and so was Trotsky, who created the Red Army."

There are, according to Nodar, many reasons why Jewish culture might make the Politburo uneasy. As in other countries, Jews constitute a minority and are highly concentrated—in urban centers. Statistics show that Jews are the best educated of all groups considered nationalities in the Soviet Union. "An intellectual is nothing but a man imbued with the pathos of criticism," notes Nodar. "And a society like Russia's can't tolerate intellectuals. So Jews, as a cultural force, are an obvious threat. Jews are generally the most Westernized, the most outspoken critics in Russia. One old saying goes, 'Jews never sleep and never allow you to sleep.'" Nodar also believes that the Soviets regard their adversary—the U.S.—as a country with a foreign policy influenced by pro-Jewish or Zionist sentiments.

Cameras never convey the absence of something, and what cannot be grasped immediately from studying Nodar's photographs is that Jewish culture and religion in Russia are, in fact, disappearing. When he visited Vitebsk, the birthplace of artist Marc Chagall—a devout Jew—Nodar noticed a run-down cemetery and a lack of Jewish customs. They had been eliminated, in large part, by the Nazis who had entered Vitebsk in 1941. Sixteen thousand Jews were liquidated there that year.

"I visited a man who looked exactly like Chagall," Nodar recalls. "If you can believe it, he lived in the same spot where Chagall had lived. But this man seemed totally removed from anything Jewish. He came down a ladder from mending his roof and insisted that if he stayed in Russia for a thousand years, he wouldn't know what a Jew was.

"I stood in his backyard. It was scattered with apples, hundreds of apples. As we talked, there was that smell that makes you drunken. And soon I saw tears in his eyes. His wife, hearing me speak of Jews and of my coming emigration, ran out of the house. She whispered, 'Go out immediately. He's forgotten he is Jewish. It is dangerous for him—for his health and soul. The last time someone made Jewish talk, he went crazy for months. Go, or I will tell the authorities you are agitating for Israel.'

"I left and they were crying on each other. But as soon as I came to the end of the bridge leading from their home, I met a boy. It was the old man's grandson. He was waiting for me with a basket of apples. I saved the most unripe one and carried it all over Russia with me until the end of my journey."

David M. Friend.

(Above) Surrounded by friends, this Israel-bound emigre toasts Mother Russia farewell.

(Opposite, above and below) Many synagogues in Russia have been closed by the Soviets. As a result, these Jews in Minsk worship in a makeshift sanctuary.

FALASHA JEWS OF ETHIOPIA

"Following the Holocaust, many of the survivors believed that the Jews of the free world, and especially the Jewish leaders of those communities, failed to fulfill their responsibilities vis-a-vis their brethren in occupied Europe. Today the Jews of Ethiopia face the danger of a similar situation. It is our obligation to do everything in our power to facilitate their rescue."

Simon Wiesenthal.

Young Falasha boy.

A less known Jewish community which is in peril is the Falasha community in northern Ethiopia. These Jews live in isolated villages. They work as farmers, smiths, weavers and potters.

The Falashas trace their origin to King Solomon and the Queen of Sheba, and have lived in Ethiopia for almost 2,000 years, clinging to Judaism through unbelievable hardship. They call themselves "Beta Israel," House of Israel, rather than *falasha* which means stranger or exile. They have survived isolation, subjugation, war, poverty, starvation, and disease. In 1970, there were approximately 23,000 Falashas. Today, their community faces extinction.

Totally isolated from other Jewish communities, only in the last century did the Falashas discover that they were not the only Jews in the world. Though for centuries they stringently observed the laws of the Bible, which they passed on through oral tradition, in their isolation they were totally unaware of the post-biblical writings and the more modern Jewish holidays.

Visit to a Falasha Village, 1868

In 1868 the Alliance Israelite Universelle of Paris sent the French Semitic scholar, Joseph Halévy, to investigate the situation in Ethiopia. On Halévy's first visit, he encountered a reaction similar to the one in the joke with the tagline: "That's funny, you don't look Jewish!" When he told the Ethiopian Jews that he too worshipped the one God of the Jews, some shook their heads doubtfully and exclaimed, "What! You a Falasha? A white Falasha! You are laughing at us! Are there any white Falashas?" The story has it that Professor Halévy, as well as his student and successor, Professor Jacques Faitlovitch, had to undergo a ritual immersion before entering villages of the Ethiopian Jews.

Howard Lenhoff.

In 1985, there were an estimated 7,000 Falashas still living in Ethiopia under extremely deplorable conditions. Famine (which has hit all Ethiopians), coupled with persecution, has motivated many Falashas to risk their lives and leave the country, often on foot.

The Forgotten People

In the sprawl of Ethiopia's north-central plateau, fortressed by forbidding mountainous terrain that has kept this country one of the poorest in the world, live a people so primitive they are cast aside by their own country. They are the Falashas, or Ethiopian Jews.

The Falashas are the object of persecution and scorn, and, indeed, may be a people headed for extinction. They are fighting for cultural survival in conditions defying human habitation, but they maintain a dignity that so far neither poverty, nor revolution, nor famine could kill.

Ethiopia is a rugged land lived in by a people whose average per capita income is $100 and the average life span, the lowest anywhere, is 36 years. It is a nation with a military government bolstered by the Soviets and trying to keep several warring factions and tribes at peace.

Since 1958 more than 3 million people have died and 4 million more lives are at stake in droughts that have afflicted the country, one of the hardest hit by Africa's current famine.

Most of the existing Falasha villages, from tiny hamlets of two to communities of 2,000, pock the rolling savannah near the city of Gonder.

It was in the open market at Gonder that I first made contact with the Falashas. Through a maze of people squatting, slithering, pushing, came a flash. A young man about 17, sporting bright red shorts and a serious smile grabbed my shoulder.

"Entu Yehudit? (Are you Jewish?)" he asked, trying to make surreptitious contact with a fellow Jew.

My feeble attempt to form a few words in Hebrew brought a look of excitement to his eyes and he was off before the stones thrown by an on-looking man in the crowd could reach him.

The young man, Ephraim, was from Wollecka, a Falasha village about 7 kilometres outside Gonder. Pulling into Wollecka, a village of thatched, round huts of sticks and mud perched in random plots on the hillside, children crowded around the car.

"Hevrit? (Hebrew?)" asked a girl of 8 in a barely audible voice.

"Hevrit, ouw! (Hebrew, yes!)", I said in Amharic, Ethiopia's national language. In a moment children formed a crowd and broke into "Oseh Shalom," a Hebrew folksong, as if presenting a gift.

At the edge of Wollecka stood a synagogue; a tuckel of cement and wood larger than the other dwellings, with a Star of David crowning the aluminum roof. Villagers entered the temple with reverence, removing their shoes before stepping onto well-worn mats of straw.

Children piled onto the floor, covering their heads with their hands if they lacked a cloth or yarmulke, boys and girls alike. A kohan, or high priest, wearing a turban with a Jewish prayer shawl dangling under his "shomma," a cotton toga draped over the shoulders and chest worn as the national dress, gave a welcome blessing in Hebrew.

The Jews in Ethiopia cannot be differentiated in appearance from other Amharas, the ruling tribe of this country which keeps over 70 ethnic groups within its border. The Semitic origins of these people give them almost "caucasoid" features: thin facial characteristics, high cheekbones and wide, almond eyes set in a coffee and cream complexion.

In their isolation, the Jewish practices of the Falashas are often combined with Coptic Christian traditions. Both religions share the liturgical language of Ge'ez and the figures of high priests and deacons. Jewish ascetics or monks are not unheard of and neither religion accepts the eating of pork. Both Christian and Jewish males are circumcised.

Ephraim waited outside the temple and motioned for me to follow. We walked toward the schooling area where two rooms of mud and cement stood side by side. In one school, a tiny space held a dozen wooden desks and benches for elementary lessons. The other school sat boarded and locked.

Here, Hebrew classes had been taught until government officials padlocked the premises two years ago and banned the teaching of the language in the village. The temple had been closed for a time as well.

Behind the school and away from the vision of other people in the village, Ephraim spoke of the hardships he faces if he remains in Wollecka, living a life without hope, without a future and in constant fear of the vicissitudes of people in power.

His people are poor, hungry and sick, and living is rough. In what English he could muster (English is taught as a second language in high schools) he discussed how Gentile neighbors treat Jews with cruelty. They believe Falashas turn into hyenas at night and eat their souls.

Ephraim talked of Israel, where he knew, as a Jew, he would be accepted. He can run. He is fast. And he can probably make it to the border. He would go in darkness and never return. Otherwise, he will likely be drafted for one war or another or summoned into prison for his suspected desire to flee....

Although no formal census has been taken, consistent estimates show there are about 20,000 Falashas [world-wide], versus possibly 100,000 at the turn of the century. Infant mortality is high in many of these villages in a region where 50 to 100 children a day perish from malnutrition and starvation.

Between war, famine, disappearance, disease and assimilation, this population of Jews may not last into the next century.

Choices are few for the Falashas and it is not a choice outsiders can make for them. Although the Ethiopian government claims Falashas have as much a chance as others to legally leave the country, those chances, involving considerable amounts of cash and know-how, are slim enough for Christians and nearly non-existent for Jews.

The underground migration out of the country, a journey which can take up to three weeks on foot, often without shoes, food, water or extra clothing, is extremely dangerous and often fatal.

Lark Ellen Gould.

Falashas celebrating Seged, a Jewish holiday indigenous to only the Falashas.

Jewish organizations from all over the world have rallied to help the Falashas emigrate to Israel. Thousands are still stranded in refugee camps in the Sudan after their arduous walk from Ethiopia.

The Israeli government organized a secret airlift which brought over 7,000 Ethiopian Jews to Israel. Though there are many problems to overcome in integrating this very unique group of Jews into Israeli life, there is now some hope for a future for this displaced Jewish community.

The Rusted Chain

My history crucified, buried under the muddy flood of time,
I, rusting in the island of sufferers,
My ancestry, my heritage to many a bookball game.
Who am I? What am I?
Speak my people of yonderland, House of Israel,
Of ruined history, of identity stolen,
Switch off your silence.

Sweet land, mother of my forefathers,
You spewed me out, you anathematized me,
From highland to lowland, from lowland to highland; So I wander,
"Falasha"...you disdain me, you accuse me, my cousin,
You pronounce me guilty for fashioning with my hands,
Ere, is it sinful to earn one's bread?
Speak my people of yonderland, House of Israel.

Ah, worse the deception that ends in false hopes,
To kiss the earth of your Orit, the land of your childhood dreams,
Only to be smeared with dust by the long-sought-for kin,
Grudgingly welcomed with a stinging, wet humility.
The rejected do also reject, the humiliated do humiliate,
They ask "Are you Jewish too?," tearing at my identity through my tired ears.
When moved by compassion some do concede "Perhaps you are of the Ten Tribes,"
Of Dan, of Asher, of Gad, of Yosef,
Or even maybe of Moses drowned or lost ones,
From the bottom of the Red Sea or the Desert.
All these speculations!
Is it my blackness or Africa's dazzling light that puzzles them?

Yosef Damana Ben Yeshaq.

EXTINCT JEWISH COMMUNITIES

Not all Jewish communities around the world have survived. Some have become extinct through assimilation; others through persecution.

A fascinating community which has disappeared through assimilation, but has left evidence of its Jewish past, is the one which existed in Kaifeng, China beginning in the tenth century. Though it was totally isolated from other Jewish communities, and never numbered more than 1,000 or 2,000 members, it managed to survive for several centuries.

The Jews of Kaifeng

During the 166 years between 960 and 1126 C.E., China was ruled by the emperors of the Sung Dynasty whose court was at Kaifeng–a bustling metropolis straddling the legendary Silk Route that linked their sprawling domain to trading partners in the West. At some time during these years, a band of wandering Jews–probably merchants, and most likely of Persian birth or descent–passed through the gates of the city and was granted an audience at the imperial palace. The emperor greeted the travelers warmly, while accepting the obligatory tribute–cotton goods from the West, in this case–that they had brought. "You have come to our China," he told them. "Respect and preserve the customs of your ancestors, and hand them down here in Pien-liang (Kaifeng)."

Chinese Jews of Kaifeng on the banks of the Yellow River.

Centuries later, in 1489, these newcomers' grateful descendents inscribed the emperor's words on a stone tablet erected in the resplendent synagogal and communal compound which had been dedicated in 1163, at the intersection of Kaifeng's Earth Market and Fire God Shrine streets. This monument (or as certain historians suggest, its replacement which was constructed after the flood that destroyed much of the city in 1642) is now among the holdings of the municipal museum of Kaifeng.

To this day, several hundred residents of the old Sung capital continue to think of themselves as bona fide members of the House of Israel. They are firm in this belief despite the fact that today they are totally indistinguishable in appearance from their neighbors; that they have had no rabbi for about 175 years; that their last synagogue was torn down a century and a quarter ago; that for generations they have had no communal organizations and they remember virtually nothing of the faith or tradition of their fathers. Surprisingly, the sign identifying the street on which many of them still live remains unchanged: "The Lane of the Sect Which Teaches the Scriptures", it reads. However, it is exceedingly rare, one may suppose, that a passerby is moved to ask himself how a street in the middle of China came to bear so un-Chinese a name. . . .

What was life like for the Jews of Kaifeng from the time they became firmly established in the city until their community fell apart?

The answer is that in its everyday, non-religious aspects the life of the Jews of Kaifeng was not very different from that of their neighbors. They dressed like the Chinese, wore pigtails (when it was decreed by the Ching conquerors of China to symbolize the submission of the Chinese to the Ching rulers), bound their daughters' feet, spoke the local dialect, and engaged in the same occupations as their countrymen: farmers, merchants, artisans, scholars, officials, soldiers, doctors, and the like. In proportion to their numbers, however, they seem to have been quite successful. Many attained mandarin rank, the most noteworthy of these being the brothers Chao Ying-cheng (Moshe ben-Abram) and Chao Ying-tou (?ben Abram) who in the 1660s held responsible government posts, and were instrumental in rebuilding the synagogue after the flood of 1642. Each of the two brothers also wrote a book in Chinese, about Judaism. . . .

The religious outlook and practice of the Kaifeng Jews was for centuries very much like that of most other Jews. They observed the Sabbath and other holy days, circumcised their male children, maintained schools which taught the language and scriptures of Judaism and ordered their lives within the moral and doctrinal parameters set forth in traditional rabbinic literature. The Kaifeng Jews, moreover, recognized one God as eternal and without physical form. They believed in Heaven and Hell, that the individual is judged in the hereafter, in the resurrection of the dead and in the existence of angels. Idols were anathema to them. They accepted full responsibility for helping the poor, the infirm and those incapable of taking care of themselves. They prayed facing westward, in the direction of Jerusalem. Their children were given traditional Hebrew names in addition to the conventional names of the country. No converts were sought, but Chinese women underwent the rites of conversion before marrying Jewish men. . . .

With the passage of time, however, Chinese teachings and traditions, particularly Confucianism, began to intrude; simultaneously, the community's appreciation and understanding of its own heritage deteriorated. . . .

Slowly, but inexorably, the knowledge of Hebrew diminished, so that when twelve new Torah books were written in the middle of the 17th century, the scribal misspellings in each of them ran into the hundreds. Even the rabbis remembered distressingly little of the ancestral language and faith they tried vainly to pass onto their people; and after the death of the last of Kaifeng's long line of rabbis, between 1800 and 1810, there was nobody to take his place. The Torah scrolls in the synagogue remained there as objects of veneration, but to read them was beyond the ability of the congregation's members. In fact, they even displayed one Torah scroll in the marketplace, together with a placard offering a reward to any traveler who could interpret its text for them. It was a futile gesture.

Chinese Woman Discovers Jewish Ancestry

Jin Sionjing is a middle-aged Chinese woman who always thought of herself as a Muslim. One day, she chanced to talk to another Muslim, a person of some learning, who told her of two brothers she knew, with the family name of Jin, who were Jewish. Jin Sionjing, her curiosity piqued—and, perhaps, some hidden spring of Jewish identity stirred—made some inquiries and learned that a Jewish community had flourished at one time in the northern Chinese city of Kaifeng, where her family, so far as she was able to trace it, had originated, and that Jin was a common Jewish family name there. Jin Sionjing journeyed to Kaifeng, where her 86-year old mother filled her in on other facts about her background, recalling among other details that her grandfather used to wear a blue *kippa*, unlike the white head coverings traditionally worn by the local Muslims. Over the generations, the Kaifeng Jewish community had been gradually effaced by intermarriage and assimilation to the Muslim majority.

Reuter News Services.

Moshe Lea, a Chinese Jewish boy, reads the Meghila in Kaifeng, China in 1967.

Synagogal services were discontinued, and the synagogue itself fell into a state of disrepair. In short, destitute Jewish families lived on its grounds—and even grew cabbages there. By 1850-51, poverty and ignorance were so widespread that the surviving Jews sold six of their Torah scrolls and several dozen other synagogal books to emissaries from the London Society for Promoting Christianity Among the Jews. A few years later, the synagogue was torn down, and in the years just prior to the First World War the land itself was sold to Canadian missionaries.

Still, there persisted throughout all this a clear feeling of attachment on the part of many descendents of the ancient Jewish community of Kaifeng to the idea of being Jewish—a tenacious sense of loyalty to the origins of their Judaic heritage, notwithstanding their almost total loss of knowledge of the barest essentials of that heritage. One finds expressions of that attachment even now, verbally and in print, and with these an occasional revelation of a deep-seated yearning for renewed association with Judaism. Given Kaifeng Jewry's grindingly long isolation from the Jewish world, and its paucity of numbers, it is not difficult to understand why most of its members were ultimately assimilated into the faiths of their neighbors. What is amazing, really, is that this beleaguered community was able to find the inner strength and the determination to carry on in the face of these overpowering obstacles for as many centuries as it did.

Michael Pollak.

A Chinese Jewish family in 1910.

173

Living in the diaspora, even in the best of circumstances, sometimes entails feelings of isolation and a loss of roots. Here is a modern story of lost and found Jewish roots.

Monte Sant' Angelo

The driver, who had been sitting up ahead in perfect silence for nearly an hour as they crossed the monotonous green plain of Foggia, now said something. Appello quickly leaned forward in the back seat and asked him what he had said. "That is Monte Sant' Angelo before you." Appello lowered his head to see through the windshield of the rattling little Fiat. Then he nudged Bernstein, who awoke resentfully, as though his friend had intruded. "That's the town up there," Appello said. Bernstein's annoyance vanished, and he bent forward. They both sat that way for several minutes, watching the approach of what seemed to them a comically situated town, even more comic than any they had seen in the four weeks they had spent moving from place to place in the country. It was like a tiny old lady living on a high roof for fear of thieves.

The plain remained as flat as a table for a quarter of a mile ahead. Then out of it, like a pillar, rose the butte; squarely and rigidly skyward it towered, only narrowing as it reached its very top. And there, barely visible now, the town crouched, momentarily obscured by white clouds, then appearing again tiny and safe, like a mountain port looming at the end of the sea. From their distance they could make out no road, no approach at all up the side of the pillar.

"Whoever built that was awfully frightened of something," Bernstein said, pulling his coat closer around him. "How do they get up there? Or do they?"

Appello, in Italian, asked the driver about the town. The driver, who had been there only once before in his life and knew no other who had made the trip–despite his being a resident of Lucera, which was not far away–told Appello with some amusement that they would soon see how rarely anyone goes up or comes down Monte Sant' Angelo. "The donkeys will kick and run away as we ascend, and when we come into the town everyone will come out to see. They are very far from everything. They all look like brothers up there. They don't know very much either." He laughed.

"What does the Princeton chap say?" Bernstein asked.

The driver had a crew haircut, a turned-up nose, and a red round face with blue eyes. He owned the car, and although he spoke like any Italian when his feet were on the ground, behind the wheel with two Americans riding behind him he had only the most amused and superior attitude toward everything outside the windshield. Appello, having translated for Bernstein, asked him how long it would take to ascend. "Perhaps three quarters of an hour–as long as the mountain is," he amended.

Bernstein and Appello settled back and watched the butte's approach. Now they could see that its sides were crumbled white stone. At this closer vantage it seemed as though it had been struck a terrible blow by some monstrous hammer that had split its structure into millions of seams. They were beginning to climb now, on a road of sharp broken rocks.

"The road is Roman," the driver remarked. He knew how much Americans made of anything Roman. Then he added, "The car, however, is from Milan." He and Appello laughed.

And now the white chalk began drifting into the car. At their elbows the altitude began to seem threatening. There was no railing on the road, and it turned back on itself every two hundred yards in order to climb again. The Fiat's doors were wavering in their frames; the seat on which they sat kept inching forward onto the floor. A fine film of white talc settled onto their clothing and covered their eyebrows. Both together began to cough. When they were finished Bernstein said, "Just so I understand it clearly and without prejudice, will you explain again in words of one syllable why the hell we are climbing this lump of dust, old man?"

Appello laughed and mocked a punch at him.

"No kidding," Bernstein said, trying to smile.

"I want to see this aunt of mine, that's all." Appello began taking it seriously.

"You're crazy, you know that? You've got some kind of ancestor complex. All we've done in this country is look for your relatives."

"Well, Jesus, I'm finally in the country, I want to see all the places I came from. You realize that two of my relatives are buried in a crypt in the church up there? In eleven hundred something."

"Oh, is this where the monks came from?"

"Sure, the two Appello brothers. They helped build that church. It's very famous, that church. Supposed to be Saint Michael appeared in a vision or something."

"I never thought I'd know anybody with monks in his family. But I still think you're cracked on the whole subject."

"Well, don't you have any feeling about your ancestors? Wouldn't you like to go back to Austria or wherever you came from and see where the old folks lived? Maybe find a family that belongs to your line, or something like that?"

Bernstein did not answer for a moment. He did not know quite what he felt and wondered dimly whether he kept ragging his friend a little because of envy. When they had been in the country courthouse where Appello's grandfather's portrait and his greatgrandfather's hung–both renowned provincial magistrates; when they had spent the night in Lucera where the name Appello meant something distinctly honorable, and where his friend Vinny was taken in hand and greeted in that intimate way because he was an Appello–in all these moments Bernstein had felt left out and somehow deficient. At first he had taken the attitude that all the fuss was childish, and yet as incident after incident, landmark after old landmark, turned up echoing the name Appello, he gradually began to feel his friend combining with this history, and it seemed to him that it made Vinny stronger, somehow less dead when the time would come for him to die.

"I have no relatives that I know of in Europe," he said to Vinny. "And if I had they'd have all been wiped out by now."

"Is that why you don't like my visiting this way?"

"I don't say I don't like it," Bernstein said and smiled by will. He wished he could open himself as Vinny could; it would give him ease and strength, he felt. They stared down at the plain below and spoke little.

The chalk dust had lightened Appello's black eyebrows. For a fleeting moment it occurred to Appello that they resembled each other. Both were over six feet tall, both broad-shouldered and dark men. Bernstein was thinner, quite gaunt and long-armed. Appello was stronger in his arms and stooped a little, as though he had not wanted to be tall. But their eyes were not the same. Appello seemed a little Chinese around the eyes, and they glistened black, direct, and, for women, passionately. Bernstein gazed rather than looked; for him the eyes were dangerous when they could be fathomed, and so he turned them away often, or downward, and there seemed to be something defensively cruel and yet gentle there.

They liked each other not for reasons so much as for possibilities; it was as though they both had sensed they were opposites. And they were lured to each other's failings. With Bernstein around him Appello felt diverted from his irresponsible sensuality, and on this trip Bernstein often had the pleasure and pain of resolving to deny himself no more.

The car turned a hairpin curve with a cloud below on the right, when suddenly the main street of the town arched up before them. There was no one about. It had been true, what the driver had predicted—in the few handkerchiefs of grass that they had passed on the way up the donkeys had bolted, and they had seen shepherds with hard moustaches and black shakos and long black cloaks who had regarded them with the silent inspection of those who live far away. But here in the town there was no one. The car climbed onto the main street, which flattened now, and all at once they were being surrounded by people who were coming out of their doors, putting on their jackets and capes. They did look strangely related, and more Irish than Italian.

The two got out of the Fiat and inspected the baggage strapped to the car's roof, while the driver kept edging protectively around and around the car. Appello talked laughingly with the people, who kept asking why he had come so far, what he had to sell, what he wanted to buy, until he at last made it clear that he was looking only for his aunt. When he said the name the men (the women remained at home, watching from the windows) looked blank, until an old man wearing rope sandals and a knitted skating cap came forward and said that he remembered such a woman. He then turned, and Appello and Bernstein followed up the main street with what was now perhaps a hundred men behind them.

"How come nobody knows her?" Bernstein asked.

"She's a widow. I guess she stays home most of the time. The men in the line died out here twenty years ago. Her husband was the last Appello up here. They don't go much by women; I bet this old guy remembered the name because he knew her husband by it, not her."

The wind, steady and hard, blew through the town, washing it, laving its stones white. The sun was cool as a lemon, the sky purely blue, and the clouds so close their keels seemed to be sailing through the next street. The two Americans began to walk with the joy of it in their long strides. They came to a two-story stone house and went up a dark corridor and knocked. The guide remained respectfully on the sidewalk.

There was no sound within for a few minutes. Then there was—short scrapes, like a mouse that started, stopped, looked about, started again. Appello knocked once more. The doorknob turned, and the door opened a foot. A pale little woman, not very old at all, held the door wide enough for her face to be seen. She seemed very worried.

"Ha?" she asked.

"I am Vincent Giorgio."

"Ha?" she repeated.

"Vicenzo Giorgio Appello."

Her hand slid off the knob, and she stepped back. Appello, smiling in his friendly way, entered, with Bernstein behind him closing the door. A window let the sun flood the room, which was nevertheless stone cold. The woman's mouth was open, her hands were pressed together as in prayer, and the tips of her fingers were pointing at Vinny. She seemed crouched, as though about to kneel, and she could not speak.

Vinny went over to her and touched her bony shoulder and pressed her into a chair. He and Bernstein sat down too. He told her their relationship, saying names of men and women, some of whom were dead, others whom she had only heard of and never met in this sky place. She spoke at last, and Bernstein could not understand what she said. She ran out of the room suddenly.

"I think she thinks I'm a ghost or something. My uncle said she hadn't seen any of the family in twenty or twenty-five years. I bet she doesn't think there are any left."

She returned with a bottle that had an inch of wine at the bottom of it. She ignored Bernstein and gave Appello the bottle. He drank. It was vinegar. Then she started to whimper and kept wiping the tears out of her eyes in order to see Appello. She never finished a sentence, and Appello kept asking her what she meant. She kept running from one corner of the room to another. The rhythm of her departures and returns to the chair was getting so wild that Appello raised his voice and commanded her to sit.

"I'm not a ghost, Aunty. I came here from America—" He stopped. It was clear from the look of her bewildered, frightened eyes that she had not thought him a ghost at all, but what was just as bad—if nobody had ever come to see her from Lucera, how could anybody have so much as thought of her in America, a place that did exist, she knew, just as heaven existed and in exactly the same way. There was no way to hold a conversation with her.

They finally made their exit, and she had not said a coherent word except a blessing, which was her way of expressing her relief that Appello was leaving, for despite the unutterable joy at having seen with her own eyes another of her husband's blood, the sight was itself too terrible in its associations, and in the responsibility it laid upon her to welcome him and make him comfortable.

They walked toward the church now. Bernstein had not been able to say anything. The woman's emotion, so pure and violent and wild, had scared him. And yet, glancing at Appello, he was amazed to see that his friend had drawn nothing but a calm sort of satisfaction from it, as though his aunt had only behaved correctly. Dimly he remembered himself as a boy visiting an aunt of his in the Bronx, a woman who had not been in touch with the family and had never seen him. He remembered how forcefully she had fed him, pinched his cheeks, and smiled and smiled every time he looked up at her, but he knew that there was nothing of this blood in that encounter; nor could there be for him now if on the next corner he should meet a woman who said she was of his family. If anything, he would want to get away from her, even though he had always gotten along with his people and hadn't even the usual snobbery about them. As they entered the church he said to himself that some part of him was not plugged in, but why he should be disturbed about it mystified him and even made him irritated with Appello, who now was asking the priest where the tombs of the Appellos were.

They descended into the vault of the church, where the stone floor was partly covered with water. Along the walls, and down twisting corridors running out of a central arched hall, were tombs so old no candle could illuminate most of the worn inscriptions. The priest vaguely remembered an Appello vault but had no idea where it was. Vinny moved from one crypt to another with the candle he had bought from the priest. Bernstein waited at the opening of the corridor, his neck bent to avoid touching the roof with his hat. Appello, stooped even more than usual, looked like a monk himself, an antiquary, a gradually disappearing figure squinting down the long darkness of the ages for his name on a stone. He could not find it. Their feet were getting soaked. After half an hour they left the church and outside fought off shivering small boys selling grimy religious postcards, which the wind kept taking from their fists.

"I'm sure it's there," Appello said with fascinated excitement. "But you wouldn't want to stick out a search, would you?" he asked hopefully.

"This is no place for me to get pneumonia," Bernstein said.

They had come to the end of a side street. They had passed shops in front of which pink lambs hung head down with their legs stiffly jutting out over the sidewalk. Bernstein shook hands with one and imagined for Vinny a scene for Chaplin in which a monsignor would meet him here, reach out to shake his hand, and find the cold lamb's foot in his grip, and Chaplin would be mortified. At the street's end they scanned the endless sky and looked over the precipice upon Italy.

"They might even have ridden horseback down there, in armor–Appellos." Vinny spoke raptly.

"Yeah, they probably did," Bernstein said. The vision of Appello in armor wiped away any desire to kid his friend. He felt alone, desolate in the dried-out chalk sides of this broken pillar he stood upon. Certainly there had been no knights in his family.

He remembered his father's telling of his town in Europe, a common barrel of water, a town idiot, a baron nearby. That was all he had of it, and no pride in it at all. Then I am an American, he said to himself. And yet in that there was not the power of Appello's narrow passion. He looked at Appello's profile and felt the warmth of that gaze upon Italy and wondered if any American had ever really felt like this in the States. He had never in his life sensed so strongly that the past could be so peopled, so vivid with generations, as it had been with Vinny's aunt an hour ago. A common water barrel, a town idiot, a baron who lived nearby. . . . It had nothing to do with *him*. And standing there he sensed a broken part of himself and wondered with a slight amusement if this was what a child felt on discovering that the parents who brought him up were not his own and that he entered his house not from warmth but from the street, from a public and disordered place. . . .

They sought and found a restaurant for lunch. It was at the other edge of the town and overhung the precipice. Inside, it was one immense room with fifteen or twenty tables; the front wall was lined with windows overlooking the plain below. They sat at a table and waited for someone to appear. The restaurant was cold. They could hear the wind surging against the windowpanes, and yet the clouds at eye level moved serenely and slow. A young girl, the daughter of the family, came out of the kitchen, and Appello was questioning her about food when the door to the street opened and a man came in.

For Bernstein there was an abrupt impression of familiarity with the man, although he could not fathom the reason for his feeling. The man's face looked Sicilian, round, dark as earth, high cheek-bones, broad jaw. He almost laughed aloud as it instantly occurred to him that he could converse with this man in Italian. When the waitress had gone, he told this to Vinny, who now joined in watching the man.

Sensing their stares, the man looked at them with a merry flicker of his cheeks and said, "*Buon giorno.*"

"*Buon giorno,*" Bernstein replied across the four tables between them, and then to Vinny, "Why do I feel that about him?"

"I'll be damned if I know," Vinny said, glad now that he could join his friend in a mutually interesting occupation.

They watched the man, who obviously ate here often. He had already set a large package down on another table and now put his hat on a chair, his jacket on another chair, and his vest on a third. It was as though he were making companions of his clothing. He was in the prime of middle age and very rugged. And to the Americans there was something mixed up about his clothing. His jacket might have been worn by a local man; it was tight and black and wrinkled and chalkdust-covered. His trousers were dark brown and very thick, like a peasant's, and his

shoes were snubbed up at the ends and of heavy leather. But he wore a black hat, which was unusual up here where all had caps, and he had a tie. He wiped his hands before loosening the knot; it was a striped tie, yellow and blue, of silk, and no tie to be bought in this part of the world, or worn by these people. And there was a look in his eyes that was not a peasant's inward stare; nor did it have the innocence of the other men who had looked at them on the streets here.

The waitress came with two dishes of lamb for the Americans. The man was interested and looked across his table at the meat and at the strangers. Bernstein glanced at the barely cooked flesh and said, "There's hair on it."

Vinny called the girl back just as she was going to the newcomer and pointed at the hair.

"But it's lamb's hair," she explained simply.

They said, "Oh," and pretended to begin to cut into the faintly pink flesh.

"You ought to know better, signor, than to order meat today."

The man looked amused, and yet it was unclear whether he might not be a trifle offended.

"Why not?" Vinny asked.

"It's Friday, signor," and he smiled sympathetically.

"That's right!" Vinny said although he had known all along.

"Give me fish," the man said to the girl and asked with intimacy about her mother, who was ill these days.

Bernstein had not been able to turn his eyes from the man. He could not eat the meat and sat chewing bread and feeling a rising urge to go over to the man, to speak to him. It struck him as being insane. The whole place–the town, the clouds in the streets, the thin air–was turning into a hallucination. He knew this man. He was sure he knew him. Quite clearly that was impossible. Still, there was a thing beyond the impossibility of which he was drunkenly sure, and it was that if he dared he could start speaking Italian fluently with this man. This was the first moment since leaving America that he had not felt the ill-ease of traveling and of being a traveler. He felt as comfortable as Vinny now, it seemed to him. In his mind's eye he could envisage the inside of the kitchen; he had a startlingly clear image of what the cook's face must look like, and he knew where a certain kind of soiled apron was hung.

"What's the matter with you?" Appello asked.

"Why?"

"The way you're looking at him."

"I want to talk to him."

"Well, talk to him." Vinny smiled.

"I can't speak Italian, you know that."

"Well, I'll ask him. What do you want to say?"

"Vinny–" Bernstein started to speak and stopped.

"What?" Appello asked, leaning his head closer and looking down at the tablecloth.

"Get him to talk. Anything. Go ahead."

Vinny, enjoying his friend's strange emotionalism, looked across at the man, who now was eating with careful but immense satisfaction. "*Scusi*, signor."

The man looked up.

"I am a son of Italy from America. I would like to talk to you. We're strange here."

The man, chewing deliciously, nodded with his amiable and amused smile and adjusted the hang of his jacket on the nearby chair.

"Do you come from around here?"

"Not very far."

"How is everything here?"

"Poor. It is always poor."

"What do you work at, if I may ask?"

The man had now finished his food. He took a last long drag of his wine and got up and proceeded to dress and pull his tie up tightly. When he walked it was with a slow, wide sway, as though each step had to be conserved.

"I sell cloth here to the people and the stores, such as they are," he said. And he walked over to the bundle and set it carefully on a table and began untying it.

"He sells cloth," Vinny said to Bernstein.

Bernstein's cheeks began to redden. From where he sat he could see the man's broad back, ever so slightly bent over the bundle. He could see the man's hands working at the knot and just a corner of the man's left eye. Now the man was laying the paper away from the two bolts of cloth, carefully pressing the wrinkles flat against the table. It was as though the brown paper were valuable leather that must not be cracked or rudely bent. The waitress came out of the kitchen with a tremendous round loaf of bread at least two feet in diameter. She gave it to him, and he placed it flat on top of the cloth, and the faintest feather of a smile curled up on Bernstein's lips. Now the man folded the paper back and brought the string around the bundle and tied the knot, and Bernstein uttered a little laugh, a laugh of relief.

Vinny looked at him, already smiling, ready to join the laughter, but mystified. "What's the matter?" he asked.

Bernstein took a breath. There was something a little triumphant, a new air of confidence and superiority in his face and voice. "He's Jewish, Vinny," he said.

Vinny turned to look at the man. "Why?"

"The way he works that bundle. It's exactly the way my father used to tie a bundle—and my grandfather. The whole history is packing bundles and getting away. Nobody else can be as tender and delicate with bundles. That's a Jewish man tying a bundle. Ask him his name."

Vinny was delighted. "Signor," he called with that warmth reserved in his nature for members of families, any families.

The man, tucking the end of the string into the edge of the paper, turned to them with his kind smile.

"May I ask your name, signor?"

"My name? Mauro di Benedetto."

"Mauro di Benedetto. Sure!" Vinny laughed, looking at Bernstein. "That's Morris of the Blessed. Moses."

"Tell him I'm Jewish," Bernstein said, a driving eagerness charging his eyes.

"My friend is Jewish," Vinny said to the man, who now was hoisting the bundle onto his shoulder.

"Heh?" the man asked, confused by their sudden vivacity. As though wondering if there were some sophisticated American point he should have understood, he stood there smiling blankly, politely, ready to join in this mood.

"*Judeo*, my friend."

"*Judeo?*" he asked, the willingness to get the joke still holding the smile on his face.

Vinny hesitated before this steady gaze of incomprehension. "*Judeo*. The people of the Bible," he said.

"Oh, yes, yes!" The man nodded now, relieved that he was not to be caught in ignorance. "*Ebreo*," he corrected. And he nodded affably to Bernstein and seemed a little at a loss for what they expected him to do next.

"Does he know what you mean?" Bernstein nodded.

"Yeah, he said, 'Hebrew,' but it doesn't seem to connect. Signor," he addressed the man, "why don't you have a glass of wine with us? Come, sit down."

"Thank you, signor," he replied appreciatively, "but I must be home by sundown."

Vinny translated, and Bernstein told him to ask why he had to be home by sundown.

The man apparently had never considered the question before. He shrugged and laughed and said, "I don't know. All my life I get home for dinner on Friday night, and I like to come into the house before sundown. I suppose it's a habit; my father— you see, I have a route I walk, which is this route. I first did it with my father, and he did it with his father. We are known here for many generations past. And my father always got home on Friday night before sundown. It's a manner of the family I guess."

"*Shabbos* begins at sundown on Friday night," Bernstein said when Vinny had translated. "He's even taking home the fresh bread for the Sabbath. The man is a Jew, I tell you. Ask him, will you?"

"*Scusi*, signor." Vinny smiled. "My friend is curious to know whether you are Jewish."

The man raised his thick eyebrows not only in surprise but as though he felt somewhat honored by being identified with something exotic. "Me?" he asked.

"I don't mean American," Vinny said, believing he had caught the meaning of the man's glance at Bernstein. "*Ebreo*," he repeated.

The man shook his head, seeming a little sorry he could not oblige Vinny. "No," he said. He was ready to go but wanted to pursue what obviously was his most interesting conversation in weeks. "Are they Catholics? The Hebrews?"

"He's asking me if Jews are Catholics," Vinny said.

Bernstein sat back in his chair, a knotted look of wonder in his eyes. Vinny replied to the man, who looked once again at Bernstein as though wanting to investigate this strangeness further, but his mission drew him up and he wished them good fortune and said good-bye. He walked to the kitchen door and called thanks to the girl inside, saying the loaf would warm his back all the way down the mountain, and he opened the door and went out into the wind of the street and the sunshine, waving to them as he walked away.

They kept repeating their amazement on the way back to the car, and Bernstein told again how his father wrapped bundles. "Maybe he doesn't know he's a Jew, but how could he not know what Jews are?" he said.

"Well, remember my aunt in Lucera?" Vinny asked. "She's a schoolteacher, and she asked me if you believed in Christ. She didn't know the first thing about it. I think the ones in these small towns who ever heard of Jews think they're a Christian sect of some kind. I knew an old Italian once who thought all Negroes were Jews and white Jews were only converts."

"But his name..."

" 'Benedetto' is an Italian name too. I never heard of 'Mauro' though. 'Mauro' is strictly from the old sod."

"But if he had a name like that, wouldn't it lead him to wonder if...?"

"I don't think so. In New York the name 'Salvatore' is turned into 'Sam.' Italians are great for nicknames; the first name never means much. 'Vincenzo' is 'Enzo,' or 'Vinny' or even 'Chico.' Nobody would think twice about 'Mauro' or damn near any other first name. He's obviously a Jew, but I'm sure he doesn't know it. You could tell, couldn't you? He was baffled."

"But, my God, bringing home a bread for *Shabbos*!" Bernstein laughed, wide-eyed.

They reached the car, and Bernstein had his hand on the door but stopped before opening it and turned to Vinny. He looked heated; his eyelids seemed puffed. "It's early—if you still want to I'll go back to the church with you. You can look for the boys."

Vinny began to smile, and then they both laughed together, and Vinny slapped him on the back and gripped his shoulder as though to hug him. "Goddam, now you're starting to enjoy this trip!"

As they walked briskly toward the church the conversation returned always to the same point, when Bernstein would say, "I don't know why, but it gets me. He's not only acting like a Jew, but an Orthodox Jew. And doesn't even know–I mean it's strange as hell to me."

"You look different, you know that?" Vinny said.

"Why?"

"You do."

"You know a funny thing?" Bernstein said quietly as they entered the church and descended into the vault beneath it. "I feel like–at home in this place. I can't describe it."

Beneath the church, they picked their way through the shallower puddles on the stone floor, looking into vestibules, opening doors, searching for the priest. He appeared at last– they could not imagine from where–and Appello bought another candle from him and was gone in the shadows of the corridors where the vaults were.

Bernstein stood–everything was wet, dripping. Behind him, flat and wide, rose the stairway of stones bent with the tread of millions. Vapor steamed from his nostrils. There was nothing to look at but shadows. It was dank and black and low, an entrance to hell. Now and then in the very far distance he could hear a step echoing, another, then silence. He did not move, seeking the root of an ecstasy he had not dreamed was part of his nature; he saw the amiable man trudging down the mountains, across the plains, on routes marked out for him by generations of men, a nameless traveler carrying home a warm bread on Friday night– and kneeling in church on Sunday. There was an irony in it he could not name. And yet pride was running through him. Of what he should be proud he had no clear idea; perhaps it was only that beneath the brainless crush of history a Jew had secretly survived, shorn of his consciousness but forever caught by that final impudence of a Saturday Sabbath in a Catholic country; so that his very unawareness was proof, a proof as mute as stones, that a past lived. A past for me, Bernstein thought, astounded by its importance to him, when in fact he had never had a religion or even, he realized now, a history.

He could see Vinny's form approaching in the narrow corridor of crypts, the candle flame flattening in the cold draft. He felt he would look differently into Vinny's eyes; his conde-scension had gone and with it a certain embarrassment. He felt loose, somehow the equal of his friend–and how odd that was when, if anything, he had thought of himself as superior. Sud-denly, with Vinny a yard away, he saw that his life had been covered with an unrecognized shame.

"I found it! It's back there!" Vinny was laughing like a young boy, pointing back toward the dark corridor.

"That's great, Vinny," Bernstein said. "I'm glad."

They were both stooping slightly under the low, wet ceiling, their voices fleeing from their mouths in echoed whispers. Vinny held still for an instant, catching Bernstein's respectful happi-ness, and saw there that his search was not worthless sentiment. He raised the candle to see Bernstein's face better, and then he laughed and gripped Bernstein's wrist and led the way toward the flight of steps that rose to the surface. Bernstein had never liked anyone grasping him, but from this touch of a hand in the darkness, strangely, there was no implication of a hateful weakness.

They walked side by side down the steep street away from the church. The town was empty again. The air smelled of burning charcoal and olive oil. A few pale stars had come out. The shops were all shut. Bernstein thought of Mauro di Benedetto going down the winding, rocky road, hurrying against the setting of the sun.

Arthur Miller.

VISIONS OF A BETTER WORLD

from The Search

Iconoclasts, dreamers, men who stood alone:
Freud and Marx, the great Maimonides
and Spinoza who defied even his own.
In my veins runs their rebellious blood.
I tread with them the selfsame antique road
and seek everywhere the faintest scent of God.

Irving Layton.

Jews have left their mark on world culture wherever they have been. Original thinking, a great need for questioning and an unrelenting search for truth, justice and knowledge have characterized the Jewish people since the time of Abraham. Albert Einstein, Sigmund Freud and Karl Marx are examples of Jewish thinkers who changed the world with their radical ideas. Jesus Christ was another great Jewish humanitarian who altered the world.

Along with their strong individuality, these great Jews had something else in common: a vision of an ideal world yet to come. This dream of a better tomorrow is steeped in Jewish tradition. Here are the words of the ancient prophet Isaiah, the ultimate Jewish prophesy of universal love and peace.

The End of Days

And it shall come to pass in the end of days.
That the mountain of the Lord's house shall be established as the
    top of the mountains,
And shall be exalted above the hills;
And all nations shall flow unto it.
And many peoples shall go and say:
"Come ye, and let us go up to the mountain of the Lord,
To the house of the God of Jacob;
And He will teach us of His ways,
And we will walk in His paths."
For out of Zion shall go forth the Law,
And the word of the Lord from Jerusalem.
And He shall judge between the nations,
And shall decide for many peoples;
And they shall beat their swords into plowshares,
And their spears into pruning-hooks;
Nation shall not lift up sword against nation,
Neither shall they learn war any more.

Isaiah, 2:1-4.

Whether or not you believe in the peaceful, perfect world yet to come, you can live your life in the Jewish tradition: with respect and compassion for all the people of the world. You are now a member of the Jewish community and a citizen of the world. *Mazel tov* to you on your Bar Mitzvah!

CREDITS

Pictures

The producers of this book would like to thank the following artists, photographers, institutions, and copyright holders for permission to reproduce material used herein. Every reasonable effort has been made to ensure that the correct permission to reproduce was obtained. Should there be any errors in copyright information, please inform the publisher of same, and a correction will be made in any subsequent editions.

Page

1   by Ted Spiegel: Copyright © Ted Spiegel.

2   by Carl Glassman: Copyright © 1980 Carl Glassman.

3   by Nir Bareket: Copyright © 1985 Nir Bareket.

4   illustration by Ruben Zellermayer: from *A Dream of Promise* by Meguido Zola. Toronto: Kids Can Press, 1980.

5   by Bill Aron: Copyright © Bill Aron Photography/Art Resource, New York.

6   by Bill Aron: Copyright © Bill Aron Photography/Art Resource, New York.

7   by Bill Aron: Copyright © Bill Aron Photography/Art Resource, New York.

8–9   by Nathan Benn © Nathan Benn/Woodfin Camp Inc.

10   by Bill Aron: Copyright © Bill Aron Photography.

11   illustrations from *To Pray as a Jew* by Rabbi Hayim Halevy Donin, Basic Books Inc., Publishers, New York.

12   (Right) by Isaac Geld: Copyright © Beth Hatefutsoth, the Nahum Goldmann Museum of the Jewish Diaspora, Tel Aviv, from "The Jewish Heritage in the Eye of the Camera": Worldwide Photo Contest Hannukka, 1981.

12   (Left) by Geoffrey Clements: Copyright © Geoffrey Clements Photography. The Jewish Museum of New York/Art Resource, New York.

13   by Ted Spiegel: Copyright © Ted Spiegel.

15   by Bill Aron: Copyright © Bill Aron Photography.

16   by Ted Spiegel: Copyright © Ted Spiegel.

20–21   by Stephen Epstein: Copyright © Stephen Epstein.

25   painting by Ben Shahn, "Allegoria". SCALA/Art Resource, New York.

27   illustration by Miro Malish: Copyright © 1985 Miro Malish. Courtesy of Reactor Art and Design.

28   by Bill Aron: Copyright © Bill Aron Photography/Art Resource, New York.

29   by Alfred Eisenstaedt: Copyright © Time Inc.

31   courtesy of the artist Tully Filmus/The Jewish Publication Society.

32   by Nathan Benn © Nathan Benn/Woodfin Camp Inc.

33   by Stephen Epstein: Copyright © Stephen Epstein.

35   by Bill Aron: Copyright © Bill Aron Photography.

36   Cecil Roth Collection, Beth Tzedec Museum, Toronto. Photo by Nir Bareket.

37   painting by Marc Chagall, "I and the Village", 1911: the Museum of Modern Art and Beth Hatefutsoth, the Nahum Goldmann Museum of the Jewish Diaspora, Tel Aviv.

39   photograph courtesy of the *Claremont Courier*.

40   by Nathan Benn © Nathan Benn/Woodfin Camp Inc.

45   by Nathan Benn © Nathan Benn/Woodfin Camp Inc.

47   YIVO Archives.

49   painting by William Kurelek, "Baber's Family Celebrating the Sabbath in Edmonton": a gift of Mr. and Mrs. Jules Loeb to The Ontario Heritage Foundation, on loan to the Toronto Jewish Congress, for display at the Lipa Green Centre. Reproductions courtesy The Isaacs Gallery, Toronto. Photograph by Nir Bareket.

50   drawing by W.A. Rogers: The Bettmann Archive.

52–53   painting by William Kurelek, "Jewish Home Life in Montreal": a gift of Mr. and Mrs. Jules Loeb to The Ontario Heritage Foundation, on loan to the Toronto Jewish Congress, for display at the Lipa Green Centre. Reproductions courtesy The Isaacs Gallery, Toronto. Photograph by Nir Bareket.

54   woodcut by Ilya Schor from *The Earth is the Lord's*: New York Public Library Picture Collection.

55   by Bill Aron: Copyright © Bill Aron Photography.

56   by Ricki Rosen: Copyright © Ricki Rosen.

57   by Peter M. Lerman: Copyright © 1975 Peter M. Lerman Photographer.

58   courtesy the Archives of the State Jewish Museum, Prague.

61   The Jewish Museum/Art Resource. Gift of Howard Dreyfous.

62   by Nathan Benn © Nathan Benn/Woodfin Camp Inc.

63   by Nathan Benn © Nathan Benn/Woodfin Camp Inc.

65   painting by Robert Guttman, "Bar Mitzvah": SCALA/Art Resource, New York.

69   (Right) painting by Marc Chagall, "King David": Property of the artist's estate. SCALA/Art Resource, New York.

69   (Left) from the collection of Dr. Fred Weinberg. Photograph by Nir Bareket.

71   engraving by Rembrandt, "Offering Isaac": The Bettmann Archive.

72–73   painting by Rembrandt, "The Benediction of Jacob": Giraudon/Art Resource, New York.

75   by Bill Aron: Copyright © Bill Aron Photography.

76   by Bill Aron: Copyright © Bill Aron Photography.

77   by Barbara Pfeffer: Copyright © Barbara Pfeffer.

79   illustration by Gail Geltner: Copyright © Gail Geltner.

80   United States Department of the Interior National Park Service photograph.

81   (Above) by Barbara Pfeffer: Copyright © Barbara Pfeffer.

81   (Below) by Carl Glassman: Copyright © Beth Hatefutsoth, the Nahum Goldmann Museum of the Jewish Diaspora, Tel Aviv, from "The Jewish Heritage in the Eye of the Camera": Worldwide Photo Contest, Hannukka, 1981.

82–83   courtesy of the Leo Baeck Institute.

84   by Nathan Benn © Nathan Benn/Woodfin Camp Inc.

89   by Nathan Benn © Nathan Benn/Woodfin Camp Inc.

90   by Nathan Benn © Nathan Benn/Woodfin Camp Inc.

91   by Mal Warshaw: Copyright © Mal Warshaw.

92   by Nathan Benn © Nathan Benn/Woodfin Camp Inc.

93   painting by Moritz Oppenheim, "Bar Mitzvah Speech": Copyright © Israel Museum, Jerusalem.

95   copyright © Beth Hatefutsoth, the Nahum Goldmann Museum of the Jewish Diaspora, Tel Aviv.

96 by Ted Spiegel: Copyright © Ted Spiegel.

97 copyright © Beth Hatefutsoth, the Nahum Goldmann Museum of the Jewish Diaspora, Tel Aviv.

101 engraving by Gustave Doré: courtesy of Nir Bareket.

103 by Roman Vishniac: Copyright © Roman Vishniac.

105 relief photographed by Nir Bareket. Courtesy of Israel Museum, Jerusalem.

107 (Left) American Jewish Historical Society.

107 (Right) by Bill Aron: Copyright © Bill Aron Photography/Art Resource, New York.

108 by Bill Aron: Copyright © Bill Aron Photography.

109 The Bettmann Archive.

110 by Nathan Benn © Nathan Benn/Woodfin Camp Inc.

111 United States Department of the Interior National Park Service photograph.

112–113 painting by Ben Shahn, "Einstein and Immigrants": SCALA/Art Resource, New York.

114 painting by William Kurelek, "General Store in Vancouver Before World War One": a gift of Mr. and Mrs. Jules Loeb to the Ontario Heritage Foundation, on loan to the Toronto Jewish Congress, for display at the Lipa Green Centre. Reproductions courtesy The Isaacs Gallery, Toronto. Photograph by Nir Bareket.

116 by Ricki Rosen: Copyright © Ricki Rosen.

118 illustration by Miro Malish: Copyright © 1985 Miro Malish. Courtesy of Reactor Art and Design.

120 by Nathan Benn © Nathan Benn/Woodfin Camp Inc.

120 by Nathan Benn © Nathan Benn/Woodfin Camp Inc.

121 by Nathan Benn © Nathan Benn/Woodfin Camp Inc.

124 copyright © Beth Hatefutsoth, the Nahum Goldmann Museum of the Jewish Diaspora, Tel Aviv.

125 by Nathan Benn © Nathan Benn/Woodfin Camp Inc.

127 by Bruce Anspach/ EPA Newsphoto.

128 painting by Marc Chagall, "The Family". Property of the artist's estate. SCALA/Art Resource, New York.

133 by Ted Spiegel: Copyright © Ted Spiegel.

134 by Nir Bareket: Copyright © Nir Bareket.

135 Zionist Archives and Library.

137 illustration by Bill Russell: Copyright ©1985 Bill Russell. Courtesy of Reactor Art and Design.

138 copyright © Beth Hatefutsoth, the Nahum Goldmann Museum of the Jewish Diaspora, Tel Aviv.

139 The Bettmann Archive.

141 Cecil Roth Collection: Beth Tzedec Museum, Toronto.

142 Zionist Archives and Library.

143 copyright © Beth Hatefutsoth, the Nahum Goldmann Museum of the Jewish Diaspora, Tel Aviv.

144 by Nathan Benn © Nathan Benn/Woodfin Camp Inc.

146 by Barbara Pfeffer: Copyright © Barbara Pfeffer.

147 by Stephen Epstein: Copyright © 1980 Stephen Epstein.

149 drawing from *Children's Drawings and Poems Terezin 1942–1944*. Edited by Hana Volavkova. Published by Artia for Schocken Books Inc. Copyright © 1978 by Artia, Prague.

150 Associated Press/ Wide World Photos.

153 Commemorative Panel: The Jewish Museum of New York/Art Resource, New York.

154 Associated Press/ Wide World Photos.

155 by Stephen Epstein: Copyright © Stephen Epstein.

156 by Nir Bareket: Copyright © Nir Bareket.

157 by Nir Bareket: Copyright © Nir Bareket.

159 by Nir Bareket: Copyright © Nir Bareket.

161 by Nathan Benn © Nathan Benn/Woodfin Camp Inc.

162 illustration by Gail Geltner: Copyright © 1985 Gail Geltner.

163 by Barbara Pfeffer: Copyright © Barbara Pfeffer.

164 (Above) by Ilene Perlman: Copyright © Ilene Perlman.

164 (Below) copyright © Beth Hatefutsoth, the Nahum Goldmann Museum of the Jewish Diaspora, Tel Aviv.

165 by Bill Aron: Copyright © Bill Aron Photography.

167 by Bill Aron: Copyright © Bill Aron Photography.

168 by Nodar Djindjihashvili: Copyright © Magnum Distribution.

169 by Nodar Djindjihashvili: Copyright © Magnum Distribution.

169 by Nodar Djindjihashvili: Copyright © Magnum Distribution.

170 by Ilene Perlman: Copyright © Ilene Perlman.

171 by Ilene Perlman: Copyright © Ilene Perlman.

172 on loan to Beth Hatefutsoth, the Nahum Goldmann Museum of the Jewish Diaspora, Tel Aviv. Credit: Mr. and Mrs. H. Forbes, Dallas, Texas.

173 copyright © Beth Hatefutsoth, the Nahum Goldmann Museum of the Jewish Diaspora, Tel Aviv.

173 copyright © Beth Hatefutsoth, the Nahum Goldmann Museum of the Jewish Diaspora, Tel Aviv.

177 illustration by Jeff Jackson: Copyright © 1985 Jeff Jackson. Courtesy of Reactor Art and Design.

180 by Nathan Benn © Nathan Benn/Woodfin Camp Inc.

Text

The producers of this book would like to thank the following authors, publishers, and copyright holders for permission to reprint material used herein. Every reasonable effort has been made to ensure that the correct permission to reprint was obtained. Should there be any errors in copyright information, please inform the publisher of same, and a correction will be made in any subsequent editions.

Page

2 Chaim Potok, from *In the Beginning*. New York: Alfred A. Knopf, 1975.

3 Leo Trepp, from *The Complete Book of Jewish Observance*. New York: Behrman House/Summit Books, 1980.

3 Meguido Zola, from *A Dream of Promise*. Copyright © Meguido Zola. Toronto: Kids Can Press, 1980.

5 Sharon Strassfeld and Kathy Green, from *The Jewish Family Book*. New York: Bantam Books, 1981.

6 Rabbi Hayim Halevy Donin, from *To Be A Jew*. New York: Basic Books, 1972.

7 Adapted from the *Aggadah* by Azriel Eisenberg, from *The Bar Mitzvah Treasury*, edited by Azriel Eisenberg. New York: Behrman House Inc., 1958.

11 Rabbi Hayim Halevy Donin, from *To Pray As A Jew*. New York: Basic Books, 1980.

12 Abraham M. Klein, from *Hath Not the Jew*. New York: Behrman House Inc., 1940.

12 Rabbi Hayim Halevy Donin, from *To Pray As A Jew*. New York: Basic Books, 1980.

14 Sigmund Freud, from *Glimpses of the Great*, by George S. Viereck. London: Duckworth, 1930.

14 Sigmund Freud, from the preface to the Hebrew translation of *Totem and Taboo*. Boston: Routledge and Kegan Paul of America Ltd., 1930.

14 Albert Einstein, from *The Bar Mitzvah Companion*, edited by

Sydney Greenberg and Abraham Rothberg. New York: Behrman House Inc., 1958.

14   Edmond Fleg, from *The Bar Mitzvah Companion,* edited by Sydney Greenberg and Abraham Rothberg. New York: Behrman House Inc., 1958.

14   Dennis Prager and Joseph Telushkin, from *The Nine Questions People Ask About Judaism.* New York: Simon and Schuster, 1981.

17   Mendele Mokher Sforim, from *How We Lived,* by Irving Howe and Kenneth Libo. New York: Richard Marek Publishers, 1979.

17   Hugh Nissenson, from *A Pile of Stones: Short Stories.* New York: Charles Scribners Sons, 1965.

24   From *The Bar Mitzvah Companion,* edited by Sydney Greenberg and Abraham Rothberg. New York: Behrman House Inc., 1958.

26   Paul Cowan, from *An Orphan in History.* Copyright © 1982 by Paul Cowan. New York: Doubleday, 1982. Reprinted by permission of Doubleday & Company, Inc., New York.

28   Jacob Benlazar, from *The Bar Mitzvah Treasury,* edited by Azriel Eisenberg. New York: Behrman House Inc., 1958.

28   David Blaustein, from *How We Lived,* by Irving Howe and Kenneth Libo. New York: Richard Marek Publishers, 1979.

30   Adapted by Solomon Simon, from *The Wise Men of Chelm and their Merry Tales.* New York: Behrman House Inc., 1952.

32   Philip S. Bernstein, from *What the Jews Believe.* New York: Farrar, Straus and Giroux, 1951.

34   Bernice Scharlach. Condensed from *Hadassah Magazine,* Vol. 63, No. 5.

36   David Cohen, from *The Bar Mitzvah Treasury,* edited by Azriel Eisenberg. New York: Behrman House Inc., 1958.

38   Linda Kerber, from *Moment Magazine.*

40   Sam Levenson, from *In One Era and Out the Other.* New York: Simon and Schuster, 1980.

41   Martin Buber, from *To Hallow this Life,* edited by Jacob Trapp. New York: Harper and Brothers Publishers, 1958.

46   A. M. Klein, from *The Collected Poems of A. M. Klein,* compiled by Miriam Waddington. Reprinted by permission of McGraw-Hill Ryerson Limited. Toronto: McGraw-Hill Ryerson, 1974.

46   Samuel Joseph Agnon. Translated by I. M. Lask, from *The Jewish Caravan,* edited by Leo E. Schwarz. New York: Holt, Rinehart and Winston, 1935.

50   Charles Angoff, from *How We Lived,* by Irving Howe and Kenneth Libo. New York: Richard Marek Publishers, 1979.

50   Rabbi W. Gunther Plaut, from *Unfinished Business.* Toronto: Lester and Orpen, Dennys, 1981.

51   Isaac Babel, from *The Collected Stories of Isaac Babel.* New York: Criterion Books, 1955.

55   Allan Gould and Danny Siegel, from *The Unorthodox Book of Jewish Records and Lists.* Edmonton: Hurtig Publishers Ltd., 1981.

56   Excerpt from *A Bintel Brief,* edited by Isaac Metzker. Copyright © 1971 by Isaac Metzker. Reprinted by permission of Doubleday & Company, Inc., New York.

57   Adapted by Francine Klagsbrun, from *Voices of Wisdom.* New York: Pantheon Books, 1980.

57   Leonard Kriegel, "Fathers and Sons" from *Present Tense,* Autumn 1979, Vol. 7.

58   Franz Kafka, from *Dearest Father: Stories and Other Writings,* edited by Brod, translated by E. Kaiser and E. Wilkins. Copyright © 1954 (renewed) by Schocken Books. Reprinted by permission of Schocken Books Inc., New York.

58   Isaac Goldemberg. Translated by David Unger, from *Voices Within the Ark: The Modern Jewish Poets,* edited by Howard Schwartz and Anthony Rudolf. New York: Avon Books, 1980.

59   Ted Allan, copyright © by Ted Allan.

60   Michael Gold, from "Jews Without Money" (1930) in *The Changing View; A Century of Jewish Writing in English,* edited by Shulamit Nardi. Jerusalem: The Institute of Contemporary Jewry, The Hebrew University of Jerusalem, 1980.

60   Irving Howe, from *How We Lived* by Irving Howe and Kenneth Libo. New York: Richard Marek Publishers, 1979.

60   Adele Wiseman, from *Old Woman at Play.* Toronto: Clarke, Irwin, 1978. Copyright © Adele Wiseman.

62   Herman Wouk, from *Marjorie Morningstar.* Copyright © 1955 by Herman Wouk.

63   Adapted by Azriel Eisenberg, from *The Bar Mitzvah Treasury,* edited by Azriel Eisenberg. New York: Behrman House Inc., 1958.

64   Philip Perl, from *A Bar Mitzvah Companion,* edited by Sidney Greenberg and Abraham Rothberg. New York: Behrman House Inc., 1958.

69   Lydia Kukoff. New York: Union of American Hebrew Congregations, 1981.

70   Stuart Schoenfeld, from "Images of Family Life in the Bible". Copyright © 1984 by Stuart Schoenfeld.

74   Yehuda Yaari. Translated by I. M Lask, from *The Confirmation Reader,* edited by Azriel Eisenberg. New York: Behrman House Inc., 1953.

76   Arnold Kiss, from *Ararat: Hungarian Short Stories,* edited by Andrew Handler. New Jersey: Fairleigh Dickinson University Press, 1977.

79   Gary Pacernick, from *Voices Within the Ark: The Modern Jewish Poets,* edited by Howard Schwartz and Anthony Rudolf. New York: Avon Books, 1980.

80   Fran Lebowitz, from *Metropolitan Life.* New York: E. P. Dutton, 1978.

84   Richard Siegel, from *Moment Magazine,* July–August 1975, Vol. I.

90   Mortimer Ostow, from "The Jewishness of Contemporary Jewish Youth" in *New Directions in the Jewish Family and Community.* New York: Commission on Synagogue Relations, Federation of Jewish Philanthropies of New York, 1974.

90   M. Ben Eliezer, from *The Confirmation Reader,* by Azriel Eisenberg. New York: Behrman House Inc., 1953.

92   Sholom Aleichem, from *The Bar Mitzvah Treasury,* edited by Azriel Eisenberg. New York: Behrman House Inc., 1958.

94   Abraham Levy, from *Jewish Education in the United States,* by L. Gartner. New York: Teacher's College Press, 1968.

95   Benjamin Artom, from *Bar Mitzvah Reflections and Remembrances,* edited by James Sanders. New York: Jonathan David Publishers, 1969.

95   Allan Gould and Danny Siegel, from *The Unorthodox Book of Jewish Records and Lists.* Edmonton: Hurtig Publishers Ltd., 1981.

96   Rabbi Howard A. Addison, from *Conservative Judaism,* Winter 1982, Vol. 35, No. 2, 1.

98   Mordecai Richler, from *The Apprenticeship of Duddy Kravitz.* Toronto: McClelland and Stewart, 1969.

101   From *The Concise Jewish Bible,* edited by Philip Birnbaum. New York: Hebrew Publishing Company, © 1976.

102   Abraham Reisen. Translated by Charles Angoff, from *A Treasury of Yiddish Stories,* edited by Irving Howe and Eliezer Greenberg. New York: Schocken Books Inc., 1973.

104   Raphael Patai, from *The Jewish Mind.* New York: Charles Scribners Sons, 1977.

106   Gustave Kahn, from *Voices Within the Ark: The Modern Jewish Poets,* edited by Howard Schwartz and Anthony Rudolf. New York: Avon Books, 1980.

106 Azriel Eisenberg, from *The Bar Mitzvah Treasury,* edited by Azriel Eisenberg. New York: Behrman House Inc., 1958.

106 Isaac Metzker. Translated by Philip Rubin, from *A Treasury of Yiddish Stories,* edited by Irving Howe and Eliezer Greenberg. New York: Viking Penguin Inc., 1973.

107 Irving Howe and Kenneth Libo, from *How We Lived.* New York: Richard Marek Publishers, 1979.

108 Alfred Kazin, from *A Walker in the City.* New York: Harcourt Brace and Co., 1951.

109 Emma Lazarus, from *The Bar Mitzvah Companion,* edited by Sidney Greenberg and Abraham Rothberg. New York: Behrman House, 1959.

109 Stephanie Bernardo, from *The Ethnic Almanac,* © 1981 by Stephanie Bernardo. New York: Doubleday & Company, Inc.

110 From Lewis Abraham, "Correspondence Between Washington and Jewish Citizens," *Proceedings of the American Jewish Historical Society,* Vol. 3 (1895). Reprinted by permission of the American Jewish Historical Society.

111 Irving Howe, from *World of Our Fathers.* New York: Harcourt Brace Jovanovich, Inc., 1976.

114 Morley Torgov, from *A Good Place to Come From.* Toronto: Lester & Orpen, Dennys, 1974.

115 Irving Howe, from *How We Lived,* by Irving Howe and Kenneth Libo. New York: Richard Marek Publishers, 1979.

115 Bill Kent, from *Inside* magazine, Vol. 5, No. 2.

117 Sylvan Karchmer, from *The Treasury of American Jewish Stories,* edited by Howard Rebalow. Thomas Yoseloff, 1958.

121 A. A. Kabak. Translated by Sora L. Eisenberg, from *The Bar Mitzvah Treasury,* edited by Azriel Eisenberg. New York: Behrman House Inc., 1958.

123 Abraham Joshua Heschel, from *The Earth Is the Lord's.* New York: Harper and Row, 1950.

126 Emile L. Fackenheim, from *Paths to Jewish Belief.* New York: Behrman House Inc., 1960.

127 "Theory and Practice," 21st edition, 1984, Federation of Reconstructionist Congregations and Havurot. FRCH: 270 West 89 Street, New York, NY 10024.

129 Sharon and Michael Strassfeld, from *The Third Jewish Catalog: Creating Community.* Philadelphia: The Jewish Publication Society of America, 1980.

134 Charles Reznikoff, from *Voices Within the Ark: The Modern Jewish Poets,* edited by Howard Schwartz and Anthony Rudolf. New York: Avon Books, 1980.

134 Solomon Goldman, from "The Function of the Rabbi" in *Crisis and Decision.* New York: Harper & Row, Publishers, Inc.

135 Grace Paley, from *The Little Disturbances of Man.* Copyright © 1959 by Grace Paley.

138 Abba Eban, from *Heritage.* New York: Summit Books/Simon and Schuster, 1984.

139 Rachel Boimwall. Translated by Gabriel Preil, from *Voices Within the Ark: The Modern Jewish Poets,* edited by Howard Schwartz and Anthony Rudolf. New York: Avon Books, 1980.

140 From *The Concise Jewish Bible,* edited by Philip Birnbaum. New York: Hebrew Publishing Company, © 1976.

142 Rabbi Hayim Halevy Donin, from *To Be A Jew.* New York: Basic Books, 1972.

143 From *The Voices of Marrakesh: A Record of a Visit* by Elias Canetti. English translation rights copyright © 1978 by Marion Boyars Publishers Ltd. Reprinted by permission of The Continuum Publishing Co.

146 Isaac Bashevis Singer, from *The Jewish Almanac,* by Richard Siegel and Carl Rheins. New York: Bantam Books, 1980.

147 Gideon Hauser, from *Six Million Accusers: Israel's Case Against Eichmann,* edited by Shabatai Rosenne. Jerusalem: *The Jerusalem Post,* 1961.

147 Elie Wiesel, from *A Jew Today.* New York: Random House, 1978.

148 Elie Wiesel, from *A Jew Today.* New York: Random House, 1978.

148 Anne Frank, from *The Diary of a Young Girl,* © 1952 by Otto H. Frank. New York: Doubleday & Company Inc.

148 From *Children's Drawings and Poems Terezin 1942–1944.* Edited by Hana Volavkova. Published by Artia for Schocken Books Inc. Copyright © 1978 by Artia, Prague.

150 Ralph Blume, from *Days of Sorrow and Pain,* by Leonard Baker. Copyright © 1978 by Leonard Baker. New York: MacMillan Publishing Co., 1978.

150 Stephen Birnbaum, from *The New York Times,* September 3, 1972.

154 Rufus Learsi, from *The Bar Mitzvah Companion,* edited by Sidney Greenberg and Abraham Rothberg. New York: Behrman House Inc., 1958.

155 Emile L. Fackenheim, from *God's Presence in History.* New York: Harper and Row, 1970.

155 Alexander Donat, from *Midstream Magazine,* July, 1970. Copyright © Alexander Donat.

158 Abba Eban, from *Heritage.* New York: Summit Books/Simon and Schuster, 1984.

158 David Ben Gurion. Translated by S. Weinstein, from Debate on the law of return and law of citizenship, July 3, 1950. Proceedings of the Knesset, Jerusalem, 1951.

158 Saul Bellow, from *To Jerusalem and Back.* New York: Viking Press, 1976.

159 Gertrude Samuels, from *The American Judaism Reader,* edited by Paul Kresh. New York: Abelard Shuman, 1967.

162 A. C. Jacobs, from *Voices Within the Ark: The Modern Jewish Poets,* edited by Howard Schwartz and Anthony Rudolf. New York: Avon Books, 1980.

163 Elie Wiesel, from *A Jew Today.* New York: Random House, 1978.

165 Sholom Aleichem, from *How We Lived,* by Irving Howe and Kenneth Libo. New York: Richard Marek Publishers, 1979.

166 Greville Janner, from "I Doubt That I Could Muster a Minyan" in *Present Tense* magazine, Autumn 1976, Vol. 4., American Jewish Committee, N. Y.

166 From the notes of Ahavia Scheindlin in "Simchat Torah on Archipova Street and Other High Holy Images from the Soviet Union," by Bill Aron. *Moment* magazine, December 1982, Vol. 8, No. I.

167 David M. Friend, from *Life* magazine, December 1981.

170 Howard Lenhoff, from *Present Tense,* Summer 1982, Vol. 9, No. 4. Copyright © 1982 *Present Tense.*

170 Lark Ellen Gould, from *Toronto Star,* Saturday Magazine, November 3, 1984.

171 Yosef Damana Ben Yeshaq. Translated by Ephraim Isaac, from *Voices Within the Ark: The Modern Jewish Poets,* edited by Howard Schwartz and Anthony Rudolf. New York: Avon Books, 1980.

172 Michael Pollak, from *The Jews of Kaifeng.* Beth Hatefutsoth, the Nahum Goldmann Museum of the Jewish Diaspora, Tel Aviv.

173 Reuter News Services.

174 Arthur Miller, from *I Don't Need You Any More.* New York: Viking Penguin Inc., 1967.

179 Irving Layton, from *The Unwavering Eye.* Toronto: McClelland and Stewart, 1975.

179 From *The Confirmation Reader,* edited by Azriel Eisenberg. New York: Behrman House Inc., 1953.